The Sage in the Cathedral of Books

Bobby and Joanne,

For our friendship.

Hwa-Wei + Mary

The Sage in the Cathedral of Books

THE DISTINGUISHED CHINESE AMERICAN
LIBRARY PROFESSIONAL DR. HWA-WEI LEE

Yang Yang

Translated by Ying Zhang

1804 BOOKS
OHIO UNIVERSITY SPECIAL PUBLICATIONS
Athens

1804 Books
Ohio University Special Publications, Athens, Ohio 45701
Copyright © 2016 by Ohio University Special Publications
All rights reserved

To obtain permission to quote, reprint, or otherwise reproduce or distribute material
from Ohio University Special Publications, please contact our rights and
permissions department at (740) 593-1154 or (740) 593-4536 (fax).

Printed in the United States of America
1804 Books are printed on acid-free paper ∞ ™

24 23 22 21 20 19 18 17 16   5 4 3 2 1

Frontispiece: At Ohio University Libraries, Hwa-Wei initiated a library automation project
by implementing the ALICE system soon after his arrival.

Paperback ISBN: 978-0-9667644-8-2
Electronic ISBN: 978-0-9667644-9-9

Library of Congress Cataloging-in-Publication Data
available upon request.

CONTENTS

WITHOUT DOUBT, Dr. Hwa-Wei Lee, a highly regarded, renowned figure, has earned a tremendous reputation in the field of international librarianship. He is greatly respected and admired by his colleagues from libraries in China as well as those working in East Asian libraries in the U.S. This high level of recognition can be attributed to his remarkable achievements in the field: Dr. Lee has reached the highest leadership position of any Chinese American library professional, and completed a body of research unsurpassed by any top-ranked professor from a Library and Information Science (LIS) program. But it is also due to his respectful, approachable, and philanthropic nature, and his superb affinity and benevolence toward others.

I, personally, got to know Dr. Lee in the mid-1990s. He was then the dean of Ohio University Libraries, the first Chinese American who had reached this level of administrative position in a research library in the U.S. His was a much different title from that of "university librarian" or "director": Dr. Lee had been given the rare title of "dean." Within Chinese culture, this would be a rare occurrence, indeed—a university librarian holding the rank of dean. In China, the professional prestige of a university librarian is positioned lower than that of a dean of an academic school.

In fact, the position of university librarian, in an American school of higher education, is usually considered a professional rather than an academic standing. Adding "dean" to the title of the head of a university library not only empowers that individual to participate in the campus decision-making process as any college dean would do; it also represents an academic honor. That title of "dean" distinguishes Dr. Lee from many university librarians at a professional level.

Back in the fall of 1998, I was a visiting scholar in the Graduate School of Library and Information Science at the University of Illinois, Urbana-Champaign (UIUC). I made arrangements to visit Dr. Lee and his library during the Christmas holiday with Jinwei Yan, the university librarian of Wuhan University, then a visiting scholar at Kent State University of Ohio.

Dr. Lee was about to retire from his position then. Upon our arrival, we discovered that arrangements had been made for us to stay on campus in a historic house, one used as a guest house for the university's distinguished visitors.

While watching television that evening, I was treated to evidence of Dr. Lee's influence in the university community: television advertisements of a local Chinese restaurant repeatedly showed a photo of Dr. Lee dining with a university vice president.

A more pleasant surprise was the news that the newly renovated library storage facility was to be named after Dr. Lee, the "Hwa-Wei Lee Library Annex." This was an honorable decision by the university administration—a retirement gift to Dr. Lee thanking him for his notable contributions to the community through his entire twenty-one-year tenure as the dean of Libraries.

Equally exciting news was the administration's recent decision to name the first floor of the Vernon R. Alden Library, the "Hwa-Wei Lee Center for International Collections." This decision was made immediately after the completion of that floor's renovation to commend Dr. Lee's remarkable achievements in globalizing the university. It is quite rare in the U.S., or anywhere in the world, for a university librarian to receive such a majestic honor from a well-recognized institution of higher education.

As the largest national library in the world, the Library of Congress (LC) is regarded as a flagship in the international librarianship arena; as such, it attracts an abundance of talented library professionals. Tung-Li-Yuan (1895–1965), a renowned twentieth-century Chinese librarian leader and a former director of Peking Library (now the National Library of China) who later resided in the U.S., worked at LC as a Chinese bibliographer for eight years (from 1957 to 1965)—a much downgraded position for a man with Yuan's qualifications.

Three years after Dr. Lee's retirement from Ohio University, Dr. Lee was hired as the Asian Division chief with a five-year contract, to serve from 2003 to 2008, after Karl Lo, interim chief, left LC. This made Dr. Lee the first Chinese American to officially serve at this position. This historic appointment clearly shows Dr. Lee's high status and great influence within the field of American librarianship.

Thus, writing a biography of Dr. Lee would not be an easy job. The writer would have to possess a rich insight, as well as be bold and fearless of the difficulties. Ms. Yang Yang happens to possess these characteristics. Not only did she do it; she did it very well.

In the early spring of this year, I received permission from Dr. Lee to be responsible for the editing and publishing of *Collected Works of Hwa-Wei Lee*. In response to my inquiry about the possibility of writing a personal memoir or having someone write a biography of him, Dr. Lee told me of Ms. Yang Yang, a journalist from China Central Television (CCTV), a former student, and a graduate student assistant to the dean at Ohio University Libraries, who had been working for several years collecting materials and in-depth interviews in preparation to writing Dr. Lee's biography.

This was truly a pleasant surprise to me. I felt it would be wonderful to have the biography and the collected works released as complementary publications, allowing readers to get a holistic view of Dr. Lee's personal life and family, as well as of his academic and professional career path. Thereafter, I contacted Yang Yang and spoke with her in person about the biography during a conference trip to Beijing. Having learned in July that 2011 was Dr. Lee's eightieth birth year, we decided to have the *Collected Works of Hwa-Wei Lee* published by the end of October so that the official release of the publication could coincide with a forum on "Dr. Hwa-Wei Lee's Library Scholarship and Thought," scheduled to be held in November. I made a phone call to Yang Yang, encouraging her to finish writing the biography by then and to come join us in celebrating the special occasion.

As a full-time CCTV (China Central Television) journalist and a mother, Yang Yang's busy schedule, with daily professional and personal commitments, would only allow her to work on the biography two hours per day, in the early morning from 5:00 to 7:00 a.m. At this pace, it would probably take more than a year to complete her writing. However, due to my constant phone calls, Yang Yang decided she had no other choice but to set aside a greater amount of her work and family duties, as well as her personal leisure time, in order to gain extra hours for writing. Her dedication and sacrifice has allowed the timely publication of Dr. Lee's biography.

There have been very few biographies or memoirs of library specialists in China, making it quite difficult to find similar published works to consult with. The scarcity of ready-to-use reference materials adds hardship to the writing of a library specialist's biography, as the writer has to collect a large amount of first-hand data, in addition to researching the historical and cultural background of the subject.

Writing a biography of Dr. Lee is even more difficult because of his extensive and diverse background in various organizations, including Ohio University and the Library of Congress; and involvement in world regions, including mainland China, Taiwan, the United States, and Thailand. This difficulty is compounded by his year-round international trips between the East and the West, through which he left his footprints on numerous cities of the two continents.

Meaningful integration of the resources necessary for a single biography is more difficult than simple resource collection. To reach readers within the general public as well as other library professionals, Yang Yang employed an admirable approach and strategy in writing this biography. Her writing from a journalistic angle allowed a more vivid portrayal of Dr. Lee, creating a story that was compelling and accessible to the general public, one that ultimately also promoted librarianship and the library sciences.

The writing of the biography features Yang Yang's in-depth reporting skill. The book begins with a prologue telling of Dr. Lee's retirement party at the Library of Congress (LC), a celebration full of compliments, attended by many high-profile admirers including Dr. James H. Billington, librarian of Congress; Dr. Deanna Marcum, associate librarian of LC; congressmen; senior officers from the federal government; and Dr. Lee's colleagues at LC. Yang Yang's decision to begin Dr. Lee's story with a flashback made the entire biography enchanting from the very beginning and enhanced the readability and charm of the book.

Divided into twenty-six chapters telling Dr. Lee's story in chronological order, each Chinese title comprised of a short four-character phrase (my suggestion), this book encompasses the personal, professional, and academic life of Dr. Lee from his childhood to his post-retirement years. Yang Yang's unique and elegant writing style depicts, on an extensive scale, in simple words, many anecdotes about books, people, things, and emotions that played an important part in the life of Dr. Lee. Rich in its humanistic approach, the biography succeeds in representing Dr. Lee, who functioned in an area of knowledge little known to those outside his field, as a wise and kind man to the general public.

During the course of writing, Yang Yang sent finished texts to Dr. Lee for review and feedback to avoid any mistakes. Once the entire manuscript was completed, Yang Yang continued to exchange ideas with me, making an effort to select an appropriate title until finally deciding upon this current one, *The Sage in the Cathedral of Books*.

Her process in choosing her title illustrates the same spirit shown in her writing—Yang Yang's striving for perfection. The two books, *The Sage in the Cathedral of Books* and *Collected Works of Hwa-Wei Lee* complement one another. Reading them together allows one to gain a holistic picture of Dr. Lee, to understand his great contribution to librarianship and library scholarship and thought, and to learn of his elegant, kindhearted, and life-affirming aspects.

Huanwen Cheng
Professor and University Librarian
Sun Yat-Sen University, Guangzhou, China
October 3, 2011

DR. HWA-WEI LEE is widely recognized as a highly accomplished, world-class library professional and administrator, as showcased in the simultaneous publication of two books: Yang Yang's, *The Sage in the Cathedral of Books: The Distinguished Chinese American Library Professional Dr. Hwa-Wei Lee,* and *Collected Works of Dr. Hwa-Wei Lee.* To an entire generation of library professionals, however, Dr. Lee is more than that: He is an ambassador of international librarianship, the first overseas library professional to come to China at the initial stage of the Chinese economic reform and open-door policy. It was Dr. Lee who held our hands and led us to the outside world.

Back in the early 1980s, I was a librarian at Peking University Library, and, like my peers, young junior scholars, hungered for the outside world beyond China. Dr. Lee's visit brought us a vivid depiction and expert interpretation of the libraries and librarianship on the other side of the Pacific Ocean, which were far richer than what we could perceive from just reading documents and reports by foreigners. Dr. Lee was always tireless and scrupulous and never seemed to look down on those of us who frequently threw brusque and ignorant inquiries of all kinds at him. He never forgot to say a few encouraging words to us after having addressed our, often, dumb questions.

Shortly thereafter, quite a few young librarians from Peking University Libraries were sent one after another to participate in the International Librarians Exchange Program at Ohio University, an exchange created and developed under Dr. Lee's administration as the dean of Libraries. I was originally on that exchange list but was later reassigned to an unsuccessful international exchange program with Australia. I have been bothered by the loss of that training opportunity at Ohio University, especially after I learned that the multi-year program, which continued from 1979 to 1999, had welcomed more than 150 librarians from mainland China from 1983 to 1999, with each participant receiving a half-year to one full year of training. Many of those librarians later became the elite in Chinese librarianship and made great contributions to the advancement of the field.

Dr. Lee's influence has been felt across all the institutions where I have worked—from Peking University, to the Library Department of the Ministry of Culture, to Shenzhen Library. He has never stopped building the connection between Chinese librarianship and American/international librarianship.

Dr. Lee is renowned as an academic ambassador of international librarianship among the Chinese library community to which he devoted many years of tireless effort. In addition to his library consultant title at Shenzhen Library (one he served during my term there), he has been invited to serve as a guest faculty member, visiting professor, and academic adviser by at least twenty institutions of higher education and research libraries including: Peking University, Tsinghua University, Zhejiang University, Beijing Normal University, Beijing University of Posts and Telecommunication, Xian Jiaotong University, Nankai University, Hunan Medical University, Wuhan University, Sichuan University, Northeast Normal University, Tianjin Polytechnic, National Library of China, Zhejiang Provincial Library, the central and branch (Lanzhou and Wuhan) libraries of the Chinese Academy of Sciences, and the National Central Library of Taiwan.

In addition, Dr. Lee was honored as a lifetime member of the Library Society of China at its 2005 annual conference. All these real and honorary titles highlight his remarkable achievements over the years.

This biography by Yang Yang shows a clear picture of an engaged and accomplished professional in the Chinese librarianship field. Dr. Lee has made at least one trip, "returning home," each year since 1982 to give lectures or attend conferences in China, making him much closer and more approachable to us. In addition, he has organized or contributed to a countless number of scholarly activities, which have exerted a tremendous impact on governmental and nongovernmental entities. It is hard to imagine that Dr. Lee accomplished all this during his busy administrative career at Ohio University Libraries and the Library of Congress. Dr. Lee's "returning home" trips have never stopped, even after his retirement from LC in 2008. He is still traveling between China and the U.S., making his tireless contribution to the "China-U.S. Librarians Professional Exchange Project," of which Dr. Lee was one of the initiators. Thousands of Chinese library professionals have benefited from the project.

The most precise and descriptive acclaim that Chinese people use to applaud Dr. Lee's accomplishment is "a hub connecting the East and the West and a bridge [connecting] China and the United States."

As the director of Shenzhen Library, I personally experienced evidence supporting how well-deserving Dr. Lee is of that acclaim. In the 1980s, a librarian exchange program was established between Ohio University and Shenzhen Library. Under this program, dozens of library professionals from Shenzhen Library went to Dr. Lee's library for an internship, training, or a visit. These elite library professionals, who gained a global vision at Dr. Lee's library, have made a significant contribution toward developing the Integrated Library Automation System (ILAS) and the 24/7 Self-Service Library, the two most advanced and influential library services from Shenzhen Library. It is hard to imagine that the field of Chinese librarianship could have become as successful as it is today without Dr. Lee's persistent and consistent effort. What great accomplishments and contributions Dr. Lee has made to us!

Zhongyan Fan (989–1052 AD), a prominent politician and literati of the Northern Song Dynasty China, wrote a song: "The distant mountain covered by cloud and the magnificent river flowing past—it resembles your majestic character which will last forever just as the high mountain and long river." This song could be a perfect portrayal of Dr. Lee's sincere heart and gentle spirit. On his eightieth birthday, I sincerely wish Dr. Lee a very happy and healthy life with continued guidance and support for a brighter future of Chinese librarianship.

Xi Wu
Director, Shenzhen Library
Shenzhen, China
September 2011

I WHOLEHEARTEDLY congratulate the debut of the book, *The Sage in the Cathedral of Books: The Distinguished Chinese American Library Professional Dr. Hwa-Wei Lee,* and thank Ms. Yang Yang for her excellent writing, which vividly portrays Hwa-Wei and his successful life. Reading through the chapters of this well-presented biography is quite moving and rewarding.

I got to know Hwa-Wei in 1982 when we both attended the IFLA annual conference in Montreal, Canada. We have kept in touch for the almost thirty years since then. It is our librarianship and our friendship that keep us connected.

The past thirty years have witnessed the economic reform and the rapid advancement in librarianship in China, along with the tireless effort and active involvement of Hwa-Wei in helping us to modernize Chinese librarianship. Owing largely to the international exchanges, especially with our American counterparts who have been flagships in the field, Chinese librarianship has made great progress in that short span of just thirty years, grown from being extremely backward at the beginning to now rising to a global standard level.

With the Sino-U.S. exchange, we have been fortunate to have as a human resource a group of diligent, dedicated, and knowledgeable Chinese American librarians who have served as ambassadors and human bridges between the two countries. Their persistent efforts have ensured the effectiveness and efficiency of the intercontinental communications: Hwa-Wei has been the most outstanding among them.

An active and well-accomplished library professional in the U.S. for decades, Hwa-Wei has worked in many important positions and has held various titles including library director, dean, professor, and consultant. However, he also has an important permanent job, one with no official title—ambassador of Sino-U.S. Cultural Exchange. As ambassador, Hwa-Wei has no assigned tasks and does not get paid. Yet, at this titleless position, he has devoted thirty years of his time and effort on a voluntary basis and with a sincere heart.

As ambassador, Hwa-Wei has made numerous trips to China from the U.S., leaving his footprint in major cities in China, even after his official retirement and despite physical health problems. As ambassador, he has also been involved in numerous programs and projects ranging from the cooperation and exchange between two national libraries, to librarian training in remote areas. To my knowledge, Hwa-Wei is without a doubt the leading person in the area of

Sino-U.S. library exchange. He has devoted the largest amount of time and effort, and has made the longest, broadest, and greatest contribution to Chinese librarianship of anyone in that field.

This statement of mine has been showcased particularly in one chapter of the book, *Library Cooperation between China and the United States*. However, what has been covered in that chapter only represents the tip of the iceberg of Hwa-Wei's achievements. Knowing of the range of his contributions, we must reach one important conclusion: Hwa-Wei's remarkable work throughout the years has made him a historical figure; his name will be deeply inscribed in the history of Sino-U.S. cultural exchange, and in the history of Chinese librarianship. Hwa-Wei will be forever remembered by history. Hwa-Wei's biography is full of excellent chapters, among which, my favorite is the one on library cooperation between China and the United States: This cooperation is creating significant change today; it promises to have an even greater, far-reaching historical impact.

Everyone who has had any contact with Hwa-Wei would be filled with admiration at his unique spiritual personality. What are the components of that personality and noble character? To name a few: dedication, innovation, hard work, tenacity, harmoniousness, self-sacrifice, helpfulness, kindness, and modesty; Hwa-Wei is a critical thinker and a practical doer. At this point, I have to admit that I feel Hwa-Wei's excellence is a complete excellence, a comprehensive excellence, and an integrated excellence—qualities impossible to summarize in such a short list. Hwa-Wei is a rare perfectionist, one who always seems to *achieve* perfect results.

This leads to another question: what is the source of Hwa-Wei's excellence, and how has he made his excellence so complete and comprehensive? The answer to the question can actually be found through learning about his background and experience. Hwa-Wei's perfect excellence originated from a combination of the profound traditions of Chinese civilization and the vigor of American culture. Hwa-Wei's perfect excellence is a successful outcome of the cultural fusion between the East and the West that has nurtured him and made him what he is.

It is not an exaggeration to say that the intertwining of Eastern and Western culture has shaped an exemplary global citizen: Hwa-Wei Lee!

The most enlightening thing that I have learned through Hwa-Wei's life concerns that East and West fusion. Hwa-Wei has made great contributions and achievements in promoting the Sino-U.S. cultural exchange. Meanwhile, he himself represents the crown of intertwined Eastern and Western culture. Cultural exchange and fusion has become one of the passions of Hwa-Wei's life; it is also the source of his excellence.

In spite of their many differences, Eastern and Western culture could essentially be mutually interlinked. A successful and meaningful fusion of the two cultures, a learning of each other's strengths, could create a new world full of new possibilities.

It is my hope that the twenty-first century will be a peaceful, cooperative, and harmonious century that features an even closer collaboration between China and the United States.

Shoujing Zhuang
Former Library Director
Peking University
Beijing, China
September 2011

THROUGHOUT *The Sage in the Cathedral of Books,* the biography of Dr. Hwa-Wei Lee, Ms. Yang Yang, the author, has portrayed the many important experiences of Hwa-Wei's life with her beautiful and eloquent writing.

Hwa-Wei, a man who was born in mainland China, grew up in Taiwan, and pursued his advanced degrees in the U.S., is a superlative intellectual possessing many Chinese traditional virtues including being family-loving and patriotic, self-effacing and persevering, hard-working and thrifty. Hwa-Wei has succeeded as an exemplary Chinese American on both personal and professional levels.

The stories about Hwa-Wei's childhood are quite absorbing. Through them, the readers of his biography will get to know more about the misery and chaos of the wars endured in mainland China from the 1930s to 1949. The Lee family's landing at the airbase in Hsinchu, Taiwan, in an air force transport plane is truly legendary.

The vividly narrated chapters on Hwa-Wei's striving to create a life in the U.S. and to successfully blend into American society are inspiring. Prior to the 1950s, Asian immigrants were often unfairly treated in the U.S. Many Chinese Americans suffered racial discrimination, making their lives difficult. However, Hwa-Wei, only twenty-six when he arrived in this foreign country, soon won the love of Mary, an American girl. They were married in 1959 and have been happily living together for over fifty years—having recently celebrated their fiftieth wedding anniversary—and have been blessed with many children and grandchildren. They were also blessed with Hwa-Wei's successful career. Shortly after his retirement from Ohio University as the dean of Libraries, Hwa-Wei was invited to work as the chief of the Asian Division of the Library of Congress and was thus able to extend his contributions to the field of librarianship.

I personally got to know Hwa-Wei in the 1990s. Back then, the National Commission of Education, now the Ministry of Education, had received a loan from the World Bank for a development program on teacher education. A total of 128 teacher colleges participated in this program. A series of trainings, involving library directors from these colleges, was arranged in order to meet one of the requirements of the World Bank loan. Due to his reputation and the success of his previous international exchange activities, Dr. Hwa-Wei Lee was hired as a foreign expert and conducted two fascinating library seminars: one at Northeast Normal University in 1995, and the other at Sichuan University in 1996.

His book, *Modern Library Management,* was well-received at both seminars. As his full-time companion, I learned a lot from Hwa-Wei's lectures and follow-up discussions. It was a pleasant and exciting experience that I still benefit from today.

Through this biography, we can learn more about Dr. Hwa-Wei Lee—his personal and professional growth, his development as an individual, and his achievements in the world of libraries.

Zhejiang Dong
Former Head of Library & Information Bureau
Department of Development and Planning
Ministry of Education
Beijing, China
September 2011

LATE IN 2007, I was invited to apply for the dean of Libraries vacancy at Ohio University. As I had researched the history of the library and asked senior colleagues about what they knew about Ohio University and the Vernon R. Alden Library, one name always came up: Hwa-Wei Lee. Everyone within the Association of Research Libraries (ARL) community knew him. Hwa-Wei, they told me, helped form OhioLINK, brought modern library technology and practices to Ohio University, earned entrance into ARL for Ohio University, amassed nationally recognized international collections, created the Shao You-Bao Overseas Chinese Documentation and Research Center, and even built a high-density storage facility that now carries his name. It was hardly surprising everyone within ARL spoke so admiringly of Hwa-Wei. And it was, frankly, an intimidating legacy for a first-time dean to follow.

Not long after coming to Ohio University, a note came from Hwa-Wei asking if we could meet for dinner. He and his wife Mary were planning a trip from their home in Florida to Ohio, and they planned a stop in Athens. And, so, on a warm July evening my wife and I met Hwa-Wei and Mary for the first time. In a small, charming restaurant tucked in the Athens countryside, we talked for hours. Instead of the distant and intimidating figure I was expecting, Hwa-Wei proved to be friendly, unassuming, and helpful. It was the first of many long conversations Hwa-Wei, Mary, and I would have. Not only were their help, perspective, and advice invaluable, the scope of all they had done for Ohio University began to become apparent.

But it wasn't until I traveled to Hong Kong, China, and Japan that I began to understand the extent of their contributions and kindness. At alumni events, library conferences, and university campuses across Asia, I met dozens of former Ohio University students, visitors, and librarians who had benefited from Hwa-Wei and Mary's generosity. So many of our international alums, who had stayed with Hwa-Wei and Mary for weeks, depended upon them for advice and looked to them as a connection to their homes that were so far away. Librarians told me of how they would visit Ohio University—sometimes for months and without adequate funding—to learn the best practices and the latest technologies in libraries. Many of those librarians are leaders in academic libraries throughout Asia today. It's hard to exaggerate, then, the influence Hwa-Wei has had on modern Asian librarianship.

His many accomplishments at Ohio University, and then at the Library of Congress, stand for themselves. More importantly, though, are the number of lives he and Mary have touched. They are both testaments to how libraries are much more than collections of books, and the power each of us has to change lives through our generosity.

Scott Seaman
Dean, Ohio University Libraries
Ohio University
Athens, Ohio, U.S.A.

DURING THE fifty years of my library career, especially before my retirement from Ohio University, many of my library friends in China urged me to write a biography in order to share my experiences, not just about my own life, but also about the drastic changes taking place in the library profession both in the U.S. since the 1960s, and in China since the 1980s, in which I have been personally involved almost every step of the way. I consider myself very fortunate to have spent fifty years of my career during the most vibrant time in modern library history. More changes have taken place in these fifty years, than in the past five hundred years. These changes have made my work most exciting and full of challenges. My humble experience, which reflected an epoch-making transformation in modern librarianship, is most memorable and worth being recorded. The key reasons that I did not follow their suggestions were due mainly to my heavy workload, a lack of time for an in-depth evaluation of my own involvement and contributions, and my hesitancy in writing my own autobiography.

In 1997, a good library friend in China, Ms. Wanping Zhang, director of Wuhan Regional Library and Information Center of the Chinese Academy of Science, sent a librarian to Ohio University as a library intern with a special assignment to collect materials in preparation for writing my biography. The librarian, Ms. Hong Lu, an excellent writer, diligently collected much of my personal information including my writings, photographs, and recorded lengthy interviews. After the completion of her internship, Ms. Lu got a job with a Chinese newspaper in San Francisco and decided to stay in the U.S. During her work in San Francisco, she wrote many articles in Chinese about me that were published in Chinese newspapers and journals. Owing to her special talent in writing and hard work, Ms. Lu has published several full-length novels and other books. She has been the editor of the literary journal *Chinese Literature of the Americas* and serves as the deputy chair of the Association of Chinese American Literary Writers.

In 2008, about the time of my retirement from the Library of Congress, a former graduate student at Ohio University, Ms. Yang Yang, who was also my student assistant during the time that I was the dean of Libraries at OHIO, expressed a strong interest in writing my biography. Ms. Yang was an outstanding graduate student and completed both her master's degree in Communication and Development Studies and her master's degree in Business Administration from Ohio University. Yang's husband, Bo Qu, a former lawyer in China, also came to OHIO and completed his master's degree in International Development.

I knew both of them very well and admired them for their diligence, academic excellence, trustworthiness, and high moral character. After their graduation, both went to work with Dr. You-Bao Shao in Hong Kong, then started their own business and raised their family in Canada, before returning to China where Yang has been working with CCTV in charge of the making and directing of several major documentary films and public programs. Bo continues his successful business enterprise.

With the support of her husband and their two daughters, Yang began her research and writing of my biography in 2009, a task that used up almost all of her free time. The work of writing a full-length biography was by no means an easy task. Being a gifted writer and director of many large documentary films, Yang was not only a good researcher but also an excellent writer. Her writing in Chinese is most beautiful and of high quality.

In 2010, Professor Huanwen Cheng, the university librarian and the dean of the School of Information Management at Sun Yat-Sen University in Guangzhou, China, together with Xi Wu, director of Shenzhen Library; and Honghui Liu, director of Guangdong Provincial Zhongshan Library and the Public Library Research Institute in China, decided to compile and publish *Collected Works of Hwa-Wei Lee* through Sun Yat-Sen University Press, as well as to hold a symposium titled, "Library Thoughts and Contributions of Hwa-Wei Lee," held November 17, 2011, at Shenzhen Library to celebrate my eightieth birthday.

Professor Cheng, who was very happy to learn that Yang was working on my biography and was nearly halfway through, immediately got in touch with Yang to ask her to finish the writing by July of 2011. He then arranged to have it published by the Guangxi Normal University Press. Both of these publications were to be officially released at the symposium in November. The special deadline for Yang to finish her writing put a great deal of pressure on her, but she worked extra hard and finished it on time.

After reading the first draft of Yang's writing, I could not help but be totally impressed and deeply grateful about Yang's beautiful writing, her profound insight and observations, and her detailed description of my entire professional life. She was able to sort out all the information gathered from my writings, recorded interviews, and others' writings about me into twenty-six chapters, which also included writing about me and our family by my wife, Mary, and by our six children in the last two chapters.

For the collecting and compiling of my collected works, I am most grateful to a team of faculty members and graduate students under the direction of Professor Xiangjin Tan, dean emeritus of the School of Information Management at Sun Yat-Sen University, and his wife, Professor Yanqun Zhao, dean emeritus of Sun Yat-Sen University Library. Both Professor Tan and Professor Zhao are well known and highly respected in China, not only for their professional accomplishments, with both holding key library positions, but also for their perfect marriage as a model couple. They were assisted by Dr. Yantao Pan, a senior faculty member, and a number of doctoral students. They spent nearly a year, including the entire summer of 2011 to work on the project, which resulted in the publication of two beautiful volumes (1565 pages) of my collected works by the Sun Yat-Sen University Press. As I learned later, despite his busy work, Professor Huanwen Cheng reviewed the entire manuscript before its publication.

For my biography, I am deeply grateful to Professor Huanwen Cheng, Director Xi Wu, university librarian Shoujing Zhuang, and Director Zhejiang Dong, all of whom are my dear friends and library colleagues in China, for their writing of the forewords. In addition to their friendship, I also benefited from their professional counsel in a joint effort to speed up library development in China as well as to promote U.S.-China library cooperation.

Before the publication of this English edition of my biography, the original Chinese edition written by Yang Yang was first published in China in 2011 in simplified Chinese characters. Later on, a Taiwanese edition in traditional Chinese characters was published in Taiwan in 2014. The Taiwan edition, which was published by Showwe Information Technology Ltd in Taipei, included not only more photographs, but also some of the sections deleted from the Chinese edition.

Since the publication of both the mainland Chinese edition and the Taiwan edition, many of my American friends and my family members wanted to know if I was to have the biography translated into English and published in the U.S. It was very fortunate that another of my good friends, Dr. Ying Zhang, a former graduate student at Sun Yat-Sen University who later completed her Ph.D. in Library and Information Science from Rutgers, The State University of New Jersey, volunteered to translate the Taiwan edition of my biography into English. Ying has a full-time job as an Asian Studies' research librarian at the University of California at Irvine, but like Yang Yang, she devoted more than a year of her leisure time doing the translation. Owning to her tireless efforts, the translation was completed in August 2014.

Because the original biography was written more than three years ago, I took the opportunity to revise and update many parts of it. Both my wife, Mary, and our son, Robert, also spent many hours editing the English translation.

I am especially grateful to Scott Seaman, dean of Ohio University Libraries, for his strong encouragement in having the biography translated from Chinese into English. Dean Seaman also contacted the Ohio University Press to have the

English edition published as one of the volumes in the Ohio University "1804 Books Imprint."

As the former dean of Ohio University Libraries, from 1978 to 1999, a major part of this biography covers the significant development of the Libraries during the period of drastic transformation from a paper-based library to a computer, networked, electronic, digital, and web-based library in fast progression. It also documented: the endeavors in creating the ALICE library automation system; the formation of OhioLINK; major endeavors in fundraising; the expansion of world renowned international collections; providing service to Ohio Valley Area Libraries; the promotion of international librarianship; and the attainment of membership status in the Association of Research Libraries.

All of these could not have been accomplished without the guidance and support of President Charles J. Ping and his successor, President Robert Glidden. Their superior leadership and the extraordinary administrative team including all the provosts, vice presidents, deans, and directors, with whom I had the privilege to be associated contributed to the success of my work. I must also acknowledge the superior teamwork of my library colleagues whose dedication, diligence, and hard work had enabled my many accomplishments. I am forever indebted to all of them.

For this English edition of my biography, I am deeply indebted to Scott Seaman, dean of Ohio University Libraries; Kate Mason, coordinator of communications & assistant to the dean; and Rob Dakin, records management specialist, who provided the necessary professional copy editing of the entire manuscript for publication. I also want to thank Ms. Gillian Berchowitz, director of Ohio University Press, and her able staff for their expertise and professionalism in the final editing and publication of this biography, which is far beyond my expectation.

After spending twenty-one years of my library career at Ohio University, it is my great honor to dedicate this biography to Ohio University for which I owe my profound gratitude.

Hwa-Wei Lee

It is already autumn in Beijing at the time of the completion of the biography of Dr. Hwa-Wei Lee. The trees outside the window, in the garden, have already begun to turn golden fall colors. This reminds me of Athens, Ohio, the beautiful and tranquil university town in the central U.S., where the fall scenery is just as gorgeous as the trees in Beijing. Back in 1993, I was pursuing a MBA and a master's degree in communication and development studies, while working as a part-time student assistant to Dr. Lee, who was then the dean of Ohio University Libraries.

I started writing this biography in 2008. Back then, Dr. Lee had just retired from the Library of Congress, but he remained as the project evaluator for the Sino-U.S. Library Professional Exchange Program. He continued to travel between China and the United States for the program and to attend other conferences, allowing me the opportunity to interview him and record his story and to complete the wish of several Ohio University alumni, of which I am one, who had been respectful and thankful to Dr. Lee.

It has been a happy writing experience. Every day, I had two highly anticipated and enjoyable time slots: one in the morning, after sending my two daughters to school and before going to the office; and the other in the evening, after the girls went to sleep. Sitting in front of the computer, I went through Dr. Lee's life as if I were experiencing an expedition. What has impressed me most, from time to time, were his trust of humanity, his calmness and firmness, and his dedication and professionalism, as well as the responsibility he had taken for his family, relatives, and friends. To me, his life has been so wise, so rich, and so balanced, even beyond his success in the library field.

In recent years, I have met and interviewed, in my role working for CCTV News Center, people from various socioeconomic backgrounds, including government and business VIPs, celebrities, tycoons, civilians, migrant workers, and mothers and children in poverty. Their personal beliefs, ideologies, and conducts have shaped my way of looking at contemporary Chinese society, and have also triggered my concerns and thoughts. I was even at the age of innocence, asking myself what kind of life would be most worthy. Over the course of writing this biography, I came to understand that a moment of glory and victory could be an astonishing magnificence, but what is really meant for a life is a sustained and balanced style, of which the quality would be measured by its breadth. The richness of Dr. Lee's life just lies in the "breadth" of his constant calmness and composure, whether granted favors or subjected to humiliation.

Through personal contact with him, I have witnessed his diligence and sincerity. He was always busy and always worked overtime. And work seemed to be the only thing he enjoyed. One day around the end of 1993, I stayed late for work. Upon walking into his office, I saw him lying on the carpet along with piles of documents while holding one document to read. I was deeply shocked by the scene, which still remains in my memory. He explained, with an apologetic smile, that his back hurt a lot and lying down made him feel better. He also told me that a surgery had already been scheduled. Thinking him always a forebearing gentleman, I guessed his pain must have been too severe to endure. I quickly handed him the document and rushed out of the office with tears in my eyes.

Most Chinese students and visiting librarians from China, like me, have been taken care of by Dr. Lee in Athens. Sometimes, he cares for people who come to him with a sense of humor. I still remember a mishap I had on campus—a falling tree branch hit me and injured my forehead. I was urged by Dr. Lee, as soon as he learned of my accident, to go to the university's health center for treatment. He also jokingly comforted me, saying that being hit by a falling tree branch would have the same low probability as winning a lottery, and I might have become lucky and should try the lottery. Later, he did drive me out to purchase a lottery ticket, which failed to win me anything. He laughed, "Too bad. Your luck seems to have run out. No wonder you did not win."

Dr. Lee has encountered numerous people and circumstances over many years through different historical periods and changing work environments, in both Eastern and Western cultural settings. Librarianship, however, has been his only ambition and passion, and the kingdom of books has always been his center. His world is vast and boundless, like a sea. We can learn so much about libraries, the place for human knowledge and wisdom, from his life and understand the revolving path of the cathedral of books. What I have done, over the course of writing, is to collect as many source materials as possible, via interviews and literature reviews, and then to put together the fragmented anecdotes to form a not-so-perfect theme of the book. Many times, I had to face a situation of more willingness than capability, which caused me irreparable regret at the end. The only thing that makes me satisfied is that I have completed this rewarding and meaningful project.

I cannot express enough thanks to Dr. Lee, his wife Mary, and his children for their help in the project. I am very thankful to Dr. Huanwen Cheng, the university librarian of Sun Yat-Sen University, for his enthusiastic assistance in writing and publishing the book. My deep thanks also go to Mr. Xi Wu, the director of Shenzhen Library; Mr. Shoujing Zhuang, the former university librarian of Peking University; and Mr. Zheqian Dong from the Ministry of Education of China for their forewords to the biography.

The completion of the project could not have been accomplished without the support and trust of my husband, who is also an alumnus of Ohio University and has been the first reader of the book manuscript. My two daughters have been extremely curious and anxious, waiting for the birth of the book. Also, I want to thank Ms. Qi Gan, an old friend of mine from school and one of the founders of the All Sages Book Garden, the first privately owned bookstore in mainland China. She has been so encouraging and offered many constructive suggestions. Without her encouragement and advice, I probably would have never rediscovered, from the depth of my heart, the desire for writing and would have never enjoyed such a wonderful authoring experience.

Yang Yang
August 2011

In this world, there are countless smart, brilliant, and successful leaders; and there are also numerous personable, approachable, and dedicated men. However, I see that there are very few people who belong to both groups. Dr. Hwa-Wei Lee is one of the few. Our profession is very fortunate to have him lead us and help us thrive.

THIS IS what I wrote in 2011 for the occasion of celebrating Dr. Hwa-Wei Lee's eightieth birthday, organized by the Chinese American Librarians Association (CALA). Anyone who wants to know the story behind these words is encouraged to read this biography. It has taken me more than a decade to learn the richness and success of his life through in-person contacts and, most recently, this biography.

Personally, I have had only a few direct interactions with Dr. Lee. But each interaction gave me an opportunity to discover one or more new traits in him. The first time I met him was sixteen years ago when I was a visiting scholar under the International Librarian Internship Program at Ohio University (OHIO) Libraries. Dr. Lee was then the dean of the Libraries. The immediate impression he conveyed was that of a "hybrid" gentleman, one possessing Confucian constraint mixed with a western "ladies-first" manner, presumably rooted in his personal experience in both cultures. As soon as I arrived, along with three other visitors from China, he took us to OHIO's guest house, a nice two-story building for special guests of the university, and assigned me, the lower-ranked visitor in the group, to the best bedroom. He said while smiling, "Ying is the only lady here, so she gets this room." The following days, we had several meetings with him. Dr. Lee, during the meetings was serious, listening more than talking. When talking, he was concise and always got to the point. Over the course of my six-month stay in Athens, I learned many times from his library employees as well as from campus and local community members about his strength, ability, and reputation.

After returning to my home institution in China, Sun Yat-Sen University, I had another opportunity to learn more about Dr. Lee. That was in 2000 during a workshop on knowledge management and metadata that was taught by Erik Jul from OCLC. Jul was accompanied by Dr. Lee, then a visiting distinguished scholar at the organization. Seeing that I grew frightened to death for being called to provide on-site translation for Jul's lectures, Dr. Lee comforted me, saying, "Don't worry. I will help you." Staring at the encouraging look in his smiling face, I felt less uneasy, standing at the podium. Dr. Lee corrected me on a few technical terms, where I failed to give precise translations. But he did this in an appropriate manner, apparently not wanting to put me in an awkward position.

In 2004, I visited him in Washington, D.C., during a National Science Digital Library (NSDL) annual conference trip. He was then the chief of Asian Division at the Library of Congress. Upon walking out of the subway station, I immediately spotted him standing up there waiting for me, perhaps already having waited for quite a while. Seeing my apologetic face, he explained on the way to the Madison Building that he had just been afraid of my having a problem in finding the place or in entering the building, due to the increased security check at the entrance. After a brief inquiry about my doctoral study at Rutgers, he talked on and on about the Asian Collection and several ongoing projects, while showing me around. Our meeting lasting several hours was filled with his work plans and library business. I could hardly tell from his high energy and passion that the gentleman in front of me was already in his seventies.

These anecdotes allowed me to get a partial impression about Dr. Lee; meanwhile, they triggered my desire to learn more about this influential and respected senior library professional. Ms. Yang Yang's biography of Dr. Hwa-Wei Lee finally came out to fulfill that desire. As soon as the book arrived, I could not wait to devour it. The reading was so inspiring and worth sharing with a broader audience. I called Dr. Lee suggesting an English version so that more people, including his family members, could learn about his wonderful life, and the tremendous efforts undertaken to reach the ultimate chapter of his life. He encouraged me to be the translator, and shortly after sent me an e-copy of the book.

The translation project did not start until February 2013, for various reasons, including my busy schedule as a research librarian at the University of California, Irvine, and, most importantly, my fear of incompetence for work requiring language proficiency. Having learned of my concerns, Dr. Lee said, "Don't worry. Just take your time. And I and my wife Mary will be here to help you." With his encouragement, as always, I finally moved forward. Over the past sixteen months, every evening, the three to four hours before bed became a fixed time for me to sit in front of my workstation, translating Dr. Lee's life, from my mother language to a second language, paragraph by paragraph, and chapter by chapter. As the first Chinese-English translation project for me, it was not easy, but it was rewarding. I have learned a lot during the process, not only of general translation skills, but also of Dr. Lee's spirit of librarianship and wisdom of life.

I know that this project would not have been completed without the support from many people. Dr. Lee, his wife, Mary, and his son, Bob, have provided ongoing and thorough review comments of all the translation manuscripts. Ms. Yang Yang graciously gave her permission for me to be the translator of this biography and also provided background information at my request. Professor Ying Hu, a Chinese literature and translation expert, and Ms. Phyllis Gottlieb, my American host family lady, frequently contributed their valuable knowledge and time. Last but not least, my parents and son were also sincere supporters, whose care and patience kept the project moving forward. I am so thankful to all these people.

Ying Zhang

The Sage in the Cathedral of Books

The Retirement Party at the
Library of Congress

Remember his resolute constancy in things that were done by him
according to reason, his equability in all things, his sanctity, the
cheerfulness of this countenance, his sweetness, and how free he
was from all vainglory; how careful to come to the true and exact
knowledge of matters in hand, and how he would by no means give
over till he did fully and plainly understand the whole state of the
business, and how patiently and without any contestation he would
bear with them that did unjustly condemn him; how he would never
be overhasty in anything; not give ear to slanders and false accusa-
tions, but examine and observe with best diligence the several actions and dispositions of men. Again, how he was no backbiter, not
easily frightened, not suspicious, and in his language free from all
affectation and curiosity . . . able through his spare diet to continue
from morning to evening without any necessity of withdrawing
before his accustomed hours to the necessities of nature; his unifor-
mity and constancy in matter of friendship. How he would bear
with them that with all boldness and liberty opposed his opinions,
and even rejoice if any man could better advise him.
                                        —*Marcus Aurelius,* Meditations

1

ON THE LAST day of March 2008 in Washington, D.C., the cherry blossoms were
in full bloom and a soft spring breeze was blowing the pink and white petals in the
air around both sides of the Potomac River. For Dr. Hwa-Wei Lee, it was the day
to say goodbye to the workplace where he had spent the past five years. Dressed
in his normal business suit, Hwa-Wei left his Clarendon Boulevard apartment and
made his usual short walk to the Clarendon metro station. It was still early (before
7:00 a.m.) and there were still empty seats in the middle section of the train.
Hwa-Wei didn't take a seat, but chose to stand near the closing doors, deep in
thought. It was a special day. Today he would step down from his position as
chief of the Asian Division and retire from the Library of Congress.

It had been five years since Hwa-Wei had become the first Chinese American appointed to this important position. A renowned senior library administrator, Hwa-Wei had served twenty-one years as the dean of the Ohio University Libraries until his previous retirement in September 1999. Originally from China, Hwa-Wei has been well regarded as a leader among thousands of Chinese American librarians, primarily because of his remarkable contribution to and influence on international collaboration among libraries. In the past thirty years, Hwa-Wei has played an indispensable role in advancing Chinese librarianship to a world-class level. His continued tireless bridging efforts between the United States and China have provided a shortcut for Chinese libraries to learn and to adapt the most advanced information technology and management practices. And his vital spirit and valued contributions have earned him a reputation among Chinese library professionals as "a hub connecting the East and the West and a bridge between China and the United States."

Hwa-Wei's retirement party was originally planned to be held in the Thomas Jefferson Building where the Asian Division is located, allowing a small gathering to take place among acquaintances, colleagues, and friends. However, the number registering to attend far exceeded the estimated headcount. A last-minute arrangement was made to relocate the party to the conference hall on the fifth floor of the James Madison Memorial Building. The hall, with a room capacity of up to three hundred people, often was used for large-scale speeches or gatherings. Having recently celebrated his seventy-seventh birthday with his wife, Mary, and his children and grandchildren, Hwa-Wei seemed ready to fully enjoy his retirement now that his service commitment to the Asian Division of LC was ending.

Hwa-Wei felt quite energetic as he walked out of the metro station and was immediately exposed to the fresh and cool spring air and the early morning sunshine. Washington, D.C., is one of Hwa-Wei's favorite cities. Prior to his tenure at LC, Hwa-Wei had taken a few trips to Washington, D.C., for conferences or tours, during which he had allocated time for sightseeing. But during his five-year-long residence, he had little chance to look around and enjoy the beauty of this capital city because of his full-time working schedule, involving even weekends. At this moment, Hwa-Wei felt a bit regretful as he knew he would soon leave this beautiful city without having further explored its many historical and cultural attractions.

Hwa-Wei sped up his pace; he hoped his last day at LC would be relaxing and his retirement party would go well. Roomy and spacious, the conference hall had been set up with a few rows of seats in the front and buffet tables with sandwiches, salads, pastries, and drinks in the back. It is a LC tradition to arrange a farewell party for each retiring employee, allowing the library's other employees a chance to summarize the retiree's contribution to the organization, express

4

their appreciation, and say goodbye to their departing colleague. The atmosphere for this kind of farewell party is usually casual, and informal because a retirement symbolizes the end of a busy public life and the beginning of a leisurely personal life with absolute freedom to arrange one's own activities 24/7.

2

As Hwa-Wei walked into the conference hall, he was immediately greeted by many familiar faces. His wife Mary, son Charles, and daughter-in-law Erika were there, mingling with administrators and his colleagues from the Asian Division and other parts of the LC. There were also reporters from the *World Journal* and other news media, as well as members of the Asian Division Friends Society. Permeating the warm party ambience was a reluctance to part from many of Hwa-Wei's friends and colleagues.

Hwa-Wei was surprised to see Dr. James H. Billington, librarian of Congress, and Dr. Deanna Marcum, associate librarian for Library Services, show up simultaneously at the party. In most cases, only Dr. Marcum, or one of the directors, would have attended such a retirement party. And, in addition to the two LC top administrators, several congressmen and senior federal officials including Mike Honda, a highly acclaimed congressman, were among the attendees. Honda, a Japanese-American, had long fought for minority rights and was the chair of the Congressional Asian-Pacific American Caucus. He was also one of the deputy chairs of the Democratic National Committee.

Dr. Billington, a renowned historian and scholar, began the proceedings with his heartwarming speech:

> Thank you for your dedicated service to the Library of Congress and the breadth of institutional and international experience that you brought with you five years ago . . .
>
> Your international librarianship and professionalism have been exceptional since your arrival at the Library of Congress on February 10, 2003. During your tenure, you worked tirelessly to build our collections and to ensure that our reference service and outreach activities served the nation in the best possible ways. The reorganization of the division; the establishment of collaborative digitization projects with major national libraries and research institutions in China, Japan, Korea, and Taiwan; your establishment and support of the Asian Division Friends Society and the Florence Tan Moeson Fund; as well as your recent establishment of the Asian-Pacific American Collection Fund will carry on your good work long after you leave these halls.

The speech by Dr. Marcum was also most sincere and personal. She had direct supervision over two-thirds of the more than four thousand employees at

LC and had been active in academia and various organizations across the country. As an efficient and demanding administrator, Dr. Marcum always appreciated dependable and hardworking library employees. She thought highly of Dr. Hwa-Wei Lee.

It is an honor to write this tribute on the occasion of your retirement. You should feel enormously gratified in knowing that you have made a huge difference in this institution, and you have touched the lives of a great number of LC staff, librarians around the world, and international scholars. The phrase "a life well lived" refers specifically to you!

You know better than anyone else how badly you were needed when the library recruited you to head the Asian Division. Collections were unavailable to the public, bibliographic records were not in the online catalog, staff relations and morale were in disrepair. You had already enjoyed a highly successful career at Ohio University as the University Librarian and, as a consultant, you set OCLC on a path to become highly influential in China. You could have insisted—with complete justification—on enjoying retirement with your family. Instead, your sense of obligation and service led you to accept the job here, and the scholarly and library communities owe you a great deal.

There is almost no comparison of today's Asian Division to the one you inherited. The reorganization has removed the language-based independent units. The staff works harmoniously and productively. The collections are well organized and can be served to the public. You have exponentially raised the public profile of the Asian Division with your seminars and the formation of a Friends group. We have partnerships with countless libraries in all parts of Asia.

At your stage of life, it would have been perfectly understandable if you had been more leisurely. But not Hwa-Wei! You have traveled hundreds of thousands of miles to form partnerships, acquire collections, and create goodwill for the Library of Congress. You have not relied solely on federal dollars, either. You have been a supremely talented fundraiser and a builder of relationships.

Finally, you have shown that you are not simply looking to others to sustain the Asian Division. When you announced your retirement, you made a substantial financial contribution to your latest campaign—the development of an Asian-American Pacific Islander collection. You have set a high standard for those who follow.

Your retirement is bittersweet for me. You certainly deserve some peaceful, more relaxed time with your family and friends, but I shall miss you very much. Your intellect, your passion, and your wisdom have given me great confidence in the capacities and capabilities of the Asian Division.

Dr. James H. Billington, librarian of Congress, praises Hwa-Wei for his accomplishments during his retirement party from the Library of Congress.

Frank Joseph Shulman, president of the Asian Division Friends Society, presents a souvenir book to Hwa-Wei during his retirement party.

Hwa-Wei accepts a plaque from a representative of the Chinese American Librarians Association.

3

The compliments from the two LC top administrators were extremely heartfelt. Immediately following the utter stillness during the speeches came prolonged applause throughout the conference hall. Standing up with a sincere and modest smile on his face, as always, Hwa-Wei nodded his head toward the audience to show his gratitude. At this moment, all his hard work over the years had been well recognized. As a library professional who had immersed his life in librarianship, what else could he ask for?

Dr. Carolyn T. Brown, who supervised all area studies divisions in the library, including the Asian Division, had been the key person to get Hwa-Wei on board. Not only did Dr. Brown persuade Hwa-Wei to take the division chief's position after his first retirement, but she also was extremely supportive of Hwa-Wei during this radical reform across the Asian Division. Dr. Brown especially noted, in her remarks to Hwa-Wei:

> When you came to the library, you promised me that you would stay for five years. We are all reluctant to see that five years have come to an end, but what an astonishing five years you have given to the Asian Division . . .
>
> If I have had a small part in your success, it has only been to explain an arcane bureaucratic system to a newcomer and to remove as many obstacles as I could so that you could be the very best that you are capable of being in the often-challenging environment. Your tenure as chief has been a triumph and demonstration of what is possible with a leader of vision and experience, one who long ago discarded the encumbrances of ego and who has led with deep appreciation for the gifts of others, with great humility, and with a rare wisdom.

4

Hwa-Wei's own remarks were concise, highlighting his appreciation to Dr. Carolyn Brown and his professional shift from working in an academic institution to a government agency. In addition, he recognized that he himself would not have accomplished as much at LC without the support of his colleagues. He also mentioned that he planned to give his prime time back to his family, while at the same time to continue his service as an advisor for the planning of the Fifth China-U.S. Library Conference, to be organized jointly by the Library of Congress and the National Library of China.

It was an ultimate honor for Hwa-Wei to have LC as the apex of his career; no other library could have given him such a strong feeling of accomplishment. When being interviewed earlier by the American Folklife Center of LC, Hwa-Wei told the interviewer Dr. Nora Yeh:

The Library of Congress is by far the world's largest and one of the most prestigious national libraries. It is therefore an ideal place for me to windup my library career. I don't think I'll go to another place for another job, because, after this, nothing could attract me to continue my work. And I want to make sure that, in my five years here, I have built a good structure in the Asian Division, under which it can continue not just on what I've done, but also could go even further to a higher plateau. I have every reason to believe that I have instilled in my staff a strong sense of mission and self-confidence. They actually have been doing a lot of great things, much more than I was hoping for them to accomplish. That's why I think they can do even more. Sometimes I teased and said to them, "Now you people can take a break after my retirement; you don't have to work that hard anymore."

But I don't think they are going to stop or slow down. They will continue. They are a group of talented and dedicated professionals. And they have a lot of good ideas. I am sure they will continue to carry on. One of the good things that I have done was to combine the best talents of newly hired staff with those who have been here many years, and have had a lot of experience. The young staff needs to learn the experience. And the old staff needs to share their experience. Often times I encourage the young staff to do things in the way they see as best for their professional development and in their own way make the library better. The combining of the strengths of these two groups of staff in a harmonious way, in my view, is very important. I have really done as much as I can to build that kind of working relationship, as well as fostering the culture of mutual respect, mutual support, and also mutual trust. This is most important for the success of any organization. I think we are now getting to have a very good working environment, and now have all these elements for success in place. So, I am very happy to leave at this time, because I feel this is the best time for me to leave. You can't find a better time for me to retire when you see that positive things will continue, and may even be better.

Working as an administrator, I want to encourage all staff members to bring out their hidden talents and feel free and encouraged to use them. Everyone has talents. But you have to give them the opportunity and create the environment for them to do it. Otherwise, hidden talents will remain hidden. That would be a waste. And they would be unhappy. So, the best management skill is to bring out the best in your colleagues and coworkers. And I think maybe that's one of my best strengths, to be able to do that because I really feel that I have great respect of the ability of my staff. I was able to empower and encourage them to do what they are capable of doing without fear of failure or reprisal.

In the past five years, Hwa-Wei had experienced an extremely complicated and difficult working environment. Yet, miraculously, he was able to transform the Asian Division from a poorly operated and notoriously divided department suffering from low morale to one that was energetic, enthusiastic, and harmonious. The pleasant outcome, however, was achieved only through a heavy workload, resulting in mental and physical exhaustion. In his mid-seventies, Hwa-Wei had to work as hard as a much younger man, frequently extending his office hours to evenings and weekends. He often felt he was at the upper limit of his physical endurance; that feeling had been getting worse.

Since the previous winter, he often felt weary. Every day, Hwa-Wei had to make several trips back and forth among the various departments through the underground tunnels connecting the Jefferson, Madison, and Adams Buildings. But just several weeks before his planned retirement, he had felt a tightness in his chest and a shortness of breath, forcing him to make several stops during one of these trips.

Hwa-Wei had suffered the same symptoms back in 2005. Then, the diagnosis from his doctor had indicated a clogged artery, necessitating a percutaneous coronary intervention (PCI) with the installation of two coronary stents. With the reoccurrence of those symptoms, his physician alerted Hwa-Wei that the state of his artery clog had been getting worse and suggested that a coronary bypass operation should be done as soon as possible. These constant and amplified signals from his body made Hwa-Wei realize that the time had come for him to say goodbye to the heavy workload. He had to face the reality of his physical limits.

5

The retirement party, including the luncheon, lasted about three hours. As the main honoree, Hwa-Wei, with his courteous and graceful bearing, expressed his gratitude to the attendees for everything they had done for the celebration. But mixed with his heartfelt appreciation was the sadness of saying goodbye to friends and colleagues.

During the past five years, this approachable and unflappable elderly gentleman had revitalized the Asian Division. Throughout the library, no one failed to pay tribute to him. Hwa-Wei was known as being mild yet courageous, lenient yet principled, steady yet determined, low-keyed as a man yet highly committed as a professional. These personal attributes made Hwa-Wei the perfect administrator—one who, seemingly, could never be defeated by any hardship, obstacle, or challenge. Rather, his tolerance and wisdom would always point the positive energy and spirit of other people in the right direction.

Ms. Judy Lu, the head of the Collection Services Department of the Asian Division, once told a *World Journal* reporter:

Dr. Carolyn T. Brown, director of The John W. Kluge Center and head of the library's Office of Scholarly Programs, hired Hwa-Wei as chief of the Asian Division at the Library of Congress.

Excerpt of a congratulatory letter, dated February 1, 2008, from Dr. James H. Billington, librarian of Congress, Washington, D.C.

Your international librarianship and professionalism have been exceptional since your arrival at the Library of Congress on February 10, 2003. During your tenure, you worked tirelessly to build our collections and to ensure that our referece service and outreach activities served the nation in the best possible ways.

Excerpt of a congratulatory letter, dated February 15, 2008, from Dr. Deanna B. Marcum, associate librarian for Library Services at the Library of Congress

You should feel enormously gratified in knowing that you have made a huge difference in this institution, and you have touched the lives of a great number of LC staff, librarians around the world, and international scholars.

The Asian Division was a "sleeping lion" five years ago, and then all of a sudden was awakened by Dr. Hwa-Wei Lee's magic stick . . . As a savior, he aroused the once-isolated Asian Division, and led us to learn walking, running, and ultimately presenting ourselves in front of the world. Under his leadership, we have been able to gain a lot.[1]

Dr. Mi Chu, the head of the Scholarly Services Department of the Asian Division, also commented on Hwa-Wei's years at LC. As an employee of the Library of Congress for thirty years, Dr. Chu had witnessed many changes; none of which, however, were comparable to those made under Hwa-Wei's administration.

He has accomplished a lot with limited funding sources, having to undergo numerous negotiations with his supervisors on the sixth floor of the Madison Building. In addition to his already busy work in the library, Hwa-Wei has given numerous speeches and lectures all over the world in the promotion of the Asian collections and has written many papers about them. The newly established Asian-American Pacific Islander Collection by Dr. Lee should have a very profound and meaningful impact.

Dr. Chu also admitted that it had been her honor to be able to work under Hwa-Wei's leadership.[2]

Hwa-Wei understood completely that all his success was reflected in the new and unprecedented public image of the Asian Division. It had been necessary to change the old public perception of the division. The Asian Division, revitalized by a positive public image combined with many improvements, now provided Asian studies readers and researchers a totally new experience. Of course, those five years were not always as rosy as were the compliments at the retirement party. At times, they seemed more like a journey full of weariness, confusion, obstacles, and even confrontation. However, once the final destination had been reached, all those unhappy moments were replaced by the wonder of the journey's completion. What remained were memories of happy moments and pictures of smiling faces taken during those years.

Hwa-Wei understood deeply that hardly anything could be done in a bureaucratic organization without fighting, when necessary, some of its rules and regulations. Indeed, much of the work he completed at the Asian Division had required great skill and patience in persuasive negotiations with powerful labor unions and offices responsible for legal matters. In order to get things done quickly within his timetable, Hwa-Wei had challenged some of the policies and rules that could have delayed or postponed the implementation of many good plans and programs.

---

1. Mao-Feng Yu, "Library of Congress Saying Farewell to Hwa-Wei Lee", *World Journal (North American Edition)*, February 19, 2008.
   2. Ibid.

For all of these reasons, this day was a very special day for Hwa-Wei—a splendid finish to a vast movement. Hwa-Wei concluded his professional life right at the summit of his career. What an impeccable decision.

Walking along the extremely quiet hallway of the Jefferson Building, his figure reflected on the marble floor, Hwa-Wei hated to say goodbye to his Asian Division colleagues with whom he had worked together for five years. Even more difficult for him was departing from the library and librarianship to which he had devoted the last fifty years. Nevertheless, he had no choice but to leave everything behind. It was time for him to get back to his personal life, to take care of his health, and to face the reality of aging.

Mary was happy about Hwa-Wei's retirement. Like many other American women, Mary, despite her graduate degrees, had worked as a homemaker ever since she married Hwa-Wei. Her family, husband, and children had been foremost in her life. She had always dreamed about an earlier retirement for Hwa-Wei, one that would allow them to fully enjoy their later years together. She had been excited about Hwa-Wei's first retirement in 1999 from his former position as the dean of Ohio University Libraries. The excitement didn't last, however: Hwa-Wei spent the next three years as a visiting distinguished scholar for the Online Computer Library Center (OCLC), traveling from Athens, Ohio, to Columbus, Ohio, three times a week. During those three years, he had also served as a consultant for the OCLC Asian Pacific Services, traveling frequently to many countries in Asia. Then Hwa-Wei was offered the position as the chief of the Asian Division at LC, which turned out to be the busiest job of Hwa-Wei's career.

For several weeks, in anticipation of Hwa-Wei's second retirement, Mary had had everything packed. All their household items were already on a moving company's truck to be hauled to Florida. The only things left in the apartment were a few pieces of carry-on luggage. The couple would take an early morning train to Florida the next day. The auto-train arrangement Mary had made included one private onboard sleeping room for Hwa-Wei and herself and the shipping of their 2003 Chevrolet minivan in a special car at the end of the same train.

Mary's thoughtful arrangements for Hwa-Wei's retirement had been made three years ago during a visit with their eldest daughter, Shirley, in Jacksonville, Florida. Shirley had taken Mary to several nearby retirement communities in the hope that her parents could settle in one of them after her father retired from the Library of Congress.

Nestled in the northeast of Florida, in a tropical zone adjacent to the Atlantic Ocean with all-year-round warm and moist weather, Jacksonville is a popular destination for the elderly and thus home to numerous retirement communities. Cypress Village was the community that Mary liked most. Luckily, she and Hwa-Wei were able to purchase a duplex in that area before his second retirement.

On the Lees' weekend trips from Washington once every few months to check on the duplex, Hwa-Wei would breathe a sigh of relief. Unlike Washington's endless traffic, very few cars were on the highway during the afternoon driving from the airport into Jacksonville. The sky was usually clear blue and cloudless. The sun was always shining. There were flowers everywhere. Even at Cypress Village, six miles from the Atlantic Ocean, he could feel an ocean breeze. With not much industry in the area, the air was fresh. It seemed like a tropical paradise. Here, Hwa-Wei felt, he would be able to feel relaxed and tranquil.

On April 9, a few days after his retirement from LC, Hwa-Wei received a phone call from Congressman Honda. He told Hwa-Wei, "Your retirement party at LC was very impressive. What you've accomplished during your tenure there is absolutely amazing. I've prepared a speech (about you) for tomorrow's congressional meeting . . ."

On the next day, Congressman Honda delivered the following speech to Congress, heaping praise on Hwa-Wei's outstanding contributions at LC. The text of the speech has been included in the Congressional Record of April 10, 2008.

> Madam Speaker, I rise today to honor the many contributions and achievements of Dr. Hwa-Wei Lee. After an esteemed five years as the chief of the Asian Division at the Library of Congress—a bookend to his dedicated fifty years in the library profession, Dr. Lee is retiring . . .
>
> During his short tenure at the Library of Congress, Dr. Lee focused his energy on completely rejuvenating and reorganizing the Asian Division. He introduced innovative programs designed to improve and expand the division's resources, collections, services, and outreach. As chair of the Congressional Asian-Pacific American Caucus, it has been my privilege to have collaborated with Dr. Lee and his dedicated staff at the Asian Division. Our shared pursuit to tell the complete Asian American and Pacific Islander (AAPI) story and dispel the cloak of invisibility and mischaracterization upon the community has given life to a new AAPI Collection at the Library of Congress. This is another milestone of Dr. Lee's storied career.
>
> Dr. Lee and his lovely wife Mary will soon move to Florida to bask in the sunny rays of retirement. But I suspect that he will not slow down, and will continue his many pursuits. As anyone who has met Dr. Lee can attest, his boundless, enthusiastic spirit will not allow him to stay idle . . .
>
> Madam Speaker, I commend Dr. Hwa-Wei Lee for his dedication and many contributions to the library profession and am especially grateful for his nurturing leadership of the Asian Division and of the establishment of the AAPI Collection at the Library of Congress . . .[3]

---

3. "Honoring Dr. Hwa-Wei Lee—Extensions of Remarks—April 10, 2008" (speech given by the Hon. Michael M. Honda of California in the House of Representatives, Thursday, April 10, 2008), E577–578, http://thomas.loc.gov/cgi-bin/.

CHAPTER I

The War Years in His Youth

One ship drives east, and another drives west,
With the self-same winds that blow;
'Tis the set of the sails, and not the gales,
Which tells us the way to go.

Like the winds of the sea are the ways of fate,
As we voyage along through life;
'Tis the set of the soul that decides its goal,
And not the calm or the strife.

—*Ella Wheeler-Wilcox, "The Wind of Fate"*

1

HWA-WEI'S ANCESTRAL home is Fuzhou, Fujian Province; however, he was born in Guangzhou on January 25, 1931. His father, Kan-Chun Lee, was then the governor of Shihui County in Guangdong Province. The third child in the family, Hwa-Wei had one brother, Hwa-Hsin, who was five years older; one sister, Hwa-Yu, who was three years older; three younger brothers; and one younger sister.

The year 1931, the Chinese Year of the Sheep, witnessed a turbulent rainy season in Southern China. The drenching rain seemed to have no intention of stopping or slowing down; instead, it kept expanding its coverage beginning in Guangzhou and moving further north. By May of that year, the rainstorms had already covered more than half the country. The water levels of several rivers, including the Pearl, Min, Yangtze, and Huaihe, rose rapidly. The fierce tides seemed to declare that this would be a disastrous year.

By June and July sixteen provinces were declared disaster areas, including Fujian, Guangdong, Guizhou, Hunan, Hubei, Jiangxi, Anhui, Zhejiang, Jiangsu, Henan, Liaoning, and Heilongjiang. Countless houses and fields across half of the nation were submerged in floodwaters. An article from *Guo Wen Zhou Bao,* a weekly newspaper from Tianjin, reported: "The current number of officially declared disaster provinces is sixteen. However, the actual number should be much more than sixteen, if we include the reports from various news sources. . . . The remaining provinces, such as Hebei and Shanxi, were also affected by considerable degrees of rainstorms and flood. It is likely that almost no province has been unaffected. This is truly a historical catastrophe."

Three townships in Wuhan, with floodwaters ranging from three to thirty-two feet deep, were among the most seriously affected areas. Scattered buildings were like isolated islands in an ocean of muddy water. Having stayed in Wuhan for a few days to inspect the situation, the head of the Nationalist government, Generalissimo Chiang Kai-Shek (Kai-Shek Chiang), acknowledged the severity of the flood in his Address to the People in the Disaster Areas: "The flood has covered a large part of the nation, south and north to the Yangtze River. The tragedy and severity of its damage is very rare throughout history . . . not only has it affected residents' daily lives, but it also has threatened the welfare of the entire nation."[1]

Facing such a peril, the Nationalist government in Nanjing lamented in its call for National Disaster Relief: "Look at the towering muddy water that is never draining away and at our vast cultural heritage in danger of being submerged. The deceased have been swallowed by fish, whereas the survivors have been suffering from the famine. What a misfortune to our nation! And what a catastrophe to our people!"

This flood, the biggest to date of the twentieth century in China, had affected so many provinces that the headcount of victims reached as high as 70 to 80 million, almost one-sixth of the national population. This serious inundation put the Nanjing government under tremendous pressure as millions of victims, overwhelmed with grief, lost their homes and sought refuge. Nevertheless, this was just the prelude to an even greater disaster.

September 18, 1931, witnessed a military conflict, the historic "9.18 Incident," in northeast China between the Chinese Northeast Army and the Japanese Kwantung Army. Bold action by pro-war Japanese military forces, combined with the pacifist policy of the Nationalist government, led to a bloodless occupation by the Japanese army of the city of Shenyang and then of all three northeast provinces, Liaoning, Jilin, and Heilongjiang. In March 1932, the Japanese invaders established the puppet state of Manchukuo with its capitol in Changchun, Jilin Province. This was followed by an aggressive expansion into other regions of China. September 18 thus became known as the "Day of National Humiliation" to the Chinese people.

Conquering China had been on Japan's national strategic agenda ever since the Meiji Restoration of the late nineteenth century. In June 1927, Prime Minister Tanaka Giyichi submitted a proposal to the emperor of Japan that said: "Conquering of China must begin with conquering Manchuria and Mongolia, and

---

1. Hongyec Guo, "The Nationwide Flooding of 1931," *Yan Huang Cun Qiu*, no.6 (2006).

conquering the world must start with conquering China." This greedy desire and ambition for continuous expansion inevitably ended in the vicious invasion of China, forcing the country into the flames of war and the suffering Chinese people into deeper misery.

Hwa-Wei was doomed to spend his childhood years in the chaos of wars and natural disasters.

2

Hwa-Wei's great-grandfather, Shun-Ching Lee, was a successful businessman in Fuzhou, capable of providing his children and grandchildren with opportunities for a good education. Hwa-Wei's grandfather, Tzu-Ho Lee, was a Xiucai, a scholar who had passed the imperial examination of the Qing dynasty, and made his living by teaching in his hometown. His career path, education, was later followed by Hwa-Wei's father, Kan-Chun Lee (whose former name was Sheng-Shu Lee), and by Hwa-Wei himself, making three generations of the Lee family professional educators.

Fuzhou, named after Mt. Fu to its north, is located south of the Min River, with warm and rainy weather typical of the south. Driving from the city center to the East Sea takes only about an hour.

For two thousand years, the city had always enjoyed a certain degree of monopoly and autonomy, given the geographic advantage of being far away from the central governments. Further, as a "blessed place," as the name "Fuzhou" implies, this ancient city, with hills behind and a sea in front, had rarely suffered from calamities caused by natural disasters and human intervention.

Fuzhou also has a poetic nickname—Rongcheng, which literally means Banyan City. Banyan trees could be seen everywhere in the city since the Northern Song dynasty (960–1120). With its continuously growing prop roots, one banyan tree can spread out, over hundreds of years, to form a far-reaching and very dense thicket, resembling from afar a lovely hill covered with green foliage. Ancient memories of this city are likely hidden in those thick tangles of banyan roots and trunks.

Unlike the natives of many other inland cities, Fuzhou people are primarily the mixed descendants of migrants from central China and local natives, with minimal regional ethnicities among them. During the Song dynasty, one thousand years ago, Fuzhou was already a well-known open-trading port on the east coast. It was, indeed, from the two harbors in Fuzhou, Mawei and Changle, the famous Admiral Zheng He (He Zheng) embarked on his seven naval expeditions between 1405 and 1433.

Fuzhou later became one of the five designated trade ports in the Sino-British Treaty of Nanjing, following China's defeat in the Opium War. As a result,

In 1931, Hwa Wei and his family visited his parents' home in Fuzhou. Returning on that visit were (*front, left to right*): two cousins; six-month-old Hwa-Wei; his sister, Hwa-Yu; and his brother, Hwa-Hsin (Min).

In 1932, Hwa-Wei's family moved to Nanjing. Shown are (*left to right*): Hwa-Wei's brother, Hwa-Hsin (Min); his sister, Hwa-Yu; his father, Kan-Chun Lee; and Hwa-Wei.

Hwa-Wei and his mother, Hsiao-Hui Wang, in Nanjing, 1932.

countless foreign diplomats, businessmen, missionaries, and adventurers flocked to the southern city. Its residents, therefore, were among the earliest Chinese people to have direct encounters with westerners and western civilization. Meanwhile, along with the introduction of Wuyi tea to the western world, the Fuzhouese started to sail across the ocean and to extend their sojourns abroad.

Whereas the ocean brought a yearning for a wandering life to the Fuzhouese, the surrounding mountain terrain cultivated conservative and traditional virtues among them, along with an open-minded nature. This is why overseas Fuzhouese descendants still preserve their traditions of family and homeland patriotism, their persistent ingrained attitudes, as well as their industry and thrift, regardless of their circumstances.

The natural and cultural environment in Fuzhou nourished the older generations of Hwa-Wei's family. Hwa-Wei's father, then Sheng-Shu Lee, received his early education in church schools. Later, he went to Yenching University to study theology and education under the guidance of John Leighton Stuart. Originally a missionary in China, Mr. Stuart later switched his focus to academia and became the founding president of Yenching University. His philosophy of academic freedom and openness was carried on through generations, making Yenching a unique institution of higher learning in China.[2] As a young student, one from a historic city far to the south, Sheng-Shu Lee was greatly influenced by Mr. Stuart and his philosophy.

Having earned his master's degree from Yenching University, Sheng-Shu went back to the south and worked as an associate professor and then as a professor at Fujian Christian University. He later served as the principal of Fujian Christian Normal School until he joined the Nationalist Revolutionary Army in 1928 and changed his name to Kan-Chun Lee in accordance with his new career identity.

From a noble family in Fuzhou, Hwa-Wei's mother, Hsiao-Hui Wang, had two siblings, a younger brother and a younger sister. All three received a good education from church colleges. Hsiao-Hui and her sister, Hsiao-Chu Wang, graduated from Hua-Nan College of Arts and Sciences in Fuzhou. Both were devout Christians.

Hsiao-Hui's brother, Tiao-Hsin Wang, was a chemistry professor, department chair, and then dean of the School of Science at Fujian Christian University (FCU). In 1948, he came to the United States to further his studies, returning to China in 1949, soon after the Communist Party took over the country, to continue his teaching and research at FCU. He was once the acting university president and also a board member of the Chinese Chemical Society. Unfortunately, he

---

2. Qing Li, *The Not Lonely Past. Jing-Po Fu: Accompanying John Leighton Stuart for 44 Years* (Hong Kong: Joint Publishing, 2009).

lost his life in the Cultural Revolution due largely to his religious affiliation and Western connection.

Hsiao-Chu Wang (Her English name is Phyllis Wang.), Hwa-Wei's maternal aunt, went to Beijing to study education at the Graduate School of Yenching University after her graduation from Hua-Nan College. She later relocated from Beijing to Guangzhou, where she worked as the head of cataloging, chief of general affairs, deputy director, and director at the Lingnan University Library. Hsiao-Chu came to the United States in 1948 on a scholarship provided by the board of Christian Higher Education in China and received her Master of Library Science (MLS) degree from the University of Illinois, Urbana-Champaign (UIUC), two years later. Because of the political situation in China and the closing of her university after 1949, she decided to settle in the United States and worked in several libraries, including the Health Sciences Library at the University of Pittsburgh.

Hwa-Wei could not remember if he ever visited Fuzhou with his parents and siblings in his childhood. However, in a later visit to Fuzhou in search of his family roots, during his first trip back to the mainland since 1949, he spoke with his uncle's wife, who insisted that the family—Hwa-Wei, his parents, older brother, and sister—had made a trip back home when Hwa-Wei was still a toddler. In spite of a blank spot in his memory involving that visit, he, interestingly enough, still had a lingering memory of the slightly sweet and astringent taste of the locally grown green olives.

On Hwa-Wei's father's side, there is only one known relative, his aunt, a medical doctor. Hwa-Wei met her only once in Chongqing and, unfortunately, lost contact with her after the family moved to Taiwan.

3

Living in a turbulent era of domestic turmoil and foreign invasion, Hwa-Wei's father, young Kan-Chun Lee, aspired to dedicate his life to his country. He was once a devout Christian and worked as the secretary general of the Christian Education Association in Fujian. However, his perception of Christianity gradually changed due to the influence of the popular "May Fourth Movement." He grew to believe that the spread of Christianity in China was a disguised form of political and cultural invasion by the Western colonial powers. Some aggressive Chinese students and intellectuals at that time even labeled foreign missionaries and their approaches as "mission and missile."[3]

He eventually chose to leave his religious work and changed his name from Sheng-Shu, "Holy Gospeller," to Kan-Chun, "Joining the Army," indicating his

3. Stacey Bieler, *A History of American-Educated Chinese Students*, trans. Yan Zhang (Hong Kong: Joint Publishing, 2010).

Hwa-Wei in Nanjing, 1935

Hwa-Wei and his siblings, Hwa-Ming, Hwa-Hsin, Hwa-Yu, and Hwa-Nin, in Nanjing, 1936. Hwa-Wei is seated fourth from the left.

Hwa-Wei's father, Kan-Chung Lee, and mother, Hsiao-Hui Wang, in Nanjing.

Hwa-Wei's paternal grandmother.

Hwa-Wei's paternal grandfather,
Tzu-Ho Lee.

Hwa-Wei's maternal grandfather.

Hwa-Wei's maternal grandmother.

transformed view of the world and his determination for a career change from academia to the military. In August 1928, he resigned from his position as the principal of Fujian Christian Normal School and joined the Nationalist Revolutionary Army. Kan-Chun started with the title of publicity department chief (a lieutenant-colonel ranking) in the Eleventh National Revolutionary Army, and was promoted one year later to director of the Political Training Academy (a colonel ranking) in the Sixty-First Division of the army. He was the governor of Shihui County, Guangdong Province, from 1930 to 1932, then transferred in 1932 to Nanjing, where he became the secretary and, later, chief of the Statistics Department of the Ministry of Interior, while also serving as a lecturer at the Political Training Institute of the National Military Commission. The entire family, including Hwa-Wei, also relocated to Nanjing with Kan-Chun.

July 1937 witnessed the Lugouqiao (Lugou Bridge) Incident, which instigated the outbreak of the Sino-Japanese War. It took only five months for the menacing Imperial Japanese Army to conquer Nanjing, the capital of the Republic of China, followed by the two-month-long historic Nanjing Massacre. The atrocities committed there by the Japanese occupiers between December 13, 1937, and February 1938 included the barbaric killing of almost three hundred thousand civilians and the destruction of one-third of the city. The Yangtze River was dyed red with the fresh blood of the victims. The notorious "Rape of Nanjing" by the brutal Japanese aggressors turned the Chinese ancient capital of six dynasties into a ghost town and a massive graveyard.

Luckily, the Lee family had already left Nanjing for Guilin of the then Guangxi Province, as Kan-Chun Lee had been hired by two regional military leaders there, General Li Tsung-Jen (Zongren Li) and General Pai Chung-Hsi (Chongxi Bai), to be the education officer in the Provincial Cadre Training Corps. The two generals highly regarded Kan-Chun's work experience as the governor of Sihui County, Guangdong.

Located in the northeast of Guangxi Zhuang Autonomous Region, Guilin has a revered reputation among the Chinese—"Guilin's scenery is the best among all under the heavens"—due to its amazing landscape with intertwined lofty mountains and flowing rivers. Guilin's famous scenic spots include the Duxiu Mountain Peak at the center of the city, Elephant Trunk Hill on the south, Seven Star Cave and Crescent Hill on the east, and Wind Cave and Folded Brocade Hill on the north.

As the Japanese invasion expanded rapidly in China, the situation in Guangxi worsened. Heavily loaded with work both day and night, Kan-Chun had little time to take care of his family. To ensure their safety, he decided to send his wife and six children to Haiphong in Vietnam, allowing them to escape the daily bombing from the Japanese airplanes. Kan-Chun and a contingent of subordinates escorted his loved ones on this journey all the way from Guilin, Nanning, and Liuzhou to Longzhou. There they crossed the border from the south of Longzhou into Hanoi and finally arrived at Haiphong.

Hwa-Wei remembers the long journey as a harsh and endless one. Along some sections of the road, they were able to take buses; on the others, only horseback riding or walking was allowed. Five out of the six children, except Hwa-Hsin, were too young to make the trip on their own. The two younger brothers, Hwa-Ming and Hwa-Nin, had to sit in large baskets, one in the front and the other in the back, of a shoulder pole carried by one of their father's subordinates. The youngest, Hwa-Tsun, had to be held or carried in a cloth sling. Seven-year-old Hwa-Wei was transported on a horse. He was afraid of falling from the horse, as rough and rugged mountain paths made the bumping and jerking horseback ride quite unstable. The rider used a rope to tie Hwa-Wei to the front of him, warning Hwa-Wei not to move. It was arranged for Hwa-Wei's pregnant mother to travel in a sedan chair carried by the men taking turns.

It is not quite clear to Hwa-Wei why his father chose Haiphong as the sanctuary for the family. It could have been that some of his father's friends were living there. As the largest harbor in northern Vietnam, Haiphong was then a French colony with arrogant police officers everywhere.

After Kan-Chun returned to Guilin, Hsiao-Hui Wang and her six children temporarily settled in Haiphong. She took good care of everything in their simply furnished rental home. Several months later, Hwa-Chou, the youngest sister, came into the world. Hwa-Wei's mother was truly an extraordinary woman, one able to manage household affairs very well, while looking after her seven children, including one newborn, in a foreign country. On the few later occasions when the family's refugee experience in Haiphong was mentioned, Hsiao-Hui always expressed thanks that all of her seven children were able to survive, something which seemed like quite a miracle during that time. She always felt happy and grateful that her family was able to escape from the war and live a simple life in a foreign land.[4]

Eighteen months later, his father arranged for the family to move back to Guilin. The trip home was somewhat easier, as all the children were better able to manage by themselves. Hwa-Chou, the youngest sister, was held in her mother's arms all the way back. When the family checked in at the immigration office in China, the mother and children were all registered as returning overseas Chinese. For that reason Hwa-Wei later went to the National Number Two High School for Overseas Chinese for his junior high education.

---

4. Hong Lu, "Extending time and space in searching and offering—the life of Dr. Hwa-Wei Lee, Director of Ohio University Libraries," *Mei Hua Wen Xue (The Literati)*, no. 25 (January/February 1999): 24–43.

Sharing the same goal of fighting against the invading Japanese troops, General Li Tsung-Jen's Guixi armed forces reconciled with Generalissimo Chiang Kai-Shek's central government and formed a temporary alliance. As the general commander of the Fifth War Area, General Li Tsung-Jen, collaborating with General Pai Chung-Hsi, directed the Battle of Taierzhuang. Due to careful deployment of the joint troops, Taierzhuang became a major victory for the Chinese, the first of the Nationalist Alliance against the Japanese army.

This victory boosted the reputation of the Guixi military. From Guangxi, a region home to impoverished but valiant people, Guixi warriors had already become well known as an "iron army" as early as the time of the Northern Expedition. Guixi forces were involved in numerous famous and extremely tough battles against the Japanese invaders. General Joseph W. Stilwell, the chief of staff to Generalissimo Chiang Kai-Shek, once marveled at the quality of this army, calling the Guixi soldiers the best warriors in the world.

A very subtle and complicated relationship of mutual exploitation and mutual vigilance existed between Li Tsung-Jen's Guixi army and Chiang Kai-Shek's central government. To get Li Tsung-Jen under control, Chiang Kai-Shek "promoted" Li in September 1943 from general commander of the Fifth War Region to chief commander of the Hanzhong Field Headquarters of the National Military Commission, a wartime senior authority between the central government and the Combined First, Fifth, and Tenth War Regions. This was a promotion in name only because, although it increased the number of war regions under Lee's supervision, it decreased his military power, as the Field Headquarters was, indeed, a paper agency.

After the Sino-Japanese war ended, Li was transferred in August 1945 to the Beijing Field Headquarters with the same rank.[5] Hwa-Wei's father, Kan-Chun Lee, already a lieutenant general, became Li's confidential advisor. Kan-Chun followed General Commander Li to Beijing where the family moved into the Qinzheng (diligence to government affairs) Hall in Zhongnanhai. The headquarters was located in the Juren (be benevolent) Hall. Originally built in the Ming dynasty and renovated in the Qing dynasty, Qinzheng Hall had once served as the offices of visiting emperors during their stays in Zhongnanhai.

Located on the west side of the Forbidden City, Zhongnanhai consists of two parts, Zhonghai (Central Sea) and Nanhai (South Sea), and was once, along with Beihai (North Sea), referred to as "Three Seas" in Beijing. With its winding streams, Zhongnanhai has a landscape differing from that of the solemn and

---

5. De-Gang Tan, *Memoirs of Li Tsung-Jen*, 1st ed. (Guilin: Guangxi Normal University Press, 2005).

respectful Forbidden City. All the emperors since the Liao (916–1125) and Jin (1115–1234) dynasties favored Zhongnanhai and invested large amounts in its expansion and renovation. Zhongnanhai became an imperial garden and political center in the Qing dynasty (1644–1911), serving as the emperors' summer resort and governance place. After the Revolution of 1911, it became one of the essential meeting venues of the Beiyang Warlord Government.

Hwa-Wei did not move with his family to Zhongnanhai. He stayed at the First Municipal Middle School in Nanjing to continue junior high school. What he knew of his family's life in Zhongnanhai, he learned from his brothers. According to them, the layout of Qinzheng Hall was rather complicated, comprising some thirty rooms of different sizes, including an anteroom, a hallway, a reception room, central and west-wing living rooms, and a dining room, as well as a very imposing home office. The home office, used mainly by Hwa-Wei's father, had a gigantic rosewood desk in which his father's documents were kept.[6]

Qinzheng Hall actually continued its political function in the post-1949 era until it was demolished in the 1970s. There Mao Zedong (Zedong Mao) would often hold his diplomatic meetings with heads of foreign countries and other dignitaries.

Under the U.S. mediation, Mao Zedong, accompanied by then U.S. Ambassador Patrick J. Hurley, flew to Chongqing in August 1945 for peace talks between the Nationalists and the Communists. An agreement to end the military conflict was reached and recorded in the meeting memo. However, under that peaceful and harmonious surface simmered the never-ending troop deployment. Before long, the Communist armed forces, having been enhanced and fortified in the northeast, launched large-scale warfare in the areas of Changchun and Siping against the Nationalist troops.

By the spring of 1946, the Chinese Civil War had spread all over northern China. The peace talk agreement eventually became invalid. The unfortunate Chinese civilians, who had been allowed no time to celebrate the end of World War II, were soon drawn into this dreadful civil war, a life or death combat between the Nationalists and the Communists. Early in 1947, the Lee family was compelled to move back to Guilin from Beijing.

There was no way for Hwa-Wei's father and older brother to stay away from the increasingly brutal war; both were inevitably involved. The winter of 1948 saw a reversal between the two parties as the People's Liberation Army won three decisive battles, Liaoshen, Pingjin, and Huaihai, over the Nationalist Army. Having sustained several successive defeats on the battlefield, Chiang's popularity dropped dramatically.

---

6. *The Bloodstained Red Sky: In Memory of the Martyrs of the Aircraft 815 of the Air Force 34th Black Bats Squadron.* (Taiwan: published by family members of the 815 Aircraft, 1993).

Meanwhile, a nationwide economic breakdown became the deathblow to Chiang's government, bringing the Communist Party to the center stage of history.[7] In order to make the new round of peace talks more effective, Chiang resigned from his presidency on January 21, 1949, appointing Li Tsung-Jen the acting president, with a primary mission of easing the tension and suing for peace. However, Li's proposal of a joint rule of China with the Nationalists to the south of the Yangtze River and the Communists to the north was immediately rejected by both the Communist government and by Chiang Kai-Shek.

Three months later in April 1949, Mao's army succeeded in breaking through the defensive line along the Yangtze River. Thus, the Nanjing Nationalist Government instantly lost its power on mainland China. On October 1, 1949, Mao Zedong proclaimed the birth of the People's Republic of China in Beijing.

As the Communist army approached Guangzhou, Li Tsung-Jen had no choice but to flee the country. He flew to Chongqing on October 13, then left Chongqing for Hong Kong on November 20, after he was diagnosed with a bleeding gastroduodenal ulcer. On December 5, Li left Hong Kong for New York City to seek medical treatment, accompanied by his wife and two sons.[8]

Li's interim government was dissolved thereafter. Chiang's Nationalist Government eventually withdrew to Taipei on December 7 after several short stays in Guangzhou, Chongqing, and Chengdu. Mainland China and Taiwan have been separated by the Taiwan Strait ever since Chiang moved to his final base.

5

Having worked for the Guixi division for many years, Kan-Chun Lee failed to get himself and his family entrance tickets to Taiwan. Facing the reality that General Li Tsung-Jen was hardly able to protect himself, Hwa-Wei's father had no other choice but to resign himself to his fate.

While the Lee family was still trapped in Guilin, the oldest son, Min Lee (whose former name was Hwa-Hsin Lee), had already withdrawn to Taiwan as an officer in the Nationalist Air Force. As an elite soldier in Chiang's army, Min was allowed to bring his family members to Taiwan. At the end of September 1949, only a few days before the founding of the new China, Min arranged a military transport plane from Taiwan to Guilin, rushed the entire family aboard, and flew back to Taiwan. Thus, at a critical moment in history, all nine members of the Lee family dramatically departed China for Taiwan onboard a special plane, thanks to Min's arrangement.

---

7. Len-Yu Huang, *Reading the Dairy of Chiang Kai-Shek from the Historical Perspective*, (Kuala Lumpur, Malaysia: Jiu Zhou Press, 2008).
8. De-Gang Tan, *Memoirs of Li Tsung-Jen*.

All the family members hurried onto the military transport plane. The inadequate safety devices and little radar guidance combined with the bad weather put the family at great risk during their escape. Because of Taiwan's high mountains, the plane, in order to land safely in the dense low clouds, had to gradually descend over the ocean before proceeding to land at the military airport in Central Taiwan. Due to these circumstances, Min and his copilot asked everyone to look out the windows and let them know immediately upon sighting the ocean so that they could control the aircraft below the low and heavy clouds.

It was Hwa-Wei's first flight in an air force aircraft, and he was very excited. Hwa-Wei and his other siblings did not feel scared at all. Instead, they all saw the endeavor as quite interesting. All started to yell as soon as they saw the dark blue sea through the windows. The plane started low-altitude flying above the ocean. Thanks to Min's superb piloting skills, they made a safe landing at the Hsinchu Air Base in Taiwan.

Four days after the Lee family escaped from Guilin, the entire Guangxi Province was taken over by the People's Liberation Army. Back then, Hwa-Wei did not realize that the next opportunity for him to return to mainland China would be thirty-three years later in 1982!

With only a few hours' notice and given limited cargo space, the Lee family was not able to take many of their belongings with them on the flight. They had nothing to call their own upon arrival in Taiwan.

Owing to years of political infighting between Chiang and Li, and Li's being away in the United States, Li's former subordinates who had managed to leave the mainland and relocate in Taiwan were unable to escape being oppressed and squeezed out of government positions. Because of his close Guixi connection, it was obvious that Kan-Chun Lee would have no chance to continue his political career in Taiwan. In addition, he, himself, had lost interest in working as a government official after experiencing so many ups and downs in politics.

Having been enlightened by reality, Kan-Chun, now in his fifties, decided to return to teaching, his previous profession. Teaching was truly an easy job for Kan-Chun due to his fluency in English and his background as a former student of John L. Stuart at Yenching University. It did not take him long to land a job teaching the English language at Taichung College of Agriculture, which later changed its name to National Taiwan Chung-Hsing University. A popular lecturer among students, he soon was promoted to the rank of full professor. This teaching job did not make the family wealthy, but neither were they poor. Compared with many other families retreating from the mainland to Taiwan, the Lees were indeed blessed and, after a short time, settled in Taichung.

Kan-Chun was an exceedingly brilliant professor. He was highly regarded and well supported by his university president. He was visited frequently by junior faculty members looking for his guidance. The recognition and respect he earned from his teaching career brought Kan-Chun true happiness. Therefore, he often told his children not to pursue a political career, citing his own experience and the vain outcome of his previous involvement in politics. In his later years, Kan-Chun felt working in academia was a more worthwhile pursuit because it brought a noble and virtuous life.

The necessity of Hwa-Wei's father returning to teaching worked out well for him; the latter half of his life became a more cheerful and comfortable time. Kan-Chun's teaching career lasted until he was almost in his seventies.

After his retirement, Kan-Chun returned to a religious life, using his previously earned missionary credentials, and became a guest minister at a Methodist church in Taichung. Kan-Chun's church service was volunteer-based, as churches in Taiwan were inadequately funded, unlike their American counterparts. Kan-Chun Lee lived a long life and passed away at the age of eighty-nine. He was buried in a graveyard in Taichung with his wife, Hsiao-Hui Wang, who died one year later, at age ninety.

6

Hwa-Wei's father had a proficiency in English; after the family relocated to Taiwan, he was able to use that skill to make a living for his family. Later, Hwa-Wei was even more impressed with his father's English when his father helped him edit and polish his application documents for American graduate schools.

Among the seven children in his family, Hwa-Wei's personality most closely resembles that of his father; he is also the child most heavily influenced by him. Nevertheless, the hardships his father had suffered were probably greater than anything Hwa-Wei has had to experience. Kan-Chun continually endured wars and political turmoil during the first half of his life. He underwent changes in his life path from his original devotion to Christianity to his dedication to the Nationalist Revolution, as a follower of General Li Tsung-Jen. The perils of those decades of military service were like treading on thin ice. Fortunately, he was able to settle down with a stable teaching job and do missionary work in his later years.

Kan-Chun took the bad with the good and honored the code of brotherhood. His limited income could barely provide the essential expenses of his big family, even under his wife's thrifty management. On many occasions when the family was unable to make ends meet at the end of the month, Hwa-Wei's mother had to trade the jewelry from her dowry to feed the family, or his father had to borrow money from one of his eleven blood brothers whose financial situation was slightly better. He had no alternative but to seek help from his

friends for the sake of his family. Hwa-Wei could feel the helplessness and ag-
ony of his father; this only increased Hwa-Wei's respect for him.

The blood brothers of his father were primarily Fujianese, known for their
strong ties with each other. Hwa-Wei met two or three of them, including I-Wu
Ho, who had once served as the secretary general of the Taiwan Legislature,
the vice chairman of the Commission of Overseas Chinese Affairs, and the president of the board of Cathay United Commercial Bank. Ho was a great help to the
Lee family and provided kind support to Hwa-Wei and his siblings with their
plans to study abroad.

Hwa-Wei's father was a family man with only a few personal hobbies, playing mahjong, smoking, and drinking with friends. His mother was a perfect
housewife who took good care of all seven children. Among the many kinds of
love, the most selfless love is the devotion of parents to their children. The adults
who are closest to a child during childhood usually shape that child's life. The
personality and character traits of Hwa-Wei's parents had a far-reaching impact
on their children. The harmonious and relaxing family atmosphere that they
created has benefited Hwa-Wei and his siblings their entire lives.

Because Hwa-Wei left home at the young age of twelve for schooling, his
mother was always very kind and loving to him whenever he came home during school recess. During his youth, Hwa-Wei suffered from chronic allergic
sinus infections and had to undergo surgeries each year for nasal polyp removal.
When providing him with meals more nutritional than those he got in school,
his mother always made him his favorite dish: five-spice red-cooked stewed
pork shoulder. Hwa-Wei has always treasured those memories of his mother
and still remembers the aromas of the food she prepared for him.

His Education during the Wars

. . . One day, enemies invaded my village.
So I've lost my family, my farmhouse, and my livestock . . .

—*"On the Jialing River"*
Lyrics by Hongliang Duanmu
Music by Luting He

1

It was not easy for Hwa-Wei's civil servant father to support a big family of seven children on his limited income. From a young age, Hwa-Wei came to understand the hardships of life. Although his well-educated parents hoped that their children could also receive good schooling, Hwa-Wei's K–12 education was constantly interrupted by endless wars and his family's frequent relocation caused by these wars.

During the anti-Japanese War, countless students, including Hwa-Wei, were forced to abandon their schools in enemy-occupied areas and flee to safer places. To help those students who were deprived of education by the war, thirty-four secondary schools were established and operated by the central government from 1937 to 1949, including one girls' school and three schools for returning overseas Chinese students from Southeast Asia. Many of these government-operated schools were quite large: twelve had over one thousand students and thirteen enrolled a student population of five hundred or more. All of those secondary schools, along with the vocational schools, offered free tuition and room and board, effectively subsidizing a refugee student's education.[1]

Located in southwest China, Chongqing served as the temporary capital of the Nationalist government during the Sino-Japanese War, providing shelters for refugees from other parts of the country. The year of 1943 saw increasing hardship resulting from the war and an even greater threat from the invaders.

Hwa-Wei and his family went first to Guilin and then moved to Chongqing, where Hwa-Wei's father worked. Hwa-Wei had just graduated from elementary

---

1. "Education in Wartime China," *The Whole History of China*, part 20, 372.

school in Guilin and was about to begin secondary school. Under an arrangement made by his parents, he and his older brother, Hwa-Hsin, were accepted by the National Number Two High School for Overseas Chinese where Hwa-Hsin was in the eleventh grade and Hwa-Wei in the seventh grade. The school was located in a remote rural area about a day's journey from Chongqing, with separate campuses about three miles apart for junior and senior high school classes. His mother was very worried about Hwa-Wei, who was then only twelve years old and had never been away from home. But she had no other choice: the government, who operated the school, would provide free education that covered room and board as well.

Founded in August 1941, the National Number Two High School for Overseas Chinese was originally located in the Cheng clan temple of the Jiangjin District, a suburb in Chongqing, as the result of a free land lease to the government for educational use by the Cheng clan. De-Hsi Wang was the school principal appointed by the Ministry of Education.

Situated in the foothills of Longdeng Mountain and alongside the Zuanjiang River, Cheng clan temple was the best building in Jiangjin. However, transportation between Chongqing and the temple was not convenient. One had to walk on foot for about two miles from the temple to Wufuchang, a small town, then another six miles from Wufuchang to Dushi, a township, then, finally, take a bus from Dushi to Chongqing.

At the beginning, all junior and senior high students boarded at school in Cheng clan temple, as they were few in number. Later, the school was expanded with the addition of another campus a short distance away due to the rising number of incoming refugee students from Southeast Asian countries that had also been invaded by the Japanese army.[2]

Hwa-Wei had quite an adventurous experience during his first trip from Chongqing to the school. His father had negotiated a paid ride with a truck driver along the highway. It was a fully loaded truck, but the driver somehow managed to find additional space by tying some goods to its top. The father and sons squeezed together in the limited space. Once the truck began to move, the tied-up goods seemed to hang by a thread. For most of the trip, Hwa-Wei kept his eyes closed and hoped nothing would fall from above.

About four or five hours later, the three got off the truck when it was about to head in a different direction. Shaking off the dust, Hwa-Wei was finally able to heave a sigh of relief. Despite their continuous jerking for several hours, the goods right above him had not fallen down at all. To complete the journey, Hwa-Wei had to walk for three or four more hours with his father and his brother, Hwa-Hsin, to reach the school.

---

2. Zhenshi Yi, "National High Schools for Oversea Chinese during the Anti-Japanese War." *Oversea Chinese Affairs First Journal*, No. 5, 2006. http://qwgzyj.gqb.gov.cn/qwhg/132/755.shtml.

After hours on the road, it was getting dark, although they had left home in the early morning hours. His father and older brother carried their light luggage. Hwa-Hsin was a thin seventeen-year-old, but he was as tall as his father, and Hwa-Wei felt somewhat secure being with his older brother. The three kept silent while walking cautiously along the potholed country road. Not far away were farmers' cottages and their surrounding croplands dotted with manure pits here and there. At times, gaunt and dark-skinned farmers would throw a puzzled look at these three neatly dressed and pale-skinned outsiders. Their skeptical gazes made Hwa-Wei feel uneasy, as if he were about to enter another world.

The outlines of the mountain in the distance were gradually obscured by the approaching sunset. In contrast to the bloody and brutal war in other parts of the country, the area seemed peaceful with curls of cooking smoke and the calls of frogs and cicadas. The father and sons hurried along heading toward Wufuchang, literally "a place with five good fortunes," and into an utterly new life for Hwa-Wei and his older brother, Hwa-Hsin.

2

The junior high campus of the National Number Two High School for Overseas Chinese was in a western-style house made of wood and bricks with an arched door and narrow windows. The two-story building was quite different from the numerous low-rise farmhouses. Local people called it Yangfangzi, "foreign house," as its original owner was a foreign missionary. About three hundred feet in front of the school flowed the limpid Zuanjiang River.

By the time Hwa-Wei entered the school, there were already some four hundred registered students distributed on the junior and senior high campuses. Educating that steadily growing student population was complicated by extremely underdeveloped facilities and a severe shortage of teaching aids, books, desks, and chairs. To cope with the lack of student desks and chairs, the school sent students to Longdeng Mountain where they would cut and bring back bamboo trunks. Local craftsmen were then hired to make school furniture. A locally made student bench called a zhukangdeng, "bamboo-supported bench," used two fire-curved bamboo trunks as legs to support another thick bamboo trunk that crossed over them.[3]

Every low-income student was eligible to receive a school uniform, made of a thick chunky cloth called Luosifubu or "Roosevelt cloth." The uniforms wore well and were good all year around. Unfortunately, all other daily commodities

---

3. "Brief History of the Second National Overseas Chinese High School", *Special Issue of the History of Private Overseas Chinese High School, the First National Overseas Chinese High School, and the Second National Overseas Chinese High School*. (Hainan: Hainan Overseas Chinese High School, May 2013. 13-23.

were of low quality. Students had only flimsy straw sandals that they would purchase or make themselves. Quite a few students were just in their bare feet.

Textbooks and notebooks, frequently in short supply, were made of a poor-quality rough paper and were often shared among the students. The rough surface made writing on those papers difficult when using a pen. Brush pens thus became the only writing tool for students, even for their English homework.[4]

The living arrangements were equally austere: seven or eight students shared one dorm room furnished with crude bunk beds made of local bamboo. A typical bed was made by loosely tying several bamboo trunks together and was covered only by a thin blanket, which often lost its original color due to sweat stains. Students had to be extremely cautious when lying on their beds so that they would not be trapped in any of the cracks between the two bamboo trunks.

In the summer, the hot and humid weather in Chongqing made the students' lives more miserable; until late at night, they felt as if they were choking, as if they were enclosed in an airtight cabin. Hungry mosquitoes thirsted for those poor students' blood. The dank winter did not make the situation better. The twelve- or thirteen-year-old children were still too young to take care of themselves properly. A lack of clean clothes and infrequent bathing resulted in constant outbreaks of lice.

Lice, the size of a sesame seed, were a type of parasite often found in the student dorms. Blood-sucking parasites of exceptional vitality, the tiny insects spread quickly. Once found on one student's body, the lice, before long, would have infested all the students sharing a room. At the beginning of the infestation, students would feel itchy over their entire bodies. Strangely, the itching feeling would eventually go away. It seemed that almost all of the refugee students had some experience with this widespread infestation of lice. Every time Hwa-Wei went back home, the first thing his mother would do was put all of his clothes in boiling water and wash his hair with liquid medicine.

Each day, the refugee students received two meals, breakfast and dinner, both seldom containing meat. A typical breakfast was up to three bowls of boiled rice soup; but three bowls represented a lucky day. A common dish was often salty beans cooked with hot peppers. Dinner was rice again accompanied by some seasonal vegetables flavored with a few slices of fat pork. The insufficient food supply felt to Hwa-Wei like a cruel punishment; his constant hunger remained deeply inscribed in his memory. It was difficult to fall asleep at night with an empty and gurgling stomach. Most of the time, Hwa-Wei kept a constant lookout for food, but that was in vain.

---

4. Ibid.

Chapter 2

In his early teenage years, Hwa-Wei started to develop an enormous appetite as his body grew. He hoped that he could get five bowls of rice for each meal, but, on most days, ended up with no more than two. The rice from greedy merchants was always mixed with lots of barnyard millet, sand, and, even, small stones, earning the rice its nickname—"Babaofan," meaning rice with eight treasures.

During dinner, students, who were always in a hurry for more bowls of rice, spent no time picking out the impurities and learned to eat those "treasures." One serious consequence of eating "Babaofan" daily was that many students developed appendicitis. Hwa-Wei was one of them.

The hardship of life, however, seemed to have little negative impact on the students' desire for learning. Instead, they all treasured their peaceful time during the war years. Every morning, reading aloud could be heard throughout the school. Every evening, study groups of three to five students each could be seen in the classroom, dining room, and courtyard. Students with good grades would volunteer to tutor other students with their schoolwork. Looking back, Hwa-Wei remembered the warm orange-colored light coming from the oil lamps in the evening at the Yangfangzi, western-style house, as a symbol of faith and hope for peace in wartime China.

Often seen together with Hwa-Wei were four boys and two girls. One of the older girls called Dejie, "big sister," really acted like a big sister, always taking good care of the others. She helped Hwa-Wei do his laundry.

Being away from their parents, the boys and girls formed a close-knit group looking after each other. Whenever one of them received a remittance from home, he or she would take the others out for a sumptuous meal, or share some money with others in need. Every time one of them received a food package, the entire group would become excited, sharing the food as if it were a holiday celebration.

During some of the weekends, a group of children would go out and spend a day helping nearby farmers in the fields picking snow peas and digging sweet potatoes, or watering and fertilizing the vegetable crops, in exchange for some pocket money and sweet potatoes. The sweet potatoes were restricted to onsite eating only, so the children wouldn't stop eating until they became extremely full. In spite of their different personalities and backgrounds, the children helped each other, depended on each other, and endured difficulties together during the national crisis.

This rural area had its unique charms. Wufuchang had abundant orange trees, with plenty of orange orchards near the school. During a golden fall season, the small town was full of ripe oranges, clusters of orange-red among the bright green leaves. The sweet and astringent odor from those ripe oranges irresistibly tempted the students, who were normally hungry, to steal them. Stealing thus became a popular student pastime.

Knowing that there would be no way to stop the children from picking oranges, the farmers came up with a smart idea: They encouraged orange tree adoption by a student at a reasonable price. Once adopted, the tree became the "property" of the student adopter whose name card would be attached to it. The student then had the right to eat as many oranges from his or her "property" as he or she could. This approach was very effective. Farmers made a profit; students gained the pride of ownership. Hwa-Wei, who was one of the adopters, took care of his orange tree. Indeed, it was the first property that he owned.

3

Almost every boy in the school was equipped with a special weapon—a slingshot —which was used for bird hunting. To those starving boys, birds represented their foremost source of meat. After school, groups of boys would often go out on bird hunts, which sometimes took longer than anticipated as the birds gradually learned their lessons and became shrewd.

Hwa-Wei was an expert bird hunter and usually made every shot count. The poor birds would end hung up to dry outside dorm windows after having their feathers torn off, insides cleaned, and their clean bodies marinated with salt. Later, they would be roasted to provide delicious food for the starving students.

Caught in the turmoil of war, the majority of students had nothing to call their own. It was hardly possible for individual refugee students to live on their own without each other's help. It was truly fortunate for Hwa-Wei to be with a group of peers who stuck together to cope with the hardship. Hwa-Wei felt lucky to have those close friends, while also being able to stay away from the cruelty of the Japanese invaders.

Experience from hardship in one's early life can become a valuable asset in one's later life. Through helping and supporting each other in difficult times, one can readily understand the power of mutual aid and the importance of sincerity, forgiveness, friendship, and thankfulness in interacting with others. From his school years at Wufuchang, the young Hwa-Wei came to realize that one can't survive on one's own, and the rules of survivorship are kindness, alliance, reverence for others, and togetherness in times of need. These rules have had a tremendous influence on Hwa-Wei and became his guide for interpersonal relationships in later years.

One's potential and endurance is essentially unlimited. The hardship Hwa-Wei experienced in his childhood set for him an ultimate minimum threshold for living. He is thankful that none of his later experiences were comparable to his years in Wufuchang. Through adversity one can learn to cherish life. The hardship of Hwa-Wei's early years toughened his soul and tempered his will. Since then Hwa-Wei felt he had nothing to fear.

Hwa-Wei's schoolmates at the National Number Two High School for Overseas Chinese were mainly from Southeast Asia. When the war ended, the students scattered in different directions. After all the years of chaotic wars and constant moving and relocation, Hwa-Wei, unfortunately, lost contact with the majority of his schoolmates and friends. Now he cannot even recall their names.

4

Government-owned schools were often more disciplined than regular schools. The Nationalist Party government instituted a rigorous core curriculum of civic education courses at the national schools. There were boy and girl scout programs in junior high and military training in senior high schools.[5]

A good number of school-sponsored extracurricular activities were also available throughout the school year, including swim competitions, ball games, and choir and drama performances, usually involving student participants. In addition to the senior high Haiyun Singing Team and the junior high Zuanjiang Chorus, the National Number Two High School sponsored highly acclaimed basketball and swim teams that were victorious against teams from several local counties. The school was visited by several Nationalist government officials including Tie-Cheng Wu, then secretary-general of the Nationalist Party Executive Committee; Li-Fu Chen, then head of the Ministry of Education; and Tao-Fan Chang, the former provost of the National Political University. Wu delivered the following speech:

> You must study hard so as to be able to make contributions to the nation. We will win the war in two or three more years. Upon return to Nanyang [at that time, the Chinese name for Southeast Asia], you could let your parents know how difficult the anti-Japanese War had been, and how the government took great effort to provide education to overseas Chinese students. This country wouldn't become prosperous and powerful without patriotic support from overseas Chinese.

Hwa-Wei has little memory about what he learned in his classes as he seemed not to have had an interest in any particular subject. What is deeply inscribed in his memory, however, are the pervasive sentiments against foreign invaders and the many popular anti-Japanese songs. Among these was "On the Jialing River" with lyrics by Hongliang Duanmu and music by Luting He, a popular and emotional piece:

---

5. "Education in Wartime China," 373.

One day, enemies invaded my village. So I lost my family, my farmhouse, and my livestock.

Now wandering on the Jialing River, I smell the aroma of soil like the one from my homeland.

Despite the same moon and flowing water, my sweet smile and dream have gone.
The river beneath is sobbing every night; so is my heart.

I must go back to my homeland for the not-yet-harvested cauliflower and starving lamb.
I must return! Return under the bullet shower of our enemy.

I must return! Return across the sword and spear jungle of our enemy;
And I will place my bloody and victorious spear at my birthplace.

The year of 1944 witnessed the steady retreat of the Chinese army as Japanese invaders reached Guizhou Province. The occupation of Dushan County in that province by a small troop of Japanese cavalry immediately put Sichuan Province at risk, and started an uproar among the students at the National Number Two High School. By order of the school administration, every student had to stay in school and prepare for last-minute relocation if needed. However, many hot-blooded young students did not obey that order and joined the Educated Youth Army or the Chinese Expeditionary Force to fight against the Japanese invaders.

Hwa-Hsin, Hwa-Wei's older brother, had a great hatred of the Japanese and registered without a second thought for the Youth Air Force Academy when he learned of the school recruitment in Chongqing. Founded in 1940 by the government, the academy aimed to train air force reserve pilots. The Chinese air force was rather weak at the beginning of the war. The situation did not improve until the arrival of the Flying Tigers, a nickname of the renowned First American Volunteer Group of the Chinese Nationalist air force, commanded by General Claire Lee Chennault.

The Flying Tigers flew the famous "Hump" air route to transport armament supplies for the Southwest Expeditionary Force and to fight against the Japanese air force. Seeing the reduced potency of the Japanese air force increased Hwa-Hsin's admiration for the Flying Tigers. He started to dream about becoming an airman.

Their parents, originally concerned about young Hwa-Wei, had hoped his older brother could take care of him, somewhat, at school. However, Hwa-Hsin had only been at the school for one quarter before he left for the Youth Air Force Academy, leaving thirteen-year-old Hwa-Wei on his own. At the moment of seeing Hwa-Hsin depart, Hwa-Wei felt panic and helplessness, and he really wanted to call out to his older brother to beg him not to walk away. However, he knew that would not work and that he had to face the future on his own. Gazing at his brother's receding figure, Hwa-Wei blinked away his tears.

5

August 1945 was a major turning point in World War II with increased Soviet involvement and America's dropping of the atomic bombs on Hiroshima and Nagasaki. Hwa-Wei's family was still in Chongqing. Every day street-corner newspaper boys would shout victorious war news. Growing excitement and joy were filling the damp air, and smiles were back on pedestrians' faces. Having endured eight years of extreme hardship from the Japanese invaders, the Chinese were ready for the long-awaited victory and peace.

With the end of the Sino-Japanese War, the Nationalist government moved back from Chongqing to Nanjing. Japan declared an unconditional surrender on August 15, 1945. Three weeks later on September 9, a mass celebration was held in the capital city. Streets were filled with cheering crowds, colorful lanterns, and bands, accompanied by the sounds of loud gongs and drums.

Some of the major avenues were decorated with archways made of pine and cypress leaves. Those archways were decorated with eye-catching golden letters, spelling the words "Victory" and "Peace," and streaming national and Nationalist Party flags, with a red "V," for victory, sign placed between the two. The gate of the Central Military Academy held two signs: "For Forever Peace" and "General Headquarters of Chinese Land Forces."

At 9:00 a.m., the signing ceremony of the Japanese Surrender (China War Zone) began at the auditorium of the former Central Military Academy. Yasuji Okamura, the commander in chief of the Imperial Japanese Army in the China-Burma-India Theater, along with six other Japanese representatives, bowed, hats off, to the Chinese government representatives led by General Ying-Chin Ho, who, ironically, was a former student of General Okamura at the Imperial Japanese Army Academy.

Japan had regarded China as a hopelessly backward country that could not withstand a single blow from modern post-Meiji restoration Japan. This perception was based on the weakness and corruption that had developed during the last century of China's Qing dynasty, founded in 1644 by Manchus, and the country's lack of unity after the 1911 revolution that ended the dynasty and established the new Republic.

The Japanese failed to realize that their invasion of this ancient country had set off a time bomb. What they had not understood was that vast and populous China had also been undergoing a reformation with westernized cultural components and an enhanced national consciousness, but one growing at a slower

Hwa-Wei (*front row, third from the left*) in his junior year at the National Han-Min High School in Guilin.

Hwa-Wei (*front, third from the left*) was a member of his high school basketball team

Hwa-Wei (*first from left*) and friends in his senior year of high school at the Provincial Taichung First High School, Taiwan.

pace than their own. Tanaka Giichi's statement about taking over China as the first step to conquering the world was ultimately proved to be wrong.

When Hwa-Wei's family returned to Nanjing in the fall of 1946, there were still many Japanese soldiers waiting to be repatriated from China to their home country. Wandering on the pier in the rain, the Japanese soldiers lined up with heads down, showing no reaction to the outrageous curses, kicks, and thrown stones from angry Chinese citizens. Seeming indifferent, those low-spirited, defeated soldiers lost their wartime swagger and moved like animated corpses.

After seeing this scene, all the hatred that had built up during the past eight years in Hwa-Wei's heart was suddenly gone. Instead, Hwa-Wei felt sympathy for those down-and-out Japanese soldiers whose expressionless faces also seemed mixed with a bit of relief—the war was over and they were going home alive. Indeed, he understood, they were merely the tools and victims of the militarism of their misguided government. The true war criminals, he felt, should be seen as those who had initiated and directed the war.

Nanjing was a city where Hwa-Wei had spent most of his childhood years. He first moved to the city with his parents at the age of two and stayed there for four to five years. His second residential period in Nanjing was between the end of the Sino-Japanese War (1945) and the beginning of the resumed civil war between the Nationalist and Communist parties in 1947. During those two years, Hwa-Wei actually stayed in the boarding school of the First Municipal Middle School of Nanjing on his own, while the rest of the Lee family relocated to Peking after a very short stay in Nanjing. There were no worries for his parents this time around as Hwa-Wei was already accustomed to life at a boarding school and had learned to take care of himself.

Hwa-Wei left Nanjing for Guilin in 1947 to join his parents and siblings, who had just withdrawn from Peking to Guilin. It was in Guilin that Hwa-Wei was able to finish his tenth and eleventh grades at the National Han-Min High School, a famous state-run school in Guilin.

CHAPTER 3

National Taiwan Normal University

Hope is the thing with feathers
That perches in the soul
And sings the tune without words
And never stops at all.

—*Emily Dickinson*

1

THE ISLAND of Taiwan became the only remaining territory of Chiang Kai-Shek after 1949. The post-war division of Korea and ensuing Korean War resulted in a flow of military and economic aid from the United States. With that aid and the natural water barrier of the Taiwan Strait, Chiang was able to resettle the Nationalist government on the island and thus establish China as a dual governance structure.

The largest city on this island, Taipei, features four major east- and westbound arterial roads: Chung-Hsiao Road, meaning loyalty and filial piety; Jen-Ai Road, meaning benevolence; Hsin-Yi Road, meaning faithfulness; and Ho-Ping Road, meaning peace. Meanwhile, many streets and alleys in Taipei are named after mainland cities and provinces. Even the layout of these streets and alleys resembles their geographic locations in mainland China, making Taipei seem a miniature facsimile of China. In addition, there are also thoroughfares with names—such as Siwei, meaning four social guidelines; and Bade, meaning eight virtues—chosen from literary allusions to primary Confucian classics.

When Hwa-Wei first came to Taipei, bicycles and rickshaws were the primary means of transportation in this simple and tranquil city; automobiles were not popular at all. Traffic signals meant nothing to pedestrians crossing the street.

With the resettlement in Taiwan, Hwa-Wei started as a twelfth-grade transfer student at Provincial Taichung First High School. After graduation, he passed the entrance examination and was admitted to the Provincial Taiwan Teachers College (renamed later as the National Taiwan Normal University), which was, back then, one of only a few institutions of higher education in Taiwan.

During the fifty years of Japanese occupation from 1895 to 1945, local students were kept from receiving education in political science and economics.

They were only allowed to study in subject areas such as education, history, literature, and medicine. The restriction remained until after the Nationalist government moved to Taiwan and instituted an educational reform. Before long, the National Taiwan University (NTU) and the National Taiwan Normal University (NTNU) rose as the two flagship universities on the island. The latter assumed a unique position in educating generations of future educators in Taiwan.

With its main campus located on the northwest side of Taipei, NTNU was founded in 1946 at the site of the former Taiwan Provincial College, which had originally been established by Taiwan's Japanese government in 1922. Many buildings on campus, featuring neo-Gothic and Gothic architectural styles, were built during the era of Japanese occupation. NTNU is just a few miles away from NTU, the other famous university established in Taiwan since the 1950s, one well known then for its academic freedom. As an institution for teachers' education, NTNU was more restrictive, known for its practice of the school motto: "Sincerity, Integrity, Diligence, and Thrift."

When the Nationalist government retreated to Taiwan in 1949, they took many influential Chinese intellectuals with them, including Ssu-Nien Fu and Shih-Chiu Liang. Fu was the president of NTU until December 1950 when he died of heart disease. The president of NTNU was Chen Liu, a renowned educator. Liu was able to recruit some distinguished faculty members from Beijing Normal University (BNU) to move with him to Taiwan in 1949, owing largely to his good relationship with BNU. These faculty members were resettled either at NTU or NTNU. Among those were Shih-Chiu Liang (English), Ming Kao (Chinese), and Liang-Kong Yang (Education).

A number of famous scholars from NTU, including Shih Hu and Mu Ch'ien, also gave lectures at NTNU. Mei-Chi Hu, Ch'ien's wife, was a classmate of Hwa-Wei at NTNU in the Department of Education. Professor Mu Ch'ien and his wife, despite the large difference between their ages, had a happy marriage. In his later years, Professor Ch'ien lost his eyesight, and his wife, Mei-Chi Hu, worked as his assistant, becoming essential to her husband's scholarly work in history and philosophy. Many of the later publications of Professor Ch'ien were the result of his dictation, recorded and edited by his wife.

Interested in civil engineering, Hwa-Wei originally applied for NTU's College of Engineering. At that time there was a unified college entrance examination on the same day for all colleges in Taiwan, except NTNU. To improve his chance of college admission, Hwa-Wei also participated in NTNU's entrance exam, using it as a backup. It turned out that Hwa-Wei's math score for the unified examination was not good enough to get him into his dream school to study engineering. His NTNU test, however, was successful. Thus, Hwa-Wei ended up in the Department of Education at NTNU. Due to his father's influence,

Hwa-Wei was interested in education and even dreamed about becoming a secondary-school principal.

There were no more than three thousand faculty and students in Hwa-Wei's first year at NTNU. In addition to free boarding and tuition, each student also received an annual set of uniforms and a regular monthly allowance. Hwa-Wei was happy to see the reduced financial burden for his parents and felt more comfortable about not being able to go to NTU for civil engineering.

NTNU was known for its strong faculty and vigorous academic requirements. It was NTNU where Hwa-Wei started his continuous and systematic education. To Hwa-Wei, the four years at NTNU have had a tremendous impact on him and his career.

At NTNU, Hwa-Wei, thin and tan, was quiet, but he was polite and got along well with others. Not being a bookworm, he was not a very good student, however. Hwa-Wei devoted many of his free hours to extracurricular activities and joined a variety of organizations, but none based on any specialty or particular strength.

One such organization was the school's drama troupe. The ineloquent and ordinary-looking Hwa-Wei was very active as the group's stage manager. He became an indispensable troupe member, busy with making room reservations, preparing costumes, and managing props and stage sets. As time grew closer to a play's opening, he became even more engaged. For example, when the sound of a storm was needed during a performance, Hwa-Wei would lead the effort of providing the live sound backstage using pots and pans.

At the time, the NTNU drama troupe was very famous among the universities in Taipei. As one of the backbones in the troupe, Hwa-Wei was highly capable, always putting the backstage area in perfect order with minimal effort. People enjoyed working with him and admired his hard work and dependability.

At the NTNU drama troupe, Hwa-Wei had two good friends, Ching-Jui Pai and Hsing Lee, who both later became influential film directors, with a huge impact on Taiwan's movie industry. Ching-Jui was an art major and started school the same year as Hwa-Wei; Hsing, two years ahead of Hwa-Wei, was also a student in the Education Department. Knowing Hwa-Wei was working backstage always made the two friends feel relieved while performing onstage. They knew that Hwa-Wei was reliable and dedicated; he never made mistakes in backstage management when in charge of lighting, sound effects, and scene changes.

Large in voice and body, but with an old head on a pair of young shoulders, Hsing Lee was the head of the drama troupe and took care of the others just like an older brother. In contrast, Ching-Jui Pai, originally from northeast China and nicknamed Little Pai, was small and ordinary looking. His personality was humorous, straightforward, and unrestrained. Despite the differences in temperament, the three friends made a good team and often planned activities together. Having no money for drinking, or even for tea, did not prevent them from one or two sumptuous meals, usually a bowl of beef noodles, a well-known night snack in Taiwan.

Hsing Lee became famous in the 1960s for his film *Beautiful Duckling* and has been regarded since then as the representative of "healthy realism" and as the godfather of the Taiwan film industry. Ching-Jui Pai also gained fame in the Taiwan film industry for *Lonely Seventeen,* after returning from Italy, where he studied film and media. Combining the two famous directors' family names, their peers jointly nicknamed them Lee Pai, one of the acclaimed ancient Chinese poets.

The two film directors stayed very close friends after their college years. Hsing Lee always gave a hand to Ching-Jui Pai, who had bad luck with his personal life and career, and passed away at the age of sixty-six. Hsing Lee is still very active in Taiwan's film industry as the president of the Taiwan Film Association. Over the years, Hsing Lee has been a member of the selection committee for the Golden Horse Awards—Taiwan's equivalent to the Academy Awards— and he himself was honored with the Golden Horse Life Achievement Award in 1995.

Despite their different life paths, Hwa-Wei and the two film directors maintained a good relationship. Every time Hwa-Wei visited Taiwan, the three friends always gathered together for drinking and talking, as if they were back in their college days.

2

NTNU produced many distinguished alumni during the 1950s. Chin-Chu Shih, former deputy minister of education of Taiwan, was a student of good character and fine scholarship from Hwa-Wei's class. Other classmates of Hwa-Wei, such as Chen-Tsou Wu, Hong-Hsiang Liu, Hsien-Kai Shen, and Wen-Chu Yin, became renowned university professors or high school principals. Another classmate, Ming-Hui Kao, after having earned his doctorate in the United States, returned to Taiwan and later served as a vice-general secretary of the Nationalist Party.

Other classmates whose superior leadership skills impressed Hwa-Wei are Chih-Shan Chang and Ping-Yu Yan. Chang and Yan, both university presidents in their later years, were leaders of the China Youth National Salvation Corps (CYNSC), which in 2000 changed to its current name of China Youth Corps. During their college years, they teamed up with Hwa-Wei in organizing summer combat training camps for college and high school students in Taiwan. Hwa-Wei still remembers his active years in CYNSC, serving as the captain of the Summer

Youth Naval Battle Camp his first year, and the chief of the Lanyu (Orchid) Island Expedition Team during his second year.

As a college student, Hwa-Wei stayed busy with extracurricular activities. He was one of the leading members of the Education Departmental Student Association. In addition to serving in NTNU's drama troupe, Hwa-Wei was involved in student publications, including a campus wall newspaper and a student literary magazine.

The wall newspaper was composed of a large sheet of poster paper on which articles and essays were written using Chinese brushes. While the design of the newspaper was created by Hwa-Wei, the news articles and essays were drafted by Hui Chen, a talented Chinese literature major. The two were also responsible for the student literary magazine, which gained quite a reputation on campus.

For the magazine, Hui served as the editor and Hwa-Wei assumed typing, publishing, and distribution responsibilities. Unfortunately, the brilliant editor Hui was not able to employ his full literary talent after he moved to the United States. He was diagnosed with melancholia, a mental disorder characterized by severe depression, guilt, hopelessness, and withdrawal. He eventually died in a tragic suicide, jumping from the forty-fifth floor of the Rockefeller Center in New York City.

Presumably owing to his gentle disposition, Hwa-Wei was constantly sought after by his friends to help with various events and activities. He never turned down invitations or requests and always enjoyed participating. Thus, his college life turned out to be much busier than that of many others. His bony body was like a gigantic energy field with unfailing vitality. As a sports lover, Hwa-Wei succeeded in basketball, as well as in track and field events. He was once the champion of NTNU's eight-hundred-meter run. This was an unbelievable sports achievement for Hwa-Wei, considering his physical condition.

Throughout his four years of college, Hwa-Wei often went to the Student Guidance and Counseling Services to obtain permission slips allowing his absence from classes. He would then hand-deliver these to his professors. Each permission slip would read something like: "Your student, Hwa-Wei Lee, will have to miss the class [on a given date] due to a scheduling conflict with a [specified] school event he will attend; please give him permission."

Many professors back then ranked academic work over extracurricular activities and thus would see a student's involvement in non-course-related programs as a sign he was neglecting his studies. Every time Hwa-Wei gave an absence permission slip to a professor, the professor would say nothing, but give a stern look. Some professors would never fail to remind Hwa-Wei of an approaching finals week, saying something like: "Hwa-Wei Lee, you'd better put extracurricular activities aside and focus on your study. Otherwise, I don't think you will be able to pass my class, as you've missed so many sessions."

Hwa-Wei at the Provincial Taiwan Teachers College in Taipei, 1950. In 1954 the college was renamed the National Taiwan Normal University.

With regret, Hwa-Wei would sincerely reply, "Thank you, Professor! Please trust me. I will study hard to make up." Luckily, Hwa-Wei was always able to pass examinations and even received better grades than his professors had expected owing to his strengths in logic, analysis, and writing, as well as his all-night cramming right before an exam.

For every exam, Hwa-Wei would usually stay up the whole night in the classroom reviewing textbooks and notes. The next morning, he would put the textbooks and notes aside, wash his face with cold water, and get ready for the exam. Hwa-Wei was only able to gain short-term memory, though, from the last-minute preparation for the exam, as everything acquired from the overnight study would soon be forgotten. His skill at cramming just before his exams won him quite a reputation in the Education Department. His professors were also surprised and started to be fond of this student who was shy when speaking but passionate about after-school programs.

It was Hwa-Wei's personality that kept him active behind the scenes of many off-school programs. It took him a while to realize the value of those extracurricular activities in shaping his leadership skills including motivating and encouraging others; cultivating fellowship and partnership; and planning thoroughly, then implementing effectively. The development of those skills proved an unexpected windfall from his college years.

Unconsciously, Hwa-Wei had already started preparing for his future through exploiting his potential. He had no idea why he was always able to get people

Hwa-Wei (*front row, right*) with fellow classmates in the Department of Education.

Hwa-Wei (*front row, far right*), who was good in sports, won first place in the eight-hundred-meter race.

Hwa-Wei accepts a trophy from the president of the university.

together and accomplish many difficult tasks. Looking back to his college years, Hwa-Wei finally came to understand that it was indeed that leadership potential he had developed in college that contributed to his career success in the United States, earning him promotions faster than his colleagues—starting with the University of Pittsburgh Library. This was a special achievement considering he was a foreign student and a non-native English speaker.

Despite the richness of its extracurricular activities, NTNU, a teachers' education institution, was rather strict on discipline. It was mandatory that girls return to their dorms before 9:00 p.m., and boys no later than 11:00 p.m. However, that regulation was not followed strictly by boys who, fed watery and flavorless food from the school cafeterias, were starving at night.

In those hours, the overpowering smell of beef noodle soup, blasting from the other side of the campus wall, became truly alluring and irresistible. Hwa-Wei and his friends often could not help but climb over the wall to savor late-night food and then climb back. The boys enjoyed their rebellious act, and even felt more excited, when they were caught right inside the wall by Chong-Le Wang, head of the student life unit of Guidance and Counseling Services, and had to run fast to escape. As the champion of the eight-hundred-meter run, Hwa-Wei had never been captured and was thus ranked by Wang among the naughtiest of the students.

An easy-going person, Hwa-Wei never had conflicts with others—with only one exception. He had a classmate who constantly abused the others. Although these classmates felt indignant, no one dared to say a word back. One day, having reached the end of his endurance, Hwa-Wei stood up and criticized the bully. Infuriated by the bony Hwa-Wei, to whom he never would have paid attention, the bully immediately picked up an ink bottle and cast it over Hwa-Wei, leaving ink splashed all over his body. Giving his shirt a shake, Hwa-Wei threw a quick and unexpected blow to the bully's face. The poor guy, never having anticipated that hard lick from the good-tempered Hwa-Wei, staggered there with a bloody face. Hwa-Wei's fist was truly relentless, knocking out one of the guy's front teeth, which cut his own hand, a wound that later formed a scar.

That was the only fight in Hwa-Wei's entire life. Hwa-Wei, himself, was no less shocked than the bullying classmate. Stunned by his own burst of energy, Hwa-Wei was also struck dumb. He had never imagined that his single blow would immediately control the opponent.

The consequence was bad. The university administration punished Hwa-Wei—regardless of his reason for the fight—with probation, two major and two minor demerits, and all the medical expenses of the wounded classmate. Luckily, Hwa-Wei was able to counterbalance the demerits using an equivalent amount of merits earned from his extracurricular activities.

What bothered Hwa-Wei most was the medical expense. One reason for his decision to go to Normal University to study education was to help with his family's tight budget, as the school provided free tuition. How could he then let his parents pay for the medical charge? If not from his parents, where could he acquire funds as an impoverished student? It became a real headache for Hwa-Wei. Knowing his difficulty, the majority of his classmates, who were on Hwa-Wei's side for his just behavior, pooled their pocket money for him. The medical expense was finally scraped together after Hwa-Wei added two more tutoring jobs.

3

The 1950s saw a constant growing tension between the two sides of the Taiwan Strait following the conclusion of the Chinese civil war. The entire island was armed and ready to counterattack the mainland at any time and hoped to receive more support from the United States when the fight commenced. Although it was a pressing desire of Chiang Kai-Shek to retake the mainland, he was not quite confident of his military strength. After all, restarting the war at that time would be a life-or-death choice. If it failed, Chiang could lose Taiwan, his last resort in the world. Having weighed the pros and cons, Chiang decided not to take further action.

Back then in Taiwan, military training was mandatory in colleges. Student dorms, supervised by full-time drillmasters, were treated as military barracks with everything, including the bed, in order. To students like Hwa-Wei, whose family income was on the low end, one big advantage of this military training was free uniforms and shoes. Under the military system, students had to stay on campus during part of their summer school breaks to undergo basic military training in drill and marksmanship.

One educational outcome was the increasingly high patriotic sentiment across the campus concerning the Republic of China. Many times the institution sent the school's drama troupe and its dance club to the offshore island of Kinmen to perform for soldiers staying on the front line. Other students also helped illiterate soldiers, who comprised a large portion of the troops, in writing letters to their families.

Hwa-Wei remembers the entrenchment in Kinmen as rather complex and concealed, spreading in all directions while also being hardly visible from the outside. He once entered an auditorium that was built just inside an excavated mountain, truly an eye-opening experience to Hwa-Wei, who had been interested in civil engineering. He was amazed at the creativity of its engineers.

Actually, Kinmen is a very small island lacking favorable geography for shelters and concealments. The best way for the Nationalist army to build structures for hidden military facilities was to excavate inside mountains. A cave airbase could be used easily for aircraft taking off and landing when its gate was opened. The Nationalist army was quite confident in the sheltering structure. One slogan stated that the Communist army would be defeated right on the beach, if they dared to come. The Communist army did not attack Kinmen in the end. Hwa-Wei wonders what those military facilities look like today as the relations between the two sides have greatly improved.

In Taiwan, every adult man had an obligation to serve in the army. The duration of service as a soldier had been two years for a new high school graduate and thirteen months for a fresh college graduate at a reserve officer rank. After that, one had to go back to the service one month each year for a consecutive five-year term. This conscription system is still proving effective.

After graduating from NTNU in 1954, Hwa-Wei received his reserve officer training at the Army Officers Academy for six months and at the Political Cadre School for another seven months. The Army Officers Academy was located at Kaohsiung, a port city in southern Taiwan. The first six months there featured strict and intensive Initial-Entry Training (IET) for all new reserve officers regardless of their subject background. The training included all basic military combat skills. The reservists also participated in actual military maneuvers using real guns and bullets, and they were exposed to dangers as if they were authentic soldiers in true battles. It was rumored that there were indeed accidental injuries and deaths.

Immediately following the six-month IET came specialized training, determined by a reserve officer's college major. For instance, an engineering graduate was most likely to be sent to the Artillery School, whereas an education major, like Hwa-Wei, was sent to the Political Cadre School, established to train future political and ideological instructors.

In the Communist army system, every company or higher unit has a designated political and ideological instructor. The Nationalist army also adopted a similar structure during the Chiang Ching-Kuo (Ching-Kuo Chiang) era, primarily due to Chiang's Soviet background. Compared to his father, Chiang Kai-Shek, Chiang Ching-Kuo did a better job of connecting with the general public and accomplished many reforms that earned him nationwide acclaim and ultimately stabilized the rule of the Nationalist Party.

Prior to his college graduation, Hwa-Wei had already thought about his near future and made four specific plans. These included becoming a high school principal, getting assigned to a teaching job, studying abroad, and pursuing a graduate-level education. For each of the four plans, he needed to prepare for either a qualification test or an entrance exam.

Hwa-Wei's original career plan was to become a high school principal, which required a candidate to pass an advanced civil service examination. To succeed

In 1953, Hwa-Wei (*front*) participated in summer military training, and was the head of the Naval Combat Team.

While in training, Hwa-Wei participated in naval combat exercises, 1953.

In 1953, Hwa-Wei successfully completed his naval combat training.

at his second plan he needed to pass the government's employment qualification test for job placement.

His third plan, to continue his effort to study abroad, was proving difficult: Hwa-Wei failed three times in earlier English-language proficiency tests for foreign studies. He seemed to have no choice but to keep trying, as his aunt in the United States, Phyllis Hsiao-Chu Wang, was trying to help him earn admission to a graduate program in education at the University of Pittsburgh with, possibly, a tuition scholarship. Meanwhile, it was not a bad idea to have an alternative plan for further education just in case his efforts in preparing to study abroad were in vain.

This led to his fourth choice: to take the entrance exam for graduate school in Taiwan. The entrance exam was very competitive. For instance, only five new students each year were admitted to NTNU's Department of Education. Indeed, Hwa-Wei took the fourth choice most seriously and gave it the largest amount of time in preparation during his spare time and during military training.

The strict and rigid military training provided no opportunities for Hwa-Wei to spend time and effort in extracurricular activities as he had done in college. Thus, Hwa-Wei was able, fortunately, to concentrate on exam/test preparations. He buried himself in studying every evening in the classroom during regular self-study hours (from 7:00 to 9:30 p.m.). That proved to be effective because he passed all four tests and exams soon after the completion of his ROTC training.

Among his four goals, passing the entrance exam for graduate studies at NTNU was the most difficult. Admission was truly meant for top students, as reflected by the limited student enrollment quota. Hwa-Wei had to work very hard for a much-improved performance on his college academic scores. On his written test, his scores were ideal, the fifth in rank, which qualified him for the next round of oral exams.

The oral exam committee was composed of three faculty members: Prof. Kang-Chen Sun, department chair of Education; Prof. Pei-Lin Tien, dean of the Education College; and Prof. Pang-Cheng Sun. Hwa-Wei was extremely nervous in front of the three well-respected scholars.

Dean Tien started the exam saying, "Hwa-Wei Lee, you have done a good job in the written exam. However, you know we only need five new students. And we want top students who will commit their time to serious research, which is quite different from undergraduate education in this regard. Are you sure you want to head toward that direction instead of spending time in extracurricular activities?"

Hwa-Wei quickly responded, "Professor Tien, you are right. I did immerse myself too much in extracurricular activities. I will definitely focus on academic work if I am admitted." Likely, Dean Tien and the other two committee

Hwa-Wei (*third row, fourth from left*) participated in the university-wide student visit to the military base on Kinmen Island.

Hwa-Wei (*second row, second from right*) graduated from NTNU, March 1954.

After graduation, Hwa-Wei's (*second row, sixth from left*) first job was dean of students at the Affiliated Experimental Elementary School of the Provincial Taipei Teachers College.

members were touched by Hwa Wei's sincere attitude, or impressed by the young man's much-improved performance in the written test, because Hwa-Wei was admitted.

Upon completion of his reserve officer training, Hwa-Wei soon started his first job as the dean of students at the Affiliated Experimental Elementary School of the Provincial Taipei Teachers College. Hwa-Wei actually got the job by chance.

Normally a newly graduated NTNU student was required to start with a one-year internship before becoming a high school teacher. The principal of the elementary school was Ta-Shih Tan. Principal Tan came to the chair of the Department of Education at NTNU, seeking his help in recruiting a college graduate from the department to fill the position of dean of students. Despite his disappointment with Hwa-Wei's academic performance, the chair was impressed by this student's ability in organizing extracurricular activities, and thus recommended Hwa-Wei to Tan as the best candidate for the position. Tan liked this modest, gentle, and quiet young man at first sight. The job offer thus came at once.

One year later, President Chen Liu recalled Hwa-Wei back to NTNU, initially as a teaching assistant. But he was soon assigned to work at the Extracurricular Activity Unit of the Student Guidance and Counseling Services overseeing student organizations. This was again a windfall to Hwa-Wei due to his strength in extracurricular activities.

Working with student organizations was a perfect fit for Hwa-Wei. He was enjoying the happiness of being an organizer and a team player, putting his accumulated experience and ideas to use. Hwa-Wei honored President Liu's five equally important principles in educating students: moral development, intellectual growth, physical education, social activity, and aesthetic appreciation. He followed those five principles during his four years at NTNU, a practice that turned out to be beneficial throughout his life.

4

Soon after he was admitted to the NTNU graduate school, his U.S. visa application went through. That was truly his lucky year. Two good friends of his, who were used to having better college grades than him, were surpassed by Hwa-Wei, ranking sixth and seventh, respectively, in the entrance written exam for graduate school. The two friends, although aggrieved, felt somehow thankful, as they were outscored by their friend and not by a stranger. They were disappointed, however, when Hwa-Wei took the quota and then gave it up to study abroad. His two poor friends had to wait another year to fulfill their graduate school dream. Constantly berated by his two best friends, Hwa-Wei had no other choice but to treat them with meals by way of apology.

Originally, Hwa-Wei's desire to study abroad was not that strong, as he had already been admitted to the graduate school of NTNU, making him feel closer to his dream profession of being a high school principal. And he was not very interested in going to the United States, a foreign country on the other side of the world, far away from his home. Rather, it was his parents and aunt who kept pushing him to pursue an advanced degree in an American university. The other reason for his initial reluctance to leave Taiwan for the United States had to do with his family's financial status. Hwa-Wei needed to raise enough money for his plane ticket and the required affidavit of financial support, things his father was unable to afford. He knew that the road ahead to study abroad would not be an easy one. Hwa-Wei actually hoped that his visa application would not be granted so that he could have a legitimate reason to stay in Taiwan.

During that time, a large percentage of Taiwanese students who came to the States were from science and engineering backgrounds. Those students were more likely to be funded by American universities and thus had a higher success rate for a visa application. In contrast, very few humanities and social sciences students ended up on this path, as they seldom were able to receive fellowships, and their families, in most cases, could not afford the high costs of studying abroad.

Hwa-Wei, with help from his aunt, Phyllis Hsiao-Chu Wang, luckily was offered a tuition waiver from the School of Education at the University of Pittsburgh. This eased his visa application. After asking a few simple questions in English, the immigration officer, blinking his blue eyes, said to Hwa-Wei in an exaggeratedly slow speed, "You are welcome to America."

It was just Hwa-Wei's luck that a better and brighter future had come to him. But to achieve that better and brighter future, he would have to work harder and face tougher challenges.

It was time for Hwa-Wei to say goodbye to the dean of the graduate school saying, "Sorry, sir—I did not expect that I could pass the English test for foreign studies. This is quite an opportunity for me. Please allow me to withdraw from the school."

Hwa-Wei promised the dean that he would study hard in the United States and come back to serve the university with a finished doctorate. The dean was very pleased, thinking that Hwa-Wei would soon be the first international student in the U.S. from his class. He simply wished him the best.

Hwa-Wei's professors and friends at NTNU were all happy for him. But for Hwa-Wei, going to the U.S. for graduate school created not just financial stress but also psychological pressure. He could feel the sincere expectations and hopes of his professors and friends at NTNU. How would he ever "have face" to return to Taiwan if his studying-abroad endeavor failed? With this concern in mind, Hwa-Wei made up his mind to strive forward!

Subsidized by the government, Hwa-Wei had received four years of free college education at NTNU. But the government subsidy was conditional and required a beneficiary student to serve in the education field for at least five years after college graduation—before receiving his diploma.

Hwa-Wei felt guilty about his lack of service length, knowing that he had worked for only two years. Eventually, NTNU made an exception in his case and mailed his diploma to him. Attached with the diploma was a note stating that the original requirement for educational service in Taiwan had been waived because of his continued service record in the American higher education system and the graduate degree in education that he had received from the University of Pittsburgh.

Hwa-Wei's service in the field of education has far exceeded his original commitment to NTNU. However, Hwa-Wei feels grateful for his college's magnanimity and flexibility in ultimately awarding him a bachelor's degree in education. He is also thankful to NTNU for his four years of rewarding experience, the impact of which on his life has proven more immeasurable than the diploma itself.

Min Unafraid to Die

Please look at me in my eyes and honestly tell me
—is there a true victor in war?

— Ying-Tai Lung,
Big River, Big Sea—Untold Stories of 1949

1

HIS WARTIME experiences during his childhood and adolescent years, especially during the Sino-Japanese War, have had a huge impact on Hwa-Wei. The city of Guilin is well known for its incredibly beautiful limestone mountains and rock formations in various shapes and sizes all along the Li River. There are many natural caves, large and small. Because of its geographical and strategic importance, Guilin was a target for Japanese bombers when Hwa-Wei and his parents and siblings lived there. They had to go with other civilians to one of the nearby mountain caves. Every time the air raid siren blared, frantic and frightened civilians dashed into caves. This kind of helpless response even got a humorous nickname, "Pao Jingbao," which literally means siren-running. Because China had only a weak air force at the time, Japan had absolute air supremacy, and Japanese aircraft were free to come and go, just like frenzied devils. They usually flew so low that the pilots' faces could be spotted.

After "siren-running," Hwa-Wei and his family often had to pass by dead bodies to go back home. One time, his mother—holding Hwa-Wei's hand—unwarily stepped on a corpse right after they walked out of a cave. Hwa-Wei was instantly frightened. A bolt of fear went through his body; he felt as if he were hit with an electric shock. That tragic death scene left a deep impression on young Hwa-Wei.

To flee from Japanese air bombings, civilians often left home at dawn for cave shelters in a nearby area carrying precooked or dried food. Outside the crowded caves, loud booms could be heard from time to time, sounds of constant explosions overhead. The caves and surrounding land trembled every time the booms sounded. Mixed with the explosions were continual whining and an ear-piercing siren.

Time passed slowly. Fear and despair seemed to be more torturous than death. Refugees dared not go back to their homes until dark. Often there would be no home left when they returned. The Japanese invaders seemingly did not want to skip a single decent house; they never neglected throwing a firebomb to burn one down. A nice street in the morning could be damaged beyond recognition by evening. Houses were burned to ruins, leaving broken structures and walls covered in smoke. On roadsides shabbily dressed refugees stood, wailing for their loss. The tragic scenes would make passersby sob. The war, blamed for so much tragic loss of lives and property, was tremendously painful, fearful, and hateful to the Chinese.

Like most Chinese youth at that time, Hwa-Wei's older brother, Hwa-Hsin Lee, had made up his mind to join the Chinese air force to fight against the Japanese. In early 1940, the American Volunteer Group (AVG), formed and headed by General Claire L. Chennault under the endorsement of President Roosevelt and the U.S. government, came to China to help in combating the Japanese aggressor. Better known as the Flying Tigers, AVG originally was comprised of some one hundred young pilots and over three hundred mechanics and nonmilitary professionals. The headquarters of the Flying Tigers was located in Kunming of Yunnan Province, and their training base was set up in Burma. This Sino-U.S. Joint Air Force entered the Sino-Japanese war in early 1941.[1]

Having fought side by side with the Chinese Nationalist Air Force, the Flying Tigers shot down countless Japanese warplanes, helping the Chinese air force gain back air supremacy. The Chinese people who lived through the war have always been thankful to the Flying Tigers and its legendary military achievement. Hwa-Hsin was one of them. It was then that he decided to go to the Youth Air Force Academy.

In 1939, General Pai Chung-Hsi, deputy chief of staff of the Nationalist Military Commission, proposed the founding of the Youth Air Force Academy in order to train more pilots. Having received its name in early 1940, the academy selected—through strict physical and academic tests—primary and junior high school graduates between the ages of twelve and fifteen.

Students admitted to the academy were taught a variety of classes in aviation in addition to the general junior and senior high school courses. The academy placed special emphasis on good nutrition and physical education. Students, after their graduation from the academy, were sent directly to the Air Force Officers School for pilot training.[2]

---

1. Hsiang-Mei Chen (Anna Chennault). *Footsteps of my Years: Autobiography of Chen Hsiang-Mei* (Beijing: China Women Publishing House, 1997), 40.
2. Chih-Wei Wu, "Young Hawks Flying in Different Directions," *Viewing the History*, no.12 (2010).

According to Shih-Cheng Lou's memoir, *We Are the Anti-Japanese Air Force Reserves*, the Youth Air Force Academy had eight recruitment centers in late 1940. These recruitment centers were in Chengdu, Chongqin, Guiyang, Kunming, Guilin, Zhijiang, Hengyang, and Nanzheng. There were nearly two thousand primary and junior high school graduates admitted to the academy in six groups. Hwa-Hsin was admitted in 1943 as a second-year senior high school student.

Similar to the general junior and senior high schools in content and length of education, the Youth Air Force Academy had, however, a different focus in curriculum. Students were given comprehensive Boy Scout training in the first three junior high years, and regular military training, aviation theory, and simulator instruction during the later three senior high years. Only those who were able to pass both the aviation-knowledge test and the physical examination could move up to the Air Force Officers School to receive real flight training. Those who met the standard of aviation knowledge, but failed in the physical examination, were sent either to the Air Force Mechanics School or the Air Force Communication School for further training. The Youth Air Force Academy was, in a way, a preparatory school for a variety of air force personnel.

Having graduated from the Youth Air Force Academy, Hwa-Hsin advanced to the Air Force Officers School in the fall of 1944. It was at that time he changed his name to Min Lee, as a statement of his commitment, following the example set by his father. The meaning of Min is described in the Chinese *Classic of History* (Shujing) as Min bu wei si, meaning intrepid and unafraid of death.

Taking the new given name of Min was Hwa-Hsin's particular and determined way of declaring his pledge of fighting to the death against the Japanese invaders as an air force officer. A family archive photo captured the young and proud Min with his fellow cadets at their training base in India. On the gate behind these young airmen, a Chinese banner proclaims this motto: "Don't enter this gate if you fear to die; and find another path if your goal is for promotion and wealth." From the very beginning, Min knew his commitment to become a professional air force pilot meant he could not be afraid to die for his country.

Min graduated from the twenty-third class of the U.S. Air Training Command, completing his advanced pilot training at Barksdale Field, Louisiana, December 10, 1946. His officer training had started with a three-month-long program in Kunming; he was then sent to the training base in India. His years at the Air Command and Staff College were spent at Goodfellow Air Force Base in San Angelo, Texas.

Regretfully for Min, it was too late for him to join the fight against the Japanese upon his return from the United States at the end of 1946, as World War II was already over, and the Japanese invaders had already surrendered in disgrace. Min was sent off to northeast China to be stationed there. His first combat mission turned out to be—after the outbreak of the civil war on May 21, 1947—to fight against the Chinese Communist army, a goal counter to his original objective for joining the air force. At that point, his dream and destiny were taken by history to an unforeseeable end.

Min was an outstanding air force officer. Already a major at the age of twenty-nine, he was promoted to lieutenant colonel at thirty-one. Throughout his thirteen-year military career, he participated in many significant battles. Owing to his distinctive military performance, Min was the first student from his class to be promoted to the rank of lieutenant colonel.

For a time after the Nationalist Government retreated from mainland China, the United States drifted away from an alliance with Chiang's government. The estrangement did not last long. Soon after the outbreak of the Korean War in 1950, the U.S. government realized its lack of intelligence information about the Peoples' Republic of China and started to work on rebuilding the bilateral relationship with Taiwan. Two years later, a joint effort was made between Taiwan's Air Force Combat Department and Western Enterprises, Inc., a CIA-affiliated company, to establish a Special Mission Unit. A mutual agreement was reached for the U.S. to equip the unit with B-17 bombers, which Chiang's air force pilots would fly over the mainland on reconnaissance missions. Information gathered during these missions was shared by those two parties. Western Enterprises, Inc., was housed in an ash-gray, western-style building on 102 East Avenue, Hsinchu 102, Taiwan.

After the Korean War, Communist China became the potential enemy of the United States. In 1955, the headquarters of the U.S. Pacific Air Forces signed an agreement with the Taiwan Air Force Intelligence Department on an Electronic Countermeasure Mission (ECM), under which the Eighth Air Force Battalion located at the Hsinchu Air Base was sent off to conduct electronic reconnaissance.

As this mission proved effective, authority over future missions was transferred to Western Enterprises, Inc., the following year by order of the CIA. The Special Mission Unit was regrouped under the Air Force Intelligence Department and changed its name in 1957 to the Technical Research Group, formally known as the Thirty-fourth Squadron. A more popular name of this group was the Black Bat Squadron, as almost all the surveillance missions were conducted in China during the night. The squadron's emblem featured seven stars beneath a black bat with its wings outstretched. Owing to his outstanding piloting skills and bravery, Min was assigned to the squadron in early 1958. His assignment was top secret, unknown even to Min's parents and siblings.

As the leading aircraft of the Thirty-fourth Squadron, the American B-17 bombers, known as Flying Fortresses during World War II, were four-engine, heavy bombers of potent, long-range and high-load capacity. Under its core

To aid in the defense of China from the Japanese invasion, Hwa-Wei's brother, Min (Hwa-Hsin), joined the Chinese air force. He received his training in both India and in the United States.

Min Lee completed his advanced pilot training at Barksdale Field U.S. Air Training Command in Louisiana, December 10, 1946.

mission, intelligence gathering, the squadron's bombers were modified to be reconnaissance aircrafts with original armaments removed and replaced by high-precision, electronic detection devices. The re-equipped (R) B-17 had no combat capacity at all and could board a maximum of fourteen crew members.[3]

The task of intelligence gathering was formidable for the squadron members who flew these RB-17s, usually leaving Hsinchu Air Base around 4:00 p.m. and entering the mainland's air space after dusk. Flight duration varied from time to time and could last more than ten hours for each flight. Relying on the most advanced electronic detection devices and superior piloting skills, Black

---

3. Hsiao-Po Meng, "Unforgettable Past—Memory of My Late Husband Min Lee," *The Blood-stained Red Sky: In Memory of the Martyrs of the Aircraft 815 of the Air Force 34th Black Bats Squadron.* (Taiwan: published by family members of the 815 Aircraft, 1993). 126–36.

Bat Squadron crews were able to fly as low as one hundred to two hundred meters—the minimum safe-altitude zone—in the dark. In some cases, a crew had to break out of the safety zone and fly the aircraft as low as thirty meters off the ground in order to avoid radar detection.

On the other side of the Taiwan Strait, the Communist air force received a counter-reconnaissance order from Mao Zedong attached with a special award to whomever shot down a reconnaissance aircraft from Taiwan. Under the order, a network of anti-aircraft guns and searchlights were deployed in strategic locations waiting for planes, their targets, to fly over. This increased the risk to the Black Bat Squadron's RB-17 bombers and their crews. Every mission was a battle against death. General Kuang-Yue Ko, former vice chief of the air force of Taiwan, said: "Each mission was targeted by more than ten missiles, more than ten attacks by fighter planes, and more than ten attacks of artillery fire."[4]

Min, a highly skilled pilot, had been able to return safely every time from his mainland air expeditions for two years until his final trip on May 29, 1959. That day, two hours after returning from one reconnaissance mission, Min received an order to back up a sick pilot on the next trip. Hsiao-Po Meng, Hwa-Wei's sister-in-law, recalled that it was a hazy day, which made her a bit worried.

Min comforted his wife by saying, "It is actually safer to fly through haze. This will be my last trip this month. And I shall be able to take a good break upon returning tomorrow." Prior to the assignment, Min had taken out his military uniform with full medals from his suitcase and polished his leather shoes because May 31, just two days away, would be a big day to him as a professional airman. On that day Chiang Ching-Kuo was scheduled to pay a visit to the Hsinchu Air Base and offer his praise and encouragement in person to the squadron members.

On May 29, 1959, Taiwan's Air Force Intelligence Agency sent off two RB-17 bombers—nos. 835 and 815, successively—to southern China. Min was the pilot on bomber no. 815, taking shifts with two other pilots, Yin-Kuei Hsu and Yan Han.

In addition to the three pilots, eleven other crewmen were on board including three electronics officers, three navigation officers, two mechanics, one communication officer, one airdrop officer, and one airdrop soldier. The mission's final destination was the southwest region of China. But to get to the region, Min and his crew had to fly over southern Guangdong Province, a risky flight-path considering the strong air defense system in the region.

At about 11:10 p.m., bomber no. 815—returning from Guangxi to Guangdong—was about to fly over a mountain to the sea on the other side. At this moment the aircraft was detected by a radar station of the Guangzhou Military Zone

---

4. Mark O'Neill, "Taipei puts Black Bats on the radar," *Sunday Morning Post* (Hong Kong), January 24, 2010.

Min and Hsiao-Po Meng were married in 1949.

Hwa-Wei and his brothers in Taichung, 1950: (*left to right*) Hwa-Ming, Hwa-Wei, Min, and Hwa-Tsun.

In this last photograph of Min Lee, taken in 1959, he stands with his wife, Hsiao-Po (*back row, second and third from right*), and several of his siblings. His son, Hao-Sheng (*front, far left*) stands alongside his grandparents. By then, Hwa-Wei was in the United States.

and was shot down, crashing into the mountain in the border area between Enping and Yangjiang Counties. All fourteen crewmen were killed.

As soon as the aircraft was hit, the crew was able to get in touch with the Hsinchu Air Force Base, reporting the fatal shot and pledging to die together with the aircraft. Back then, Taiwan's air force had a stringent regulation for its airmen: no one should be allowed to become a captive of the Communist army, and every crewman should be willing to die for his country. Obeying the regulation, the entire crew rejected the use of parachutes to escape—their only opportunity for survival—and chose to crash into the mountain with their bomber.

The weather was slightly muggy in Hsinchu. The night of the tragedy, Min's young wife, Hsiao-Po, felt worried and could hardly fall asleep. She had always been on tenterhooks every time her husband Min was out on duty, but never so much as on that night. The dawn finally arrived. Hsiao-Po opened the window and saw a round hole with a diameter of seven inches that had been dug by Lucky, the family dog. She was shocked. Believing that dogs have an incomprehensible capability of sensing a master's misfortune, air force family members had always feared seeing a family dog crying or digging a hole. This foreboding sign left Hsiao-Po instantly breathless; she did not know what to do.

It did not take long for the tragic news to spread throughout the Hsinchu Air Force Base. Min's colleagues and classmates showed up unexpectedly. Their grieving faces suggested something bad had happened. Among them was a friend of Min who had been on the same reconnaissance trip with Min just one day earlier on May 28. He started to cry as soon as he was seated. Seeing the seasoned air warrior fail to control his sorrow, Hsiao-Po came to realize that a family tragedy had happened.[5]

According to an official military announcement, bomber no. 815 was lost in the air space over Guangdong during its mission; it was then unknown whether the crew members were alive or dead. The Air Force Command covered up the truth to the families of the victims, allowing them to believe that their loved ones were missing while a full search was still going on. Family members clung to any small ray of hope: perhaps their loved ones had made a safe parachuting or had been captured.

Handsome and strong, Min was the idol of his siblings and the pillar of his family. When Lee's family first moved to Taiwan, Min often helped his father, Kan-Chun Lee—who earned a meager salary as a college professor—with the family expenses by using a part of his monthly income from the air force service. A good husband and father in his own household, Min managed with limited resources to accompany his wife each weekend to dances at the Officer's Club

---

5. Hsiao-Po Meng, "Unforgettable Past," 126–36.

or to movies at a local theater. He would also take his son out for snacks and pastries. His son, Hao-Sheng Lee, recalled that many pieces of the family's furniture, including tables, bookcases, benches, and chairs, had been homemade by Min. What most impressed Hao-Sheng was a motorcycle assembled by his late father using spare airplane parts.[6]

Hwa-Wei was finishing up his Master of Education degree at the University of Pittsburgh when the tragic news reached him. The news was a cruel blow; Hwa-Wei—in spite of limited time together with his brother—had shared a strong bond with Min. In desperation, Hwa-Wei searched every Chinese newspaper that he could find about the aircraft incident with his brother onboard.

Finally, a Hong Kong newspaper article was retrieved from the University of Pittsburgh Library. According to the news report, a Taiwan military aircraft was shot down by the Chinese air force and all its crewmen were found dead. The Communist officers who contributed to this successful attack were to receive awards from Mao Zedong in person. The photo of the airplane wreckage clearly identified bomber no. 815, his brother's plane. At that point, Hwa-Wei believed that all the crew, including his brother, were dead; what he did not know was that bomber no. 815 had actually been attacked twice.

As the first attack imposed no immediate threats, the crew tried to flee toward the south at the lowest safe altitude. However, as the modified bomber had no defensive weapons, it was soon attacked by a MiG-17. Hit by an air-to-air missile, the plane exploded into pieces 2,625 feet above Enping, Guangdong Province. It was later learned that the air-to-air missiles had been recently acquired by the Communist Chinese air force from the Soviet Union.

Knowing his brother would never come back home alive, Hwa-Wei carefully saved the newspaper piece in his personal file hoping it would be useful someday in the future in locating the crash site. Meanwhile, he could not bear to tell the truth to his parents; they had, however, already learned the heartbreaking news with the assistance of a friend in a high position in the Nationalist Government. Learning of the disastrous loss of her oldest son, his mother aged rapidly. Her hair turned completely gray in just a few days, and she developed heart disease. She was deprived of joy and happiness during the later years of her life.

Min was just thirty-three years old at the time of his death; he was survived by his wife, Hsiao-Po Meng, and his son, Hao-Sheng Lee. The military uniform and leather shoes, which he had prepared for the occasion of Chiang Ching-Kuo's visit, waited, neatly pressed and shined, in the closet on May 31, 1959, for their owner, who would never return.

---

6. Hao-Sheng Lee, "Scattered Memories of My Beloved Father," *The Bloodstained Red Sky* (Taipei,1993), 138–41.

Chapter 4

On the other side of the Taiwan Strait the pilot Zhelun Jiang, who had shot down bomber no. 815 was celebrated as a hero. Jiang received a special medal from Mao Zedong, a high honor at that time. Having originally joined the air force to fight against Japanese invaders, Min ended his life in an aircraft crash while on a reconnaissance mission over Communist China.

2

In 1982, Hwa-Wei was invited by the International Development Research Centre (IDRC) of Canada to join a team of library experts to conduct a special seminar: The Management of Scientific and Technical Information Centers in Kunming, China. The two-week seminar was jointly sponsored by the Institute of Scientific and Technical Information of China and IDRC and was attended by information-center directors from national and provincial government agencies. The trip to China was the first for Hwa-Wei since his leaving China in 1949, thirty-three years before. It opened the door for Hwa-Wei to be invited back to China annually for lectures and consultation by the national library, national and regional scientific and technical libraries, and major academic libraries.

During each of these trips, Hwa-Wei's father urged him to try his best to find the whereabouts of Min's remains, as locating them had become his only wish. Taking out the Hong Kong newspaper clip he had kept for some twenty-three years, Hwa-Wei confirmed that the crash site should be somewhere at Dawang Mountain, close to Jinji Village of Enping County in Guangdong Province. However, after arriving in Enping and looking at Dawang Mountain from the foothills, he began to realize how impossible it would be to locate the exact spot. Whenever he inquired, local government officials and villagers replied uniformly, "We don't know." In fact, as Hwa-Wei realized then, without appropriate approval from the higher military authorities, they dared not tell the truth, even if they knew it.

Several follow-up trips also were in vain, even with help from many of his friends in the library and academic fields. It wasn't until 1987, several years later, that Hwa-Wei's sister-in-law, Hsiao-Po, was finally able to connect with Yichun Zhang, the deputy chief of the Unification Working Committee under the Chinese People's Political Consultative Conference (CPPCC), via De-Kuang Liang, a former colleague of Min Lee.

With the assistance of Zhang, the second son of the former Nationalist Party General Zhizhong Zhang, the Hong Kong, Macau, and Taiwan Liaison Office of the Guangdong Provincial CPPCC issued an official letter to its subordinate committee in Enping requesting "assistance in investigating the whereabouts of Min

Lee, a Nationalist Air Force pilot."[7] The chairman of the CPPCC Enping branch, Diechu Zheng, assigned Han Situ, the head of the Secretariat Division, to assume the responsibility.

The late 1980s witnessed a thaw in the relationship between the two sides of the Taiwan Strait. The investigation of Min's whereabouts soon produced a positive result. The date was June 20, 1987. The planned investigation site on that day for Situ and his team was Hengpo Zhen, a township near the crash site. Jinrong Liu, the local police chief, happened to be a former member of the militia who had been responsible for onsite security. According to Liu, bomber no. 815, after being hit, crashed into pieces halfway up the mountain. All devices and instruments recovered from the wrecked plane were removed by security personnel, and the dismembered bodies of the victims were buried without any marks in an abandoned gray brick furnace. Below is the witness report Situ collected from Liu:

> The accident occurred around 11:00 p.m. on May 31, 1959 [correct date: May 29]. The crash site was on the mountain near Jinji Village, Heshan Township, Yangjiang County of Guangdong Province (the common border between Enping County and Yangjiang County). The crash killed the entire crew. Militias were immediately called upon for onsite protection. The next morning, Guangzhou Military Command set up a temporary command post in Hengpo Zhen dealing with the aftermath. The decisions made by the post include:
>
> Enping County [will] be responsible for the onsite protection till noon, June 1;
>
> Yangjiang County [will] be charged for the burial of bodies and disposal of wreckage.
>
> It was said that all the bodies (approximately twelve in total), except two, were broken into pieces of different sizes. Yangjiang County hired a local farmer [deceased now] [who] buried all the bodies and body parts in an old brick furnace.

Situ also wrote the following memo after the investigation:

> Based on the information provided by Comrade Jinrong Liu, we carried out a further onsite investigation, and found the burial site for Min Lee and the others, which is now already an overgrown marshy land, in spite of the still clear outline of the old brick furnace. Presumably, the remains are still inside the furnace. According to local people, the burial site should be on Dawang Mountain, the northeast of Jinji Village, Heshan Township of Yangjiang County. The specific location should be at about 592 feet above sea level, the back of the third mountain where there is an old, broad-leaved tree.[8]

---

7. Hwa-Wei Lee, "Record of My Efforts in Finding the Remains of My Brother and His Comrades in China and Bringing the Ashes Back to Taiwan for Burial," *The Bloodstained Red Sky* (Taipei, 1993), 48–54.
8. Ibid.

Chapter 4

Some thirty years had passed. The furnace was now covered by wild trees and shrubs. Finding it would be a matter of luck. Hope remained, however, as long as someone knew the whereabouts of Min and the other crewmen. Hwa-Wei immediately rushed to Enping to meet Jinrong Liu. Liu told Hwa-Wei that it had been a long time since someone had climbed up the steep Dawang Mountain, ever since a rumor started among superstitious local villagers about ghosts haunting an area halfway up the mountain in the middle of the night. Gradually, even the mountain trail had disappeared.

Liu suggested Hwa-Wei hire some locals to create a trail and take him to the burial site. Under Liu's coordination, Hwa-Wei started his journey early the next morning with several villagers, who were armed with tools. Liu was right. It was weedy all the way up. Those farmers worked on creating a trail as they climbed up the mountain. They finally uncovered the gray brick furnace at a location with good feng shui. In answer to Liu's question about whether to dig the remains out, Hwa-Wei felt the importance and the necessity of seeking input from the family members of the victims. This was about the lives of fourteen deceased airmen; further attached to those lives were the lives of their families who had been tormented, without hope, for thirty years.

Hwa-Wei reported the trip to his sister-in-law Hsiao-Po. Hsiao-Po was too ill then to make the trip to Enping in person to arrange a memorial service for her late husband. But she did wish to bury Min's remains in a grave with a nice gravestone. The local government's response to her wish was that building a grave, following local custom, was permitted at a family's own expense, but erecting a gravestone was not acceptable.

Hsiao-Po eventually made the trip in December 1992. She told Hwa-Wei by phone that she was hoping to unearth the remains of Min and the other crewmembers for cremation, so the ashes could be taken back to Taiwan for burial. To assist his sister-in-law in her wish, Hwa-Wei made an immediate decision to accompany her on the trip. They scheduled to meet in Guangzhou on December 9 and then travel together to Enping.

Prior to their trip to the mainland, Wen-Hsiao Liu, a military historian of Taiwan, attended upon invitation "The Research Forum on the Occasion of the Eightieth Anniversary of the Death of Ru Feng, the Pioneering Chinese Pilot," which was held in Enping. The historian inquired about the whereabouts of bomber no. 815 and learned that Min Lee's widow and brother were on their way to Enping. Upon his return to Taiwan, Liu wrote an article on the "Feng Ru Memorial Museum" with the following report:[9]

The author made an effort to explore the whereabouts of the "B-17 Flying Fortress" and its crewmembers. Mr. Zhongren Guan, the conference sponsor,

---

9. Wen-Hsiao Liu, "Feng Ru Memorial Museum," *Global Defense Journal*, no. 98 (October 1, 1992): 70–75.

was extremely helpful. Having made contact with the local CPPCC branch, Mr. Guan found out that Min Lee's American family members started the inquiry back in 1987 according to the copies of the investigation files held by the branch.

Because the mission of the Thirty-fourth Squadron back then was in strict confidence, and the attack on the aircraft was very sudden, the Taiwan military authority was unable to identify the exact crash site, thus making it impossible to inform the families of the crewmembers with more details. According to the official casualty record, crewmembers lost in the mission include three pilots (Min Lee, Yin-Kuei Hsu, and Yan Han), three electronics officers (Ting-Chang Fu, Su Ma, and Chen-Huan Yeh), three navigation officers (Fu-Chow Huang, Cheng-Chiu Chao, and Hui-Hsiang Fu), two mechanics (Shih-Wen Huang and Ti-Chou Song), one signal officer (Chun-Sheng Chen), one airdrop officer (Te-Shan Lee) and one airdrop staff (Ya-Hsing Chen). The total number of casualties is fourteen. As of early 1991, however, only Min Lee's family member in the U.S. had been working on the investigation. The other thirteen families were presumably uncertain about what to do.

This report reached the wife and daughter of Ting-Chang Fu, one of the three electronic officers. Fu's daughter, I-Ping Fu, was the associate chief editor and the head of the international news center at the *United Daily*—one of the best-known newspapers in Taiwan. Having been looking for information about her father, Ms. Fu had mixed feelings of joy and sorrow after reading the military historian's report.

She contacted Hwa-Wei immediately and soon published a feature article entitled "My Father Will Be Back" in the *United Daily*, in which she called on the families of bomber no. 815 crewmen to get in touch with her. The article was well written and very moving to read.

Ms. Fu also arranged for two other featured commentaries by Wen-Hsiao Liu and Tai-Sheng Weng, respectively, to be published in the November 23 issue of the *United Daily*, filling one-half page of the paper. Owing to the popularity of the *United Daily* in Taiwan and the power of those three articles, only twenty hours passed before the families of all the deceased crewmen responded to the call. Arranged by Ms. Fu, the fourteen crewmen's families gathered in Taipei on December 5, 1992, to discuss and prepare for the trip to Enping. Hwa-Wei attended the meeting and was chosen as the trip leader.

On December 9, 1992, a total of some fourteen family members of the crew of bomber no. 815 traveled from Taiwan and the United States all the way to Guangzhou. The following morning, they boarded a chartered bus heading for Enping. The real search for remains of their loved ones would begin around 9:00 a.m. the next day.

The search group also included a few local officials including Zhongren Guan, former vice chairman of the CPPCC Enping Branch, and Han Situ, head of the Secretariat Division of the branch, who assisted the family members in making the trip arrangements and in hiring village labor.

All the family members were in a depressed mood, matching the gloomy weather that day. Their inability to hope—a numbness that had developed over their previous thirty-three years of suffering, totally disconnected with their loved ones and knowing nothing about the last moments of their life or death—returned due to hours of bumping along the mountain road. After a one-and-a-half-hour drive, the group finally arrived at Jinji Village. It took them approximately another half an hour to get to the foot of Dawang Mountain by foot.[10]

The uninhabited mountain was fully covered with woods and brush. It hadn't had any trail until a few weeks prior to that day when a simple track was created. Climbing along the steep track, the group finally arrived at the point of the mountain where the gray furnace, eight feet in diameter, was located. The memorial service began with fourteen bouquets of flowers, fourteen sets of scented candles, and fourteen cups of watery wine offered by the fourteen family members on the deserted furnace. Then the eulogy was read, followed by the calling of the names of the deceased and a ritual burning of paper money by family representatives, one after another. A floating mist and a sweeping wind, as if of conscious souls, arose, completing the moment. Everyone was sentimental; everyone was crying. The Chinese Communist Party (CCP) officers and the villagers who witnessed the ceremony were deeply touched with emotion.

The villagers removed weeds that covered the furnace and started to dig into it with spade after spade. As they got a few feet deep, bits of bluish debris that looked like pieces of a parachute and a military jacket started to emerge. An hour or so later, they had reached a depth of six-and-a-half feet, but there was still no sign of any human remains. The contracted village workers thought it might be a good time to quit. But the family members, feeling heavier and heavier of heart, begged the villagers to continue. After another half an hour, a leg bone suddenly came in sight followed by broken skulls, teeth, and finger bones.[11]

The fourteen skulls with visible teeth were essentially well preserved, but the other body parts were heavily damaged. Having been buried together for thirty years, the remains of the crewmen were indistinguishable; it was impossible to tell which bones belonged to which crewmember. Although this way of being buried, together in the same place, seemed to represent the fellowship

---

10. Yi-Jie Fu, "Climb up the Jingji Mountain to Recover the Remains of the Lost Ones by Family Members," special news report from Enping County, Guangdong, US-Canada Center of *United Daily*, Dec. 11, 1992.

11. Ibid.

among these battle companions, it was truly heartbreaking to the family members who had traveled all the way there in hopes of locating their own loved one. Now they could only call the names of their deceased relatives who were already in a different world, hoping their lost souls could finally return home.

The mixed remains were carefully collected and put into a number of bags to be carried by family members back to Enping for cremation that evening. The ashes were contained in a special urn, carried to Guangzhou on December 13, then finally to Taipei via Hong Kong the next day. During this time, Taiwan's military authority was informed and representatives of the media were eagerly awaiting further information. Because of concern that the Chinese Communist government, especially its military, would intervene to prevent the success of the mission, publicity was kept to a minimum and Taiwan's media people were asked to stay away until the group was out of China.

3

Sitting on the seat of the China Airlines flight from Hong Kong to Taipei, Hsiao-Po held her late husband's ashes tightly to her chest. Hsiao-Po had never been on her late husband's aircraft, so it was the first time for Min and Hsiao-Po to be on the same flight, but they were now in two different worlds, at the opposite sides of the border between life and death. Hsiao-Po was expressionless, unaware of the two lines of tears running down her cheeks.

Having met and fallen in love in Northeast China, Min and Hsiao-Po had had a very happy marriage together. Min's passing had completely changed Hsiao-Po's life path. She moved to the U.S. in 1962, and had been living in California on a government pension. Their son, Hao-Sheng Lee, had been only nine at his father's death. After finishing his K–12 and college education in Taiwan, Hao-Sheng came to the States for graduate school in 1978 and settled in California with his mother after graduation.

His remembrance of his late father was frozen forever on May 29, 1959.

It was an overcast and rainy afternoon, May 29, 1959.

And it was at the Shulintou Air Force Military Community, the 1st W. Wuling Road, Hsinchu, Taiwan.

And there were tall trees and Japanese-style houses.

I was then a third-grade elementary student at the Air Force Children's School. No school was held that afternoon. Because of the rain, I had to stay home and play alone on the Tatami mat by the window, which was quite boring. The bedroom door was opened, and my father in a pilot uniform walked out toward the entrance. As usual, he put on his hat and shoes and left home for the base, while I kept playing, not being distracted. What was

The ashes of Min Lee and his thirteen comrades were buried in a mass grave in the Air Force Cemetery, Bitang. Their tombstone was engraved with a brief biography of each of the airmen.

Hwa-Wei and Mary inside the entrance to the Air Force Cemetery, Bitang.

Two published books about the Black Bats' Squadron.

unusual that day, though, was that father soon returned and left again with a dark blue military raincoat. This time, he looked back at me, and I glanced up and said, "Bye" to father.[12]

Determined to be a professional airman, Min Lee chose to sacrifice his life in a way that seems as perfect as his life's ideal. What exactly was the faith that he and his fellows held as they boarded that vulnerable aircraft and carried out their missions over flak zones without any hesitation? What was indeed the reward of the life of this once ambitious youth who had been wholeheartedly devoted to fighting for his country? War is cruel, and war has no victors.

After fifteen air force planes had been shot down, one after another in mainland China, the Taiwan government came to conclude that this high cost of intelligence gathering, this unnecessary trading of life for information was not worth it.

Communication technologies in the U.S. had advanced to the point where human intelligence work could now be accomplished by satellites. Statistics have shown that the Black Bats' Squadron carried out a total of 838 missions from 1953 to December 1967, among which fifteen planes ended in catastrophic crashes. Two-thirds of the squadron members, 148 in total, died at their post.

4

The successful return of the ashes of the fourteen brave air crewmen made headlines in all news media in Taiwan. When the Chinese airplane landed in Taipei on the afternoon of December 14, 1992, the family members were met by high officials from the Nationalist Air Force accompanied by a military band and ceremonial guards. The urn of ashes was taken to the Air Force Cemetery in Bitang, outside Taipei, and a formal memorial service was held. Later on, the urn of ashes was buried in a specially constructed long grave with a brief biography of each airman engraved on its tombstone. It stated that Min had been promoted posthumously to the rank of air force colonel.

Several years after the declassification of a part of the records of the Black Bats' mission by the United States in 1992, some surviving former airmen in Taiwan and other family members of those deceased airmen decided to establish a "Black Bats' Squadron Memorial Hall" in Hsinchu. With the assistance and support of the city government of Hsinchu, the memorial hall was officially opened on November 11, 2009. The initial collections were mostly donated by surviving airmen and the family members of the deceased airmen.[13]

---

12. Hao-Sheng Lee, "Scattered Memories of My Beloved Father," 138–41.

13. *Black Bats' Squadron Memorial Hall*, brochure (Hsinchu, Taiwan, ROC). http://www.hcccb .gov.tw/.

CHAPTER 5

Studying in the United States

The traveler has to knock at every alien door,
To come to his own,
And one has to wander through all the outer worlds,
To reach the innermost shrine at the end.
My eyes strayed far and wide,
Before I shut them and said, "Here art thou!"

—Rabindranath Tagore, Gitanjali

1

HWA-WEI CAME to the United States in 1957 at the age of twenty-six for his graduate studies. San Francisco was his port of entry. Carrying a half-full suitcase, Hwa-Wei had inexplicably mixed feelings of excitement and uncertainty, feelings most likely shared with other international students from Taiwan. The future was suddenly wide open; he, just like the explorers coming to the North American continent more than four hundred years ago, faced a new life of adventure. He had no way to foretell what kind of future he would have.

Hwa-Wei was among the early generation of Taiwanese students to come to the U.S. During the 1950s, citizens of Taiwan were facing a difficult and insecure livelihood. The two sides of the Taiwan Strait were at the height of military confrontation, each side aiming to defeat the other, and Taiwan's economic recovery was still at the beginning stage.

Walls in Taiwan and mainland China were covered in political slogans such as "Building the base in Taiwan and taking back the mainland," "Fighting against Russia and eliminating the Communist gangs," and "Liberate Taiwan." The widening conflicts between the two sides offered the younger generation in Taiwan very little sense of security and certainty; many students hoped to go to the U.S. for a brighter future.

Before coming to the States, Hwa-Wei was a junior staff member at National Taiwan Normal University earning a meager salary. To save for an airplane ticket to go to the U.S., he had to live cheaply while working evenings as a private tutor, his only source of savings. The combined monthly earnings from the two jobs was, however, still too low to cover the cost of an airline ticket to the U.S.

When preparing for his trip, Hwa-Wei spent a portion of his two-year savings on two sets of custom-made suits, which at that time were luxury items for him. However, these two suits along with all the other essential items he had packed for his trip abroad were stolen during a dorm burglary just a few days before his departure. Staring at his emptied suitcase, Hwa-Wei felt rather upset about the mishap. Only by sheer luck was his travel cash fund not in the suitcase; it was thus saved. Otherwise the outcome would have been much worse. Some of the inexpensive stolen items—the shirts, pants, and underwear—were easily replaced, but the two western-style suits were too costly.

When Hwa-Wei's father came to Taipei to see his son off, he took off his own western suit and gave it to Hwa-Wei. He felt it was very important for his son to dress properly abroad and not be disrespected. Although the suit was too big for Hwa-Wei, it was the only western suit he had to take with him.

To support his son's study-abroad trip, his father had already invested $1,000, which included the family's entire savings and loans from friends. This was quite a lot of money back then. The airfare would cost $460; the rest of the money could be reserved for later expenses in the U.S. Hwa-Wei's father said, "This is all I can do for you. Please take care of yourself and be safe."

For financial reasons, Hwa-Wei chose to take the train from San Francisco to Pittsburgh, a hilly city in the East. It was a four-day railway trip: Hwa-Wei passed through wild deserts and canyons in the western region, crossed the Rocky Mountains, and traveled through boundless Midwest farmland and highly populated Chicago, to eventually arrive at his final destination.

Located on the winding bank of the Ohio River and backed by the ancient Appalachian Mountains running up and down like camel humps to the east, Pittsburgh—known as the Steel City—was quite different from the cities Hwa-Wei had visited before. The Fort Pitt Bridge was made from steel and seemed ready to fly, its shape evoking the gigantic stretched-out wings of the city soaring up to the sky. On the river were boats fully loaded with coal and iron, often blowing their steam whistles. These boats looked just like drifting hills.

A large city in western Pennsylvania, Pittsburgh was once one of the busiest inland river ports in North America. There the Allegheny and Monongahela Rivers join to form the Ohio River, which then runs west for about 1,300 miles, eventually flowing into the Mississippi River system.

The natural advantage of the Ohio River and the railway system built along the river, gave this inland city tentacles extending in all directions, allowing it to readily absorb the nourishment needed for the city's development. By the early initial stages of American industrialization, Pittsburgh had already risen to become a prominent steel town. That steel industry brought the city immense fortune and attracted many wealthy people from around the world.

Capital from that industry also benefited the city's public welfare and educational system. The city's residents had gained much from the generosity of Andrew Carnegie, an entrepreneur and philanthropist. Born to a poor Scottish immigrant family, Carnegie had moved to Pittsburgh at the age of thirteen with his parents. He started his career as a telegram delivery boy, his keen eyes learning every corner of the city, while also studying it to devise a plan to make a fortune.

Carnegie rose up to become the tycoon of a steel empire, one as famous as Henry Ford, the king of automobiles, and John D. Rockefeller, an oil magnate. This ambitious industrialist's intake of wealth was indeed phenomenal. A believer of "money is power," Carnegie amassed a fortune, but at the same time he recognized that "surplus wealth is a sacred trust, which its possessor is bound to administer in his lifetime for the good of the community."

In his later years, Carnegie devoted his life to large-scale philanthropy. Amongst his charities, free libraries were his highest priority. Carnegie never forgot his early years when the free library in downtown Pittsburgh founded by Colonel James Anderson specifically for working boys was his primary source of education. The library, which had served as his study hall, kept him occupied after working hours. Due to this early experience, Carnegie used a large portion of his donations to build public libraries, thus empowering the poor to change their destiny.

Carnegie explained, in *The Autobiography of Andrew Carnegie and the Gospel of Wealth*:

> It was from my own early experience that I decided there was no use to which money could be applied so productive of good to boys and girls who have good within them and ability and ambition to develop it, as the founding of a public library in a community which is willing to support it as a municipal institution . . . Colonel James Anderson—I bless his name as I write—announced that he would open his library of four hundred volumes to boys, so that any young man could take out, each Saturday afternoon, a book which could be exchanged for another on the succeeding Saturday.

Between 1893 and 1919, a total of 1,689 public libraries were built in 1,400 communities across the country with Carnegie's support, making him the first person in the United States to bestow upon its towns and cities such a large number of library buildings. It is legitimate for him to claim that he succeeded in his "efforts to make the earth a little better than I found it."[1]

These anecdotes about Carnegie were legends of the city of Pittsburgh. The young Hwa-Wei, soon upon his arrival in the United States, was exposed to

---

1. Alberto Manguel, *The Library at Night* (New Haven, CT: Yale University Press, 2008), 104.

libraries such as he had never seen before, and he soon began to establish an indissoluble bond with them.

2

The University of Pittsburgh (Pitt), named after the city, is an important icon of this steel town. It started as the Pittsburgh Academy as early as 1787, just twenty years after the municipal founding date. The founder, Hugh Henry Brackenridge, was a Pennsylvania Supreme Court judge and renowned American writer. As one of the oldest institutions of higher education in the U.S., the school's fame rose rapidly in the first century of its founding. In 1908, the university adopted its current name.

Situated in the neighborhood of Oakland, the University of Pittsburgh occupies a large area of the city's southeast region. Two busy city streets, Fifth and Forbes Avenues, pass through the campus, eliminating any physical boundary between the school and the city.

Hwa-Wei's scholarship from the graduate department of the School of Education was largely due to his aunt, Ms. Phyllis Hsiao-Chu Wang, a serials librarian in Pitt's medical library (later named Falk Library), who was quite familiar with the university.

An outstanding woman in her youth in China, Phyllis had been educated at Hwa Nan College for Women in Fuzhou and then Yenching University in Beijing. After graduation, she worked at Lingnan University in Guangzhou. She served in a variety of library positions including head of cataloging; chief of general affairs; deputy library director; interim library director; and, then, library director at the university library from 1935 to 1948. In 1948, sponsored by the United Board for Christian Colleges in China, she came to the U.S. to pursue her master's degree in library science (MLS) at the University of Illinois at Urbana-Champaign. By the time she had earned her MLS in 1950, the Communists had already taken over mainland China. Because it had been a missionary-supported university, Lingnan University was closed soon thereafter. Phyllis Wang decided to call off her original plan to return and stayed to work in the U.S.

Hwa-Wei's mother, Hsiao-Hui Wang, and aunt, Phyllis Wang, both graduated from the same Christian college in Fuzhou. They were among a very small number of Chinese women in the early twentieth century who were fortunate to be given the privilege of an education, thanks to their open-minded parents. The higher education that they received broadened their vision and provided more life and destiny choices to the two siblings.

His mother, Hsiao-Hui, chose family as the center of her life; his aunt, Phyllis, spent her life in a completely different way. She attached great importance to professional development and personal freedom. A brother, Tiao-Hsin Wang, born between the two sisters, was also well educated and served as a professor of chemistry, dean of the College of Science, and acting president of Fujian Christian University. After 1949, Fujian Christian University was renamed Fujian Normal University. Tiao-Hsin, due to his Christian background and affiliation, died during China's Cultural Revolution at the hands of the Red Guards.

Having never married, Phyllis was very independent and totally dedicated to her library career. She often commented about her own success: "Look at me as a lady who has been striving for a life being independent and with a good career."

As his scholarship covered his tuition, Hwa-Wei only needed to take care of a small portion of his expenses, such as rent, meals, textbooks, and educational supplies. Phyllis paid for Hwa-Wei's room and board for the first year; Hwa-Wei had only to cover his daily expenses with the $500 that he had brought from Taiwan. His aunt urged Hwa-Wei to watch every penny that he spent.

From the late fifties until the early eighties, Chinese students in American universities were primarily from Taiwan. As international students, they—just as the students from mainland China who started to arrive in the eighties—had to deal with two major problems: poverty and the language barrier. Those international students had no choice but to study hard and be careful of their spending. Since the year 2000, however, the situation for newly arrived Chinese students has improved much due to rapid economic development on both sides of the Taiwan Strait.

3

Another challenge Hwa-Wei faced was a cultural gap that included the differences between the learning environments and the methods of teaching in Taiwan and the U.S. In Taiwan, as in most other Asian countries, the classroom atmosphere was far more restrictive. Students did not ask questions or express their views unless they were called upon by their teachers. In the U.S., the situation was quite different. In Hwa-Wei's graduate classes, students were encouraged to raise questions and express their views. There was much interaction between teachers and students as well as among students themselves.

Class presentations and group discussions were also frequently required. Hwa-Wei, not accustomed to public speaking and handicapped by his limited English, found adapting to the new environment difficult. Another pedagogical difference was the change in emphasis from note taking and memorizing, two methods of learning with which Hwa-Wei was very familiar and had mastered, to critical thinking and problem solving. He needed to make this adjustment very quickly in order to catch up with the new pace of learning.

In classes, Hwa-Wei was able to comprehend only half of the lecture content and frequently fell behind in answering questions and during group discussions. He had to spend more hours after class, often many more hours than his peers, to finish the same amount of homework. He started with intensive reading, word by word, using English-Chinese dictionaries. He soon abandoned this approach as being too time-consuming and impractical, replacing it with a speed-reading of the full text to get a general overview of the contents, then supplementing that reading with a selective reading of the key parts. After he had worked hard using the new approach for a period of time, Hwa-Wei noticed a big improvement in his English-language reading skills and comprehension.

Graduate study requires a lot of essay writing in addition to routine quizzes and exams. Hwa-Wei found that writing in English was preferable to speaking and reading, as it allowed him to spend more time sorting out his ideas and weighing his words. To simplify his professors' work grading his essays, Hwa-Wei devised a special format for his homework, adding a summary and a brief table of contents on the first page of an essay to immediately clarify the essay's main argument and structure. This format was well received by his professors.

Hwa-Wei's college education and teaching experience in Taiwan had provided him with a solid foundation for his graduate studies. His theoretical knowledge was enriched through many core courses including the history of education, educational psychology, pedagogy, and philosophy of education; his statistics and practical knowledge were enhanced by his two years of teaching.

Because of this background, Hwa-Wei was able to grasp the essence of the subject matter and contents of his graduate classes at Pitt. Thus, the only issue left was the language barrier, which, he recognized, might take some time to overcome. Knowing his strengths and weaknesses, Hwa-Wei felt less pressure and was able to improve.

The university library was Hwa-Wei's favorite place. It was here, he felt, he could find the knowledge he needed. To him, the library represented a gigantic and sacred place in which human wisdom, having accumulated over centuries, was waiting for him. Hwa-Wei enjoyed its quiet, broken only by the occasional soft clip from the flipping of book pages or the taking of notes. He was happy acknowledging his natural fondness for books and his strong appetite for knowledge.

To achieve academic excellence in school was a special way for Hwa-Wei to motivate himself and to gain respect from others. He believed that this was something he could do and must do in order to succeed as a foreign student. So he studied much harder than ever before and found new self-confidence.

Befriending books and learning turned out to be Hwa-Wei's lifestyle in the United States well into his later years.

4

Due to the cultural differences between Taiwan and the U.S., Hwa-Wei found the need to assimilate himself to the new environment as quickly as possible. He encountered many "culture shocks," but, due to his strong ability to learn and adapt, he was able to make quick adjustments to the new environment.

His first year at Pitt, Hwa-Wei lived in a graduate student dormitory, which housed very few international students. His roommate, Ahma Esthete, was from Ethiopia and majored in public health. The two got along very well despite their different living habits and cultural backgrounds. This roommate went back to his country after graduation, where he served as the state minister of Health. Tragically, he died in a military coup a few years later.

As a boarding graduate student, Hwa-Wei was required to dine in the campus cafeteria. The food there was quite pricey, but rich in variety. Hwa-Wei, however, could only afford one large meal per day. He came up with smart ways of fighting hunger, including applying more butter, which digested slowly, to his bread to extend the length of time between his two daily meals.

Church activities were very popular among students. Many international students were also invited to participate, especially in the Roger Williams Fellowship of the First Baptist Church, to which Hwa-Wei belonged.

Rev. Paul Offenhiser, a dear friend of his aunt, Phyllis, was the Baptist pastor overseeing student activities at Pitt. The reverend had gained a great popularity among international students because of his kindness and enthusiasm toward them. "Mr. O," as he was affectionately called by those students, took especially good care of Hwa-Wei. During Hwa-Wei's first summer months at Pitt, the reverend made a special arrangement to send Hwa-Wei to work in a church camp in Green Lake, Wisconsin.

Located in a beautiful lakeside campground, the camp hosted several hundred campers every week for Christian spiritual fellowship and activities. Besides Hwa-Wei, there were thirty to forty other students with summer jobs at the camp. All of them were American students of college age. Besides working in the dining hall and serving three meals daily, these student workers also sang at church services and gave performances on stage. Since Hwa-Wei already had extensive experience in stage management, he was able to handle backstage work easily while the American students performed on stage. Apart from those duties, one thing Hwa-Wei loved doing was singing Christian hymns in the church choir. To him, those spiritual songs were simple, beautiful, and touching.

Newly arrived in Pittsburgh, Pennsylvania, in September 1957, Hwa-Wei was ready to begin his graduate studies at the University of Pittsburgh.

His aunt, Phyllis C. (Hsiao-Chu) Wang, and the Rev. Paul Offenhiser were instrumental in making it possible for Hwa-Wei to come to the United States for his graduate studies.

Mary (*first row, far left*) and Hwa-Wei (*second row, second from left*) participated in many campus activities at the University of Pittsburgh.

The income from the summer camp job was minimal. Many Chinese students preferred to stay in Pittsburgh or go to larger cities, such as New York, to work in Chinese restaurants as waiters and waitresses, delivery boys and girls, or kitchen assistants, because they could earn more money. Hwa-Wei, however, felt he would gain more value and meaning by getting himself immersed as quickly as possible into the American way of life. As a gregarious person fond of group events and wide social interaction, Hwa-Wei saw his working experience at the summer camp as a great opportunity for him to get acquainted with American culture.

Hwa-Wei's father had been a Christian from his early years; his mother had studied at missionary schools. Whereas they both were pious Christians in their later years, Hwa-Wei's parents were open minded and gave their children the freedom to choose their own religions. Even though he never became a Christian, Hwa-Wei likes the spirit of all religions, especially Buddhism; he does not care for religious superstitions, mysticism, or radicalism. He admires the kindness and benevolence of the Buddhist goddess Kuan Yin in her applying the principles of compassion, mercy, and love to all beings.

When summer was over, everything went back to normal on campus. The busy school life, pleasant and steady, filled Hwa-Wei's days at Pitt with hope. He started to work in the university library as a part-time student assistant in order to earn his living expenses. He was able to finish his master's degree in education in one and a half years.

In February 1959, while preparing for his doctoral program application, Hwa-Wei was selected to become a librarian trainee by the university librarian, Ms. Lorraine Garloch, who saw the hard-working Hwa-Wei as someone with the potential to be a good librarian. The librarian trainee program was a new program of Pitt Library.

To complete the program, Hwa-Wei was required to pursue a master of library science (MLS) as a part-time student within the three-year-long training period and work full-time in the library in various departments. Hwa-Wei was very fortunate to be assigned to the departments of cataloging, circulation, and government documents, and to the branch libraries of the School of Social Work and the Graduate School of Public and International Affairs. He worked in each area for a duration of three to six months. The practical experience gained from working in all of these different areas of the university's library system proved to be most valuable to Hwa-Wei in his library career.

The library not only paid his salary, which was minimal pay in the beginning, but also his full tuition. To earn his MLS, Hwa-Wei enrolled in the Carnegie Institute of Technology (later renamed Carnegie Mellon University) as

Pitt did not have a relevant program back then. Luckily, the institute's School of Library Science was located at the Carnegie Library of Pittsburgh, just across Forbes Avenue from the Pitt campus. His contract stipulated that once Hwa-Wei completed his MLS degree he would be hired as a full-time librarian.

Without difficulty, Hwa-Wei worked full-time and completed his MLS degree in two years, one year ahead of schedule. In 1961, he started to work as the first assistant in the Acquisitions Department, the first professional librarian's position he held. Among his many assigned responsibilities was the acquisition of Chinese materials for the soon-to-be-established East Asian Collection of the Pitt Library.

While working in the library, Hwa-Wei resumed his doctoral study in education as a part-time student. Being a professional librarian, he was able to get a tuition waiver for his doctoral study.

Upon his arrival at Pitt, there had been a Chinese faculty and staff club but not a Chinese student association. All the students were busy enough with their own lives. The situation remained unchanged until about 1961 or 1962 when Hwa-Wei initiated and organized—after completing his MLS and becoming a full-time library employee—an intercampus Chinese student association. There were about seventy to eighty members, including many from other colleges and universities in Pittsburgh.

Later, Hwa-Wei also joined a Chinese academic organization named the Rho Psi Fraternity, with a membership comprised of Chinese American scholars and specialists from all over the country. Its Pittsburgh-based members included faculty, doctors, researchers, and engineers. The organization had regular meetings and activities through which Hwa-Wei made a few very good friends with whom he has kept in touch for decades.

CHAPTER 6

Love Story in a Foreign Land

The village church, among the trees,
Where first our marriage vows were given,
With merry peals shall swell the breeze,
And point with taper spire to heaven.
—*Samuel Rogers*

1

THE CATHEDRAL of Learning is a landmark building in Pittsburgh. The gigantic forty-two-story Gothic Revival Cathedral, standing tall and majestic on campus, features long and narrow stained-glass windows and hand-carved Roman columns, layer after layer rising to the vantage point atop. Seen from a distance, it resembles an ancient European church. The name of the building was given, perhaps, to suggest a similarity between religion and education—both of which require seriousness and dedication.

After its groundbreaking in 1926, the Cathedral took a lengthy eleven years to complete. The construction was suspended once in 1933 during the great economic depression due to a funding shortage. To make certain it was completed, construction began both from the bottom up and the top down. For a few years, the central floors remained incomplete. Donations from countless local residents including pocket money from children secured the completion of this magnificent edifice.

One noteworthy feature of the building is its beautiful Commons Room, a central three-story stone hall with gothic arches. Around the hall are twenty-nine unique nationality rooms—a tourist attraction to be sure, but one used primarily for most of the university's undergraduate classes. Each room has a unique style representing the culture and, in some cases, history of each country. Included among them is a Chinese room. It differs from the other rooms—in which the chairs are placed as in a regular classroom—in that it has one large black lacquer table, with ten surrounding chairs, that is used for graduate seminars. The most impressive thing in the room is a life-size, etched, gray-slate figure of Confucius.

Committees from Pittsburgh's different ethnic communities have helped design and fund the rooms, bringing materials, artists, and some furnishings from their native countries. The decor of the Chinese room was initially designed and furnished by the Chinese government. At Christmas time, each group decorated its room and/or Christmas tree in native styles. Mary Kratochvil volunteered as one of the hall's guides, trained to show visitors the rooms when no classes were in session.

Hwa-Wei and Mary met on the twenty-seventh floor of the Cathedral of Learning, in an audio-visual education course, Hwa-Wei's first class in the United States. Because of his language difficulty, he chose a seat at the back of the classroom. Right before class began, Mary rushed in and took a seat by him.

The professor, Ivan Hosack, knowing Hwa-Wei was a newly arrived international student, came to the back to check with Hwa-Wei at the end of class. He asked if Hwa-Wei could understand the lecture. Hwa-Wei confessed that he was having some difficulty but was able to take some notes. After looking at those notes written mostly in Chinese with a few simple English keywords, Professor Hosack, turned to Mary and said, "This young man may need some help. Would you be willing to let him borrow your notes each class?" Mary readily agreed. The professor added that perhaps she could also arrange to meet with Hwa-Wei to show him where the next class would be held since they were changing to a new classroom. And so began a new destiny for the two.

2

Hwa-Wei borrowed Mary's notes on a regular basis, returning them as arranged. The notes were very helpful and eased his course work. Hwa-Wei did very well in the class. He was very clever. And he could type, a skill many of the students did not possess. The professors loved his easy-to-read typed papers with their summaries and tables of contents.

When they met, Mary was a senior undergraduate in the College of Education. As she planned to pursue a graduate degree, she chose to take a few graduate courses in advance. One such course was Comparative Education taught by Dr. William H. E. Johnson, who happened to be Hwa-Wei's academic advisor. For her term paper topic, Mary chose a research study comparing education in Taiwan with U.S. education. Dr. Johnson advised her, "I know someone who would be a good resource person for you." Later, the two professors, Hosack and Johnson, both proudly claimed to be the one who had brought Mary and Hwa-Wei together. Both became lifelong friends of the young couple.

Mary was very studious. She and Hwa-Wei sometimes ran into each other in the library reading rooms. They also often saw each other in the Tuck Shop, a cafeteria in the basement next to the Undergraduate Library where Hwa-Wei often worked. Hwa-Wei was always happy to bump into her there. The cafeteria was a place where students could spend their time between classes, which were often scheduled many hours apart. And, as many students commuted to the university, they would wait in the booths there for their rides home.

On Saturdays, when there was a home football game, many students walked up the hill to Pitt Stadium. For the first game, Mary asked Hwa-Wei if he wanted to join her. He did. So they met and joined the crowd of students headed to the game. Here began a clash of cultures. Mary didn't know that at Hwa-Wei's university in Taiwan when a boy singled out a girl to accompany him anywhere, their relationship was considered a permanent commitment; if broken off, the boy was to blame. Hwa-Wei didn't know that in the States, platonic friendships between males and females, ones based on qualities other than a physical attraction for each other, were quite common.

Mary had two brothers whose friends were her friends. She lived in a neighborhood with a lot of boys, and she joined in their ball games. For two years, she commuted to Pitt in a carpool with several boys who also commuted the thirty miles each day. At Pitt, she had several good friends who were male students, and she especially enjoyed the company of pre-ministerial students, always searching for what they might have learned that others would never know.

Hwa-Wei thought he was being invited on a date. Mary was not attracted to Hwa-Wei at first. Initially, he had been wearing a single gold band. When Mary asked about it later, he said it was from his mother and that it was customary for a mother to give such a ring to a son who was going away. Mary came to respect Hwa-Wei for who he was and all that he had experienced and endured during the Sino-Japanese war and the subsequent civil war between the Nationalist Government and the Chinese Communists. But she respected and admired him long before she came to love him. She knew he was dependable, trustworthy, and had great perseverance.

At Pitt, Thanksgiving break came quickly. Winter was near, and the weather was getting cold. Pittsburgh has four distinct seasons: summer sunshine, winter snow, spring flowers, and autumn fruits. Thanksgiving, a special holiday for Americans to commemorate the Pilgrims' first settlement in the colonies, is celebrated on the fourth Thursday of November. Family members go home and, customarily, invite visitors or single friends to join in the traditional turkey dinner. Mary invited Hwa-Wei to join that year's family gathering at her parents' home in Jeannette, about thirty miles southeast of Pittsburgh. Hwa-Wei could have a chance to experience one of the most important American holidays and to meet Mary's parents, her two brothers, Charles and Robert, and their families.

Jeannette is a small town, small enough that children can all walk to their local school and families can walk to a local church on Sundays. As in many small towns in suburban areas, government, public services, banks, and convenience stores were all on one street.

Jeannette is known as the Glass City. At its peak, 70 percent of glass products worldwide were coming from the town. Unfortunately, as cheap labor overseas began to offer higher profits, those glass factories moved out, one after another. Only four remained in the 1950s when many students, Mary included, took summer jobs in them because of the high wages that could be earned in a few months.

Mary's parents were employed in the glass industry. Mary's mother was a secretary at Ro-An Laboratories, later named McKesson-Robbins Co., a supplier of the raw materials used in making glass. Mary's father was the plant manager and arranged the receiving of shipments, storage, mixing of chemicals, and delivery to factories.

Mary's father, John (Jack) W. Kratochvil, was very skilled with his hands and involved in many things in his leisure time. Before Christmas, he would go to their vacation home 150 miles north of Jeannette and cut pine trees that he had planted there to bring back and sell from his backyard. Besides renovating the family's weekend vacation home in Cooperstown, Pa., he bought land nearby in Utica, divided the large house there into apartments, then, by himself, built four cabins for fishermen and a large two-story recreation center. He kept a cabin right on French Creek for his own family and friends. After retirement, he bought an apartment building that he rented out in Utica and then built a small grocery store that he and his wife ran until he died.

Early on in her schooling, Mary knew that in high school she would have to be first in her graduating class and be active in school and her community in order to receive one of the two half-tuition scholarships that Pitt offered each year to her school. Mary was the valedictorian of her class in 1954 and did get her scholarship. Maybe it was just a coincidence—or maybe it was fate—that Mary became interested in Taiwan when she was still in high school. To her, it seemed that the United States should provide as much help as it could to Taiwan, which had been in need of assistance.

In her valedictory speech at graduation, she expressed that it was important for everyone to think about giving a hand to underdeveloped regions and countries such as Taiwan and the Philippines. Her speech was entitled "Trust in God but Tie Your Camel." She told her audience that they could trust that all would be well in the world, but each should take part in helping to make it so. In other words, trust that no one will steal your camel, but take every precaution to tie it up anyway.

At that time, many of her fellow students didn't know of a place called Taiwan on the other side of the world. Mary, herself, was interested in becoming a medical missionary and dreamed about someday being able to travel to the Philippines to help people there. She was originally enrolled in the five-year nursing program at Pitt. After a year, however, she was no longer interested in being a nurse or a missionary. She wanted to be a teacher, changing to the School of Education with a major in English Literature and minors in German and Spanish.

Hwa-Wei didn't expect that he would ever be friends with such a beautiful and kind-hearted girl and share with her the different culture he brought to the United States. It was through Mary that he came to a better understanding of American people and culture. Although he once had a girlfriend in Taiwan, Hwa-Wei really had limited experience in interacting with and dating girls. In the 1950s, college students in Taiwan were rather conservative, especially about dating and serious relationships. Also, as a teacher's training university, National Taiwan Normal University (NTNU) had strict rules about on-campus dating.

When at NTNU, Hwa-Wei had once admired a classmate. The girl, lively and attractive, had many secret admirers. Whether or not she knew of Hwa-Wei's interest, she would always prefer to go out with a group of friends instead of with Hwa-Wei alone. Potential dating opportunities were thus turned into group outings. Later, finding that he had many strong rivals in the class, Hwa-Wei lost his courage to take further action in expressing his admiration for her, except for a few letters he wrote. Many years later, the girl also came to the United States and became a librarian. They met again at one of the library conferences. Both were married then, and the girl told Hwa-Wei—playfully—that she knew of his interest back then and teased him for not openly pursuing her.

Shortly before his graduation from NTNU, Hwa-Wei got to know another girl, a sophomore at the same university, who was also active in extracurricular activities. The two spent a lot of time together through those activities. They started letter writing after Hwa-Wei left for his military service. The girl thus became Hwa-Wei's official first love. Their relationship continued until Hwa-Wei left Taiwan for the United States.

The friendship between Hwa-Wei and Mary started slowly at first but grew rapidly after Hwa-Wei returned from summer camp in Wisconsin. From the beginning of the second school year in the fall of 1958, he and Mary saw each other much more often and fell deeply in love. Hwa-Wei decided to propose marriage to Mary.

They became engaged in January 1959. A few of their student friends arranged a small party for them at a friend's home in Pittsburgh. Hwa-Wei's parents, who had received a westernized education in China and were open-minded,

Mary was Hwa-Wei's classmate at the University of Pittsburgh. Her volunteering to help him with his English resulted in a close friendship between the two.

Hwa-Wei with Mary's parents, Mr. and Mrs. John W. Kratochvil.

On March 14, 1959, Hwa-Wei and Mary were wed in the First Methodist Church, Jeannette, Pennsylvania.

liked the idea of an American daughter-in-law. His father sent a personal letter to Mary to tell her that he and Hwa-Wei's mother were very happy and would bless them remotely from Taiwan. Humorously, he later sent Mary a pair of pointed chopsticks urging her to learn to use them. He also gave Mary a stone seal carved with Mary's Chinese name.

Throughout the winter and toward the spring, while both of them were finishing their master's degrees in education, they were very busy preparing for their wedding. For Hwa-Wei, the feeling of heaviness seemed to be gone: his wandering in a foreign land was over. He now felt surrounded by happiness. Walking on the lawns in front of the Cathedral of Learning, Hwa-Wei could sense the frozen field was thawing and the grass was growing green. He felt light-hearted and joyful.

The wedding took place at the First Methodist Church in Jeannette. Following traditional American custom, the wedding arrangements were made by the bride's family. Mary's parents were happy to have Mary and Hwa-Wei come home to have their ceremony. Hwa-Wei was moved by the happy outcome. So were his parents. Hwa-Wei's father wrote a special letter in English to Mary's parents in which he expressed support and blessings to the marriage, as well as apologies for not being able to attend the wedding in person and to share the wedding cost due to his family's financial constraints. Mary wrote him back explaining that, due to American custom, it was only fair to have the bride cover all the costs of a wedding held in the United States. She added that she looked forward to celebrating with them later in Taiwan, as she and Hwa-Wei originally planned to return to Taiwan after the completion of Hwa-Wei's graduate studies.

The wedding was held the evening of March 14, 1959. Among the wedding attendees were Aunt Phyllis Wang; Rev. Paul Offenhiser; international students from thirteen different countries who drove the thirty miles from Pittsburgh to Jeannette; and Mary's family, friends, relatives, and neighbors. The guests—a total of sixty to seventy people—gathered at the church. The bridesmaid was Mary's roommate, Somsong Limsong, a student from Thailand. Kuei Nam Rhee, Mary and Hwa-Wei's friend from Korea, sang "The Lord's Prayer" a cappella in Korean. It was a moving and unforgettable moment. Everything went beautifully as planned.[1]

During their courtship before, and even after their wedding, Hwa-Wei and Mary spent a great deal of their leisure time, mostly during weekends, in beautiful Schenley Park in Pittsburgh. Situated between the neighborhoods of Oakland, Greenfield, and Squirrel Hill, and just a short walking distance from the Pitt

---

1. Mary Frances Lee, interview by the author.

Shown here dressed in his graduation robe, Hwa-Wei completed his Ph.D. from the University of Pittsburgh in June 1965.

Some years later, Mary and Hwa-Wei returned to visit the campus of the University of Pittsburgh.

campus, Schenley Park was a top attraction for university students, local residents, and outdoor enthusiasts.

Most of all, Hwa-Wei and Mary enjoyed the remarkable Phipps Conservatory and Botanical Gardens, which displays beautiful flowers and plants of different seasons all year round. They found it a wonderful place to relax and to walk through holding hands. Besides the conservatory and gardens, the park is also home to Carnegie Library and Carnegie Museum—two major cultural institutions—which host special exhibits and programs. The hiking trails on the 456 acres of the park also offered a nearby escape from busy campus life.

From 1959 to 1961, Hwa-Wei was attending classes at the Carnegie Library School, one of the graduate schools of the Carnegie Institute of Technology. He was also working as a librarian trainee at Pitt Library. His classes were held at the Carnegie Library of Pittsburgh, just across Forbes Avenue from the Cathedral of Learning, making life very convenient for Hwa-Wei since the two places had only ten minutes of walking distance between them.

Two years after Hwa-Wei's completion of his master of library science degree, the library school was transferred to Pitt and the Carnegie Institute of Technology (Carnegie Tech) was renamed Carnegie Mellon University.

The transfer of the library school from Carnegie Tech to Pitt was very good news for Hwa-Wei: he could add library science as a minor to his Ph.D. studies in education. In the early 1960s, very few library schools in the United States had a doctoral program. The new Graduate School of Library and Information Sciences at Pitt was in the planning stage to offer a doctoral program in library science. Dr. Harold Lancour, dean of the Graduate School of Library and Information Sciences at Pitt, and Dr. Andrew D. Osborn, a famous library science professor at Pitt, were pleased to serve as members of Hwa-Wei's doctoral dissertation committee in education at the invitation of Dr. William H.E. Johnson, Hwa-Wei's major advisor and chair of the Department of Educational Foundation.

During the years of his graduate studies at the Carnegie Library School, Hwa-Wei and Mary celebrated the birth of their first child, Shirley, a beautiful and lovable child who brought much joy to the new family. Three years later, the second child, James, was born, a handsome and strong boy with a gentle nature.

While Hwa-Wei was busily working on his dissertation, two years after the birth of James, their third child, Pamela, was born. Shirley and James looked like Mary, while Pamela looked very much like Hwa-Wei, having distinctive Chinese facial features and dark hair. Pamela even exhibited Hwa-Wei's personality traits of strong will and independence. When Mary was editing Hwa-Wei's dissertation, soon after the birth of Pamela, Hwa-Wei tried to bottle-feed formula to Pamela, but he found that Pamela always wanted to hold the bottle herself.

Over the years, Mary became the mother of six children (Edward and Charles, born in Edinboro, and Robert, born in Bangkok) and spent a tremendous amount of time and energy managing the big family, of which she was the center. She did everything possible to free Hwa-Wei from worries about home, so he could devote his full attention and energies to his full-time library work, his part-time graduate studies, and, later on, his much-expanded professional commitments, including research, speeches, and writing throughout his library career.

The children, being exposed to both eastern and western cultures, were able to develop mature and tolerant personalities. Growing up in a harmonious family and seeing little conflict between their parents, they seldom exhibited signs of teenage rebellion. Hwa-Wei feels this all should be credited to Mary, who has maintained a very close relationship between herself and her children and has also encouraged close relationships among the children themselves. Hwa-Wei came to realize the similarities between Mary and his own mother, despite their different national and cultural backgrounds. These two most important women in his life share the same disposition: they both are kind hearted and special.

CHAPTER 7

Beginning His Library Career

Written texts are the most priceless treasures in the world. Broadly speaking, they pass on knowledge from generation to generation; more narrowly, they take down mundane things from day to day. They facilitate communications of ideas and sharing of feelings among people without temporal and spatial limitation. They help people succeed and gain reputation. They expand one's view and experience. Through reading written texts, one could gain knowledge and understand concepts with ease. Are they not the most priceless treasures in the world?

—*Emperor Kangxi (1654–1722), fourth emperor of the Qing dynasty,*
Disciplinary Principles to His Children, "Respect and Value [of]
Written Texts, the Most Priceless Treasures in the World

1

STUDENTS AT the University of Pittsburgh usually took courses during the fall, winter, and spring quarters and chose to work during the summer. The tuition-waiver scholarship that Hwa-Wei received was originally for only one academic year. The earnings from his summer job at the church summer camp were small—covering only some of his living expenses—so Hwa-Wei was very happy when his tuition scholarship was extended for the second year.

In searching for a part-time job to further meet his financial needs, the first source that came to his mind was the library; it was the building he most frequented and, therefore, the most familiar place on campus. He usually went to the library to study when there was no class and had even become an acquaintance of several librarians there. He asked one of the librarians, "I need a job. Can I get a student assistant job here?" He was told to talk to the librarian in charge of human resources.

The first question from the human resources librarian was, "What kind of work can you do in the library?"

"I guess I can work in the book stacks in the evening hours and on weekends. I know that I am a responsible worker who can keep the stacks neat and orderly and can expedite the process of locating needed books for readers, " replied Hwa-Wei.

The head of human resources was amused by this applicant's response. And Hwa-Wei got his first student job on campus, twenty hours a week in the library. The job itself was easy, but the income was minimal. Hwa-Wei, however, was quite happy to be able to make money on his own.

Back then, closed stacks for library collections were very common among American academic libraries. Library patrons had no direct access to the bookshelves within the closed stacks. They had to use a card catalog to find the books they needed, write down the call number and brief bibliographic information of each book on a three-by-five-inch slip of paper, and submit these slips to library staff behind the service counter. The staff would then send the slips to the workstation, located in the closed stacks, where student assistants would use the information to find the books requested and then deliver them to the patron. It could take half an hour for a staff member to run through the huge stack area to obtain a few books from different shelves. The long waiting time often made patrons impatient, and the dashing back and forth was laborious for staff members.

Every day, Hwa-Wei spent four hours working in the library. He worked diligently in the stacks and walked as fast as he could so as to save the patrons' waiting time. He was a service provider when racing through the stacks. But outside the stacks area, as a graduate student, he became a service user. This role reversal helped him better understand user needs.

Many times Hwa-Wei, as a library patron, would invest a tremendous amount of time in finding a potentially relevant book based on the limited information in the card catalog, then find the book was not exactly what he had wanted. So, he would be forced to go through another time-consuming loop of looking and waiting. Some situations could take several loops before he found the right book to meet his needs. Thinking this mishap could happen to other patrons, Hwa-Wei began to look for a way to improve the system. Eventually, after having familiarized himself with the stacks, he came up with one approach. Every time he was asked to search out a title, in addition to the exact title or titles requested by a patron, he would bring out several other books with similar contents for the patron's reference. In many cases, patrons ended up with the additional books—and appreciated the add-on service. Hwa-Wei was pleased to see the positive outcome.

One day while working in the stacks, Hwa-Wei suddenly heard Ms. Lorena A. Garloch's voice coming over a loudspeaker, "Mr. Hwa-Wei Lee, this is Ms. Garloch, the university librarian. I want to talk to you. Please come to my office." Ms. Garloch was known to be a demanding administrator, one who often set high standards for her staff. Therefore, she was feared by many of the library employees.

Hwa-Wei stopped his work and started to feel nervous. He wondered whether he had done anything wrong and was at risk of being fired. Other student assistants on duty, all knowing the toughness of Ms. Garloch, showed their concern. One student approached him, tapped him on the shoulder and said, "Hey Hwa-Wei, be careful and good luck!" Hwa-Wei did not want any bad luck to happen to him because this library job, the source of his bread and butter, was so important to him. However, he was also puzzled because it would be unusual for a library director to fire a student worker herself.

The result turned out to be totally different than what he had anticipated. Ms. Garloch was gentle and affable. She asked Hwa-Wei to take a seat and started to talk to him in a slow-paced voice, "I have received many reports about your work efficiency and dedication. I was told that you had figured out a better way to meet patrons' needs. I wish every library employee could do the same thing as you did." She was referring to the add-on service Hwa-Wei provided to library patrons with additional books. While Hwa-Wei himself considered that additional service a modest change, some faculty and students felt differently. They expressed their gratitude with comments to Ms. Garloch. The result was quite a relief to Hwa-Wei.

The conversation continued. Hwa-Wei told Ms. Garloch that the idea came from his own experience as a graduate student, one who happened to be a heavy library user, who had encountered difficulty in locating the right books to read. Providing patrons with a few more alternate titles could be helpful. It was really an easy deed, he said, nothing special.

Ms. Garloch, with a soft look in her eyes, said: "Because of your thoughtfulness of library users and their needs, you have the potential to become a good librarian. Have you thought about a professional career in librarianship?"

The question was somewhat unexpected. "Ms. Garloch, I do like my library work very much. Do you think I can become a professional librarian with a master's degree in education?" Hwa-Wei responded respectfully.

"A graduate degree in education is very helpful. However, in order to become a professional librarian you need to study for a second degree, a master of library science. We can help you to accomplish this since many professional librarians do have two master's degrees," replied Ms. Garloch.

Ms. Garloch continued to explain to Hwa-Wei that the university had recently received a federal grant for establishing an Asian Studies program and a library collection to support the program. The library was therefore looking for the right person to build the Asian Studies collection. Furthermore, in order to recruit and train more new library professionals, the library had started a

Library Professional Trainees' Program. Ms. Garloch told Hwa-Wei that she would like to hire him to be one of the librarian trainees in the program and at the same time to work on the library's Asian Studies collection.

Being told that Hwa-Wei would have one more quarter of study to complete his master of education degree, Ms. Garloch assured Hwa-Wei that after he began to work as a librarian trainee he could continue to complete his master of education degree on a part-time basis. After that, he would have three years to complete the second degree, a master of library science, while working full-time as a librarian trainee. The library would pay him a full-time salary as well as his tuition.

This sudden offer was beyond anything Hwa-Wei had anticipated. What he had done was just a spontaneous thing to him, an act based on his nature. As one thoughtful to the needs of others, he had always tried to do his best to reach a better—more productive and thorough—outcome. To Ms. Garloch, those characteristics revealed his potential for becoming a library professional. Something truly amazing had happened. An ordinary action, based on good intent, set off a succession of pleasant results and led Hwa-Wei to his destiny.

2

Thus, in November 1958, Hwa-Wei started his first full-time job as a librarian trainee in the Cataloging Department, responsible for the acquisition and cataloging of Chinese books. His supervisor was an experienced librarian who had worked in the department for decades. She was very knowledgeable about cataloging rules, but she was also conservative and obstinate, with few creative ideas. Even when dealing with the unfamiliar, including Chinese-language materials, she would stick to her rules.

At the beginning, Hwa-Wei had a hard time adapting to this type of working environment; at times, he felt resentful. Nevertheless, he was still very respectful to the experienced librarian, who provided him with strict by-the-rules training. Later, he was thankful to that somewhat inflexible supervisor, as her strictness and rigidity helped him build a solid foundation in cataloging works.

Hwa-Wei received a very structured professional training at the university library. Ms. Garloch had arranged for him to rotate every three months to a different position in a different department, allowing him to familiarize himself with all aspects of library work. At the same time, he would continue his work in the acquisition and cataloging of Chinese publications a few hours each week.

Hwa-Wei completed his master of education degree at the University of Pittsburgh and started his graduate studies toward his master of library science (MLS) degree at Carnegie Institute of Technology (now CMU). The library science program at Carnegie was not large, and its course offerings were quite practice-oriented. Hwa-Wei was particularly impressed by Dr. Sarah Vann, one of the program's faculty members. Dr. Vann taught several graduate courses covering library management, collection development, cataloging, serials, and government publications; Hwa-Wei felt she was an excellent teacher. Benefiting from both Dr. Vann's courses and the senior librarian's training, Hwa-Wei became the top student in the cataloging class.

Dr. Vann was a special faculty member who cared about her students. In addition to teaching, she also served as an advisor for the students' career planning. Her advice to graduating students was that one should not stay in one position for too long. It would be better to change jobs every three or four years, but with two preconditions—a promotion and a pay raise. Interestingly, in the 1960s, Hwa-Wei did manage to change jobs every three years in his early career, at a time when the majority of universities were in rapid expansion. And for Hwa-Wei, every move came with a promotion and a large pay raise. Dr. Vann's parting advice seemed to predict her student's career path.

After CMU, Dr. Vann went to teach in the Graduate School of Library Studies at the University of Hawaii from which she retired. She and Hwa-Wei have kept in touch over the years. Already in her nineties, Dr. Vann has been very pleased with Hwa-Wei's accomplishments in the library profession. To celebrate his retirement party at Ohio University, she even sent him a lei of Hawaiian orchids.

3

After getting married, Hwa-Wei moved with Mary into a government-subsidized apartment in the Hill District of Pittsburgh. He became extremely busy, spending sixteen to seventeen hours each day on a full-time job, then studying part-time in the graduate program. Hwa-Wei started to employ strict time management, adjusting to the fast-paced life as if he were an athlete in an intensive training program. His physique and body endurance improved greatly. This fast-paced lifestyle continued throughout his career.

Unlike his peers in the graduate program, Hwa-Wei was equipped to make the connection between learned theory and library practice because he was simultaneously both a MLS student and a library employee. This allowed him to relate everything he learned in class to its use in practice, giving him a deeper and more flexible understanding of libraries and librarianship.

Hwa-Wei completed the three-year program in just two years. Upon earning his MLS degree in the summer of 1961, he became a formal library employee and was hired as the first assistant in the Acquisitions Department.

As one of two core technical service units in American libraries, an acquisitions department is responsible for selecting and acquiring books. A cataloging department, upon receiving the books, systematically lists them using established standards to make the titles searchable. Hwa-Wei, gentle and diligent as always, was well liked by his colleagues. Not only did Ms. Garloch offer him a full-time job, but she also explored this young Asian man's potential to become an outstanding library professional.

Luck kept favoring Hwa-Wei. The 1960s saw a rapid growth in American higher education, bringing greater opportunities in academic libraries than ever before. At the time Hwa-Wei earned his degree, fresh graduates of master in library science programs were in short supply. Each of Hwa-Wei's peers ended up receiving at least two or three job offers. The decade also witnessed the establishment and development of East Asian libraries, one after another across the nation, supported by special government funding. A huge demand grew for specialized personnel who had Chinese, Japanese, and Korean language and cultural backgrounds.[1] Many international students, arriving from Taiwan, took this opportunity to change their major to library science. Hwa-Wei, as an earlier arrival in the field, had a bright future waiting for him. And he was constantly learning, preparing for the challenges ahead.

Shortly after Hwa-Wei had earned his master of library science degree, the Carnegie Library School was transferred to Pitt, giving him the opportunity to pursue a doctorate in education at Pitt, majoring in educational administration, with library science as a minor.

4

One day the following year, Hwa-Wei received an unexpected phone call from Ms. Eleanor McCann, the university librarian of Duquesne University Library. "Mr. Hwa-Wei Lee," she began, "we met recently at a library conference. I am the university librarian at Duquesne University and was informed about your great performance at the University of Pittsburgh Library as the first assistant in the Acquisitions Department. We have a vacancy for the head of Technical Services. Would you be willing to come to work for us? The position supervises both the Acquisition Department and the Cataloging Department. We will pay you 50 percent more than your current salary."

Ms. McCann's invitation was direct and straightforward because she already knew about Hwa-Wei from various sources. As he hung up the phone, Hwa-Wei could not help but recall the advice from Dr. Vann. It had been over

---

1. Cunxun Qian, *American Memories: Recollection of My 60 Years of Life in the U.S.* (Anhui: Yellow Mountain Books, 2008).

three years since he started working at Pitt. Maybe it was time to start a different position and to try new opportunities. However, he faced a true dilemma: should he leave Pitt Library as Ms. Garloch had been so good to him?

A few days passed. Hwa-Wei decided to talk with Ms. Garloch. Entering her office, he laid out the situation, "You've brought me to this career and offered me much guidance. My performance has been good. Now I've received an offer from the library director at our neighboring university, which sounds very attractive. But I am having a hard time deciding whether or not to accept it. I would like to seek your advice. And I will decline the offer if you think I should stay at Pitt."

After hesitating, Ms. Garloch responded. "Hwa-Wei, as your director, I am very reluctant to let you go. Thinking from your end, however, it is an unusual promotional opportunity, and thus you should accept it. Frankly speaking, it will take at least three to five years before an assistant librarian could possibly advance to the head of the Acquisition Department and another three to five years to have the chance to rise to the head of technical services. This is definitely a shortcut for you. Although Duquesne University Library is smaller, it can give you more opportunities for growth." Ms. Garloch also told Hwa-Wei that the university librarian at Duquesne was her friend. She would call her and let her know what a marvelous librarian she would be getting.

Hwa-Wei felt extremely thankful after hearing these words from Ms. Garloch, who was apparently a person with a warm heart. Being the first to recognize his talent, Ms. Garloch had provided him with many opportunities in training and professional development. On top of that, she had also given him the freedom to choose his own future. Ms. Garloch, Hwa-Wei felt, was a very good example of an open and free-minded American, one who respected others' opportunities. Not only did she not stop Hwa-Wei from seeking better opportunities; she also encouraged him. Hwa-Wei has been forever grateful to her.

5

Founded in 1878 near downtown Pittsburgh, Duquesne University is a private Catholic university with a medium-sized library. The dual job titles given to Hwa-Wei were the head of Technical Services and the Africana Special Collection librarian. Taking charge of two library departments was by no means an easy task. Furthermore, the Africana Special Collection was a totally new area for Hwa-Wei. He knew about Asia but knew very little about Africa; his only exposure to that culture came from his African roommate in his first year at Pitt. At the time, there were no more than forty full-time library employees at Duquesne University Library, of which twelve to thirteen were under Hwa-Wei's supervision.

The library's Africana Special Collection was well known in the United States. It was originally built with personal collections of the Holy Ghost Fathers, whose missionary work once covered the entire African continent, beginning in 1778. The Fathers' special interests in African civilization and history have been kept up at Duquesne's Institute of African Affairs, established in 1956 and regarded as one of the oldest African research centers in the United States.

Beginning in 1960, an African Language and Area Studies Center was launched as part of the Institute of African Affairs and was subsidized through a contract with the U.S. Department of Health, Education, and Welfare under the National Defense Education Act of 1958. That government funding enabled the Institute of African Affairs at Duquesne to expand its programs and activities.

The library also received a large amount of money for building the Africana Special Collection. In 1963, one year after Hwa-Wei assumed his job at the library, the collection grew to 4,500 volumes of books and government publications, approximately one thousand pamphlets, and some 217 periodical and newspaper titles. The focus of the special collection was broadened from East Africa to the entire African continent; its range grew from language, history, anthropology, sociology, economics, and missionary work to include all subjects. There were some ninety-six African languages represented in the collection.[2]

While at Duquesne, Hwa-Wei wrote and published his first two professional papers. From then on he has continued to research, write, and publish some 130 articles and papers on a variety of library topics and authored or co-authored eight books throughout the fifty years of his library career. (A list of his publications is appended at the end of this biography.)

It was a big change, as Ms. Garloch said, for Hwa-Wei to move from the position of assistant librarian in the Acquisitions Department at Pitt to the head of Technical Services at Duquesne. In the small, but comprehensive library setting, he got to familiarize himself with the entire management workflow including acquisition, cataloging, collections management, special collections, and librarian training. This turned out to be a critical period of professional growth in his career. Everything started naturally and proceeded smoothly. As he was recruited by the director herself, he received special attention and full support from the library administration. In return the library was rewarded with his highly satisfactory work ethic and capabilities. Those three years of solid and

---

2. Hwa-Wei Lee, "Africana at Duquesne University Library," *African Studies Bulletin* 6, no. 3 (October 1963): 25–27. "Africana—A Special Collection at Duquesne University," *The Catholic Library World* 35, no. 4 (December 1963): 209–11.

thorough experience at Duquesne laid a firm foundation for Hwa-Wei's library career. As an introvert, Hwa-Wei did not talk much in public. Rather, he chose to let others express their opinions while he listened attentively. As an administrator, however, he had to speak on different occasions and in English, which was difficult for him at first. To cope with that situation, he would always draft speech notes with key points and rehearse them several times beforehand, a habit he has kept throughout his life even after he became accustomed to public speaking. Hwa-Wei's introverted personality proved a rare strength; being a doer was better than being a talker. Before taking action, though, Hwa-Wei preferred to review the big picture, seek input from coworkers, and weigh the pros and cons in order to develop a plan of action. When the time to speak out came, he would go for it—but in a measured way, with confidence.

In terms of administrative management, Hwa-Wei had come to understand that the experience and conduct of an organizational leader could exert direct impact on the performance of that organization. According to Confucius, a leader must continuously learn and sharpen his own competencies. For this reason Hwa-Wei never gave up opportunities to learn and to grow at work—just like a big tree with its branches and leaves constantly stretching for the essence of the sun, air, and rain, and its tangled roots digging deeper for the nourishment of the earth.

Initial Success in
His Early Library Career

Every librarian is, up to a certain point, an architect. He builds up his
collection as an ensemble through which the reader must find a
path, discover his own self, and live.

—*Michel Melot, director of the Centre Pompidou Library in Paris*

1

THE LIFE of Hwa-Wei and Mary was growing busier and busier. Their first
three children—Shirley, James, and Pamela—joined the family one right after
another while Hwa-Wei was working in the library full-time and studying for
his master of library science degree and his Ph.D. in education on a part-time
basis. Mary loved children. She had once said, half-jokingly and half-seriously,
that she wouldn't mind having twelve children.

Hwa-Wei also loved children and was a tender and patient father whose
children were fond of pestering him. In the evening, he often held his children
in his arms, patting them and swaying while walking, until they fell asleep. After
placing them in bed, he would start another round of work—library and/or
course related—often working through the night. He would then take a nap at
dawn to get recharged for another busy day.

Hwa-Wei became more and more adapted to the highly demanding routine and was able to deal with a full agenda of various tasks with ease. Meanwhile, he managed his own time well for his doctoral studies, which covered a
wide range of major courses in the foundations of education including educational administration, teaching materials and pedagogy, educational psychology, comparative education, educational statistics, history and philosophy of
education, and educational research. These course studies were very useful for
a library administrator considering the library's position as the center of a university with its core mission of supporting and serving education. Because all
faculty and students have to use the libraries to find information and knowledge
for their teaching, learning, and research, it was considered extremely important

for library administrators to have a good understanding of educational theory and practice.

Subconsciously, Hwa-Wei thought that he had to work much harder than his American peers in order to succeed in his new country. The land of opportunity, as the United States was known and viewed with hope by new immigrants, still had a shadow of racial discrimination. But Hwa-Wei trusted that, as long as he could build himself up by learning and hard work, he would eventually receive recognition from Americans. He studied and worked tirelessly for a better future.

Since the late 1950s, American universities have undergone unprecedented change and growth. After the successful launch of the first man-made satellite in 1957 by the (then) Soviet Union, the federal government began to emphasize the importance of education in relation to national security. One year later, on September 2, 1958, the National Defense Education Act was passed by Congress, marking an epoch in American educational history. The act has had a huge and long-lasting impact on the development of science education and research in the United States. Under the act, a vast number of student loan programs were established and an increasing number of research grants were offered.

The year 1964 also saw the passage of the Economic Opportunity Act, under which federal funds were allocated to colleges and universities through state governments to create the College Work-Study Program for the part-time employment of students from low-income families. The direct outcome of the act was a rapid growth in student enrollment as access to higher education expanded, including not just the elite but also the general public.[1]

The Higher Education Act of 1965 carried President Lyndon Johnson's "Great Society" principle to its acme. Title II of the act, including its amendments, authorized an annual appropriation of millions of dollars of public funds, in a succession of seventeen years, to support college library development in the areas of library building, acquisition of research materials, and training of library professionals. The government's financial support continued until the Reagan administration.

In 1965, Hwa-Wei completed his doctorate in education and library science from the University of Pittsburgh. That same year Dr. Thomas Miller, president of Edinboro State College in Pennsylvania, made a phone call to Pitt's Department of Education to recruit a deputy library director, a position for which a doctorate was required. Hwa-Wei's academic advisor immediately recommended

---

1. Nicholas A. Basbanes, *The Eternal Library II—Patience & Fortitude* [in Chinese], trans. Chuan-wei Yang. (Shanghai: Shanghai People's Press, 2011), 82. Originally published as *Patience & Fortitude: A Roving Chronicle of Book People, Book Places, and Book Culture* (New York: HarperCollins, 2001).

him, and, meanwhile, told the president, "My student is excellent and definitely among the top students I have ever taught. He is currently the technical service department head at Duquesne University Library. He has the right experience and educational qualifications that you are looking for. And I trust that he can do exceedingly well."

Edinboro State College had recently been upgraded from Edinboro State Teachers College, in 1960, and was in the process of moving up to university status—Edinboro University of Pennsylvania—according to a master plan approved by the state government. To achieve the goal, one important necessity was to raise the percentage of faculty with doctorates from less than 25 percent to a minimum of 50 percent. Therefore, whenever a vacancy arose, the recruitment priority would be given to candidates with doctorates. With perfect timing, Hwa-Wei had just earned his doctorate in education and library science. Although he had only a few years of library experience, Hwa-Wei, with his academic advisor's recommendation, decided to give the position a try.

After a brief phone conversation with President Miller, Hwa-Wei made a trip to Edinboro for the on-site interview, meeting with the academic vice president, library director, and President Miller. Immediately, at their first meeting, the president started to like this self-composed and confident young man, especially his gentle smile, calmness, and self-confidence. The president even gave him a library tour in person and told him that the vacancy was for a deputy director, who was expected to be promoted to library director as the then director, Mildred Forness, was going to retire in a year. Hwa-Wei felt that the opportunity was so promising that he should go for it. In spite of his limited experience in top library administration, he did have a doctorate, which was in high demand at Edinboro.

As he drove back to Pittsburgh, it was already late evening; trees on both sides of the road flashed in fading lights. But Hwa-Wei had no feeling of fatigue. He was longing to return home and let Mary know the great news. At the age of thirty-four, in only the eighth year since his arrival in the United States, Hwa-Wei had already earned two master's and one doctorate degree. He had begun to make a name for himself in the library field and would soon rise to be a senior administrator. Few contemporary Chinese American librarians could claim comparable achievement.

All of this seemed beyond his expectations, but, as no one worked as diligently as Hwa-Wei did, those achievements were within reason, just rewards for his hard work. Unable to refrain from laughing, he once again recalled the advice from Dr. Vann. Whether by coincidence or destiny, he did manage to stay on in each position for about three years and had already changed two positions —from Pittsburgh to Duquesne, and now from Duquesne to Edinboro—in that short span of six years, with each new position coming with a promotion. And both were steady and flawless professional leaps.

Destiny at that moment became especially generous and made a shortcut for Hwa-Wei, as if it were compensating for all the suffering he received during his childhood and his endurance throughout his life up to that point. His career path was set far beyond his original goal, to be a high school principal. He appeared to have a broader career capability surpassing his initial wishes, as his doctoral academic advisor had already observed. And the advisor was right . . . Hwa-Wei could go much further.

2

Edinboro State College is located in northwestern Pennsylvania's Edinboro Township. The town's earliest residents were primarily immigrants from Scotland, and many township streets, buildings, and schools were named after their hometown of Old Town, Edinburgh, Scotland. The town keeps its Scottish traditions alive in many ways including the annual Highland Games festival. Celebrated for a succession of three days, local residents—those who have inherited a bold spirit and talents in singing and dancing—perform ethnic songs and dances, play bagpipes, and participate in all kinds of traditional highland games. Bagpipe and drum players from the college band, a well-known musical group in the town, wear traditional Scottish dress while playing brave and courageous Gaelic music. These wonderful performances evoke, for the townspeople, memories of lodges, shepherds, and boundless remote grasslands, a return to their spiritual home of freedom.

The Edinboro campus, with its red brick buildings and verdant lawns, is beautiful and quiet. It is only about twenty miles away from Lake Erie, one of the five Great Lakes in North America. Broad and vast, Lake Erie resembles an endless sea more than a lake. In Edinboro, there is another beautiful lake, albeit one much smaller than Lake Erie. It is a favorite place for local residents during the summer months to enjoy the scenic lake view and warmer weather. Hwa-Wei and Mary would take the children to the lakeside for picnics and to let them run around enjoying the sunshine.[2]

Hwa-Wei started his tenure at Edinboro in the fall of 1965 as its deputy library director. That was the year the state government promised funding for a new library building to show its support of the college's expansion; the old library building was aged and already at full capacity for books and the existing student enrollment. Thus, the first thing Hwa-Wei was assigned to do was form

2. Edinboro University, www.edinboro.edu. The Borough of Edinboro, www.edinboro.net. "Edinboro University," Wikipedia, http://en.wikipedia.org/wiki/Edinboro_University.

Chapter 8

a four-member planning committee for the new building. None of the committee members, though, including Hwa-Wei, had sufficient knowledge or experience in designing a library building. Having never tried to understand a library
from its architectural angle, Hwa-Wei saw this challenging work as a highly satis-
fying opportunity. Through a careful investigation, a review of numerous references, and site visits to several famous libraries, the committee, led by Hwa-Wei,
soon came up with a detailed proposal.

Spatial design is extremely important to a library. The architecture and design of a place for books can have an impact on the relationship between the
books and their readers. Reading a book in a round room creates a different
feeling from reading it in a square room. So, too, does reading a book in a room
with a high ceiling, as opposed to in a room with a low ceiling. When readers
indulge themselves in books, the reading atmosphere and, consequently, the
reading experience can be positively or negatively shaped by the readers' physical surroundings, including the distance between shelves, bookshelf density,
light intensity, and even those elements affecting the senses of touch and smell.[3]
Readers may not be consciously aware of these various influential factors, but
they are subconsciously affected by them. And different combinations of these
factors may generate totally different effects.

Indeed, library architecture is highly domain specific and function specific.
This design is all about books, for books exist for patrons to read and for staff to
manage. Therefore, the anticipated growth rate of a library collection becomes
a critical factor to consider when designing a library building. The collection
determines the size of the building and the designation of areas within the building for different purposes, such as bookshelves, study areas and work space.
Meanwhile, operational workflow—the most reasonable and efficient way to
unload books and pass them on to the Cataloging Department, for example—
should also be taken into account.

Also important is a detailed design for different types of shelving units, study
seat appropriation, and workspace assignment among staff members of various positions and work relationships. Each concrete design should be reasonable. In addition to basic specifics and soundness from a technical viewpoint,
every design element has to reflect library operations and principles while also
being extensible to meet the demands of library growth in future decades.
Meeting the practical and psychological needs of every library patron and staff
member provides a professional and intellectual challenge for a designer.

Owing to his outstanding learning ability and his devoted and down-to-
earth personality, Hwa-Wei was able to comprehend the complicated details

---

3. Nicholas A. Basbanes. *Patience & Fortitude*, 82.

involved in library space planning and management and to conceive of a plan that placed the greater emphasis on the needs of patrons and staff. To him, the user service areas are the core of a library, and each library should set up service areas of various sizes with the largest one on the main floor and smaller ones on other floors—at least one for each—for the convenience of patrons. Stack areas should also be sensibly designed with high-use books on lower levels of the building and low-use materials on higher levels. Meanwhile, staff working space should be reasonably distributed in relation to the other two areas. These three interpenetrating areas can be defined to meet the various functional requirements of a library.

Unsurprisingly, the committee's design was well received by the college administration. In addition to attending routine meetings for project status and progress reports, Hwa-Wei paid frequent personal visits to the construction site on his way to or from home, feeling just like a farmer expecting a harvest from his crop field. He was fascinated to see a library building being constructed from scratch under his efforts. He recalled that civil engineering had once been his dream major back in Taiwan, perhaps an indicator that he had possessed the potential to become an architect. Unfortunately, he had had no luck back then with the engineering school of National Taiwan University.

Regrettably, Hwa-Wei's tenure at Edinboro was only three years. Before the completion of the new library building, Hwa-Wei was already far away in Thailand. Nevertheless, the experience he had at Edinboro gave him knowledge of library architecture. Later, he was able to apply his newly gained expertise when designing and implementing the Asian Institute of Technology Library in Bangkok, Thailand, for which he was chiefly responsible.

In 1966, Hwa-Wei was promoted to the library director of Edinboro State College upon the former director's retirement. At the time, there were only a few Chinese Americans in such positions, and they were directors of East Asian libraries, area-studies libraries with a narrower focus on Asian languages and culture only. Thus, Hwa-Wei became the first Chinese American to achieve the highest administrative position in an academic library. His educational background, knowledge structure, and management style, far more than his strengths as a Chinese American, had won him the approval of his American library colleagues.

3

To Hwa-Wei, his time with Edinboro State College Library as a deputy director and then as the director was an important period in his career. Although his position was at the senior administrative level, he faced professional and psychological challenges in terms of inadequate work experience and insufficient language proficiency in English. He had no choice but to grow, as quickly as possible, his professional and administrative capabilities, especially in the areas of library administration, personnel supervision, and project management. To do so, he had to watch his step and stick to established rules, as people wanted to see whether this alien administrator could get things done well, rather than whether he could do things innovatively. As a young man in his thirties, however, Hwa-Wei preferred to try new ways of doing things. The opportunity came sooner than he anticipated.

Early in the summer of 1968, Edinboro was holding its annual graduation commencement. The invited keynote speaker was a high-ranking foreign-service officer from the U.S. Department of State, who delivered a speech on international education. After the ceremony, Hwa-Wei, the only college administrator with an international background, was invited to join the luncheon in honor of that official. One topic discussed at the luncheon was the importance of international education, which happened to be Hwa-Wei's strength.

The guest speaker was deeply impressed by Hwa-Wei's fresh and unique thoughts and mentioned that among his current projects abroad was the establishment of the Asian Institute of Technology (AIT) in Bangkok, Thailand. He asked Hwa-Wei directly: "We have a multinational project in Thailand to be launched soon. In order to confront the problem of 'brain drain' of Asian college students we, in cooperation with a dozen other countries such as Australia, Canada, France, Germany, the Netherlands, and the U.K., are in the process of establishing a graduate school of engineering in Bangkok, Thailand, for the training of future Asian engineers, who after their graduation will stay in Asia to work for the development of their respective countries. Now we are looking for a library director for the graduate school. Would you like to join the American team to be sponsored by the U.S. Agency for International Development?" It was truly an unexpected request to Hwa-Wei, one equally unexpected by President Miller. After a short consideration, Hwa-Wei responded, "It is really a good opportunity. I think I would take it if President Miller could grant me a one-year administrative leave."

Perhaps just to be polite to the distinguished guest, the president did not oppose. He replied with a smile, "Okay Hwa-Wei, I will grant you a leave of absence for one year and will visit you in Thailand to see your work there."

Here came another stroke of luck. Hwa-Wei had been at Edinboro for just three years. It seemed that all his luck had to do with "three years," the preferable number of years one should stay with any position according to Dr. Vann's advice to her graduating students in the 1960s.

Relocating to Edinboro Township had been quite a big life change for Hwa-Wei and Mary. With Hwa-Wei's nearly doubled salary, they could afford to purchase a suburban house and welcome two more children, Edward and

Hwa-Wei's father, Luther Kan-Chun Lee (b. September 22,1893, d. March 1, 1983), and his mother, Hsiao-Hui Wang (b. March 27, 1894, d. August 6, 1984), celebrate Kan-Chun's seventieth birthday in Taiwan.

Charles, into the family. With five little ones and small age gaps in-between, the family was as lively as a kindergarten. Mary was awfully busy taking care of the big family of seven members, and never mentioned again her twelve-child plan. The country scenery was so beautiful. Often, Hwa-Wei drove the entire family to Lake Erie for weekends and holidays.

The only thing Mary disliked about Edinboro was its weather. Close to Lake Erie, Edinboro, situated in the so-called "snow belt" of North America, becomes extremely cold in winter. Its snow season could last six months, from November to April of the next year. Heavy snowdrifts sometimes could reach as high as a roof; normal accumulated snow still could cover boots. Overcoming the winter snow and cold became a huge headache for Mary. Trapped inside the house with no outdoor activities, the children kept getting sick. They were often down simultaneously, first with measles, due to expired vaccines, followed by chicken pox, and then strep infections. Winter turned out to be the most dreadful season to Mary.

Thinking that Mary would not be interested in moving to a foreign country, Hwa-Wei, tentatively, started a conversation with her. The conversation was surprisingly short and straightforward. Mary had only one question, which was about the weather in Thailand. After hearing her husband's response: "It will be very different from Edinboro in that Thailand is situated in Southeast Asia. Its climate is largely tropical, hot and humid all year around with temperatures in the 82–95°F range. Unlike Edinboro, there is no snow." She replied quickly. "Good. That is a good place to live! How soon can we move?"

To receive the official job offer, Hwa-Wei still had to go through an interview with the project director from Colorado State University, who was in charge of the AIT project. For Hwa-Wei's convenience, the interview was held at Erie International Airport. The entire Lee family was invited.

Hwa-Wei and Mary arrived at the airport with their five children. Hwa-Wei told Mary to walk away and look after the little ones, thinking the officer wouldn't need to talk to her. The project officer only had a short conversation with Hwa-Wei before he asked Hwa-Wei to watch the children while he talked to Mary. He told Mary about the scorching hot weather and unpleasant smell everywhere in Thailand. He also emphasized that some foreign-service members ended up leaving the country because their wives could not stand the environment there, especially the unpleasant odor. Mary replied with humor, "As a mother who has changed diapers for five children, what smells would bother me?"

The officer could not resist laughing. He was satisfied with Mary's answer. One month later, passports, visas, and immunizations were ready for the entire family to embark on their international trip. Hwa-Wei received his official contract in June 1968. Two months later, the Lee family arrived in Thailand.

Leaving Edinboro was exactly what Mary had been looking for. It turned out to be her first trip abroad. She had not even traveled beyond Pennsylvania. All of a sudden, her entire family migrated to an unfamiliar country on the other side of the earth. Compared to Edinboro, the Thai tropical scene seemed just like paradise to her. The children got to eat fresh fruits all year around and were able to play outside all day long. Mary no longer needed to worry about their health. They were so healthy that most of them didn't need to visit the doctor even once in seven years.

The local staff of AIT took very good care of Hwa-Wei's family. While waiting for their luggage to arrive, arrangements were made for the family to stay in a large suite at the newly opened four-star Montien Hotel. The two-month hotel stay gave Hwa-Wei and Mary enough time to find an apartment in a large residential compound with a swimming pool and a large playground. The high-class residential compound was also within walking distance to the Bangkok International School where the older Lee children were enrolled.

4

Hwa-Wei was a lucky fellow among early international students in the United States. He felt fortunate to be introduced by chance to the library field and quickly made his mark in it with his dedication and administrative skills. In fact, the United States had many outstanding international students from Taiwan during the 1950s and 1960s, similar to those students from mainland China who arrived during the 1980s study-abroad boom. Due to political, economic, and cultural reasons, most of these students experienced a dual hardship, physically and psychologically. Some students were able to get through, whereas others were not.

Hui Chen was one of Hwa-Wei's best friends in college. Hui, a Chinese literature major, was a gifted student at National Taiwan Normal University known for his superb talent in publishing a well-received campus literary journal. In spite of the differences in their major and disposition, the two, as close as brothers, trusted and admired each other.

At the time Hwa-Wei came to the United States, Hui went to Singapore to teach Chinese literature in a high school there. Later, he also moved to the States. Hwa-Wei once introduced him to library science but, as Hui was not interested in that field, he eventually dropped out of the program. Due to the pressure of failing to land a job that matched his talent, he had to work as a waiter at a Chinese restaurant in New York City. As time went by, the arrogant, gifted man found no way to fit himself into the snobbish and indifferent metropolitan society and the Chinese restaurant setting. Neither could he find a way to get along with people. Later, he developed schizophrenia with auditory hallucinations, always feeling that everyone was trying to hurt him. Poor Hui also suffered from drug addiction.

Hwa-Wei tried to persuade him to go back to Taiwan and look for a suitable job in teaching and writing. However, Hui insisted that he would lose face in doing so. Coming to the United States was once a dream for many Taiwan youth of their generation. Hui did not want to give up his American dream. One day, Hwa-Wei received a phone call from him saying, "Hwa-Wei, come to New York at once; I want to kill myself. I have thought about it several times already. However, thinking that you are working hard, and you have been helping me, I feel I will owe you a debt if I leave the world now." In the middle of a heavy workload as the library director at Edinboro State College, Hwa-Wei had no choice but to ask his sister, Hwa-Chou, who was then a doctoral student at Columbia University in New York, to take care of the matter. Hwa-Chou and her college roommate rushed to Hui's place, where no one answered the door. After three hours of waiting outside, they finally had the police break into Hui's room where they found everything in a mess. Hui finally came back. The two took him to their apartment and cooked him a meal. Seeing Hui calming down, Hwa-Chou called her brother, assuring him of the positive outcome.

However, Hwa-Wei and Hwa-Chou had no way to predict that Hui would still commit suicide. Around 10:00 a.m. the following day, Hui jumped from an open window on the forty-fifth floor of Rockefeller Center. Like a falling autumn leaf, his body was torn into pieces by electric wires during his fall. By the window he left a pair of shoes. The city was the same, still bustling New York, busy but indifferent. An alien young man was suddenly engulfed in the racket, leaving no trace.

It was November 6, 1967. Hui's death was so distressing to Hwa-Wei that he had a hard time accepting it. Just a year earlier, he had received two poems from his friend.

Untitled

Throwing bright sunlight onto billowing dust,
How much senseless gambling could one have in his life,
and how many prominent fighters are blunted by lost years?!

Picking up by chance a few seeds of understanding, and a bit of solemn and stirring,
as sensitive as mimosa, never staying the same
between perseverance and numbness.

Being in a hurry to finish a journey,
and race against the clock,
Among the billowing dust are spiral-shaped roads.
Noontime had passed, and the sun still shines.

Written on the Night of Stirring Time

From past to future, like blowing wind and falling leaves,
on this autumn night not yet in fall season,
Drifting like snow, and rolling like dust and sand.

Taipei, Singapore, getting further and further away,
time passes just like flowing water;
Hometown and childhood, both have gone out of sight,
Looked from afar, they appear to be myths.

Hui sent Hwa-Wei another poem a few days before his death. When the mail arrived, he had already departed. This poem became his farewell to this world and to his friends.

Low and then high, on the ocean of time and space
I, the barefoot Robinson, am running on an isolated island in the ocean.
Gather and part with ease, in the infinite time and space,
It is an ancient battlefield, ever since the human history,
Loneliness of living, loneliness of dying,
Wind, coming from old places, and going to remote destinations.
Tonight,
sleepless memory, crying emotion, and angry will,
I will, however, lie on wind waves, putting desolateness aside!

Reading these words, "loneliness of living, loneliness of dying," and "sleepless memory, crying emotion," Hwa-Wei's heart broke sorting out memories from the years that he and Hui spent together. He wrote a eulogy for his friend, which was published in the *United,* a quarterly magazine of the Chinese Student Union in America. Many of their schoolmates back in Taiwan did not know of Hui's suffering.

Having been together at the National Taiwan Normal University for four years, Hui and I, though from different schools, were very close to each other. I admired his brilliant talent and poetic gift. Hui was known, among fellow students, for his sharp mind and rich emotion. And he was a person dominated by feelings . . .

From his poems, we could know that he led quite a bitter life in the past years, both physically and emotionally. His experiences are not unique and are shared by many.

We are often exhausted struggling between schoolwork and financial needs, like those determined soldiers who cross a river to fight the enemy and burn their bridges behind with no way to retreat. Hereby, I urge government agencies to take more care of international students—especially those who have difficulty in making the adjustment.

The Seven Years in Thailand

Dig anywhere in the earth and you will find a treasure, only you
must dig with the faith of a peasant.

— *Khalil Gibran, "Sand and Foam"*

1

ONE OF the largest countries in Southeast Asia, Thailand was a major military
ally of the U.S. in the Indochina Peninsula after World War II. In the summer of
1968, the entire Lee family moved to Bangkok, the capital and the largest city of
Thailand. During that time, on the far east of the peninsula, the Vietnam War
escalated into a stalemate.

The 1960s saw the Cold War confrontation between the United States and
the Soviet Union. Southeast Asia had been regarded as a potential critical battlefield in the Cold War. American troops were sent six thousand miles away to join
with Ngo Dinh Diem's South Vietnamese army to fight against North Vietnam.

The American involvement was seen as essential to prevent the Communist North Vietnamese army from taking over South Vietnam. However, the
war did not proceed as the Americans wished, for their military paid a high
price on the foreign land full of rice fields and lush forests. Instead, the U.S.
government was placed in a more complicated and difficult situation. As the war
went on and on, a rising disappointment grew among the American public. An
anti-war campaign started on a small scale in universities, then intensified, eventually becoming a nationwide movement by the end of the 1960s. Both liberals
and conservatives in the United States started to attack President Lyndon Johnson
and his government. A large majority of American news media also joined the
anti-war camp.

As a part of the U.S. strategy, President Johnson proposed a protection plan
for the Mekong Delta, the rice granary of Southeast Asia. The largest and longest
river in Southeast Asia, the Mekong River originates at the northeast slope of
China's Tanggula Mountain, then flows downstream through Myanmar (Burma),
Laos, Thailand, Cambodia, and Vietnam before draining into the South China
Sea, a total length of 2,700 miles (4,350 km). The Mekong River forms part of
the international border between Myanmar and Laos, as well as between Laos

and Thailand.[1] As part of the protection plan, the U.S. foreign aid program was to develop local talents, especially much-needed engineers and technical specialists, for the many development projects in the Mekong Delta region.

In the plan's early stage, many bright native youths from Asian countries were sent to the United States and Europe to study engineering and technology. However, many didn't return to their home countries, causing the problem of a "brain drain." For those who did go back, the knowledge they acquired turned out to be quite inapplicable to local needs, thus creating the second problem of "brain waste." The founding of the Asian Institute of Technology (AIT) was to fill one of the strategic needs related to the Mekong Delta plan, to train local engineers and technologists with appropriate knowledge and skills suitable for the needs of their respective countries.

With a mission to develop highly qualified and committed professionals who would play a leading role in the sustainable development of the region and its integration into the global economy, AIT was established through a U.S. initiative. With the support of the host country, Thailand, AIT was joined by many other countries including Australia, Canada, France, Germany, Japan, the Netherlands, Taiwan, and the U.K.

Hwa-Wei was one of thirteen American scholars and experts recruited and sent by Colorado State University under contract with the U.S. Agency for International Development (USAID), many of whom were well-known professors from Ivy League schools including MIT, Yale, and Cornell, all selected by USAID. Hwa-Wei's primary responsibility was to oversee the operation of the AIT library. Along with these American scholars and experts were thirteen faculty members from the U.K. and a dozen others from Australia, France, Japan (Tokyo Polytechnic University), and the Netherlands. Many of these countries had once established colonies in Southeast Asian countries including Great Britain in Burma, Cambodia, and Malaysia; France in Vietnam; the Netherlands in Indonesia; and the United States in the Philippines. All these former colonies eventually gained independence after World War II.

The Asian Institute of Technology (AIT), formerly the Graduate School of Engineering of the Southeast Asian Treaty Organization (SEATO), was founded in 1959.[2] At the time of Hwa-Wei's arrival, the school, which was still quite small, was undergoing a reorganization with a very ambitious master plan. Its original campus was in a building borrowed from Chulalongkorn University, the oldest and most prestigious university in Thailand, founded in 1917 by King Chulalongkorn, a great monarch in the history of Thailand.

---

1. Jeffrey W. Jacobs, "Mekong River," *Encyclopedia Britannica,* www.britannica.com/place/Mekong-River. "Mekong River," Wikipedia.org, http://enwikipedia.org/wiki/Mekong.

2. Asian Institute of Technology, http://www.ait.ac.th/.

During the king's reign of more than half a century (1868–1919), Asia was the target of colonialism of the European powers. The king launched a modernization reform aimed at self-support and self-improvement that was regarded as an exemplary model for Asian-Pacific countries. Its impact was second only to Japan's Meiji Restoration. Through his superior diplomatic skills, the nation's independence was saved. Thailand was the only sovereign country in the Southeast Asia region that was never colonized.

As a graduate institute, AIT provided master's and doctoral programs only. The school was in a very healthy fiscal situation at its early stage, benefiting from the financial assistance of twenty-three countries. The assistance was provided in various forms, first by sending faculty and staff, with wages and benefits covered by their original countries. The second form of assistance came by providing scholarships to students—up to $8,500 per person ($7,000 tuition and fees and $1,500 living expenses). The generous scholarships ensured that AIT had the best students from Asian countries because it, essentially, gave them a free education. The third form was through the donation of instructional equipment, facilities, and buildings. Throughout the AIT campus stood buildings contributed by different countries including ten faculty houses on AIT's new campus donated by New Zealand. Hwa-Wei was among those who chose to live in one of those houses.

At the time of Hwa-Wei's arrival, AIT had about five hundred students and only one temporary building borrowed from Chulalongkorn University. Both the library space and collections were very small in size. They were located on the second floor of the borrowed building. Although AIT already had its land for a new campus granted by the Thai government, the new campus was still in the planning stages. It took three years to build the initial campus from the ground up.

The new campus, built on former farmland acquired by the Thai government, was located in Khlong Luang, Pathum Thani Province, about twenty-five miles (forty kilometers) north of Bangkok and fifteen miles beyond the Bangkok International Airport. Due to Thailand's humid climate and its winding waterways in all directions, the campus construction had to start with river flow alteration and land reclamation, which was then followed by landscaping work.

The finished campus featured a beautiful layout of lakes and canals. Benefiting from the tropical weather and rich soil, the well-planted trees and flowers grew rapidly and provided much needed shade and color along the sidewalks and in the open spaces. Architecturally, AIT shared more similarity with American universities than with Thai institutions.

The new campus library was developed at a rapid pace. Specialized collections were built to meet the needs of the new student population and the continuing advancement of research programs on campus. Thanks to donations from various countries, the AIT library had a remarkable engineering collection of all types and from different areas, eventually earning a distinguished reputation in the Asian-Pacific region. The collection was not large; however, it was highly specialized and included a small, but first-class, special collection that was rich in reference materials and tools pertaining to Asia.

2

At the library, all staff members were native Thai, except Hwa-Wei, who was the director and who was "donated" by the U.S. government. Hwa-Wei still remembers well the first meeting with his staff members. They were most polite and showed the traditional respect of Thai people to their senior supervisors. Whenever they came to see him or were just passing by him, they always bowed their heads so as to never have their heads higher than Hwa-Wei's. Hwa-Wei was also most impressed by their smiles, which supported Thailand's nickname "The Land of Smiles." Thais are very friendly to Chinese because of the similarities in their cultures and traditions. The staff members were pleased to know that their director was a Chinese American.

Along with the completion of the new campus was the increase in library staff from the original seven to more than two dozen. Hwa-Wei found the Thai staff most pleasant to work with, for they were hardworking, dedicated, and highly dependable. They were also always very sincere and friendly.

To the Lee family, Thailand was a paradise. Because of the sunshine and an average temperature of ninety degrees Fahrenheit all year around, the children never had colds or flu. When the Lees first arrived in Bangkok, they lived in an apartment complex designed especially for foreign aid experts. Everyone was able to have maids, a cook, and a driver. Children went to the International School of Bangkok (ISB), with an enrollment of up to 3,650 students, making it the largest international school in the world. In the early 1970s, there were two hundred thousand Americans living in Thailand; the majority of them resided in Bangkok. Many of the Americans were family members of U.S. military servicemen or foreign-service personnel.

The 24/7 outdoor pool at their complex was heaven to the Lee children. They spent daytime either there in the pool or in the central lawn playing soccer. They were tanned and healthy. With servants to take care of the children, cook, and do the housework, Mary became a happy hostess and led a life very different from the one she had in the United States The pace of life in Thailand was much more relaxed. Men got off work every day at 5:00 p.m. with little or no overtime or take-home work. Once Hwa-Wei was home, all his time belonged

In August 1968, when Hwa-Wei was hired by Colorado State University to work at the Asian Institute of Technology under the sponsorship of the U.S. Agency for International Development, the entire Lee family moved to Bangkok, Thailand. Shown here are (*clockwise from top*): Mary, James, Pamela, Charles, Edward, and Shirley.

The Lee family enjoyed their stay in Bangkok from 1968 to 1975.

While in Thailand, the family liked to visit Thai temples.

The tropical environment of Thailand was a drastic difference in weather from the snowbelt of Edinboro, Pennsylvania.

to Mary and their children. The family spent time together by going out to eat, watching movies, or traveling. Mary was pleased and even suggested, "Let's just settle down here and not move back."

Mary's unintentional words turned out to predict the Lee family's seven years of living in Thailand. The original contract with AIT was for one year only, as Hwa-Wei had promised to go back to resume his library director position at Edinboro. However, AIT, or perhaps Thailand, succeeded in retaining him. From then on, his contract with USAID got renewed every two years until 1975 when the Vietnam War ended and many of the foreign-aid programs ceased.

As a special treat, foreign-aid scholars and experts in Thailand could become members of the Royal Bangkok Sports Club. However, due to the popularity of the club's horseracing track, the membership application was quite difficult and could take about two years, with applicants going through a waiting period. The club featured a first-class dining facility, swimming pool, and golf course. Spending weekends there was quite comfortable and cozy for families—children swam and adults lounged around the pool.

As family of a USAID-contracted staff member, the Lees were also allowed to use the U.S. Officers Club and were given the privilege of shopping at the commissary and the P.X. duty-free shop that was run by the U.S. government at its military bases. They had a rich supply of different commodities imported from the States including grocery items, cigarettes, wine, and even cars that were made in the United States—just as if it were a real American store. The Lees bought their piano and a new station wagon there. The Officers Club served genuine American meals and had special shows, free of charge, that were often given by famous American entertainers with whom one might hardly ever meet back in the United States.

During long breaks, Hwa-Wei usually drove two hours to take his family to Pattaya beach for vacation. Although the roads in Thailand were not good in the 1970s, people still felt enthusiastic about taking driving vacations. Known for its beautiful night scene, Pattaya features cool and pleasant sea winds, somewhat similar to Florida beaches.

Back in Thailand, Hwa-Wei and his family could enjoy all the privileges given to American overseas staff, including a two-month-long, home-leave trip every two years for a vacation back to the United States. Since traveling from Bangkok to Pittsburgh was halfway around the world, they had an option to go either by the western hemisphere or the eastern hemisphere. They chose to make it an "around the world" trip.

Every time, Hwa-Wei and Mary came up with a thorough vacation plan: they flew on a Pan American global flight that made stopovers in transit cities for a few days each. In total there were three home-leave trips in Hwa-Wei's

Mary and Hwa-Wei pose in front of the Siam Continental, one of the top Thai hotels in Bangkok.

Every two years during one of their scheduled leaves for "home," the family traveled around the world—like this London trip to 10 Downing Street.

Hwa-Wei and Mary hiking the Acropolis in Athens, Greece.

Mary and four of the Lee children with their tour guide at the local market in Mumbai, India.

The children pose alongside a statue inside Taipei's Taiwan Historical Museum.

Mary and her children at Sun Moon Lake in Taiwan.

seven years of tenure in Thailand, through which the Lee family visited most of the famous cities en route including New Delhi, Mumbai, Istanbul, Rome, Athens, Frankfurt, London, Madrid, Paris, Tokyo, and Honolulu. During every trip, Hwa-Wei also managed to make a detour to Taiwan to visit his parents and meet with old friends. On their way to Osaka for the 1970 World Expo, they also toured other cities in Japan such as Tokyo, Nara, and Kyoto.

It was not an easy job traveling with six small children. Mary came up with a good way to manage. She dressed them in the same style and color of clothes, like uniforms, making them easy to spot in a crowd. The children grew up while traveling around the world and enjoying vacations with Hwa-Wei and Mary. This special experience became a rare and precious treasure in their life.

3

As a true international institute of higher learning—a miniature United Nations (UN)—AIT had faculty, students, and staff from a wide variety of countries and regions who had their own traditional holidays. Since AIT honored all important national holidays and traditional festivals, there were frequent celebrations with special programs organized by students from different nationalities. During festive seasons, there would also be celebration parties at embassies and consulates of different nations, to which international experts and staff members of UN and NGO agencies were invited. Each year, the Taiwan Embassy in Thailand would invite Chinese, Chinese Thai, and students from Taiwan to attend its grand celebration event for the Chinese New Year, which featured a twelve-course traditional Chinese dinner and entertainment from Taiwan. As frequently invited guests, Hwa-Wei, Mary, and the children also got to enjoy the event.

The Lee children's favorite festival was the Thai traditional Loy Krathong, which takes place on the fifteenth day of the twelfth month in the Thai lunar calendar, usually in November, the best season of the year in Thailand, just past the rainy season. On the night of the full moon, Thais launch their Loy Krathong, decorative floats made of banana leaves carrying flowers and lighted candles, onto drifting water to express their devotion and respect to the gods, and also to pray for a blessed new year. Under the cool moonlight, stretches of decorative floats on rivers and lakes are fully loaded with the piety of human hearts drifting away with the stream. The glittering candlelight shining with starry rays forms a unique vision.[3]

3. Bangkok.com, "Loy Krathong 2015 in Bangkok," www.bangkok.com/whats-on-events/loy-krathong/. Graduate School, "Loy Krathong Festival," Chang Mai University, http://www.grad.cmu.ac.th/eng/index.php/loy-kratong-festival. "Loi Krathong," Wikipedia.org, http://en.wikipedia.org/wiki/Loi_Krathong.

Mary and Hwa-Wei sit in front of a small temple in Hong Kong.

A family portrait taken in Bangkok.

Hwa-Wei poses with his six children. He is holding Robert, the youngest member of Lee family, who was born in Bangkok, Thailand.

The Lees enjoyed going to a park and launching their homemade Loy Kra-thongs onto the lake. Sometimes they also held small home parties watching fireworks in their yard with invited international neighbors. The children en-joyed it as much as their Christmas celebrations back in the States.

During the first three years in Thailand, the Lees lived in an apartment complex for international experts. Their neighbors were from different coun-tries including Japan, Italy, Lebanon, and India. The children, finding it easier to get along with each other than did the adults, started to play together before long, entirely bypassing the language barrier. There was a spacious lawn at the center of the complex that served as a soccer field. The Lee children—all sports lovers—quickly started as a team to play against other children. Hwa-Wei loved to play soccer with them and sometimes even joined their matches. Actually, he was the only father on the soccer field and thus was voted the best father by several Japanese housewives. These Japanese mothers told Mary that their hus-bands, although wanting to also play, were too restricted by their customs to join the games and could only stay behind curtains watching, from a distance, their own children at play.

Thailand became a second homeland to Hwa-Wei and Mary. Their young-est son, Robert, was born in the American Military Fifth Field Hospital in Bang-kok, one of the best memories they had of this foreign country. Robert was born at midnight; a few hours later, while Mary was still resting in the ward, a nurse rushed in waking her up saying, "Go get your baby! It is time for breast-feeding!" As a military hospital at that time, they were short of staff. After tak-ing Robert back to the ward, Mary still had to get medicines and breakfast on her own. Hwa-Wei joked with Mary, "We actually could have gone to a Thai hospital where you could have had our maid stay right in the same room to help with these things."

It was always a concern to Hwa-Wei that Mary and the children would not easily adapt to life in the foreign country. It turned out that their adaptability surpassed his imagination. In a letter to his father, James, the oldest son, men-tioned those days in Thailand:

> My fondest memories are of the weekend mornings at AIT. All us kids would climb into bed with you and mom and you would trap us between your legs and tickle us. We'd laugh and talk and ask you and mom questions about all sorts of things . . .
>
> Thanks also for the opportunity to be raised in Thailand and traveling around the world to exotic places . . . The life experiences you've given me have truly had a very strong, positive effect on my personality and maturity.[4]

---

4. Mary Frances Lee, interview by the author.

Mary and the children at a stopover in Hawaii to visit an old friend, Laura Lum.

The Lees pose for a family picture in Bangkok—just before their return to the United States.

4

Most Thais that Hwa-Wei and Mary met were well educated and well mannered. They were polite, thoughtful, and kind. The couple visited remote villages where people were leading a simple life with no television or modern entertainment, as if separated from the rest of the world. Thailand was known as a rice barn in Southeast Asia for its good climate and fertile land. One sowing and harvest in a year was enough for life's necessities. Villagers lived a stable and comfortable life without having to work too hard. They were happy and carefree, in sharp contrast to the people in cities such as Bangkok and Pattaya.

One time, Hwa-Wei and Mary were dining at a local restaurant in a village, where the owner was very attentive, and the food was delicious. With great satisfaction, they left a tip on the table following the American custom. As they turned on the car engine and got ready to leave, the owner hastily chased out with the tip in hand calling to them, "Hey, you forgot your money!" Having listened to Mary's explanation, he was very grateful and said, "Thank you" many times. When Hwa-Wei's car was already far away, the owner was still standing there waving his hand goodbye.

Besides their warm encounters with villagers, the Lees met other very special Thais. By chance, Hwa-Wei became acquainted with the director-general of the Thai Police Department, a Thai of Chinese descent. The director-general was very hospitable and often invited Hwa-Wei and the Lee family to his family farm for a visit. There was a large orchard at the farm. When lichee (or litchi) was in season, invited guests could take a bag to the orchard to pick the fresh fruit to eat. The director-general also had a superb family cook, whose hot-rock-roasted chicken was the children's favorite. The way he made it was quite a marvel. It would start with building a stove with stones on the ground and then heating it. Meanwhile, the cook would cover a whole chicken, still with its feathers, with special clay, but with insides cleaned and filled with stuffing, and throw it into the heated stone stove. The constantly heated stones cooked the chicken thoroughly. The clay layer outside would be stripped off, along with all the chicken feathers, leaving the chicken meat extremely tasty.

The director-general also gave Hwa-Wei his business card, on which he wrote a few words in Thai, essentially commanding his subordinates to protect the person who holds this card, in case of trouble. Hwa-Wei only used it once for a traffic issue. It was not easy to drive around Thailand, mainly due to traffic disorder and a lack of road signs in English. One time, Hwa-Wei mistakenly drove onto a one-way street because no proper signage was displayed at the entrance. As he wondered how to get off the street, he was approached by a police officer. In panic, he suddenly remembered the director-general's card and decided to give it a try. Upon seeing the card, the police officer's expression immediately went from stern to respectful. After a salute, he led Hwa-Wei off the one-way lane. Through this, Hwa-Wei truly experienced the director-general's authority and enjoyed a privilege that he would never have had in the United States.

In Thailand, Hwa-Wei met not only the special Thai official but also a special American who was his son Jim's baseball coach, an upright and easygoing gentleman. As the boys on his baseball team were all from families of American troops in Thailand, he and his boys' parents fared very well. "Colonel" was the intimate form of address from those parents to the coach, who was indeed a colonel of the U.S. Army.

Ten years after his return from Thailand, Hwa-Wei received a phone call from Washington, D.C. "Do you remember me? I was your son Jim's baseball coach." After a simple greeting, the colonel told Hwa-Wei, "Currently, there is a vacancy for the library director at the UN Headquarters in New York City. For a long time, the position had been held by a Russian. Now, she has finally retired. We hope that her successor will be an American. And I think you are the best candidate."

His remarks were truly a shock to Hwa-Wei. The colonel continued, inadvertently revealing a secret, "I was the one who did the security check on you every two years while you were in Thailand. So I know you very well. I am now holding your personnel file in hand. We are impressed by you, including your outstanding work at AIT. You are the most qualified candidate for the position."

Hwa-Wei knew that all Americans sent to AIT had to go through a security check every two years at the time of his or her contract renewal. Thinking it was just a routine requirement, Hwa-Wei did not pay much attention to it. After receiving the phone call from the colonel, he came to understand the underlying rationale. He recalled that the Indian porter at his apartment complex once stopped him with mystification saying, "Mr. Lee, I want to tell you something. Just now, an American army man was here investigating you. He asked me a lot of questions about you and your family including what people visited you." Ten years later, Hwa-Wei finally got to solve that mystery. According to the colonel, he was the CIA station chief in Bangkok.

Hwa-Wei did not accept the offer. He knew by then that the UN position was highly political and that it was not in his best interest to get involved. Furthermore, he liked his job at Ohio University very much and didn't want to make a change to relocate his family to New York City even though the salary and benefits at the UN might have been slightly better.

Many years later, before being offered the position at the Library of Congress (LC), Hwa-Wei underwent a stricter background check, one that would normally take many months. However, it only took Hwa-Wei six weeks to pass the check. The very short turnaround time was a surprise to the human resources personnel at LC. To Hwa-Wei, the amazing speed was perhaps owing to his past security-check records. He was somewhat curious about his personnel file at the CIA and was hoping to have a chance to get a copy of it under the Freedom of Information Act.

During his seven years in Thailand, Hwa-Wei was very involved with many UN agencies that maintained regional offices in Bangkok. He was frequently asked by these agencies to serve as their library consultants. As a result, he organized an International Librarians Club and served as its founding chair. The International Development Research Centre, a Crown corporation created by the Parliament of Canada to help developing countries. The Centre, due to its strong involvement in Southeast Asia, not only supported the library program at AIT but also enlisted Hwa-Wei to be a consultant for library projects in that region after Hwa-Wei had returned to the United States.

Because of his strong interest in education, Hwa-Wei was also involved with one of the best Chinese schools in Bangkok, Huanghun High School, and served as its honorary advisor. By Thai government laws, Chinese schools can only operate in the evenings and on weekends. The school, which had a reputation in Chinese-language teaching, attracted many excellent teachers and enrolled over five hundred students. Hwa-Wei took advantage of this opportunity, hiring one of the teachers as a private tutor to teach Chinese to his children at home on weekends. This teacher, Vivian Chen, and her family became close friends of the Lees, and after settling in the States many years later, have maintained contact with and visited the Lees.

CHAPTER 10

Endeavoring for Innovation

Library is a common dining table for thoughts, at which guests sit around finding their favorite food. Library is a repository for some people to deposit their thoughts and inventions while others could retrieve them as needed.

—*Alexander Herzen*

1

PARTICIPATING IN the U.S. foreign aid program in Thailand was the most favorable opportunity Hwa-Wei had taken. He was able to broaden his library management experience in a brand new institution and in a completely different and challenging environment where he could try new things and be free to be creative and innovative.

Most Thai cities were small, except Bangkok. In the capital city, there were over a dozen colleges, constituting almost all the educational resources in the country. Among these colleges and universities were two flagships: Chulalongkorn University (CU) and Thammasat University (TU). CU, a comprehensive university, was well known for its science, engineering, and technology departments, whereas TU's strengths were in the humanities and social sciences.

The Asian Institute of Technology (AIT), however, was totally different. Developed under foreign-aid programs of different countries, the institute was staffed by leading international experts and scholars from those countries. In a way, it was a new experiment, innovative and unbound by any rules and traditions. From the beginning, AIT's mission was to be a regional graduate school of engineering and technology with an aim to become "a first-class postgraduate school of engineering, advanced technology, management, and planning in Asia"—"the MIT of Asia." As a means to achieve that goal quickly, AIT placed an emphasis on innovation, considered to be the necessary approach in order to promote technological change and sustainable development in the Asian-Pacific region.

A new school is just like a blank piece of paper with unlimited possibilities. At AIT, where there was no institutional bureaucracy and historical burden, Hwa-Wei got the opportunity to do things his way. Young, healthy, and energetic, Hwa-Wei had gained nine years of management experience in American libraries, giving him a strong combination of knowledge and skills. The AIT library was destined to become a new starting point in his career, allowing him to spread his wings. In fact, all the institute's staff felt the same way. Everyone was eager to work hard in order to meet any challenges and achieve common goals.

Dr. Za-Chieh Moh, recruited from Yale University, was one of the American staff at AIT; he later became the vice president of the institute. A Chinese American, Dr. Moh was a very good friend of Hwa-Wei's and very supportive of his work.

Hwa-Wei's major responsibilities were to quickly develop a modern library to support the graduate programs offered by AIT at its temporary campus, and, at the same time, to begin the planning and designing of a new library on the new campus. The new library was to be located on the second floor of a core instructional building. Distinct from the old cramped library at Chulalongkorn University, the new library would be spacious and equipped with new facilities.

Because of his previous experience in designing the library at Edinboro State College, Hwa-Wei did not take long before coming up with a blueprint. Meanwhile, he also assisted the AIT president in contacting IBM to request the donation of a computer system. As a pioneer in the computer industry, IBM nearly dominated the global market. With a regional office in Hong Kong, the company was striving to open its Asian market. They agreed to give AIT a brand new set of their latest models, shortly after the company's Asian chief representative met with Hwa-Wei and the university president.

In order to make the AIT Computer Center a showcase for IBM computers in Asia, IBM not only agreed to send their technicians to assist in the installation and operation of the donated computers but also provided fifty scholarships each year to AIT's computer science students. This generous donation by IBM also triggered financial support from USAID to construct a new building for the computing center.

2

After reviewing the institutional mission of AIT and the role of its library, Hwa-Wei had a creative idea: to expand the library's traditional role from collection development to information processing. To reflect its new role, the facility was renamed the Library and Information Center. Library services would be greatly expanded, allowing the collections to be easily accessed by students, faculty, researchers, and specialists from near and far through a wide range of information tools including printed periodical indexes, technical document abstracts, and a union catalog of engineering materials at AIT. Access was also available through other national or specialized scientific and technical information centers in the Asian-Pacific region.

With its core mission of collection development and management, cataloging and classification, and user services, a traditional library is similar to a stacked room where valuable resources are just stored for use without any information processing and value-added services. In contrast, an information center, as proposed by Hwa-Wei, would continue to highlight the library's collection but would also feature information reprocessing, an expanded and extended library service for its users.

Under the new name, the AIT Library and Information Center (AITLIC) expanded its collections from books and journals to include technical publications, in-progress research, and engineering projects covered by AIT's instructional, research, and outreach programs. Through his consulting work, Hwa-Wei was able to advise many national scientific and technical information centers in ways of developing their national S&T document databases for joint use.

Covering the areas of civil, hydraulic, environmental, mechanical, and structural engineering, and transportation, many of these searchable databases were utilized for AITLIC's regular abstract and in-progress research publications and were available free to local users and by subscription to remote users. These innovative information tools introduced many valuable, yet previously unknown, technical information resources to people who could then benefit from their use. Under Hwa-Wei's leadership, AITLIC also established a number of specialized information centers.

At this time, many Asian countries were undergoing rapid development with endless construction projects here and there, making the region resemble a large bustling construction site. Many engineering companies came to AITLIC seeking firsthand information prior to their bidding on a project or during the early design stages of airport, road, tunnel, bridge, reservoir, dam, or building construction.

One of the major problems for developing countries in Asia had been the information gap faced by their people. Scientists, engineers, and other professionals in those countries lacked the effective channels to keep their fingers on the pulse of emerging cutting-edge knowledge in science and technology. Their work efficiency was hampered perceptibly by the information gap between them and their peers in developed countries, resulting in a huge waste of human and monetary resources.[1]

Many Asian countries recognized this problem and strove to seek solutions through a variety of means, among which was the building of scientific and tech-

---

1. Hwa-Wei Lee, "The Application of Information Technology to Close the Information Gap" (paper presented at the First Conference on Asian Library Cooperation, Tamsui, Taipei, August 19–22, 1974).

Hwa-Wei with his library staff at the Asian Institute of Technology.

nological information networks and centers at the core of their efforts. UNESCO reported in 1972:

In each country visited there is active interest in the development of scientific and technical information, and plans (including financial commitments in Indonesia, Malaysia, the Philippines, and Thailand) for improvement of the present system. In Indonesia, a Ford Foundation mission recently advised on the establishment of a national network of science information centres to be coordinated by the National Scientific Documentation Centre, and the Government has requested UNDP (United Nations Development Programme) consultant services to assist in the actual planning. In Malaysia, a mission was carried out in late 1971 under British Council sponsorship to advise on "Scientific and Technical Library and Information Services in Malaysia." In Singapore, there has been no direct follow-up on the 1969 UNESCO sponsored "Proposals for the Setting-up of a Scientific and Technical Information Centre," but there is active interest in revising this study to bring it in line with [the] changing situation in Singapore. In the Philippines, the NSDB is setting up a new National Science Information Centre, which will serve as the national co-coordinating body and as the linkage to regional and international networks or systems. The Government has requested UNDP advisory services in planning the Centre. In Hong Kong, the Committee for Scientific Co-ordination has set up a Sub-Committee on Scientific and Technical Information to consider the establishment of a "Centralized Technical Information Service." In Thailand, the Thai National Documentation

Center (TNDC), which is already well established, is planning further services, and the Asian Institute of Technology has advanced plans for development of a complete information service on a regional level.[2]

The scientific and technological information needs triggered by the rapid regional growth provided the developmental direction for the AIT Library and Information Center (AITLIC). In July 1971, the annual conference of the Asian Geotechnical Engineering Society was held in Bangkok. Conference attendees expressed an urgent need for an effective and efficient geotechnical information service. As a follow-up, the conference passed a resolution to entrust AITLIC to establish the Asian Information Center for Geotechnical Engineering (AGE), which would be funded by the International Development Research Center in Canada. AGE's mission was to find, select, and acquire relevant formal and informal literatures from Asia in all languages.[3]

Officially established in January 1973, AGE was jointly managed by the Library and Information Center and the Department of Geotechnical Engineering. Utilizing the catalog and information retrieval system developed at AITLIC, AGE compiled, edited, and published a series of secondary sources, technical information guides, including *Current Awareness Service, Asian Geotechnical Engineering Abstracts, Conference Proceedings List, AGE Journal Holdings List, Asian Geotechnical Engineering in Progress,* and *Asian Geotechnical Engineering Directory.* The areas covered by these secondary sources included soil mechanics, foundation engineering, rock mechanics, engineering geology, and earthquake engineering.

Many Asian countries were supportive to AGE and supplied a large quantity of extremely valuable engineering documents and materials from various related agencies. In the field of civil engineering construction, for example, data collected concerning various construction projects were made available. This data included information about the soil and rock formation, as well as the geological composition of these proposed sites, gathered prior to building project foundations; it also contained rigorous feasibility assessments, foundation depth calculations, and identification of potential problems. This precious data would normally lose their value and even be discarded once a construction project was completed. At AGE this data was collected and made available to other engineers allowing them to save time and efforts in designing other construction projects.

---

2. *Report of UNESCO Fact-Finding Mission on the Regional Information Network for Science and Technology in Southeast Asia* (SCP/4252-25) 1972, 20.

3. Hwa-Wei Lee, "The Experience of a Specialized Information Service in Asia—AGE" (paper presented at the Round Table Conference on Documentation Problems in Developing Countries, Khartoum, Sudan, April 10–11, 1975, sponsored by FID/DC and FID National Member in Sudan), in *Journal of Library and Information Science* 1, no. 2 (Oct. 1975): 82–93.

The unforeseen turnout of the initiative at AIT's library brought Hwa-Wei fame within the Asian library community. Although Hwa-Wei presents a calm and sober appearance, he is passionate about innovation in his heart. In fact, he is never fond of sticking to the status quo. The foundation of his library knowledge management has always been to maximize the use of library collection through the improved use of bibliographic tools and outreach services.

3

Apart from his daily administrative work in the library, Hwa-Wei also traveled to neighboring countries for acquisition trips. He cultivated solid professional relationships with government agencies and science and technology information centers in many Southeast Asian countries. He was able to receive engineering materials from those agencies and centers through the mail or during those trips, thus benefiting from the relationships.

Hwa-Wei had a great adventure in 1970 during one of his acquisition trips. He usually chose to travel by air. But his travel companion, Ted Brand, AIT geotechnical engineering professor, had just bought a new car. Ted insisted on driving from Bangkok, Thailand, to Kuala Lumpur, Malaysia. Traveling by car was somewhat risky as Thailand, a Buddhist country, had quite a few Malay Muslims living in the south who often had conflicts with the government. The rebels were very active at the border area. In addition, the road conditions in the south were not good, with some roads still under construction.

Perhaps because they were still young, Hwa-Wei and Ted had little fear of potential danger along the way. But they did take their friends' advice—never driving at night, not hitting the road too early in morning, and stopping to find an inn to rest at about four o'clock in the afternoon. They traveled with caution, doing their best to avoid harassment by rebels when approaching the border.

Even so, something unanticipated happened one day. Around noon the two arrived at the border of Thailand and Malaysia. In front of them was a large tract of rubber trees. On the body of each tree was a tire inner tube containing white milk-like sap, raw material for natural rubber, dripping out slowly. The lush branches and leaves of those rubber trees blocked the tropical sun. So they decided to take a rest in the woods.

Shortly after getting out of the car, Hwa-Wei saw from a distance vague figures swaying in the woods. Seeing that the figures were quickly getting closer, Hwa-Wei felt far from comfortable and started yelling, "Ted, run!" The two hurried back to their car and quickly started the engine. At that moment, the people in the woods began shouting and shooting. As whistling bullets flew by the car, Ted floored the gas pedal, accelerating the car to its maximum speed limit, and frantically drove forward. As they heard the gunfire and shouting getting farther and farther behind, the two men realized that they had managed to free themselves from a disaster.

As they were around the same age, after that trip to Malaysia, Ted and Hwa-Wei became Damon and Pythias to each other. Hwa-Wei's many projects at AIT were completed with generous help from Ted, an authoritative engineering expert who knew well what resources to collect and what not to collect. Later, the two also traveled together to Laos and Cambodia, where they experienced no danger, but had all sorts of funny encounters.

During one trip from Thailand to Cambodia, Hwa-Wei and Ted were at the border of the two countries, which are separated by a river. As not many people crossed the border at this location, the custom offices on both sides were simply furnished and only had one or two officers in each. Having heard that bribing custom officers could avoid troubles, they gave five dollars to a Thai officer, a successful trade for a smooth inspection, and did the same at the Cambodian office. Thinking that they would return in two days to the same office, Hwa-Wei asked the Cambodian about the office's daily closing time and arranged to meet him there around four o'clock in the afternoon for reentry to Thailand. The conversation went very well: the custom officer seemed like a straightforward type of person and talked with the two travelers just like a friend. He promised to wait for their return.

By the time Hwa-Wei and Ted rushed back two days later at 4:00 p.m., however, the office was locked. They started to worry about what to do as the border area was rather deserted, and it was hardly possible for them to find an inn in which to stay. While looking around, they saw a little boy standing next to the office door and asked: "Have the people in the office already gone? Do you know where to find them?" The boy replied, "Yes, I know where they are. If you give me ten dollars, I will take you there."

The boy was apparently an experienced bargainer. A deal was reached for Hwa-Wei and Ted to pay five dollars up front and another five dollars once the officer was located. After a short walk passing by two or three buildings, they were brought to the officer, who was playing cards with a few others in a house filled with smoke. The officer seemed to have completely forgotten the promise that he had made two days earlier and said, with an embarrassed look on his face, "We just started playing. How about waiting till tomorrow?" Hwa-Wei and Ted had no choice but to give him more money. He then started to walk back impatiently to the custom office.

Many years later, Hwa-Wei and Ted were still impressed by that officer, whose original frankness had fooled them. They had not anticipated such a trap. Starting with the closed office, to the little boy by the door, to the card-

playing scene—everything seemed to have been carefully planned by that officer, based on his knowing the two travelers' return time. Through his trickery,
he managed to receive twenty dollars, not five dollars, quite a bit of money back
then in Cambodia. Hwa-Wei and Ted admired the shrewdness of the Cambodian, but meanwhile sighed about the pervasive bribery culture in Southeast
Asian countries.

Hwa-Wei and Ted left AIT in 1975, the same time the foreign-aid program
ended. After that, Ted worked in Hong Kong for ten years as the director of a
civil engineering and development department. A number of bridges and tunnels were built during his term.

4

In addition to its most comprehensive engineering collection, AIT's Library and
Information Center also developed a computer retrieval system, an elementary-
level library-automation system. Such a library-automation system back then
was a new thing, even in the United States. Hwa-Wei had started his computer
experience in Edinboro, when that state college was promoting the use of computers by requiring each department to send selected staff members to receive
training. At that time, most people had probably never heard of computers
and were not knowledgeable about what one could do; Hwa-Wei was one of
just a limited number of technology geeks. He even learned FORTRAN, a first-
generation computer language, and used it to develop circulation, acquisition,
and cataloging systems in the library. The programming itself was very basic,
but its concept was extremely innovative.

Back then, Hwa-Wei already had a keen feeling that computer technology
would someday become a driving force of human advancement and that libraries
would also be redefined. Thus, he kept trying various ways of applying computer
technologies to library services, so-called unconventional attempts to accomplish
conventional work. Instead of regarding himself as a thinker, Hwa-Wei believed
that he was a doer who practiced what he preached. The seven years in Thailand offered him a great opportunity for making those innovations.

Hwa-Wei wrote computer programs for the acquisition and cataloging of
library journals and books. To people nowadays, those early computers seem
rather simple and primitive with a limited function despite their huge size. The
operation of those computers relied on punch cards where each line could take
some seventy characters, essentially adequate for title and author fields but certainly not enough to contain more information. But even at that limit, developing
automated library catalogs on those computers was an unbelievable leap. At
AITLIC, newly acquired engineering materials, including project plans and

reports from different Southeast Asian countries, were cataloged through computer programs written locally and grouped into different categories. Eventually, these catalogues were published by Hwa-Wei and his colleagues in various specialized bibliographies for others to use.

What Hwa-Wei and his library had accomplished was clearly beyond the basic functions of a conventional library. Rather, it was a highly specialized service formed through a partnership between library professionals and subject experts from different engineering departments. Some engineering faculty and students assumed the responsibility of library document organization. Guided by librarians, these subject specialists represented and organized acquired engineering resources in a way that could meet and fit the needs of engineers. Each month, AITLIC was able to publish one issue of the only bibliography of engineering resources in Asia. The bibliography turned out to be very popular with enthusiastic subscribers from engineering departments, schools, and agencies all over Asia.

Before long, AITLIC upgraded its computer system from an already overloaded IBM 1130 to an IBM CDC3600. The library and information center also welcomed a new deputy director, Stephen W. Massil, an excellent library-automation expert and a former contributor of the online MARC systems at the University of Birmingham, Aston University, and the Birmingham public library system in the U.K. Since Massil took the post, AITLIC was empowered to make further advances in the area of library automation and information retrieval systems in Asia.[4]

The success of AITLIC caused a stir in Thailand; Hwa-Wei's fame was rising high throughout the Southeast Asian librarianship field. He was invited to become a part-time faculty member at the Library Science Department of Chulalongkorn University, teaching library automation and consulting at UN agencies. He also went to libraries of many countries upon invitation to offer help, as UNESCO was then striving to establish national science and technology information centers in every country, for which AITLIC undoubtedly provided a successful model.

The course in library automation Hwa-Wei taught at Chulalongkorn University was noteworthy. He developed it himself, and it proved innovative even for American library schools. The course, its design based upon Hwa-Wei's own projects, basically concerned programming languages and the practical skills related to computer applications in libraries. His class, originally an elective, was flooded with enrollees, young CU students with keen eyes on new things. One student even translated the syllabus, which became influential and widely disseminated, into Thai. In the 1970s when most people were still using type-

4. Hwa-Wei Lee, "The Application of Information Technology to Close the Information Gap."

writers, library automation was just a pie in the sky with an irresistible charm and influence.

Hwa-Wei's work at AITLIC actually reached beyond a library director's normal responsibilities. Through his consulting on library management and development, Hwa-Wei got to know many library colleagues and established good professional relationships with libraries across Southeast Asia. He was invited to many countries including Malaysia, Indonesia, and the Philippines to present papers about his management experiences at a variety of conferences. His work also brought him his first invitation to lecture in China as a specialist.

His potential for being a great leader was maximized in the free environment in Thailand, and Hwa-Wei has maintained a special relationship with the Thai library community. Even some twenty years after he left the country, Hwa-Wei was invited back. On September 11, the time of the terrorist attacks in the United States, he was in Thailand at the Department of Library Management at Chiang Mai University, on a six-week Fulbright Senior Specialist program to help the department plan and design its graduate program.

With the maturation of library science undergraduate education across Thailand, Chiang Mai University started to establish its graduate program, with an aim of enhancing library education. Hwa-Wei advised the university to go beyond the traditional courses and pedagogy and add more weight to knowledge management in libraries.

One of the preparatory committee members was a faculty member at the School of Management, who shared his thoughts with Hwa-Wei. The two men complemented one another. Lifting the core concept of library management from information management to knowledge management required a reflection of the latter in the graduate curriculum. With the professor's influence on campus, a complete curriculum design was completed in six weeks as well as the successful professional training of a number of faculty and staff.[5]

Hwa-Wei was very pleased to see that the introduction of knowledge management to the graduate program curriculum opened a new world to the Department of Library Management at Chiang Mai. Meanwhile, he had other fresh thoughts about knowledge management in libraries. He continued his research in this field, systematically collecting and reviewing relevant resources. The final product of this research was an influential academic monograph entitled *Knowledge Management: The Theory and Practice,* co-authored by Hwa-Wei and two scholars from Peking University, Dr. Xiaoying Dong and Dr. Meiyun Zuo.[6]

5. Ratana Na-Lamphun and Hwa-Wei Lee, "Focusing on Information and Knowledge Management: Redesigning the Graduate Program of Library and Information Science at Chiang Mai University," *Information Development* 18, no.1 (March 2002): 47–58.

6. Hwa-Wei Lee, Xiaoying Dong, and Meiyun Zuo, *Knowledge Management: Theory and Practice,* Twenty-first Century Library Science Series [in Chinese] (Beijing: Huazhi Publishing, 2002).

CHAPTER II

Returning to the United States

Comin' home to a place he'd never been before
He left yesterday behind him,
You might say he was born again,
You might say he found a key for every door.

—*John Denver, "Rocky Mountain High"*

1

W HEN THE foreign-aid program of USAID came to an end in the summer of 1975, American experts started to leave AIT. At that time, because his reputation as an innovative library leader was well known throughout Southeast Asia, Hwa-Wei received an offer from Hong Kong Polytechnic (renamed Hong Kong Polytechnic University in 1994) to become a deputy library director. This was a late invitation; Hwa-Wei had already been offered the position of associate director of libraries with a rank of professor of library administration by Colorado State University (CSU), based on a strong recommendation from the dean of its College of Engineering.

CSU had served as the administrative agency of the American foreign-aid program at AIT, contracted by USAID. Hwa-Wei's work at AIT was also well known by top administrators of CSU. When offered the position, Hwa-Wei happily accepted, deciding to return to the United States to continue his library career. Mary and the children were all in favor of his decision. Being away from the U.S. for such a long time, they were excited to be home again.

Located in Fort Collins in the northern part of the state of Colorado, CSU, founded in 1870, has had over one hundred years of history. A public research university, CSU is the state's land grant university and has been traditionally strong in agriculture, veterinary medicine, engineering, and technology, with a particular focus on applied science and research. The university is also well known for its research in infectious disease, atmospheric science, clean energy technology, environmental science, and biomedical technology. Similar to other university towns in the United States, the growth of Fort Collins benefited from the university. At the time the Lees lived in that city, many of its 150,000 residents were CSU employees and students; a large percentage of the remaining residents were also engaged in university-related work or business.

Located five thousand feet above sea level, Fort Collins is situated at the western edge of the Great Plains and at the base of the Rocky Mountains. The ancient and majestic Rockies stretch thousands of miles all the way from the north to the south of America. Covered with snow all year around on the peaks, those steep and jagged cliffs are monumental and majestic to view.

On the mountain plateau, the sunshine is strong, the sky is blue, and the air is extremely refreshing. This was a totally different world from tropical Thailand. Having lived in Thailand for seven years and having experienced several international tours, the Lee children adapted quickly to the new environment. It did not take them long to familiarize themselves with their neighborhood and to start biking around on bike paths alongside the wide four-lane streets. The children liked this place. Beautiful and picturesque mountains were right out there within sight of their new home.

The Lee family experienced their first snow in Fort Collins not long after they settled into their new house. The blowing and drifting snow lasted two days, a misery to them after just returning from Thailand. Back in Thailand, the children were used to wearing short-sleeve school uniforms or casual blouses and never had the need for warm clothes.

Mary, realizing the need for winter clothes, rushed to all the local garage sales and found many like-new used items of clothing, including jeans, coats, hats, gloves, and boots. Dressed in those heavy clothes, the six children had to reacquaint themselves with the cold weather they had long forgotten. To Mary, the most dreadful thing was dealing with her children's wet clothes and boots and making sure that they could dry quickly. She decided to buy a dryer, a machine she had never used before. Having to do all of this work herself, without any assistance from domestic help, was a little hectic for Mary. Fortunately, fourteen-year-old Shirley was sensible and capable, and she became a great help.

CSU had a large Asian student population. Shortly after taking the post in the library, Hwa-Wei was invited to become a faculty advisor for the Thai and the Taiwanese student associations. His home often served as the best place for students to meet. In February 1976, the Lees hosted an in-house dinner party for a group of seventy people to celebrate their first Chinese New Year at Fort Collins.

The Lee family kept their passion for travel. Surrounding Fort Collins were a number of national parks. And Denver, nationally famous for its scenic beauty, was not far to the south. During weekends or long holidays, Hwa-Wei would take the entire family out on road trips. Other times, they went skiing in the Rockies. Hwa-Wei enjoyed seeing all his children playing and laughing in the snow. His son, Jim, recalled those days in a letter to his dad:

I still don't know how you took the time to take us all around Colorado, and to take us to places like the Grand Canyon and Yellowstone National Park. I've lived in Denver longer than we lived in Ft. Collins, and I still haven't taken my kids to these places.

2

As one of the two deputy library directors at CSU, Hwa-Wei oversaw all the technical service units, including cataloging, acquisition, collection management, and information technology; the other deputy director was responsible for public services and library instruction. The two collaborated very well. In the area of collection development, Hwa-Wei was in close contact with faculty members of different colleges and departments so as to better understand their research and teaching needs.

Fort Collins proved a soft landing place for Hwa-Wei, allowing him to return to routine administrative work in an American university library after being away in Thailand for seven years. His new American colleagues soon found that this gentle and polite deputy director was always passionate and capable of getting things done remarkably well. Furthermore, he possessed unbelievable energy and kept himself always busy, seldom giving himself a break. Behind his calm manner was an extraordinary drive for excellence.

Hwa-Wei's work at CSU went very well. He earned tenure in just three years, which meant that he could stay at CSU as long as he wanted, enjoying the blue sky and picturesque mountain views in Fort Collins throughout his library career. Hwa-Wei, however, with over fifteen years of administrative experience and appropriate academic credentials, wanted to explore the possibility of moving to a library director's position at another university library.

A "glass ceiling" existed in the United States for Asian Americans and other ethnic minorities, preventing them from moving up to top positions in organizations, including libraries. Hwa-Wei wanted to try to break through that glass ceiling. This desire motivated him to apply for director's positions at other academic libraries even though this meant he would have to give up his tenure, the protection and job security he had just earned from CSU.

In the short span of three years at CSU, Hwa-Wei gained valuable experience and came to a more complete understanding of library administration in a large American research library. As a member of the Association of Research Libraries (ARL), the CSU Library was known for its strength in research collections in several subject areas. Hwa-Wei did not realize back then that these valuable experiences had equipped him well for the library director's position he would soon assume at Ohio University. He was moving steadily up, preparing to go through the glass ceiling.

With a total number of 126 large research library members from the United States and Canada, the Association of Research Libraries (ARL) is composed of eight national libraries and archives,[1] two famous public research libraries,[2] and 116 university libraries from the top institutions of higher education. Each year, ARL ranks its member libraries in terms of collection size as well as by other quality indicators.

Becoming an ARL member is considered an honor and a special recognition, as only those libraries with impressive research collections can meet the competitive criteria for membership: an ARL member library usually possesses a research collection that has attained very high standards both in size and in quality. Statistics show that the 126 ARL member libraries house nearly 50 percent of all library resources in North America.[3]

Apart from his administrative work in the United States, Hwa-Wei had maintained a good professional relationship with major libraries and international and regional organizations in Asia. Almost every year, he would have one or two opportunities to serve, upon invitation, as a consultant to libraries in the East and Southeast Asian regions. In 1976, he was invited jointly by UNESCO and the National Library of Thailand to design the Regional Centre for the International Serials Data System (ISDS) in Thailand.[4] In 1978, upon the invitation of Canada's International Development Research Centre, he gave a special talk on the "Impact of International Information System and Programs on NATIS" at the Fourth Congress of Southeast Asian Librarians on Regional Cooperation for the Development of National Technical Information Services.[5]

In his dual role as a senior administrator in an American research library and an expert on Southeast Asian librarianship, Hwa-Wei was capable of exchanging and transmitting advanced knowledge on library and information management across the Pacific without any cultural barrier. This type of role was very special and important, and Hwa-Wei, along with only a few others, had these capacities. He had turned into a uniquely international librarian.

1. The eight national libraries and archives are The Library of Congress, the National Library and Archives of Canada, Canadian Institute of Scientific and Technical Information, U.S. National Archives and Records Administration, National Agricultural Library, National Library of Medicine, Smithsonian Institution Libraries, and the Center for Research Libraries.

2. The two research-type public libraries are Boston Public Library and New York Public Library.

3. Nicholas A.Basbanes, *Patience & Fortitude: A Roving Chronicle of Book People, Book Places, and Book Culture*, trans. Chuanwei Yang (Shanghai: People's Publishing House, 2011), 78–81.

4. *The Possibility of Establishing a Regional Centre for the International Serials Data System in Thailand* (SC-76/WS/7), (Paris: UNESCO, 1976). In *Collected Works of Hwa-Wei Lee*, vol. 2 (Guangzhou: Sun Yat-Sen University Press, 2011), 856–71, 874–81.

5. "Impact of International Information System and Programs on NATIS" (SCP/4252-25), *Regional Cooperation for the Development of National Information Services: Proceedings of the Fourth Congress of Southeast Asian Librarians, Bangkok, Thailand, June 5–9, 1978* (Bangkok, Thailand: Thai Library Association, 1981), 133–46.

A Lee family photograph from their first winter in Fort Collins, Colorado, just after their return to the United States from Thailand.

It had been more than two years since Hwa-Wei came to CSU Libraries. He seemed ready for another professional move, again following Professor Vann's graduation advice. His job search for library director positions started in late 1977. On April 13, 1978, Hwa-Wei received his official appointment letter as the director of Libraries from Ohio University in Athens, Ohio. The job was to begin on August 1, 1978. A year later he was also appointed an adjunct professor of curriculum and instruction in the College of Education, so he could serve on a number of dissertation committees for doctoral students whose research topics were on aspects of education concerning Asia.

3

Founded in 1804, Ohio University (OHIO) was the first state college in Ohio. Having a much longer history than Ohio State University, OHIO was already, at the time of his arrival, a rather sizable comprehensive research university, with ten colleges and sixty-two departments offering bachelor, master's, and doctorate degrees. The university ranked third among eighty public and private higher education institutions in the state of Ohio.

Named after the Ohio River, the state of Ohio is situated between the Ohio River and Lake Erie. Ohio University, about ninety minutes away from the state capital of Columbus, is situated in Athens, a city in Southeast Ohio. A typical university town, Athens has nearly sixty thousand people, of whom over half are OHIO faculty, staff, and students. At that time, the primary city street was Court Street, which passed right through the campus. Pedestrians on the street were mostly young and bright students striding confidently ahead carrying bulging bags on their shoulders.

Athens is a vibrant and lively place when the university is in session. One of its exciting fall events is Halloween. It has been said that many ghost stories and supernatural legends are associated with Athens, adding to the city's mystery. As the night approaches, people from all the nearby counties pour into the city. They dress up in various costumes, disguised as elves, ghosts, witches, demons, monsters, zombies, vampires, angels, and aliens. The Halloween crowd is large, and the carnival lasts well past midnight.

For the Lee family's relocation from Fort Collins to Athens, Hwa-Wei hired a moving company for furniture and household items. He drove their family station wagon with a total of nine people on board: Mary, Hwa-Wei, their six children, and his younger sister's five-year-old daughter, Elizabeth. Elizabeth's parents had gone back to Taiwan for a trip, leaving her with the Lees for the entire summer. While Mary took care of the seven children, Hwa-Wei drove the entire family for almost a thousand miles with stops in four states: Nebraska, Iowa, Illinois, and Indiana.

Not long before their big move, Hwa-Wei and Mary were lucky to find a three-story house with six bedrooms, a spacious living room, and a full-size basement on the south side of Athens. The house was for sale by a faculty member, who also had a big family and was about to move to Arizona for another teaching job. Without hesitation, Hwa-Wei and Mary decided to purchase it. It would become the family's new home in Athens; the Lee children would grow up there. At the time of their arrival, the new house looked very messy with furniture, unpacked boxes, suitcases, and the various souvenirs that the family had brought back from Thailand scattered here and there.

The Lee children were always excited about settling into a new place. They did not seem tired at all after the long journey. At night on the same day of their arrival, while the exhausted Hwa-Wei fell asleep, Mary spotted her children in their dark bedrooms already beginning to make new friends with the four Ellis children in the house next door. They were sending flashlight signals through the windows, exchanging code words, with the lights flickering and lengths staggered. Mary was happy to see the children's adaptability. The speed at which they made new friends was beyond many adults' imaginations. As the children of the two families were about the same ages, they became lifelong friends.

Mary, feeling tired, needed a good night's sleep, as tomorrow would be a busy day. According to Hwa-Wei, Ohio University President Charles J. Ping would pay a family visit to their home. So Mary had to sort things out as soon as possible in the house, or at least in the living room. With the help of all the children, the two front rooms were in perfect order when President Ping arrived.

4

Hwa-Wei became the director of Ohio University Libraries in August 1978. Shortly after the initial excitement, he came to realize that everything would not be as easy and relaxed as the welcome party thrown by the president. In fact, early during his job interview, Hwa-Wei already understood that OHIO needed a new library director with strong administrative experience and leadership ability because the library had been facing a number of difficult problems that required prompt and effective action.

As Hwa-Wei learned in his first week of work in his new position, there had been a demonstration in front of the president's office in Cutler Hall, led by the library staff and joined by students and some faculty members, over the long-term issue of the frequent breakdowns of the central air-conditioning unit in the Vernon R. Alden Library. The poor condition of the unit made it impossible for library staff to work and for students to study in the first and second levels of the library during the summer months. The demonstration had taken place just two months before Hwa-Wei's arrival.

Another serious problem concerned the library's roof, which leaked on the top level of the seven-floor building whenever there was rain. Since most of the library collections were housed on the sixth and seventh floors, some valuable book and journal collections had been damaged by the leaking water despite the fact that some shelves on the seventh floor were covered with large sheets of plastic, which was, in itself, very inconvenient to both the library users and staff.

During their first few meetings Hwa-Wei and his immediate supervisor, Provost Neil S. Bucklew, discussed these two serious problems, agreeing that solutions were clearly needed for both. In addition, the provost suggested that disciplinary action for the acting library director and those staff members who had led the demonstration would also be necessary. Hwa-Wei didn't follow through with this suggestion since he felt the staff's actions were justified because of the unbearable working conditions.

For more than two years—since the former library director, Thompson Little, left OHIO to become the vice president of Online Computer Library Center (OCLC)—the position of director had been vacant. The acting director William Rogers, originally the associate director, was an experienced library administrator with an easy-going personality, one well liked by the library staff.

When the director's position became available, however, Rogers did not apply; he was satisfied serving as the associate director. He made it very clear to Hwa-Wei at their first meeting that he would support Hwa-Wei wholeheartedly to improve the library's operation after two years of inaction. He turned out to be a great help to Hwa-Wei over the years.

In 1978, Hwa-Wei was hired by Ohio University in Athens, Ohio, as the director of Libraries, where he worked in the Vernon R. Alden Library for twenty-one years.

During his tenure at Ohio University, Hwa-Wei welcomed many visitors from Chinese libraries to the campus.

Hwa-Wei and his family stand outside their home in Athens, Ohio.

President Ping had very high expectations for the library. As a scholar himself, he attached great importance to excellence in teaching and research. He also emphasized the significance of the library as the center of all academic activities and believed in the necessity of having a robust library. He thus hoped that Hwa-Wei could lead Ohio University Library in expanding its research collection expeditiously and in providing high standards and state-of-the-art services to meet the teaching and research needs of the different colleges, schools, departments, and centers.

Furthermore, both the president and the provost also counted on Hwa-Wei's leadership to qualify Ohio University Library to rank as a member of the Association of Research Libraries (ARL). ARL membership was actually a critical factor affecting OHIO's national ranking. In the United States, a first-class university must have a first-rate library.

A huge gap existed between this hope and reality as the then medium-sized University Library, ranked below 120th among North American research libraries, had much to accomplish to meet ARL membership requirements. To maintain its prestigious position, ARL had set very strict standards for its members, and membership was by invitation only. A library had to lift its ranking to fall within the top 75 libraries, that is, to surpass one third of the 116 member libraries at that time, in the areas of collection and service before it could be eligible to be assessed and audited for a possible invitation for membership. In addition to the quantitative standards, another area of assessment concerned whether or not the library had well-recognized research collections of national and international reputation.

It was obvious that OHIO's library was overwhelmed with a critical mix of old problems and new challenges, requiring Hwa-Wei to quickly formulate a strategic plan with clear goals and plans for action. He was very happy to recognize that most of the library staff were highly competent and dedicated. They were very eager to work with him in order to regain their position of importance in the university as the center of learning and scholarly pursuit.

As a team player himself, Hwa-Wei was able to quickly gain the confidence and support of his staff. As a member of the Deans Council, he quickly built up a good working relationship with all the vice presidents and the academic deans. Through the University Library Committee, Hwa-Wei got to know many of the key supporters among faculty members in the various academic departments and disciplines. In order to reach out to all the constituencies among administrators, faculty, staff, students, and Athens community leaders, Hwa-Wei kept very busy, oftentimes working overtime from early morning to the closing of the main library at midnight.

This hard work did pay off handsomely; many of the initial challenges were overcome, and Hwa-Wei was recognized by the university's Administrative Senate in 1982 with the Outstanding Administrator Award. One of the basic rules of the award required a nominee to have been an administrator at the university for at least three years. Hwa-Wei was nominated for the award as soon as he reached the three-year requirement. The nominators, as Hwa-Wei learned later, included his immediate boss, Provost Bucklew.

The citation of the Outstanding Administrator Award reads as follows:

> The award recognizes the superior performance of your responsibilities as director of Libraries. Your professional knowledge, creativity, and dedication have resulted in a new leadership and direction for the Ohio University Library.
>
> Your introduction of new and innovative technologies has led to an improvement in the quality, quantity, and accessibility of information and to a marked increase in the use of library services.
>
> Your ability to acquire additional grants and donations has made the modernization of facilities and many of the improvements in resources possible.
>
> Your professional recognition internationally has allowed the library to participate in international internship programs and has made you an ambassador for Ohio University.
>
> Your contributions to the University and to your profession have enriched the educational experience available in the academic community at Ohio University.
>
> Presented May 18, 1982

The award certificate was signed by John C. Ray, chair of the Selection Committee; Gary O. Moden, chair of the Administrative Senate; and Charles J. Ping, president of Ohio University. It was the first major award that Hwa-Wei had received during his long and meritorious library career. While he truly deserved such recognition, a more valuable part of this honor was the impact it had on his library staff in terms of building pride and solidarity, and winning Hwa-Wei full staff support.

Implementing Ambitious Plans

The library is far more than a collection of books or a building. It is
the intellectual heart of the university, a vital element of university
life with an essential role in teaching, learning, and research.
—*Dr. Vernon R. Alden, fifteenth president of Ohio University*

1

UPON TAKING his post, Hwa-Wei learned that William "Will" Rogers, associate
library director, was well liked by the staff for his impartial and caring nature.
The reason for his involvement in the demonstration was simply because he
saw no other options. The library building, since its completion, had never had
its air conditioning fully maintained. Because the library's air conditioning
frequently broke down, Will Rogers had already contacted the director of
Campus Facilities Management several times seeking to have it fixed. The
problem, however, remained unresolved, due to the lack of funding to cover
the $250,000 service cost. That day, the weather was extremely hot, and the
library building felt like a sauna, which was unbearable to most staff. Will
thought that it was his obligation to join the protest for the rights and benefits
of the library employees.

Hwa-Wei met with Will and told him frankly about the university's stand-
point on the protest. Will confessed that his way of handling it had been inappropriate, but, really, he felt it had been his only choice. Thinking it was not all
Will's fault, Hwa-Wei went and interceded with the provost, with a promise of
handling similar situations in the future in a more proper and rational manner.

Shortly afterward, Hwa-Wei began to contact the director of Campus Facilities Management and urged him for a full repair of the library air conditioning.
He also visited the associate vice president for Facilities and Auxiliaries, as well
as both the vice president for Administration and the vice president for Finance
to seek their support. After his persistent efforts, the university authorities finally
agreed to allocate sufficient funding to replace the system and to fix the leaking
roof. As he was able to remain in his position as the associate library director,
Will knew that he owed Hwa-Wei a debt. Having seen the new director's work

ability, Will offered his full support to Hwa-Wei, and the two worked closely and harmoniously together.

Hwa-Wei's first accomplishment at the new library post won him popular support from his staff. Above all, of course, his work ethic and passion earned him trust and admiration. His hard work and sincerity in improving library collections and services also earned him the respect and support of faculty members across the campus, especially those faculty members who served on the University Library Committee.

Hwa-Wei realized that transforming Alden Library to a first-class academic library would require a comprehensive enhancement, and becoming an ARL member library could be the breakthrough. He submitted a report to the president and the provost, comparing Alden Library with other medium-ranked ARL libraries. In the report, he pointed out that it would take at least fifteen years for the library to reach its goal, mainly because of the size of its collection and the level of quality of its research resources, especially those in several academic areas that were supposedly strong areas for Oho University. These included the Southeast Asia and fine arts collections and the Cornelius Ryan Collection on World War II. Hwa-Wei went one step further by outlining, in detail, strategic plans for the future of Alden Library.

University President Charles J. Ping, a very distinguished scholar in higher education administration, was a remarkable leader. Dr. Ping immediately had a long talk with his new library director, appreciating his pragmatism and persistence. With explicit excitement, Ping encouraged him saying, "Hwa-Wei, just go for it. You have my full support." Thanks to Ping's superb personnel management skills, every Ohio University senior administrator was dedicated and cooperative and worked collaboratively with Hwa-Wei to raise the library's status.

To meet ARL's membership qualifications, the first necessary step was to build up the library's organizational strength. Hwa-Wei embarked on a comprehensive upgrade of collections and services. Besides the main campus in Athens, OHIO has five regional campuses spread throughout Southeast Ohio, located between forty and one hundred miles away from the Athens campus; each regional campus has a branch library. Hwa-Wei proposed to merge the five regional libraries with the main library into an integrated university library system. Under the old structure, those regional libraries were partners of the main library, operating under the direction of the regional campus deans.

Hwa-Wei invested a tremendous amount of effort to coordinate the structural change. With support and assistance from Dr. James Bryant, vice president for Regional Higher Education in charge of the regional campuses and distance education, Hwa-Wei was able to complete the merger quickly, creating

Hwa-Wei worked closely with Phyllis Field, chair of the Library Committee, to introduce ALICE to the OHIO faculty.

Hwa-Wei Lee, Director General Chen-Ku Wang, and President Charles Ping celebrate Wang's honorary doctoral degree from Ohio University.

Library directors of major Chinese universities visited the Ohio University Libraries. Dr. Ying Zhang, the translator of this biography, stands on the far right.

a unified university library system in which all of the library resources, both collections and human resources, were shared among all campuses.

That proved to be a well-conceived plan of action; the library system as a whole showed a measurable increase in total funding, staffing, and collection size—a major step to approaching the membership requirement of ARL. Meanwhile, the regional libraries not only received more funding and staff support from the main library but also enjoyed more direct access to collections within it, a huge benefit to faculty and students at the regional campuses. Thus, the move served multiple purposes.

Hwa-Wei's next attempt was to strengthen research and special collections, an important review criterion for ARL membership. Back then, the Southeast Asian Collection at OHIO mainly focused on Malaysian resources. Over a long time period, due to funding from the U.S. Department of Education, the College of Education had set up a special civil service training program at Mara Institute of Technology in Kuala Lumpur.

Meanwhile, a joint MBA program between Ohio University's College of Business and Mara was taught by rotating faculty members from OHIO. In addition, more than two hundred Malaysian students were attending Ohio University with financial support from the Malaysian government. To broaden the cooperation, the Malaysian government established a Tun Abdul Razak Chair in Malaysian Studies at OHIO's Center for International Studies and sent scholars to teach at the university, for terms of two years. With this close relationship and cooperation, the Malaysian government, through its prime minister's office, also donated many of its government publications to Alden Library.

Upon taking his office, Hwa-Wei attached great importance to further relations with Malaysia. There were hundreds of middle- and high-level officials in the Malaysian government with graduate degrees from Ohio University; those unique personnel resources, without a doubt, had helped to build better relations between Malaysia and OHIO. A successful effort was made in obtaining an annual budget allocation (50,000 Ringgit) from the Malaysian government to acquire Malaysian books and journals through the National Library of Malaysia (NLM) for Alden Library. This annual funding was in addition to the regular donations of official publications from the Malaysian government.

The current NLM director, Dr. Donald F. K. Wijasuriya, coincidentally, was Hwa-Wei's old acquaintance from back in Thailand. The director was thrilled knowing his friend had become the library director of Ohio University and would be working with him on the government book project. Thereafter, the two became more closely connected, and the library's Malaysian collection was greatly enhanced in both quantity and quality.

Hwa-Wei's talent for strategic planning was starting to shine; the collections were steadily growing. He decided to broaden the range of his enhancement strategy. He proposed to establish a Malaysia Information Resource Center at Alden Library on the strength of the library's existing Malaysian collection, hoping that through this center the library could serve as a resource to publicize and promote Malaysia in the United States through its unique information resources. Meanwhile, the library could revitalize its Malaysian collection by providing scholarly services to researchers and others who were interested in Malaysia.

The success of the Malaysia Information Resource Center owed largely to Hwa-Wei's extraordinary vision, which put a strong emphasis on developing relationships with foreign governments and national libraries in order to expand the OHIO Libraries' international collections.

Since the Center for International Studies at OHIO has three main programs —Southeast Asian, African, and Latin American Studies—Hwa-Wei was able to use the Malaysian model in establishing similar national information resource centers for two African countries, Botswana and the Kingdom of Swaziland; and one Latin American country, Guatemala. Under an authorized agreement with each of the governments, Alden Library was able to become the official depository of publications of these countries through their national libraries. This win-win model for international cooperation, deployed by Hwa-Wei, was the first of its kind among American academic libraries. It not only greatly expanded the library's international collections in both size and quality, but the cooperation also boosted the reputation of Alden Library's international resources.

The rapid expansion of the international collections at Alden Library, which included the addition of many donated rare artifacts from Southeast Asia, was due largely to the addition of Dr. You-Bao Shao's collection of resources on overseas Chinese in Southeast Asia, and the establishment of the Chubu University Commemorative Japanese Collection, developed with annual donations from that university. In a short period of time the international collections required an extension of their physical space. Originally housed in a quarter of the first floor in Alden Library, those collections expanded to occupy nearly the entire floor, turning that floor into the most exotic place in the library. At the time of Hwa-Wei's retirement in 1999, Ohio University named the first floor of Alden Library the "Hwa-Wei Lee Center for International Collections" in recognition of his contributions.

During the time the OHIO Libraries were striving to attain ARL membership, the university went through two presidents: Dr. Charles J. Ping and Dr. Robert Glidden. Both men were highly committed to the established goals, attached great importance to the library, and provided it with strong support to ensure the steady growth of its collections.

When Hwa-Wei took the post in 1978, there were 700,000 volumes of books, 600,000 reels of microfilms, 5,500 titles of current serials, 260,000 pieces of varied resources—and a collection budget of $620,000 dollars. Under his persistent efforts, however, at the time of Hwa-Wei's retirement in 1999, the numbers had increased to: 2,230,000 books, a greater than 300 percent increase; 2,960,000 microfilms, a 500 percent increase; close to 20,000 current serial titles, a 400 percent increase; and $3,983,221 for the collection budget, a greater than 600 percent increase.

In 1995, Alden Library successfully earned an ARL membership with a rank of seventy-third. It was listed as a significant accomplishment in Ohio University's 1995 yearbook. If ARL had not imposed a three-year freeze on accepting new library members, the Libraries could have become an ARL member in 1992 or 1993 as originally planned.

2

Another important achievement for Hwa-Wei was his effort in bringing library automation to Alden Library. Because of his knowledge and expertise in computer applications for library operations and service, Hwa-Wei began to investigate the possibility of acquiring an integrated library automation system for the library in 1979.

The state of Ohio has been well known for its pioneering effort in library automation and networking in the United States. The best known case is the establishment of the Ohio College Library Center (OCLC) in 1967, which was soon expanded into a national as well as an international Online Computer Library Center (retaining the original initials OCLC but with a worldwide coverage in library membership).

As early as 1965, a computer-assisted cataloging system had been established at the Library of Congress (LC), then regarded as a sign of unprecedented progress and a remarkable milestone in library automation. The new system was actually intended to employ a standardized Machine Readable Cataloging (MARC) format to computerize cataloging of library materials.

The state of Ohio was the first in the United States to respond to this innovative approach by taking collaborative action to utilize the benefit of MARC. At their regular quarterly meetings, library directors from thirteen state universities made a joint decision to adopt the Library of Congress's MARC standard and to establish the Ohio Computer Library Center (OCLC) in 1967. The decision was supported unanimously by the presidents and provosts of those universities.

Frederick G. Kilgour, a library automation expert from Yale University, was hired as the founding president to lead the development of the first statewide

Hwa-Wei and his family entertained many international students in their home, including Yang Yang, the author of this biography, standing in the center of the photograph.

The Lee home often became a home-away-from-home for many international students and visiting scholars.

Dr. You-Bao Shao, a Hong Kong businessman and philanthropist, was honored for his contribution in the establishment of the You-Bao Shao Overseas Chinese Documentation and Research Center at Ohio University Libraries. Holding the plaque in his honor are (*left to right*): Daniel Shao, OHIO President Glidden, Dr. You-Bao Shao, Dean of Libraries Julia Zimmerman, Chancellor of the Ohio Board of Regents Roderick Chu, and Dr. Hwa-Wei Lee.

library computer and cooperative cataloging system. Through the system, each member library could utilize preloaded MARC records in cataloging provided by the Library of Congress so as to reduce duplication of efforts by each library. Member libraries could also upload their cataloging records to the online system developed by OCLC to form a union catalog in which both the cataloging records and library collections could be shared among member libraries. This system changed interlibrary loan (ILL) service from a manual operation to an online catalog of library collections, resulting in a great improvement in the sharing of resources and in a faster ILL service.

The great success of OCLC's catalog and resource-sharing network soon attracted libraries in many other states and nations. Within ten years, OCLC had become a global library network, and its membership extended to include libraries of other types and varying sizes, archives, and museums. The annual report of OCLC in 2011 showed the number of member libraries, archives, and museums had grown to 23,815 covering some 110 countries. The OCLC online catalog—later named WorldCat—comprised approximately 2 billion items including 151 million books, 7.4 million serials, 4.8 million visual items, 5.3 million sound recordings, 2.9 million maps, and 4.4 million musical scores.

Hwa-Wei was very interested in the development of OCLC while he was working at the Asian Institute of Technology in Thailand. He visited the center each time during his home leaves between 1970 and 1975. In 1979, the second year of his tenure at Ohio University, Hwa-Wei submitted a proposal to acquire an integrated library automation system that would enable Alden Library to draw greater benefits from OCLC's online catalog and to expand its usefulness to other parts of library services such as automated acquisitions, cataloging, serial records, circulation, public access catalog, ILL, and reference services.

The proposal was supported and funded by the university. After public bidding, selection, and installation of the initial system were completed, the Virginia Tech Library System (VTLS), was acquired and put into operation in 1981. As one of OCLC's founding members, Alden Library has contributed numerous MARC records to the system. In fact, on August 26, 2011, the fortieth anniversary of the start of WorldCat, Ohio University Libraries was recognized as the library that inputted the very first MARC online cataloging record to OCLC. Alden Library had cataloged a total of 133 books online on August 26, 1971, the first day of OCLC's network operation.

Furthering their reputation as a leader in library automation, the thirteen state university libraries decided again in 1989 to establish a statewide library network named the Ohio Library and Information Network (OhioLINK). The reason for forming OhioLINK was to more effectively share library resources among all college and university libraries in the state of Ohio. Hwa-Wei was one of its initiators.

OhioLINK was intended to forge a connection among some eighty college and university libraries in Ohio, both public and private, through sharing their library collections, including microform and audiovisual materials, so that faculty and students from those colleges could utilize shared resources from peer institutions in a timely fashion—usually within forty-eight hours of the online lending request being sent. In addition, with state government subsidies, a consortium was formed to acquire electronic databases, e-books, and multimedia resources jointly, proving a great saving to individual libraries, especially to the smaller ones. Also, at OhioLINK, distributed databases were centralized and stored in the state supercomputer system for easy access.

The mission statement of OhioLINK reads as follows:

> OhioLINK creates a competitive advantage for Ohio's higher education community by cooperatively and cost-effectively acquiring, providing access to, and preserving an expanding array of print and digital scholarly resources; by efficiently sharing the collections of member libraries; and by centrally hosting digital content to advance teaching, learning, research, and the growth of Ohio's knowledge-based economy.

OhioLINK soon became a model followed by other states. It is worth noting that the concept of OCLC and OhioLINK was adopted in the early development of the China Academic Library and Information System (CALIS). This was due to Hwa-Wei, who introduced the concept to China through his frequent consulting trips and lectures.

3

Another innovative achievement of Hwa-Wei was his effort for OHIO Libraries to serve as a resource library for the public libraries of ten Southeast Ohio counties, which had organized a regional library consortium with the name of Ohio Valley Area Libraries (OVAL).

This region of Southeast Ohio had been known for its coal mines, but because of pollution and the competition of low-cost gasoline products, most of the coal mines had closed, leaving the region poverty stricken. As a result, public libraries in the region also suffered from the lack of adequate tax revenue to support their basic operation.

In working with the State Library of Ohio, Hwa-Wei was able to work out a contractual agreement with OVAL to provide reference, interlibrary loan, and staff training for the OVAL members. Under this contract, Ohio University Libraries was reimbursed annually by federal funds. In 1998–99, the last year of the contract, the annual reimbursement was $45,000.

Through the outstanding effort of Ms. Karen William, a dedicated reference librarian from OHIO Libraries who was assigned as the OVAL librarian, the services provided to the OVAL members were rated most satisfactory, each and every year, by library directors at all OVAL branches.

Being a strong proponent of library development in the state of Ohio, Hwa-Wei was very active in the Ohio Library Association (later named Ohio Library Council in the 1990s) and served on its board as well as on several committees. In 1987, he was named the Ohio Librarian of the Year. When he retired from Ohio University in 1999, Hwa-Wei was recognized as a Hall of Fame Librarian.

4

Beginning with President Ping's tenure in 1975, Ohio University experienced a new wave of growth and expansion. This was reflected in the library, too, since Hwa-Wei became the library director in 1978. Under the guidance and support of President Ping and Provost Bucklew, Hwa-Wei was able to make dramatic changes on many fronts, successfully placing Alden Library at the center of learning and research on campus. As the first Chinese American library director of a major university, Hwa-Wei broke through the glass ceiling that had often prevented people of Asian American heritage to reach the top in their professional careers. In recognition of Hwa-Wei's outstanding accomplishments as the library director, his official title was changed to dean of Libraries at Ohio University in 1991.

Because of his reputation in the library world, Hwa-Wei was invited to serve as a library consultant in many international projects. In August 1991, he traveled—upon invitation from the Asia Foundation—to Papua New Guinea to help the Commission of Higher Education and the Library Council of Papua New Guinea in designing a nationwide program titled "Library Development, Resource Sharing and Networking among Higher Education Institutions in Papua New Guinea."

Located in the southwestern Pacific region, the country of the Independent State of Papua New Guinea occupies over six hundred islands with a population of 6.3 million and a complex racial composition including people of Melanesian, Papuan, Micronesian, Polynesian, Chinese, and Caucasian descent. There are more than eight hundred different local dialects. A young country, only independent since 1975, Papua New Guinea had kept the customs of headhunting and cannibalism until the nineteenth century.

Port Moresby, the capital, had a very bad reputation for public safety, despite its natural advantage of being located on a hillside facing the sea with a beautiful and pleasant view. Prior to his trip, Hwa-Wei was told that the local sponsor had already arranged for a bodyguard to protect his safety throughout the trip. This made Hwa-Wei and Mary nervous, for the need of a bodyguard could be an indicator of extreme danger. As soon as he stepped off the plane, Hwa-Wei was greeted by a tall, dark-skinned man, with extraordinarily bright eyes and teeth. The man threw a quick smile and a nod at the visitor, then resumed a stern, silent demeanor. From his swift action and reaction, Hwa-Wei guessed that this man had a professional military background.

In the days that followed, the bodyguard carried out his duty with integrity, accompanying Hwa-Wei everywhere with a high level of alertness. Because of its rugged topography, the result of frequent earthquakes, tsunamis, and volcanic eruptions, Papua New Guinea had an underdeveloped road system, which meant traveling between major cities and outer islands relied heavily on small aircraft.

Just as if he were a Hollywood star, Hwa-Wei kept changing transportation carriers, accompanied by a tough bodyguard. Throughout his visit to seven cities and forty-one libraries in three weeks, he obtained a large amount of firsthand information. Based upon the trip and the information he gathered, he wrote a final report and recommendation, which was published by the Commission on Higher Education in Papua New Guinea in December 1991.[1]

His 1989 trip to the Philippines proved more dangerous. Invited by the Canadian International Development Research Centre (IDRC) to assess the Renewable Energy Information Center, which received grant funding from IDRC, Hwa-Wei arrived in Manila at noon on Sunday, November 31, checking into the Hotel Nikko Manila. After taking a short walk in a crowded downtown business district near the hotel, he suddenly heard shots ring out; pedestrians began screaming and running around in panic. "A military coup!" someone shouted. With no other place to flee, he rushed back to the hotel, the last place he should have gone to, as it had already been taken over by the rebel soldiers, who were using it as their temporary headquarters.

Armed rebel soldiers ordered all guests to return to their rooms at once. Hwa-Wei had no choice but to obey. After sunset, the gunfire became more intense, joined by huge explosions throughout the night. Over the hotel loudspeaker came an announcement from the rebels asking everyone to remain in their rooms and to stay away from the windows while waiting for room-service delivery of drinks and simple meals. All room communication channels had been cut off. The only two sources of information were the rebels' broadcasts and the room-service attendants. Even though he was aware of the local eco-

---

1. Hwa-Wei Lee, *Library Development, Resource Sharing, and Networking among Higher Education Institutions in Papua New Guinea: Final Report and Recommendations* (Port Moresby, Papua New Guinea: Commission for Higher Education, December 1991), 48 pgs. In the *Collected Works of Hwa-Wei Lee*, vol.1, (Guangzhou: Sun Yat-Sen University Press, 2011), 446–76.

Chapter 12

nomic recession, political unrest, and military coups that had taken place in the Philippines in the earlier half of the twentieth century, Hwa-Wei did not anticipate becoming a hostage in that country.

The coup had been launched by more than three hundred soldiers loyal to former President Ferdinand Marcos. Since the early morning of December 1, these soldiers had held control of the two television stations and four airbases—Villamor Airbase, Fort Bonifacio, Sangley Airbase, Mactan Airbase in Cebu—battling over a fifth, Camp Aguinaldo. Aiming to overthrow the reign of President Corazon Aquino, the rebels headed directly to the presidential palace with fierce offensive attacks.

President Aquino turned to the United States for help. The U.S. Air Force in the Philippines quickly dispatched F-4 Phantom fighter jets that circled over Manila. The hovering U.S. aircraft, without a single gunshot, assisted the Aquino government in regaining air supremacy and reversing the unfavorable situation. The rebels were resentful of the Americans and started to yell through the hotel broadcasting system, threatening to kill all American hostages as a revenge for U.S. involvement. Fortunately, the Canadian embassy in Manila had told the hotel to list Hwa-Wei as a Canadian.

Hwa-Wei felt a jolt of nervousness as the fear of war, forgotten after so many years, reoccupied his mind. At that moment, he worried most about Mary and their children, not knowing that the Canadian embassy in Manila had, during his five days of captivity, kept in daily contact with Mary, updating her concerning the situation in the Philippines. Luckily, the rebels finally surrendered to the government on December 5, after five days of the insurgency, and released all hostages. Watching CNN live news, Mary saw Hwa-Wei walk out of the hotel to line up with the others; she felt great joy and eternal gratitude to the Canadian government.

The Philippine government arranged for special buses to transport all foreign hostages to the Manila airport for departure. Thinking his mission was still undone, Hwa-Wei returned to Metro Manila and tried to check in at another hotel only to be delayed because of a bomb threat there. On the second day, the staff of the National Renewable Energy Information Center cried out with surprise when they saw Hwa-Wei enter the center. Remaining calm and composed as if nothing had ever happened to him, Hwa-Wei told them he was just fine. His courage and professionalism impressed everyone.

5

In searching for ways to further strengthen the Southeast Asian Collection of Ohio University Libraries, Hwa-Wei noticed the collection's inadequate coverage of the overseas Chinese in Southeast Asia. During his seven years of work in Thailand with frequent travel throughout Southeast Asia, Hwa-Wei had become aware of the important contributions made by overseas Chinese in most of the Southeast Asian countries. In the 1980s, there were very few libraries that were dedicated to the collection of overseas Chinese materials. Hwa-Wei saw an opportunity to build an overseas Chinese collection within the Southeast Asian Collection at Ohio University.

Hwa-Wei managed to establish the Dr. You-Bao Shao Overseas Chinese Documentation and Research Center as a part of the Southeast Asian Collection with a sizable donation from Dr. You-Bao Shao, a banker, businessman, civic leader, and philanthropist in Hong Kong.

Dr. Shao had served on the Consultative Committee in the drafting of the Hong Kong Basic Law and had participated in the Sino-British negotiations during the return of Hong Kong from British rule to China as a special administrative region under Chinese sovereignty on July 1, 1997.

After the transfer, Dr. Shao served as an advisor to the Hong Kong and Macao Affairs Office of the State Council of the People's Republic of China and the Hong Kong office of Xinhua News Agency. When the new Hong Kong airport was planned, Dr. Shao served as a member of the Consultative Committee on the new airport and related projects and was the convener of its financial and monetary team. Another of his civic involvements was serving as one of the board directors for the One Country Two Systems Research Institute.

Hwa-Wei knew Dr. You-Bao Shao through his son, Dr. Daniel Kung-Chuen Shao, an OHIO alumnus serving as a board director of The Ohio University Foundation, who had helped in organizing Ohio University alumni chapters in Hong Kong, Japan, Korea, and Taiwan. Both father and son were most generous with their time and financial support to Ohio University; both were awarded honorary doctoral degrees by the university in 1993 and 1998, respectively, for their outstanding public service and philanthropic activities.

Since its founding in 1993, the Shao Center has devoted great effort to collecting current and past publications as well as historical documents about overseas Chinese in Southeast Asia including government documents, private manuscripts, genealogies, inscriptions, and oral recordings. In addition, the center has also created online databases for information relating to the studies of overseas Chinese and other connected topics.

As an integral part of its mission, every three years the Shao Center also convenes an international conference of institutes and libraries for overseas Chinese studies. The first conference was held at Ohio University in 2000. It was at that conference that participating institutes and libraries for overseas Chinese studies decided to establish the World Confederation of Institutes and Libraries for Chinese Overseas Studies (WCILCOS) with headquarters at the Ohio University Libraries.

Since the inaugural conference in Athens, Ohio, four more conferences have been held thus far: The second one, in partnership with the Chinese University of Hong Kong, was held in Hong Kong in 2003. In 2005, a third conference, in partnership with thirteen institutions in Singapore, including the Chinese Heritage Center and the National University of Singapore, was held in Singapore. The fourth conference was held in partnership with Jinan University in Guangzhou, China, in 2009. In partnership with the University of British Columbia, a fifth conference was held in Vancouver, Canada, in 2012.

The significance of the Dr. You-Bao Shao Overseas Chinese Documentation and Research Center is clearly reflected in the following objectives of the Third International Conference of Institutes and Libraries for Chinese Overseas Studies:

> Chinese overseas migration began many centuries ago. In the long process, Chinese contacts were established with the vast maritime world in Asia. This development in turn ushered in the world of maritime Chinese, which spread from the Asia-Pacific to the Indian Ocean littoral.
>
> The Third International Conference of Institutes and Libraries for Chinese Overseas Studies with the theme "Maritime Asia and the Chinese Overseas" (1405–2005) coincides with the six-hundredth anniversary of Admiral Zheng He's first of seven voyages to the South Seas and the Indian Ocean. The Zheng He expeditions in the early fifteenth century contributed to the development of the Asian maritime world, of which the Chinese diaspora was a key Asian component. The Europeans subsequently entered this maritime world and participated in its trade activities. All these developments contributed to many important aspects of interaction among the Asians themselves, including the Chinese, and between the Asians and the Europeans. There emerged, as a result, the convergence and mutual adaptations of the various civilizations.
>
> The primary objective of the Third International Conference of Institutes and Libraries for Chinese Overseas Studies is to explore the long process of these interactions and the role played by the Chinese overseas. It will trace both the early and modern developments in the various aspects. The geographical areas, which the conference will cover, include the Asia-Pacific, Southeast Asia, Australia, New Zealand, India, the Middle East, and East Africa.

Hwa-Wei, even after his retirement, was invited by Ohio University to personally be involved in the planning of all of these conferences. He, subsequently, was elected deputy chair and the chair of WCILCOS at the fourth and fifth conferences, respectively.

Library Cooperation between China
and the United States

> I am told this is on a classroom wall in Athens' East Elementary School:
>> We must study geography so that for us
>> There is no foreign place.
>> We must study humanity so that for us
>> There is no foreign person.
>
> The commitment of Ohio University described in the Educational Plan
> is "to international community, to education for interdependence."[1]
>
> —*Dr. Charles J. Ping, eighteenth president of Ohio University*

1

IN THE early summer of 1979, the city of Athens and Ohio University welcomed a group of special guests. It was the first high-level delegation of Chinese university officials led by Peiyuan Zhou, a renowned physicist and the president of Peking University, and accompanied by Peisong Tang, a famous botanist. The two scientists had received their educations in the United States in the early twentieth century and had been "re-educated" at "niu-peng" (cattle depot) during the Great Proletarian Cultural Revolution from 1966 to 1976.[2]

When this question was posed to Tang, "What could a scientist in this dormant period [be] do[ing]?" Tang answered, "Waiting for the germination."[3] The group's visit was a follow-up to the U.S. visit by the new Chinese leader, Xiaoping Deng, in early 1979.

The mission of the visit was to initiate programs for an educational exchange with American institutions of higher learning in the post-Mao era. The univer-

---

1. Charles J Ping, "International Education at Ohio University: The Search for International Community and Education for Interdependence," *Ohio University in Perspective: The Annual Convocation Addresses of President Charles J. Ping, 1975–1984* (Athens: Ohio University Press, 1985), 130.

2. "Niu-peng" refers to a type of jail-like places where, during the Cultural Revolution, a large number of so-called "rightists" were tortured and forced to perform hard labor in order to be re-educated.

3. Stacey Bieler, *A History of American-Educated Chinese Students*, trans. Yan Zhang (Hong Kong: The Joint Publishing, 2010), 408–9.

sities the group visited included Stanford University and UC Berkeley on the West Coast; the University of Illinois and Ohio University in the Midwest; and a few other well-known universities on the East Coast.

The Chinese delegation's visit to Ohio University was big news. It was hard for Americans to understand why the Chinese government had chosen a university in such a rural area. Later, they learned that the selection was made based upon an investigation conducted by the Chinese Embassy in Washington, D.C. Its finding stated that college towns with a relatively rural environment, like Athens, Ohio, would be more suitable for government-funded students, allowing them to concentrate on their academic work, in comparison to universities situated in large cities.

During his second year, Hwa-Wei and Henry Lin, the dean of the College of Fine Arts, were chosen as members of the welcoming team. Both men were representative of the Chinese faculty members on campus; both also held high administrative positions. Hwa-Wei was thrilled. He had a hunch from his time in Thailand that China would eventually open up to the West in the post-Mao period and begin to change its course of modernization.

Before long, the first group of twenty government-sponsored Chinese students arrived at Ohio University and entered the colleges of arts, science, and engineering. Since then, numerous Chinese students have come to OHIO, perhaps owing to President Charles Ping and his favorable policies for international education.

Since the establishment of an educational exchange program between the two nations in 1979, the number of Chinese students enrolled at Ohio University has grown rapidly. Nationwide statistics showed that over 100,000 Chinese students came to the United States for the purpose of education and research from 1979 to 1990 including 60,967 state-funded students and visiting scholars, and 41,501 self-supported students. The Chinese student population from that ten-year period was more than twice as many as the total population from the previous one hundred years, from 1860 to 1950 (approximately 30,000 students).[4]

With the continuing improvement of diplomatic relations between China and the United States, the number of programs for educational exchanges also increased. After Hwa-Wei left China in 1949, he didn't have an opportunity to visit mainland China until he was invited as a library consultant in December 1982, a span of thirty-three years. That trip was for a two-week workshop, Management of Scientific and Technical Information Centers, held in Kunming and co-organized by the International Development Research Centre of Canada (IDRC) and the Institute of Scientific and Technical Information of China

---

4. Nin Gu, "The culture exchange between China and U.S. from 1979 to 1992—A review and thoughts," *World History*, 1995, no. 3.

(ISTIC). The workshop attendees were directors of scientific and technical information centers at national and provincial levels. Hwa-Wei was one of the two overseas Chinese experts invited by IDRC. The other expert was Dr. T. C. Ting, chair of computer science at Worcester Polytechnic Institute.[5]

Kunming in the 1980s was an older city. Its streets had essentially no automobiles except for a few military jeeps. The popular transportation was bicycles. Pedestrians could walk in the center of the streets without having to worry about blocking traffic. Its citizens led a simple, frugal life. Their clothes were mostly black, blue, and gray in color. International visitors had to use foreign exchange certificates (Wai hui quan) for commodity purchases.

Among the workshop attendees were high-ranking officers from national, ministerial, and provincial scientific and technical information centers. Hwa-Wei was able to make friends with many of them including the director of Fujian Institute of Scientific and Technical Information. Learning that Hwa-Wei was originally from Fuzhou of Fujian Province, the director asked whether he still had any relatives in his hometown, and, if so, whether he would like to go back for a visit. Upon hearing the name of Hwa-Wei's aunt and her home address in Fuzhou, the director grew excited, banged his fist on the table, and said, with emotion, "What a coincidence! I know your aunt! I know her well!"

His story began with a tragic incident involving Hwa-Wei's uncle, Dr. Tiao-Hsin Wang, a renowned chemist. Hwa-Wei remembered Tiao-Hsin as an easygoing, loving, and venerable scholar. Tiao-Hsin had received his college education from Fujian Christian University, then later earned his doctorate from Cornell. Being a patriot, Tiao-Hsin was excited at the time of the founding of the People's Republic of China (PRC) in 1949 and gave up his chance to stay and work in the U.S., instead returning immediately to mainland China. He was among the earliest group of Chinese studying or working abroad to return home at that time.

Back in China, Tiao-Hsin served in several positions including department head, dean, and acting president of Fujian Christian University, and as the board director of the Chinese Chemical Society. However, his religious background and education abroad doomed him to suffer during the Great Proletarian Cultural Revolution.

It was rumored that the Red Guards found a radio during the ransacking of his home. To them, a radio was evidence that he was a foreign spy. With that

---

5. Hwa-Wei Lee, M. Beckman, and Jianyan Huang, "Management of Scientific and Technical Information Centres: Aspects of Planning a Course Sponsored by IDRC (Canada) and ISTIC (China)" (paper presented at the International Federation for Information and Documentation (FID) Pre-Congress Workshop on Curriculum Development in a Changing World, The Hague, September 3–4, 1984), 19. In the *Collected Works of Hwa-Wei Lee*, vol. 2 (Guangzhou: Sun Yat-Sen University Press, 2011), 650–57.

accusation, he was denounced, beaten, and physically tortured. As a result of the torture, he suffered a stroke and was partially paralyzed. He passed away two years later.

The late wife of the director was a graduate student of Tiao-Hsin, who felt indignant after seeing the brutal treatment of Tiao-Hsin by the Red Guards, and spoke out for her academic advisor. She just wanted to tell the Red Guards that her professor, Tiao-Hsin, could never be the type of person that they accused him of being. Nevertheless, her message was not fully heard because the irrational Red Guards threw her from a second-floor window, killing her instantly. The director himself also suffered from the Cultural Revolution and was sent to the countryside for re-education. He was not even able to recover the body of his wife to have her buried.

The madness and inhumane behavior of the Red Guards may sound harsh to today's society. Ugliness, bigotry, and cruelty against other human beings were out of control, surging just like apocalyptic floods. Any personal pains, no matter how tragic and desperate they might be, were endured in silence. Fortunately, the director did survive the disastrous Cultural Revolution even after being sent to the countryside for re-education.

After the Kunming workshop, Hwa-Wei paid a visit to Fuzhou and Beijing to establish contacts with libraries in both places including Fujian Normal University (the former Fujian Christian University), the National Library of China (NLC), Peking University, and Tsinghua University.

His second trip to China in 1984 was at the invitation of ISTIC and many other university libraries. By then, Chinese universities and research centers were entering a new phase of development, and their libraries were eager to learn about new practices in western countries. Hwa-Wei was thus invited to give lectures and presentations at various universities including Peking, Tsinghua, Beijing Normal, Nankai, Wuhan, Xi'an Jiaotong Universities, and Beijing University of Posts and Telecommunications. Since then, Hwa-Wei has returned to China almost every year, lecturing as a visiting professor at more than a dozen universities and serving as a consultant at NLC, National Science Library of Chinese Academy of Sciences, Shanghai and Shenzhen Libraries, and Zhejiang Provincial Library.

Later, Hwa-Wei was also involved in a World Bank funded teachers' education and development program, which provided training to librarians from various teachers' colleges and universities across the nation. As the program was a partnership between the World Bank and the Chinese Ministry of Education (CME), Hwa-Wei's cooperation with mainland China expanded from the academic community to include the government. He made friends with Zheqian Dong, a bureau chief at CME in charge of the library administration of all colleges and universities in China. Dong was kind enough to accompany Hwa-Wei to a number of the training programs. Hwa-Wei's lectures covered a wide range of topics on modern library management and library automation. His lectures were eye-opening experiences to Chinese librarians.

2

As early as 1979, Hwa-Wei managed to establish an international librarian internship program at Alden Library with funding support from various sources including UNESCO; United Nations Development Programme; U.S. Agency for International Development; Asia Foundation; Yen-Ching Education Foundation; Lingnan Foundation; and Blackwell North America, Inc. The program was developed to train librarians from developing countries in Asia, Africa, and the Middle East. Groups of librarians from Taiwan National Central Library, Tamkang University, Feng Chia University, and Provincial Taichung Library came to Ohio University as library interns in the initial years of that program.

The Thai Royal Library presided over by Her Royal Highness Princess Maha Chakri Sirindhorn also sent two librarians to Ohio University for training. Princess Sirindhorn specifically met with Hwa-Wei in the grand palace in 2002, during his visit to Chiang Mai University as a Fulbright senior specialist, to express her appreciation.

Through his frequent trips to mainland China, Hwa-Wei perceived the importance of Chinese librarians acquiring new knowledge and experiences by visiting other libraries, attending seminars and workshops, and participating in international library internships and conferences. To make this education more readily available to these librarians, Ohio University's International Librarians Internship Program began accepting a growing number of library trainees from China. Statistics showed that, in the fourteen years between 1985 and 1999, as many as 150 Chinese librarians completed their library internship at OHIO Libraries. They came from the National Library, and from major academic, special, and public libraries in many parts of China.

While Hwa-Wei was still in Thailand, he met Ms. Sizhuang Liang, deputy library director of Peking University, at the IFLA annual conference in Manila, Philippines. Ms. Liang is the daughter of Qichao Liang, a well-known Chinese scholar and reformer during the transition from the Qing dynasty to the founding of the new republic. In 1982, Hwa-Wei met Professor Shoujing Zhuang, director of Peking University Library, at the annual conference of IFLA in Montreal, Canada. The two soon became close friends.

Professor Zhuang, a visionary library leader and a pioneer in library reform, was strongly committed to library automation and modernization. After hearing

Thirty-three years after he left China in 1949, Hwa-Wei was invited back as a library consultant for a two-week workshop held in Kunming, December 1982.

In 1996, Hwa-Wei was the coordinator of planning for the first China-U.S. Library Conference held in Beijing, China.

Hwa-Wei was appointed a visiting professor at Nankai University in China.

that Alden Library had installed the first generation of a library automation system, Professor Zhuang arranged with Hwa-Wei to send, successively, two groups of ten library staff, five each year, to OHIO to receive training. After many years of effort, Professor Zhuang transformed Peking University Library into a model library in China. Years later in the hands of his successors, Longji Dai and Qiang Zhu, the flagship library in China ultimately grew into a world-class library.

Around the same time, library directors and senior librarians from Tsinghua University, Beijing University of Posts and Telecommunications (BUPT), and other Chinese universities were visiting Alden Library, one after another. The visit from Tsinghua's library director Professor Guilin Liu and its automation department head, Ms. Shulan An, led to a close cooperation between their libraries and Ohio University Libraries. Ziwei Ma, the BUPT library director, wrote a book, *Library and Information Automation*, based upon his research at OHIO.

Similarly, Professor Weihan Diao from East China Normal University finished her book, *OCLC Compact Disk and Online Cataloging*, during her visit, and Ms. Ping Sun, a senior librarian from Tsinghua and a former visiting scholar at OHIO, compiled an important reference book, *English-Chinese Dictionary of Library and Information Science*.

In 1987, Hwa-Wei, in coordination with Professor Xinxia Lai, the library director and highly regarded historian of Nankai University in Tianjin, was able to arrange mutual visits between Chinese and American academic library directors. For two weeks, a group of university library directors from Ohio visited libraries in Tianjin, then a group of academic library directors from Tianjin visited libraries in Ohio for two weeks. These visits aroused the American library directors' interests in Chinese libraries and brought about a series of bilateral collaborative projects, an important chapter in the history of U.S.-Chinese librarianship.

During the 1980s, it was not easy for Chinese librarians to pursue education and training abroad. The International Librarians Internship Program at Ohio University was offered twice a year, with each session lasting three months. A session began with a week-long orientation covering library organization, administration, acquisitions, cataloging, technical processing, collection management, library service, and computer application.

After the general introduction, each intern was assigned to a library department based on his or her library position and specialization at home. According to the special needs of each intern, some would stay in one department for the remainder of the session, while others would rotate from one department to another. During the three months, field trips were also arranged for the interns to visit OCLC, OhioLINK, and other libraries.

The cost of the international travel for the library interns was covered by their home institutions; their living expenses in Athens were paid by Ohio University. In order to justify the payment from OHIO, each intern was required to work at least half of the time in their assigned department. Those interns who paid their own travel costs depended on Ohio University's funding to earn their living in Athens.

To make it possible for library interns to enter the United States, Hwa-Wei also worked closely with the Office of International Students and Faculty Services in issuing letters of invitation and sending the necessary application forms for a J-1 visa. Upon their arrival at the Columbus airport, about a two-hour drive from Athens, the interns would be met by either Hwa-Wei, driving his own vehicle to the airport to pick them up, or a student assistant whom he had arranged to meet them. For newly arrived library interns, this service was vitally necessary because there was no scheduled public transportation from the Columbus airport to Athens. A taxi would cost a minimum of one hundred dollars per trip, and the cost would double if an intern arrived late at night.

Prior to the interns' arrival in Athens, Hwa-Wei and his student assistant would try to find a suitable rental apartment for each of them. However, this was not always that easy, and many interns would stay at Hwa-Wei's home for a few days before settling into a new apartment. Hwa-Wei and Mary often purchased used bicycles, tables, chairs, and utensils from garage sales for use by the library interns, since their stays in Athens were only temporary.

In addition to obtaining the necessary funding for the internship program, Hwa-Wei and many of the library staff also provided valuable time and effort to ensure that each of the interns would receive the best possible training during their brief stay at Ohio University. Librarian interns who completed this program were deeply grateful to Hwa-Wei and his staff for the special care and attention each of them received.

In order to provide opportunities for more international librarian interns, especially those from China, Hwa-Wei raised $250,000 from his good friend Dr. Daniel Kung-Chuen Shao, the eldest son of Dr. You-Bao Shao. This generous endowment would generate enough interest to support five Chinese librarian interns each year for as long as the program lasted.

Dr. Daniel Shao studied at OHIO in the 1960s. Upon graduation, he returned to Hong Kong and engaged in trade and international business with China, Japan, and Southeast Asian countries—a family business operated by his father. Being a loyal OHIO alumnus, Daniel has been a generous donor for many Ohio University projects. It was through the financial support of his father, Dr. You-Bao Shao, that University Libraries was able to establish the You-Bao Shao Overseas

Among his many accomplishments at Ohio University were Hwa-Wei's collaborative agreements between OHIO Libraries and other international libraries. Here, such an agreement between Shenzhen Library, China, and Ohio University Libraries is celebrated in a signing ceremony.

Mary joins library directors from universities in Tianjin, China. Exchanged visits between Chinese library directors and their counterparts from state universities in Ohio were frequently arranged as part of Hwa-Wei's plan for global library cooperation.

In 2007, Hwa-Wei (*front, far left*) was a speaker at the Chinese Culture & Publishing Shanghai Forum.

Chinese Documentation and Research Center in 1994. It was regrettable that after the retirement of Hwa-Wei from Ohio University in 1999, the International Librarian Internship Program ended. With the consent of Dr. Daniel Shao, the remainder of his endowment was transferred to the endowment fund for the You-Bao Shao Center for Overseas Chinese Documentation and Research.

The library internship at OHIO was the first and the largest of its kind in the United States during the 1980s and the 1990s. According to the statistics compiled by Ms. Shuyan Wang, one of Hwa-Wei's graduate student assistants, the OHIO Libraries, from 1981 to 1999, provided nineteen training sessions with an enrollment of over 190 librarians, including 150 interns from China. Over twenty of the Chinese librarians were directly supported by Dr. Daniel Shao's library internship fund. It was a far-reaching training program, and many of the intern librarians from China later became leaders of Chinese libraries.[6]

Although a number of similar programs were offered by other American universities in the 1990s, those programs were somewhat limited and short-lived. Only recently have the number of new training programs begun to expand as the contacts and programs of academic exchange between the universities of the two countries have deepened. Comparable programs have been developed at the University of Illinois at Urbana-Champaign, Seton Hall University in New Jersey, and the University of Pittsburgh. In addition, Harvard-Yenching Library has also started to fund one or two visiting librarians from China each year.

The internship program at OHIO, renowned among Chinese librarians, played a critical role in the development of Chinese librarianship in the 1980s and 1990s. As most interns enrolled in the program were in middle- and high-level administrative positions in their home libraries, they were able to apply the new knowledge acquired in the United States about library operations and management to their daily work upon returning home.

Having suffered during World War II, the Chinese Civil War, and the destructive Cultural Revolution, libraries in China were in disarray. Collections had been destroyed, and many library staff had not been properly trained. In rebuilding, the modern operations and practices of American libraries became the model for Chinese libraries to follow. By the hard work of a few library leaders, combined with the strong support of the Chinese government, libraries of major universities, together with the National Library, Shanghai Library, the Institute of Scientific and Technical Information, the Chinese Academy of Sciences, and the Chinese Academy of Social Sciences, played a key role in modernizing their library operations and services, making remarkable progress within a short period of thirty years.

---

6. Ohio University Libraries, https://www.library.ohiou.edu.

That fast rate of growth among Chinese libraries, including the expansion of library and information science education, has enabled many Chinese libraries to quickly approach, or even surpass, library development in some of the more advanced countries in the world. In creating a bridge between China and the United States, Hwa-Wei has made remarkable contributions to the regeneration of modern library concepts and practices in China.

Among the library interns and visiting scholars at OHIO were librarians from the National Library of China (NLC); major public libraries such as Shanghai Library, Zhejiang Library, and Shenzhen Library; key universities such as Peking, Tsinghua, Nankai, Fudan, Jiaotong, and Wuhan; the Chinese Academy of Sciences; and the Institute of Scientific and Technical Information.

Heping Zhou, deputy director of NLC, who was later appointed as the director of NLC and then deputy minister of the Ministry of Culture, also paid a visit to Alden Library accompanied by Ms. Liping Sun, the director of NLC's International Liaison Department. With his rich administrative experience and eagerness to bring the National Library up to international standards, Zhou did a careful observation of the library management system and asked questions about the latest developments during his week-long visit at Ohio University. Later, he also visited the Library of Congress and several other major libraries in the United States. He once commented that his trip to the U.S., especially his time at Alden Library, had inspired and benefited him a great deal.

3

The inspiration behind the first China-U.S. Library Conference came from studying the success of a similar bilateral library conference, the U.S.-Japan Library Conference, held at regular intervals for many years. Hwa-Wei felt the same model should be applied to strengthen the increased library cooperation between the Chinese libraries and the American libraries.

By then, Hwa-Wei had accumulated substantial experience in planning and organizing international conferences including "Library Development and Cooperation in the Asian Pacific Region," held in the U.S. in 1983; "New Technologies in Libraries," co-sponsored by Ohio University Libraries and Xi'an Jiaotong University Library in 1988; "Information Technologies and Services," held in Shanghai in 1994; and "Information Resources and Social Development," held at Wuhan University in 1996.

In order to achieve the maximum visibility for and, thereby, ensure a positive result of the first China-U.S. Library Conference, Hwa-Wei decided to contact library leaders from the U.S. National Commission on Libraries and Information Science, Library of Congress, American Library Association, Association of Research Libraries, and Chinese American Librarians Association to form a U.S. organizing committee. Being the only Chinese American on the committee, Hwa-Wei was responsible for the liaison work between the U.S. organizing committee and its Chinese counterpart.

In order to enable more top American library leaders to participate, Hwa-Wei scheduled the first conference to be held just a few days before the Sixty-second IFLA General Conference which was to convene in China in August 1996. (This was the first time an IFLA conference was held in that country.) The close proximity of the dates made it possible for high-level American delegates to attend both conferences in one trip. Members of the original U.S. organizing committee were Michael Dowling, Hwa-Wei Lee, Beverly P. Lynch, James G. Neal, Isabel Stiring, Gary Strong, Winston Tabb, and Peter R. Young, with Dr. Lynch serving as the committee chair for the first four conferences.

Hwa-Wei's counterpart in China was Heping Zhou, the NLC's director. Zhou knew Hwa-Wei well and was very supportive of the idea of organizing the first bilateral conference. With the endorsement of the Ministry of Culture, the Chinese organizing committee was formed and included several prominent Chinese library leaders such as Ke Du of the Ministry of Culture, and Heping Zhou, Beixin Sun, and Chengjian Sun of the National Library of China.

Conference cost was a key issue for Hwa-Wei. It was imperative to seek funding to cover the cost of local accommodations and lodgings for all attendees, international airfare for some American representatives, and rent of the conference venue, as well as other expenses. Being the key organizer of the conference, Hwa-Wei's role also included this fundraising. After investing a great amount of time, he was able to raise over $15,000 from the U.S. National Commission on Libraries and Information Science; the Council on Library Resources and Commission on Preservation and Access; OCLC; and a number of library companies including Blackwell North America, Inc.; Congressional Information Services, Inc.; EBSCO Subscription Services, Inc.; Innovative Interfaces, Inc.; and Silver Platter Information, Inc.

Prior to the conference, the two sides worked harmoniously to select its theme, "Global Information Access: Challenges and Opportunities," and two keynote speakers, one from each side. The theme was then broken down into a series of topics; again two experts, one from each side, were assigned to lead topic discussions. Each side sent forty participants. Five of the CALA members also served as interpreters: Mia Wang Bassham, Susana Juh-Mei Liu, Amy D. Seetoo, Angela Man-Lin Yang, and Shali Zhang.

The conference was held at NLC in Beijing, located near White Stone Bridge in the west suburb area of Beijing and next to the Purple Bamboo Park. The nineteen-story twin tower building of NLC, built in 1987, was considered one of the "Beijing Top Ten Buildings in the 1980s." Built with white walls and black roof tiles, it is filled with architectural elements of the Han and Tang dynasties.

The joint conference went smoothly, a result of the careful planning and close coordination. Nearly one hundred library leaders from both countries actively joined discussions around the conference's theme. Proving a success, the conference and its highlights became part of Sino-U.S. cultural-exchange history, representing a milestone of library cooperation between the two nations. Chinese media reported the following:

> One hundred thirty years after the Chinese government donated one thousand volumes of rare books to the Library of Congress of America in 1869, nearly one hundred library directors, specialists, and scholars from the two nations finally stood side by side on the doorsteps of the National Library of China to celebrate that historic event."
>
> Mr. Winston Tabb, associate librarian of the Library of Congress commented, "not only has the event strengthened bilateral professional cooperation, it also has enhanced mutual understanding among people of the two nations."
>
> Ms. Beixin Sun, an admirable lady and deputy director of NLC who had worked some forty years in the library, was deeply impressed by the refreshing library management concepts [that] she had learned from American counterparts during the conference. She highly praised Hwa-Wei for all his efforts.[7]

Shortly after the inaugural conference, Hwa-Wei started to plan the second conference, scheduled to be held at the Queens Library in New York and the Library of Congress in Washington, D.C., immediately prior to the 2001 IFLA Annual Conference in Boston. The success of the second conference was a credit to Gary Strong, director of the Queens Library, and Winston Tabb, associate librarian of the Library of Congress. Since then, every three or four years, library professionals from both countries gather together either in China or in the U.S.

The third conference was held in Shanghai and was hosted by the Shanghai Library under the leadership of Dr. Jianzhong Wu, director of Shanghai Library. The fourth conference was held in Dublin, Ohio, and was hosted by OCLC under the leadership of Jay Jordan, president and CEO of OCLC. In its fifth meeting the conference returned to NLC in Beijing in September 2010. Dr. Deanna Marcum, associate librarian of Congress, assumed the leadership role of the U.S. organizing committee. All these conferences resulted in improved communica-

---

7. Hong Lu, "The role of knowledge managers in the 21st century—Special interview of Dr. Hwa-Wei Lee, Chief of Asian Division, Library of Congress," *Silicon Valley Times*, July 20, 2003.

Chapter 13

tion, better understanding, and closer cooperation among libraries and library professionals in China and the U.S.

The fourth joint conference hosted by OCLC in the U.S. contributed to an official collaboration among Chinese and American libraries known as the China-U.S. Librarian Collaboration Project, jointly sponsored by the U.S. government's Institute of Museum and Library Services (IMLS) and China's Ministry of Culture (MOC). The project was officially launched in 2008 with an agreement signed by IMLS and MOC at the Library of Congress.

In the U.S., IMLS awarded the project to the libraries of the University of Illinois at Urbana-Champaign (UIUC), which acted as its chief administrative agency; UIUC was joined by the Chinese American Librarians Association (CALA) as the project partner. The Chinese administrative agency was the Library Society of China under the direct supervision of MOC.

Hwa-Wei, having already retired from the Library of Congress, was contracted by UIUC to be the project evaluator. The project was designed to send teams of American library specialists to conduct advanced library seminars in various provinces and autonomous administrative regions in China, to invite Chinese library leaders to the U.S. for visits, and to help Chinese libraries in making their digital resources available online to American libraries and researchers. As stated in the final report of this highly successful project:[8]

> Building on a June 2007 cultural accord, on November 16, 2008, the Institute of Museum and Library Services (IMLS), along with the National Endowment for the Arts (NEA) and the President's Committee on Arts and Culture (PCAH) entered into a Partnership for Cultural Exchange with the Ministry of Culture of the People's Republic of China to strengthen cultural cooperation between the two countries. A major portion of this agreement concerned libraries and museum professionals in both the United States and the People's Republic. The agreement calls for sharing best practices in library services, including enhancement of public service and access to information in libraries, promotion of youth engagement, and applications of new technologies in libraries and museums to engage audiences and increase the availability of information online.
>
> Under the auspices of the Laura Bush Twenty-first Century Librarian Program, IMLS funded the University of Illinois at Urbana-Champaign Library, in partnership with the Library Society of China and the Chinese American Library Association, to develop a partnership between librarians in the U.S. and China to enhance communication and relations between U.S. and Chinese librarians and to enrich the variety of information and services

---

8. *A Partnership to Enhance Communication and Relations between Libraries in the U.S. and China, September 1, 2008–August 31, 2012. Final Report*, (final project report), UIUC 032613.pdf.

that U.S. librarians can offer their users. This is the first government cooperation project between the library community in China and the United States. The project is providing workshops for Chinese librarians and library educators, in both the U.S. and China, on American practices in library public services. Conversely, U.S. librarians are learning about Chinese resources that can be made available online. The project has developed a Web-based portal at www.library.illinois.edu/China.

The grant-supported professional development activities have occurred both in the United States and in China. More than thirty U.S. experts in library management and services, language materials, and digital libraries traveled to China to present twenty seminars of three days each in duration, and some forty-three leading Chinese librarians visited the United States to attend professional conferences, special continuing education events, and to visit a wide range of American libraries. As of August 31, 2012, the project has included forty-four cities in thirty-one provinces in China and forty-five cities in fifteen states and Washington, D.C., in the United States. More than seven thousand U.S./Chinese librarians have directly participated in the professional development component of this project.

4

By 1994, the global computer network, known as the Internet, was already developing quickly. However, only a very small number of Chinese research institutions—such as Peking University, Tsinghua University, and the Chinese Academy of Sciences—were able to connect to a special intranet communication network through Stanford University. This was dissatisfying to the Chinese academic community, who saw synchronized access to information with the rest of the world as critical in an increasingly globalized era.

That year marked a momentous time when the Chinese government also acknowledged the importance of being connected to the Internet, something it had originally hesitated to pursue because of security concerns. Before making a decision, Vice Premier Minister Lanqing Li solicited input from academia. Hwa-Wei, who was then at Tsinghua attending a conference, clearly expressed his viewpoint: "It is essential for China to join the global network; otherwise the nation would remain an isolated state." Later that year, Tsinghua was ordered by the government to develop the China Education and Research Network (CERNET) with the goal of developing a national network that would connect Chinese academic institutions to the World Wide Web.

Immediately after the establishment of CERNET, Hwa-Wei took the opportunity to introduce the idea of OCLC and OhioLINK to libraries in China. Operating with a successful global inter-library cooperation and resource-sharing

In 2009, Hwa-Wei spoke at the International Seminar on the Trends for Developing Library Computer Management Systems in Hefei, China.

Hwa-Wei (*first row, third from left*) was one of the participants in the Librarians Professional Development Seminar, part of the China-U.S. Librarians Professional Exchange Project, held in Shanghai, China, in 2010.

In 2010, Hwa-Wei spoke at the Academic Library Directors' Forum in Shanghai, China.

model, OCLC had already been interested in reaching out to Chinese libraries. Before long, an agreement was signed between Tsinghua University Library and OCLC that enabled Tsinghua to serve as the Chinese partner of OCLC, which opened its first Chinese office there. Hwa-Wei was an invited guest at the opening ceremony of the OCLC China Center.

OCLC did not generate the stir in the Chinese library community that was originally expected. This was due to the higher charge of cataloging Chinese language materials, and OCLC's inadequately developed Chinese operating system. Nevertheless, the OCLC model still inspired Chinese library professionals throughout China to develop similar programs including cooperative cataloging, union catalogs, interlibrary loan, and resource sharing on their own at a more affordable cost.

Thinking the concept of OhioLINK might be more practical to China than OCLC, Hwa-Wei introduced it to Peking University, where the China Academic Library and Information System (CALIS) was established with the coordination of Qiang Zhu, deputy director of the university library. Hwa-Wei was instrumental in bringing the Chinese library delegation with members from many universities to visit OhioLINK in Ohio, resulting in the successful adaptation of the OhioLINK model in resource sharing among Chinese academic libraries.

When Hwa-Wei first went back to China in 1982, Chinese libraries were still recovering from the destruction of the Cultural Revolution. At that time, he estimated, Chinese libraries would need at least twenty years to catch up with their American counterparts. However, the hard work of a few determined library leaders, combined with increasing support from the government, has allowed the recovery process to exceed Hwa-Wei's expectation.

The most important assistance needed by Chinese libraries, Hwa-Wei felt, were opportunities to learn about new library developments in other more advanced countries, such as the U.S. and some European nations. This could be done by encouraging Chinese librarians to attend international library conferences such as IFLA, ALA, and others organized by UNESCO; by providing training opportunities abroad; by inviting foreign experts to conduct library seminars in China; and by establishing sister-library relationships between Chinese libraries and foreign libraries.

With these concepts in mind, Hwa-Wei began in earnest to expand his International Librarians Internship Program at Alden Library to Chinese librarians by establishing sister-library relationships with a score of Chinese libraries, by traveling to China to conduct library seminars, and by organizing the China-U.S. Library Cooperation Conferences.

Ohio University's Alden Library was very pleased to establish sister-library relationships with many key Chinese university libraries including ones at Peking,

Tsinghua, Nankai, and Beijing Normal Universities. In addition, Alden Library also formed fruitful relationships with the Wuhan and Lanzhou regional library and information centers of the Chinese Academy of Sciences, Shanghai Library, and Shenzhen Library. Many librarians from these libraries participated in OHIO's International Librarians Internship Program. In reciprocation, a number of librarians from Ohio University also visited libraries in China to gain knowledge and first-hand experience about library development in China and to strengthen ties with the sister libraries.

As a direct result of Hwa-Wei's promotion, a group of library automation staff from Shenzhen Library went to Alden Library to study the integrated library automation system there in order to design and develop a similar library automation system for Shenzhen Library, keeping in mind the different language requirements, cost factors, and operating environments. The initial success made by Shenzhen Library caught the attention of the Chinese Ministry of Culture; it was selected as one of the key development projects funded by the government. The library automation system developed by Shenzhen Library was named Integrated Library Automation System (ILAS) and soon was installed in many other libraries including academic, public, and special libraries throughout China. This locally developed library automation system was very popular due to its low cost, good backup service, and, most importantly, its suitability to Chinese-language applications.

At the Twentieth Anniversary Forum of ILAS Technology in 2009, Ping Yu, head of the Science and Technology Division at the Ministry of Culture, commented: "The twenty years of ILAS development represents twenty years of great progress in Chinese library automation. In the past twenty years, ILAS has had a steady growth along with Chinese library automation, from a state-funded, core research project to a library-automation-management product with thousands of library clients nationwide." This outcome pleased Hwa-Wei.

The history of Chinese library and information science education dates back to 1920 when American-trained librarian Mary Elizabeth Wood established the first library school in China, Boone Library School, in the city of Wuchang; the school was later incorporated into Wuhan University.

Before the establishment of the People's Republic of China in 1949, a few other universities in China had begun offering courses on librarianship, but the library education program at Peking University had been the most prominent. After 1949, the library education programs at Peking University and Wuhan University were transformed into four-year, undergraduate-degree programs. Unfortunately, however, due to the destructive Great Leap Forward movement and the Cultural Revolution in China in the 1960s, all educational programs were interrupted, including library science education. Not until 1972

Hwa-Wei (*second from right*) joins other members of the Chinese American Librarians Association (CALA) in honoring Heping Zhou, director general of the National Library of China, for his support in promoting library cooperation between China and the United States.

Hwa-Wei and two participants at the Eighth Conference on Cooperative Building and Sharing of Chinese Digital Resources, held in Taipei.

were the library science education programs reinstated at Wuhan University and Peking University.

The 1970s ushered in the transformation toward library and information science. In 1978, Wuhan University established the first information science specialty program under its library science department. Following that lead, other universities including Peking University, Jilin University of Technology, Nanjing University, Nankai University, and Sun Yat-Sen University also established similar programs.

In 1981, institutions including Peking and Wuhan Universities officially launched their Master of Library and Information Science (LIS) education programs. In 1990, Peking and Wuhan Universities were authorized to offer Ph.D. degrees in library and information science. By 2010, there were approximately

180 programs that offered master's degrees in library and information science and archives studies.[9]

Because of the fast growth of library and information science education in China in the 1980s and the 1990s, Hwa-Wei was invited to be a visiting professor at Peking, Nankai, Sun Yat-Sen, and Wuhan Universities. The list expanded very quickly to include over twenty universities before Hwa-Wei's retirement from Ohio University in 1999.

5

Those Chinese library professionals who were sent to the training program at OHIO all held middle or upper administrative positions in their libraries. Most of them were highly dedicated and hardworking. They showed an eagerness to learn library operations and management in American libraries, especially in the areas of computer application and library networking. With the exception of a small number of the library interns who chose to stay in the U.S. after their internship to further their studies at other universities, those who returned to China were able to implement their newly gained knowledge into good use.

Besides those librarian interns, Ohio University also attracted a large number of Chinese students and visiting scholars. Those who came as students found that life in a foreign land was not at all easy. This was especially true in the early 1990s when a majority of Chinese students faced not only economic hardship but also a language barrier and culture shock. As a faculty advisor to the Chinese Students and Visiting Scholars Association on campus, Hwa-Wei remembered well his own hardships when he first arrived in the U.S. In his position as dean of Libraries, Hwa-Wei did his best to provide a number of highly qualified Chinese students with part-time employment in the library as student assistants.

In his dealings with Chinese students, Hwa-Wei had to handle many emergency situations. One of the more complex ones concerned an official from the China Academy of Agricultural Sciences, who came to Ohio University as a visiting scholar in the department of economics with government funding. Upon finishing his program as a visiting scholar, he decided to continue his study for a master's degree in economics on his own. He found being a degree-seeking student completely different from taking courses as a visiting scholar. His heavy course load plus his limited English proficiency brought him extreme hardship and led to a nervous breakdown.

---

9. Feicheng Ma and Minjie Chen, "Library and Information Science Education in China: Development and Trends," (paper presented at the International Symposium on Library and Information Science Education: Trends and Visions (Taipei: National Taiwan University, 2011), www.lis.ntu.edu.tw/50symposium/submissions/IP004.pdf.

One day after seeing a news report on television about a plane crash at Guangzhou Baiyun International Airport, that scholar suffered a terrible delusion, deciding that his wife and daughter must have been on that flight and had lost their lives. As a result, he locked himself in the bathroom in his apartment and stabbed himself with a kitchen knife more than ten times.

Fortunately for him, his roommates discovered his suicide attempt and reported it immediately to the campus police. He was sent to the local hospital for emergency treatment. Hwa-Wei, the faculty advisor for Chinese students, received a phone call soon after this student was admitted to the hospital. As this student had no close relatives in the U.S., Hwa-Wei became his only source of support. Having found the home phone number of the student's wife, Hwa-Wei made an urgent phone call to China and confirmed that both his wife and daughter were fine and had not gone on any trips. Hwa-Wei then made special arrangements to connect this student on the phone with his wife to prove that his loved ones were safe. The student's condition improved steadily thereafter and, after his wounds healed, he was sent to a local mental hospital for further psychiatric rehabilitation. His mental health gradually improved in the succeeding two months.

Founded in 1874, the Athens Mental Health Center (the Ridges) was one of the oldest public service facilities in the state of Ohio. Many soldiers traumatized by war had been receiving psychiatric treatment there. Most of the patients were suffering severe trauma and, therefore, were confined to their rooms with limited mobility; this was not a good long-term solution for the Chinese student. A final decision was made to send him back to China for recovery. Acting as his guardian, Hwa-Wei signed his discharge release. He also helped him secure travel funds from the university to cover the airfare and to apply to Athens' social welfare department for a waiver of the $30,000 medical expenses.

On Christmas Eve Hwa-Wei drove the student from Athens to the Columbus International Airport for his early morning flight back to Beijing. It was a snowy night; snowflakes hit the windshield, melting into bright drops of water. There were very few cars on the road. Several residential towns they occasionally passed through were full of Christmas decorations; most visible were the warm lights in the dark. The student did not say a single word. Hwa-Wei could not think of any way to comfort him. After almost two hours of driving, they finally arrived at the airport. Having checked the student into a hotel near the airport, Hwa-Wei said goodbye to him, but the student became very nervous and asked Hwa-Wei if he would stay with him.

That Christmas morning, only Mary was with their children. At the time they were opening their gifts, Hwa-Wei was away, staying in that hotel room with the Chinese student. The man had gone through considerable suffering and was now waiting to reunite with his wife and daughters; thankfully, due to his family's care upon his return, the student fully recovered. He and his wife have been extremely grateful to Hwa-Wei. Later, their two daughters also came to the U.S. and earned their doctorates.

6

While working closely with libraries in mainland China, Hwa-Wei kept in touch with libraries and educational institutions in Taiwan and Hong Kong. He was invited by the government in Taiwan to attend the National Reconstruction Conference, held every two or three years, and served as a member in the Cultural and Educational Session. At this conference Hwa-Wei got to know Dr. Ying-Ming Liao, president of Feng Chia University, one of the top private universities in Taiwan. The friendship that developed between President Liao and Hwa-Wei led to the establishment of a sister-university relationship between Feng Chia University and Ohio University. Over a period of fifteen years, the two universities exchanged students. The presidents and senior administrators of both universities also exchanged visits. Many faculty members and graduates from Feng Chia came to OHIO for graduate studies with tuition waivers; at the same time, an equal number of Ohio University graduates, about five to seven each year, went to Feng Chia to study Chinese while teaching English with their living expenses paid for by Feng Chia.

OHIO also established similar programs with Tamkang and Ling Tung Universities and provided educational opportunities to faculty members and graduates of those schools.

Representing Taiwan, a large number of librarians from the National Central Library, National Taichung Library, and Tamkang University have participated in the International Librarians Internship Program of Ohio University from its inception. Hwa-Wei was invited to attend and present papers at many library conferences in Taiwan.

Hwa-Wei's professional relationship with Hong Kong's academic libraries started early and was long-lived. The former president of Hong Kong Baptist University (HKBU), Dr. Daniel C.W. Tse, and his wife, Mrs. Kitty Tse, were fellow students with Hwa-Wei at the University of Pittsburgh. President Tse and Hwa-Wei received their doctorates and Mrs. Tse received her master in library science (MLS) in the same year. Upon their return to Hong Kong, Dr. Tse served as the president of HKBU, where his wife Kitty served as the library director. Whenever Hwa-Wei traveled through Hong Kong to China, he stayed in their home.

Originally HKBU was a private liberal arts college in Hong Kong. However, under the outstanding leadership of Dr. Tse, HKBU grew into a public university with the same status as Hong Kong University, The Chinese University of Hong Kong, and Hong Kong University of Science and Technology. At the initial construction stage of the HKBU library, the Tses invited Hwa-Wei to be the consultant because of his expertise in the design of university library buildings. Their friendship continued and further developed into an inter-institutional relationship between HKBU and Ohio University into the 1990s.

Under the leadership of Dr. James Bryant, OHIO's vice president for regional higher education, a joint degree program and an extension center at HKBC was established, taught by faculty members sent from OHIO together with HKBC faculty members. At the height of this program, several hundred Hong Kong students earned their first two years of education at HKBC and then finished their last two years of education at Ohio University. Students who successfully completed the degree requirements were conferred their bachelor degrees jointly by both universities.

At the preparatory stage of the Hong Kong University of Science and Technology (HKUST), Hwa-Wei received an invitation to become its first library director. Lord Christopher Patten, the last governor of Hong Kong, was the current university president. The vice president, Chien, enthusiastically contacted Hwa-Wei in person, saying, "We are aiming for a top-rated university in Asia. We need to invite the best experts and scholars to join us." In order to lure Hwa-Wei, HKUST offered an attractive deal: a 20 percent salary increase plus a bonus of one full year's wages at the time of renewal three years later. Due to the high housing cost, the rent subsidy was even greater than the salary. Apparently it was a sincere invitation, but it came at the time of the Tiananmen Incident of June 4, 1989.

Worrying that Hong Kong might be impacted, Mary said to Hwa-Wei, "Maybe we should hold off for now." On the OHIO side, the university administration offered counter benefits, not wanting to lose Hwa-Wei, who had been playing a significant role in advancing the Ohio University Libraries to become a member of the Association of Research Libraries. Weighing the options, Hwa-Wei decided to turn down the offer from HKUST.

Another good friend of Hwa-Wei in Hong Kong is Dr. Wah-Tung Poon, then library director of the City University of Hong Kong (CUHK), and, later, library director at the University of Macau. Dr. Poon repeatedly invited Hwa-Wei to be a consultant of the CUHK library. In the early 1990s, Dr. Poon spent two summers at Alden Library researching and helping Hwa-Wei to prepare for his lecture on modern library management, one Hwa-Wei would present in China.

Hwa-Wei Lee came to the United States for graduate studies at the University of Pittsburgh in September of 1957.

Mary Frances Kratochvil was also a student taking graduate classes at the University of Pittsburgh in 1957.

Hwa-Wei and Mary both received their master's degrees from the University of Pittsburgh in June 1959.

Hwa-Wei received his Ph.D. from the University of Pittsburgh in June 1965.

Hwa-Wei Lee at Ohio University, 1978

Mary Lee, 1978

Hwa-Wei and Mary in front of Ohio University's Hwa-Wei Lee Library Annex, named in his honor, 1999

Hwa-Wei was honored with a private meeting with Her Royal Highness Princess Maha Chakri Sirindhorn of Thailand in the Royal Palace, 2001.

Mary and Hwa-Wei pose for a portrait after Hwa-Wei's retirement from Ohio University, 2002.

A symposium in honor of Hwa-Wei Lee was held at Shenzhen Library, Guangdong, China, November 17, 2011. Attendees included (*left to right*): Dr. Daniel Shao, Director Xi Wu, Dean Scott Seaman, and Hwa-Wei Lee.

Yang Yang, author of *The Sage in the Cathedral of Books,* spoke at the Shenzhen symposium, 2011.

Hwa-Wei was conferred an honorary doctorate degree by Ohio University, June 9, 2012.

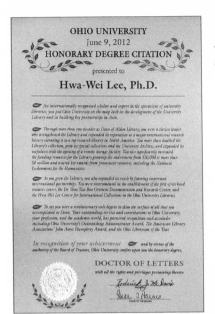

The Ohio University Honorary Degree
Citation presented to Hwa-Wei

Mary and Hwa-Wei stand in front of a sign announcing a symposium and special exhibit
honoring Hwa-Wei, held at National Taiwan Normal University, Taipei, Taiwan, on
December 9, 2013.

Hwa-Wei and Mary stand at the entranceway to National Taiwan Normal University. Hwa-Wei had graduated from the university in 1954.

Successful Fundraising

I want to paint the earth full of windows;
So all eyes accustomed to the darkness would get used to bright light.

—Cheng Gu

1

AMONG THE several professional books that Hwa-Wei has written is *Fundraising for the 1990s: The Challenge Ahead: A Practical Guide for Library Fundraising: From Novice to Expert*, co-authored with his deputy library director, Dr. Gary A. Hunt. Written during their spare time, with a constant push from their publisher to finish the manuscript as soon as possible, the book took only about six months to complete. Based on Hwa-Wei and Gary's actual experience in fundraising, this book was quite popular among academic libraries because, then and now, fundraising has become a necessary requirement for academic library directors.

By the early 1990s, the reputation of Hwa-Wei's adept fundraising skills had spread across the library community. Having sensed this business opportunity, an Ohio publisher contacted Hwa-Wei in 1991, inviting him to write a book to share his experiences.

In the United States, state government appropriation is normally the primary funding source for public universities. However since the early 1980s, that funding has been decreasing, leaving those public colleges and universities, which were accustomed to relying on government funding, in dire straits. To cope with the situation, public universities had to draw on the model used by private institutions for additional money: they had to increase the amount of donations from private sources. Harvard, Princeton, Stanford, and Yale each have billions, even tens of billions, of dollars in the form of endowment funds. By sound investment, those endowment funds can generate a large sum of annual income to support university operations.

A large percentage of donors are elite alumni. Having decided to follow the established success of private universities, public institutions of higher learning started to seek support from their alumni as well. Many of them created a position responsible for public relations and fundraising and for establishing a foundation to manage the raised funds. Meanwhile, college deans and heads of major administrative units in public institutions of higher learning were also required to develop fundraising plans and goals and to be actively involved in fundraising.

There are essentially two types of fundraising approaches. One is the annual giving by donors through solicitation by direct mailings, phone calls, and special fundraising events. The amount of funds raised by these means is normally modest. The other is through major fundraising campaigns, conducted once every few years with a set ambitious goal. The latter approach tends to be aimed at the substantial amount of funds needed for major projects.

The funds raised through these two campaigns are generally used in two possible ways. Funds can be used within a specified period of time according to the purpose of the project and the wishes of the donor. An alternative approach is the creation of an endowment fund, managed and invested by the university foundation, with only the interest or a portion of the interest to be used. An endowment is linked to a specific, designated expense such as a scholarship fund, a building fund, an endowed professorship fund, or a library fund.

Projects can also be funded by grants from government sources and private foundations. Applying for these grants requires expertise in proposal writing as available grant funds are matched with a particular need. Hwa-Wei was very fortunate to have the assistance of Gary Hunt and Kent Mulliner; both men excelled in "grantsmanship." Kent was the special assistant to the dean. He and Gary gave Hwa-Wei excellent administrative support.

Before Hwa-Wei assumed the position of library director at Ohio University, the total amount of the Libraries' endowment was about $20,000, ranked last among the seventeen cost centers on campus (ten colleges and seven administrative units). There were many reasons for this low amount. Chief among them were the lack of an organized program and little desire for fundraising. Since libraries do not have alumni, it is difficult to identify potential donors.

As a new library director with little previous experience in fundraising, Hwa-Wei faced quite a challenging task. However, Jack Ellis, OHIO's vice president for public relations and development, just happened to be his neighbor. Jack was organizing a large-scale fundraising activity and encouraged Hwa-Wei to participate. He also suggested that many Ohio University alumni might prefer to support the Libraries instead of their academic departments or colleges. Furthermore, Jack encouraged Hwa-Wei to begin cultivating donor relationships with non-alumni including faculty members, members of the Ohio University Board of Trustees, community leaders, and philanthropists.

Encouraged by this good advice, Hwa-Wei decided to give it a try. A distinguished alumnus from the College of Engineering and Technology, Paul Stocker, had given $20 million to the college. Stocker had been highly praised by the university as a model alumnus. As frequent visitors to OHIO, Stocker and his wife, Beth, were always warmly welcomed at special events of the college. At one of those receptions, Hwa-Wei met Mrs. Stocker. During the course of their conversation, Hwa-Wei found that she was actually very interested in the library. Hwa-Wei took the opportunity to invite her to visit Alden Library, and she immediately accepted.

At that time, Hwa-Wei had just created a preservation department at the library. Because many library books were old and badly damaged through wear and tear from each circulation, staff members, apart from routine repair work, sometimes had to replace missing or torn pages by inserting photocopies of pages from books that were borrowed via interlibrary loan from other libraries. This type of repair work was very common across almost all libraries. However, at most libraries, there were only one or two designated staff members to do the work; few had a preservation department.

The head of this new department was Ms. Patricia Smith, an outstanding librarian with a MLS degree from Columbia as well as specialized training in preservation from Stanford. Patricia had been offered opportunities to work at Yale and Stanford upon graduation, but chose Ohio University instead because the position as head of the newly established Preservation Department was much more attractive to her. Furthermore, she was interested in the expanded role of the department, incorporating the microfilming and digitization of selected library materials. At Ohio University, she had her own office, a full-time assistant, several part-time student workers, and a number of volunteers.

During the visit, Mrs. Stocker showed an interest in the work of Patricia's department. She was touched by meeting so many volunteers and by the enthusiasm of the department head, who displayed a great passion for book repair and preservation. Mrs. Stocker was enchanted by Patricia's demonstration and constantly threw out questions. Hwa-Wei told her that professional preservation was a cutting-edge concept in the library community, and the department was in urgent need of expansion and new equipment. Mrs. Stocker immediately expressed her willingness to help.

Two months later, right before Christmas, Beth Stocker mailed a $100,000 check with this attached note:

> Dr. Hwa-Wei Lee, I would acknowledge that you are leading an excellent library. I am especially interested in the book preservation part. Here is my donation of 100,000 dollars to support your new endeavor. I plan to continue my support through annual gifts.

That was a very special Christmas gift for the Ohio University Libraries. Since then, every year before the holiday, Mrs. Stocker's scheduled donation would arrive. By the time of Hwa-Wei's retirement, she had donated a total of $1.3 million to the Library Preservation Endowment.[1] With the donation and annual income from the endowment fund, Patricia was able to utilize her expertise fully, making the preservation department a successful model for other libraries to follow. She later became the wife of the associate dean, Dr. Gary Hunt.

2

The preservation project funded by Mrs. Stocker was the first fundraising project Hwa-Wei brought to fruition. It was such a good start that it made him eager to seek more external funding.

At about the same time, the National Endowment for the Humanities (NEH) had launched a Challenge Grant to encourage fundraising at institutions of higher education to promote arts and humanities education. The grant stipulated that a participating institution with an approved proposal and a set fundraising goal could receive one dollar of NEH money for every three dollars raised. The duration for each approved proposal was three years. For example, if a library had set a goal of $450,000 and was able to raise the full amount in three years, it would receive an additional $150,000 from NEH, thus bringing the total to $600,000 for use in enhancing programs in the arts and humanities.

In his first NEH fund application, Hwa-Wei set his fundraising goal at $450,000 for a $150,000 Challenge Grant. He was uncertain whether he could reach the goal. But it was clear to him that he had to cultivate new donors within the next three years. He again turned to his neighbor Jack Ellis for advice. Three years later, Hwa-Wei achieved and exceeded his goal with a total of $600,000 raised.

The success not only boosted Hwa-Wei's confidence but also raised his expectations. Soon after the required one-year waiting time had passed, he submitted another Challenge Grant application to NEH. The second Challenge Grant application was for $750,000. According to the NEH guidelines, a returning grant applicant had to raise four dollars in order to receive a one dollar grant, which meant that Hwa-Wei had to raise $3 million in the succeeding three years in order to receive the $750,000 from the NEH.

To achieve the new goal, Hwa-Wei had to double his fundraising efforts. Jack was most helpful by assigning a full-time fundraising staff member, Ms. Salinda Arthur, to serve as the Libraries' assistant dean for development. With the expert skills of Salinda, the library was able to surpass the fundraising goal

1. "Market Value of Established Library Endowments as of June 30, 1999," *Ohio University Libraries 1998–1999 Annual Report* (Athens: Ohio University Libraries, 1999), 26.

required by the second NEH Challenge Grant application. Salinda left Ohio University shortly after Hwa-Wei's retirement. She is now the vice president for university advancement at the University of Southern Georgia.

In order to solicit public support, Hwa-Wei also established the Friends of the Libraries group soon after his arrival at Ohio University. Members of the Friends included faculty, alumni, and community leaders. As time went by, many of the Friends became very active in fundraising and donated their time and monetary gifts.

On the average, Hwa-Wei spent three hours per day on fundraising activities. In addition to the Friends of the Libraries, he also created a National Library Advisory Council to reach out to prominent alumni and Friends, many of whom were recommended to him by Jack Ellis.

To Hwa-Wei, a successful fundraising effort has to begin with the successful operation of an organization. Only with a well-recognized reputation could an organization attract funding from prospective donors. Because of Hwa-Wei's good work at the library, many members of the Ohio University Board of Trustees and the Ohio University Foundation, became very interested in OHIO's Libraries. Among them were Charlotte Eufinger, Donald A. Spencer, Dr. Grasselli Brown, Sydney E. Buck, Sanford D. Elsass, and Dr. Daniel Shao. These members not only actively participated in fundraising for the library, but they also made significant donations. For example, upon learning about the library's effort to build a strong African American Studies collection, one board member, Donald A. Spencer, donated $90,000 to establish an endowment fund for the collection.

Another significant donation came from Dr. Frederick Harris, an American living and working in Japan for over forty years, who had married a charming Japanese lady, Kazuko Harris. Dr. Harris owned an interior design firm, The Design Studio, in Tokyo, Japan, and was well known for his mastery of the Japanese "Sumi-e" painting technique.

As a collector of art books, both of the Eastern and Western arts, Dr. Harris had a personal library of over six thousand books and was thinking about donating his collection to an elite American university. Since Dr. Harris had neither a relationship with Ohio University, nor had ever heard about it, he never thought that his treasured collection would end up at Ohio University Libraries.

Thanks to Robert Fallon, a personal friend of Harris, Hwa-Wei learned about this treasured collection. Fallon, a loyal OHIO alumnus and a member of the Friends of the Libraries, was then Chase Manhattan Bank's chief representative in Asia. Through Fallon's introduction, Hwa-Wei visited Dr. Harris in Tokyo and received a warm welcome. Dr. Harris gave Hwa-Wei a personal tour of his home and an enthusiastic introduction to his impressive art collection. Hwa-Wei took this opportunity to introduce him to Ohio University Libraries' fine arts collection, which had gained quite a reputation among American libraries. It was here that Hwa-Wei asked Dr. Harris if he would consider donating his personal collection to Ohio University, allowing the library's fine arts collection to be further enriched and internationalized. However, Dr. Harris was quite frank and quickly said, "I know nothing about Ohio University, and really can't think of any reason to donate my collection to its library."

Hwa-Wei recognized the validity of Dr. Harris' comment, and saw the necessity of arranging a campus visit for him, so he could see the Fine Arts Library for himself. Learning that Dr. Harris would be visiting his ailing brother in New York, Hwa-Wei invited him to visit Athens, Ohio, and promised to arrange for a university plane to pick him up at one of the airports in New York City.

This special VIP treatment worked out quite well. Dr. Harris was picked up in New York City and landed safely at Ohio University's Gordon K. Bush Airport, where Hwa-Wei was waiting to greet his guest. Situated nine miles west of the Athens campus, the university-owned airport was designated for use by VIPs of the university and for university-related programs, including research in aviation engineering and pilot training.

Dr. Harris's trip to Ohio University was very pleasant. The fine arts librarian, Anne Braxton, who had an extensive art background, gave him an in-depth tour of the fine arts collection. The two enjoyed their conversations, hitting it off like two old friends. Under a special arrangement with the College of Fine Arts, Dr. Harris also gave a guest lecture to faculty and students. Upon leaving Athens, Dr. Harris said, "Hwa-Wei, I've decided to donate my books to your library."

Later, Hwa-Wei paid several more visits to Dr. Harris during his business trips to Japan in connection with Chubu University, a sister university of Ohio University. Dr. Harris was notable not only for his widely acclaimed fame in the Japanese art world but also for his strong sense of patriotism. Having lived in Japan as a highly respected American for nearly forty years, he once served as the president of the Tokyo American Club. In the late 1980s and early 1990s when American ships and troops were still stationed in Japan, Dr. Harris arranged for those U.S. Navy sailors to be guests of Japanese families to enhance their mutual understanding and friendship.

Through their frequent contacts, shipments of the Harris' book collection began to arrive at Ohio University Libraries. Hwa-Wei soon became a close friend of Dr. Harris and his wife, Kazuko. At the recommendation of Hwa-Wei, Dr. Harris was conferred with an Honorary Doctorate in Fine Arts from Ohio University in 1997.

Before Hwa-Wei's retirement in 1999, Dr. Harris decided, in support of the fine arts collection, to donate $500,000 for use in its continuing acquisitions and operations. Because of his generosity, Ohio University Libraries decided to name the collection "Frederick and Kazuko Harris Art Collection."[2]

3

Upon first arriving in Athens, Ohio, Hwa-Wei noted the name of the library, the "Vernon Roger Alden Library." He soon learned that Vernon R. Alden was the fifteenth president of the University, serving from 1962 to 1969, and that the library building was built during Alden's presidency. Dr. Alden, when only thirty-nine years old, had moved from the Harvard University Business School as the associate dean to become the president of Ohio University. The move from Boston to Athens, Ohio, was quite a change for him and his family.

A visionary and energetic leader, Dr. Alden greatly enhanced OHIO's academic status by using his prestigious academic background and his extensive connections. The 1960s saw a rapid expansion of the university. During Alden's seven-year tenure, the student and faculty body doubled in size, and many buildings were constructed in the distinctive traditional style, with large white window frames and plain red-brick walls surrounded by expansive green lawns and large trees.

Under Dr. Alden's leadership, Ohio University spearheaded the economic revitalization of Southeastern Ohio, including the development of the Appalachian Highway Network and the re-routing of the Hocking River, which had often flooded the OHIO campus. In addition, as president, he established six regional campuses to accommodate the growing educational needs of the region. Thus, he ensured that Ohio University was to be a prominent university in the state of Ohio, despite its rural location.

Dr. Alden made great efforts to secure government funding for a new library. The construction of the new building took five years and was finally completed in 1969, the last building built during his term. Upon his resignation from the university in 1969, the Board of Trustees named the new building in his honor, the Vernon R. Alden Library. With the new building ready, the library collection moved from the Edwin Watts Chubb Library, constructed in 1931 on the northwest corner of the College Green, which had reached its storage capacity, to the Vernon R. Alden Library to meet the ever-increasing needs of collections and readership.

The late 1960s also witnessed a surge of nationwide college student protests against the Vietnam War. This student movement was extremely active at Ohio University. On the day of the library's opening ceremony, some students

---

2. Fine Arts Library, "Frederick & Kazuko Harris," OHIO University Libraries, https://www.library.ohiou.edu/about/collections/fine-arts/frederick-kazuko-harris/.

broke into the building and ate the refreshments on the main floor that had been prepared for VIP guests.

More alarming was a demonstration held in front of Dr. Alden's residence, with radical students shouting and throwing stones and bottles into the front yard, frightening Mrs. Alden and their young children.

In fact, the anti-Vietnam War movement in the late 1960s had spread to many American college campuses. Student anti-war demonstrations were extremely intense across college campuses in Ohio. On May 4, 1970, some members of the Ohio National Guard fired at protesting students at Kent State University (KSU), killing four and wounding nine students. Ohio National Guards were also stationed at Ohio University.

Seeing the students out of control and the university to which he had devoted so much of his efforts erupting into chaos, Dr. Alden felt understandably disappointed. Soon after this unfortunate event, Dr. Alden decided to accept a position as the chairman of the Boston Company and left his tenure as president of Ohio University.

From then on, Dr. Alden has had a very successful career in the business and financial world. He transformed an essentially local financial company into a national and international corporation. Beyond this business endeavor, Dr. Alden also devoted his interest to the arts, education, and international affairs. In 1985, the Emperor of Japan conferred upon him the Order of the Rising Sun, Star Class. In 1996, His Majesty the King of Thailand presented him with the Most Noble Order of the Crown of Thailand. As a recipient of thirteen honorary degrees from various universities, Dr. Alden was also elected to the Ohio University Hall of Fame in 2006. Hwa-Wei felt great sympathy about the tough situation Dr. Alden had encountered during the last year of his presidency at OHIO and had a profound gratitude for his farsightedness in seeking the funding for and overseeing the construction of the new library building, a facility which all students and faculty in later years deeply appreciated.

The second year after Hwa-Wei joined Ohio University happened to be the 175th anniversary of the university. Coinciding with the anniversary would also be a celebration of the Libraries' acquisition of its one-millionth volume. Hwa-Wei thought it might be a good opportunity to invite Dr. Alden back for a visit.

It was a warm afternoon. The celebration was held at Alden Library. Dr. and Mrs. Alden returned to the campus through arrangements made by President Charles Ping. At the ceremony, Hwa-Wei recalled, with sincere appreciation, numerous meaningful and lasting contributions that Dr. Alden had made during his tenure, in particular, the construction of the library. Owing to his foresight, the new library building was built with ample space, to allow continued growth of the Libraries' collection and user needs.

Mary, Hwa-Wei, and Vern Alden, the fifteenth president of Ohio University (1962–69), stand near the busts of Dr. Alden and his late wife, Marion. The busts were commissioned by the Ohio Fellows to commemorate the fiftieth anniversary of Dr. Alden's inauguration. The Aldens were very generous donors to the Ohio University Libraries.

Dr. Frederick Harris stands in front of the Frederick and Kazuko Harris Art Collection inside Ohio University's Vernon R. Alden Library. Dr. Harris donated his personal collection of fine arts books and a substantial amount of money to the fine arts collection at the library.

Representatives of Ohio University including (*left to right*): Josep Rota, Hwa-Wei Lee, Sandra Geiger, Alan Geiger, chair of the Board of Trustees, President Robert Glidden, Rene Glidden, Mary Lee, and Daniel Shao stand in front of the Forever Blooming Bauhinia sculpture in Hong Kong. The bauhinia flower is regarded as a symbol of wisdom by the people of Hong Kong.

Dr. and Mrs. Alden had mixed feelings about their revisit. Ohio University had not forgotten them. The heartfelt appreciation and gratitude from the university and the library more or less soothed over the pain from the time of their departure. The charming and beautiful Mrs. Marion Alden offered a generous donation of $200,000 immediately to the library for its Southeast Asian Art Collection, benefiting both the Southeast Asian Special Collection and the Fine Arts Library. Dr. Alden also accepted the invitation from Hwa-Wei to serve as honorary president of the Friends of the Libraries. Thereafter, the Aldens began to return annually to participate in many university activities.

Dr. Alden kept a close personal association with Hwa-Wei, admiring the library dean's calm and humble personality, as well as his prudent and realistic way of doing things. He once told Hwa-Wei on a private occasion that he was very satisfied with the library development and that he would make an even larger donation to the Libraries in the form of a planned gift. His public declaration to donate $5 million to the library was made in 2000, and was, by far, the largest single donation the Ohio University Libraries had ever received.

4

When Hwa-Wei first arrived at Ohio University Libraries, there was only $20,000 in the library endowment fund; by the time of his retirement the number reached $9,086,611, raising the library's total endowment from last place to fourth place among the seventeen budget units on campus. According to the policy of the Ohio University Foundation, the Libraries would be able to use about 4 percent of the annual income from endowment funds for various designated purposes.

That $9 million represented what was already in the endowment fund. There was actually an additional $3 million that had already been spent in compliance with donor intents. In addition, there was also nearly $6 million committed for future donations such as planned giving,[3] like the gift from Dr. Alden, who had already given a total of over $700,000 to the library during Hwa-Wei's tenure to establish the Vernon & Marion Alden Library Endowment ($479,469) and the Marion Alden Endowment Fund for the Southeast Asian Library Collection ($223,966).

Through his many remarkable fundraising projects, Hwa-Wei, with his charming personality and demonstrated success in library operations, was able to build lasting friendships with current and potential donors. As his fundraising reputation kept rising, he became one of the most prominent and accomplished fundraisers in the library field.

---

3. Planned giving comprises large or small donations, made during a donor's lifetime or willed at death as a part of his or her overall financial and/or estate planning.

In general, fundraising should start with a long-range plan: an itemized to-do list of important projects and their corresponding costs, and a brochure outlining these goals and funding needs, thereby allowing potential donors to make informed decisions. With the assistance of the Development Office, Hwa-Wei was able to have a beautiful brochure made for use in the Libraries' fundraising. As the subtitle of Hwa-Wei's fundraising book indicates, *From Novice to Expert,* Hwa-Wei had learned a lot from his years of experience. He felt strongly that it is no longer adequate to merely demonstrate one's needs. Today, libraries must be able to convince prospective donors of their value, worth, and benefits to society.

Below are guidelines to judge whether a library is ready to launch a successful fundraising program:

1. There is a general feeling that the library is essential, provides useful services, and is under excellent leadership.
2. There is an active group of library supporters.
3. The library's parent organization is committed to help.
4. The library staff is sufficiently motivated to take part.

In Hwa-Wei's fundraising book, he listed ten basic principles for successful fundraising. These ten principles are as follows:

1. Develop a positive image.
2. Find the right market niche: what specific themes should the library emphasize to reach the philanthropic market?
3. Pick the best leadership for the fundraising team.
4. Target prospects carefully.
5. Successful fundraising requires commitment in terms of time and necessary expenses.
6. Concentrate on relationship—the "cultivation" step in fundraising.
7. Make the request—the "solicitation" step in fundraising.
8. Listen and be patient.
9. Never forget a donor, including appropriate donor recognition.
10. Accountability—effective stewardship that inspires the confidence of the donor. [4]

By applying those ten principles, Hwa-Wei and his team were able to accomplish most of their goals. The most rewarding experience from fundraising, as recalled by Hwa-Wei, was the opportunity to meet so many wonderful, generous, and public-minded people with whom he was able to build lasting friendships.

---

4. Hwa-Wei Lee and Gary Hunt, *Fundraising for the 1990s: The Challenge Ahead: A Practical Guide for Library Fundraising: From Novice to Expert* (Canfield, Ohio: Genaway and Associates, 1992).

CHAPTER 15

Management Principles

Most of our societies (by no means all) have assembled around a
book, and for these the library became an essential symbol of power.

—*Alberto Manguel*

1

IT WAS the winter of 1993. The city of Athens was experiencing unusually heavy snow, and everything had already turned to pure white. Vehicles that were parked along the streets were almost buried in snow, but the snowflakes kept falling, neither too fast nor too slow. Those large heavy flakes soon resulted in three feet of snowfall. All the schools and shops were closed.

At that time, Hwa-Wei was in Columbus, Ohio, undergoing surgery for the treatment of his lumbar disc. When he was to be released from the hospital, a section of the road between Athens and Columbus was not passable, so Mary was unable to pick him up from Columbus. Fortunately for Hwa-Wei, Tommy and Jenny Wang, his good friends in Columbus, took him to their home for a few days.

The surgery was a success. During his recovery, he had extra time to work on his book, *Modern Library Management,* under a recent publication contract with San Min Book Company in Taiwan. In the book, he would generalize his experiences in library management and incorporate findings from literature reviews. Luckily, he had already collected abundant materials through his lecture trips in China and Taiwan over the years.

Hwa-Wei avoided working on purely theoretical and academic writings because of his extremely busy administrative work and his personal preference for empirical research. Often, he was invited by organizers of professional conferences and editors of academic journals to write papers, especially about his recent innovative practices. Thus, the papers that he wrote were primarily about his professional work at different times of his career. His first paper was written about the African Collection at Duquesne University. While in Thailand, his writings, which mainly drew upon his experiences at AIT while doing consulting work in Southeast Asia, focused on innovations at the Library and Information Center, collection development and management, computer technology applications, specialized information services in engineering and technology, the creation of national science and technology information systems, regional library cooperation, and information resource sharing.

After Hwa-Wei returned to the United States, his publication topics were expanded to include modern library management, library fundraising, adaption of science and technology in library automation, Sino-U.S. library cooperation, international librarianship, and knowledge management in libraries. The writings on these topics were essentially reflections of his views and understandings of specific issues from his daily work. After joining the staff at the Library of Congress (LC), the focus of his publications transitioned to Asian collections, the Asian-American and Pacific Islanders Collection, and Chinese research resources at LC.

At the time, academic library directors in the United States generally focused their efforts on library administration. Their spare time was limited and often did not allow much time to research or write. Writing articles, especially scholarly papers, was also extra work for Hwa-Wei. However, he didn't seem to mind being invited to share his valuable experience with others. To do so, he had to find time from his busy administrative work and utilize much of his scarce free time. With an average of two papers per year, he worked extremely hard, and his workload reached its limit.

Throughout the decades of his library career, Hwa-Wei authored or co-authored a total of 130 scholarly papers, published eight monographs, compiled three conference proceedings, and served on the editorial board of seven academic journals. His published books include *Librarianship in World Perspective: Selected Writings, 1963–1989*, published in Taiwan by Student Book Company in 1991; *Fundraising for the 1990s: The Challenge Ahead: A Practical Guide for Library Fundraising: From Novice to Expert*, co-authored with Gary Hunt, and published in Canfield, Ohio, by Genaway & Associates in 1992; *Modern Library Management*, published in Taiwan by San Min Book Company in 1996; *An Introduction to OCLC Online and CD-ROM Cataloging*, co-authored with Weihan Diao and Andrew H. Wang, and published in Shanghai by East China Normal University Press in 1999; *Knowledge Management: Theory and Practice*, co-authored with Xiaoying Dong and Meiyun Zuo, and published in Beijing by Huazhi Publishing in 2002; and *Collected Works of Hwa-Wei Lee*, a two volume set published in Guangzhou by Sun Yat-Sen University Press in 2011.[1]

In most cases, in order to be granted tenure from an American institution of higher education, faculty are required during their first six years of employment to publish a certain number of papers in peer-reviewed academic journals, to have an outstanding performance in teaching and research in their respective

---

1. For a full list of Hwa-Wei Lee's publications, please see Appendix B.

areas of specialization, and to engage in university and professional services. Hwa-Wei, however, due to his remarkable performance, was able to gain tenure within his three years of employment at Colorado State University. His writing, therefore, had nothing to do with career pressure but resulted, rather, from his personal commitment to excellence. The hectic work pace that he had developed over the years, because of his personal approach to life and his drive for professional satisfaction, had became a part of his extraordinary personality traits.

2

Having received his education and training in China, Taiwan, and the United States, Hwa-Wei's management philosophy and style effectively integrated Eastern and Western cultural influences. Through years of administrative and managerial practices, he had formed a unique management style—a fusion of Eastern and Western philosophies, combined with the latest management theories and practices, as well as a strong belief in following new developments in information technology applications and in the concept of knowledge management.

In his perspective, Western management practices are heavily grounded in laws and regulations, emphasizing strict compliance to an organization's policies, regulations, and procedures. However, Chinese management practices are heavily based on human relationships or personal favoritism. Placing emphasis on either "laws and regulations" or "human relationships" has its shortcomings. To seek a balance between the two, ancient Chinese sages advocated the employment of "rationality" as a middle-of-the-road approach to bring the two extreme approaches together into a harmonious relationship. Confucius' "Doctrine of the Golden Mean" shows the wisdom of that balance.

To Hwa-Wei, the management of people is very important, and harmony in interpersonal relationships is the key to successful organizations, including libraries. As a people-oriented person, Hwa-Wei enjoys working with his colleagues, the faculty, the students, and the university administration in a harmonious way. In working with his library colleagues, he values the talent and ability of each of them. He sees his role as a facilitator for a pleasant work environment where each staff member is empowered and given the opportunity to do his or her best in achieving the shared vision and goals of the library.

Hwa-Wei was also a good delegator and gave each staff member sufficient power to be innovative in order to facilitate success. Hwa-Wei did not hesitate to reward good performance of his staff, but he would also bear the burden for unintentional failure due to exploring new approaches in advancing library work. He was fair and considerate and did not play favorites.

Betty Hoffmann-Pinther, a paraprofessional in the cataloging department of Alden Library, worked diligently as the assistant to the head of the department for many years. Before the retirement of the department head, due to his poor health, Betty was doing most of his work and kept the department running smoothly. When the library became a member of the newly established OCLC, Betty learned the new OCLC cataloging system, and was the individual who inputted the first cataloging record into the online cataloging system on August 26, 1971, an historic moment for OCLC. In addition, Betty also helped in training other staff in OCLC cataloging, and, later on, in the selection of the library's first library automation system, the Virginia Tech Library System (VTLS), from its installation to operation.

After the department head retired, the library administration began an open search for a new department head. Even though Betty didn't have a master of library science degree, she was encouraged by many of her colleagues to apply since she was already doing most of the work of a department head. After reviewing all qualified applicants, Hwa-Wei decided to offer the position to Betty, bypassing several other professional catalogers in the department—most of whom agreed with Hwa-Wei's choice. The employment action was considered an exception to common practice because Betty didn't have the required professional qualifications for the position. This exceptional appointment turned out to be the correct decision by Hwa-Wei. Betty later proved her extraordinary competency in her work as the department head. Her appointment was not only fair, it also gave hope to other paraprofessionals that they too, by outstanding work, could be promoted.

Besides his support of the application of a management principle balancing laws and human relationships with rationality, Hwa-Wei is also a strong believer in harmony in every working environment. In his office he displayed a Chinese proverb, "Harmony is Precious," encapsulating his beliefs. To him, the core of successful management is in building trust, which must begin first in himself. Another of Confucius' teachings that guides Hwa-Wei in dealings with his colleagues is "Earning trust from others should start with cultivating self-discipline." By respecting and treating others with fairness and kindness, he was able to build an atmosphere of trust in the workplace.

3

This concept of building trust runs through Hwa-Wei's entire book, *Modern Library Management,* which introduces advanced Western management concepts such as management by objective, participatory management, total quality management, and knowledge management—concepts which he practiced at OHIO Libraries.

These four management concepts have been very popular in the business world in the United States from the 1960s. The first two have been widely adopted in academic libraries, but Hwa-Wei found the other two concepts of great interest, also. He always stressed the importance of applying the concept of total quality management and knowledge management in his work.

In the application of management by objectives, Hwa-Wei would seek opinions from his colleagues in order to develop the library's vision, mission statement, goals, and objectives. He would establish a special task force to solicit input and draft the library's statement for action. To Hwa-Wei, any organization's goals and values have to be in line with the interests and desires of its staff members. Only through this shared vision can staff members gain incentives and maximize their efforts to achieve both for the organization as well as for themselves. The idea of balancing interests of all parties and eliminating conflicts to reach a win-win situation coincides with Hwa-Wei's management principles.

For the purpose of long-term planning, Hwa-Wei emphasized the concept of strategic planning in order to be forward thinking and not restricted by short-term goals and objectives. Dr. Donald E. Riggs, the author of *Strategic Planning for Library Managers,* was a good friend of Hwa-Wei. They both shared a common desire to promote the application of strategic planning in academic libraries.[2]

In order to involve library staff in library planning and operations, Hwa-Wei was very mindful of participative management by encouraging staff involvement at all levels of management and decision-making. By doing so, he encouraged and empowered staff to take initiatives at work while receiving support, not restrictions, from their supervisors, just as long as the actions supported the goals and objectives of the library.

For the creation of a favorable atmosphere for participative management, Hwa-Wei set the example by making library administration more democratic, transparent, humanistic, and accountable. To achieve the desired results, he also placed great emphasis on staff development and encouraged staff to attend relevant library conferences and in-service training programs. Furthermore, Hwa-Wei encouraged staff to pursue continuing education in order to advance their professional careers.

The principles behind total quality management (TQM) were implemented in Japan in 1948 by Dr. W. Edwards Deming, "the father of the quality evolution," in order to revive the Japanese economy and the manufacturing industries that had been destroyed by World War II. Because of the successful results Deming's "Fourteen Points" achieved in Japan, they were adopted extensively within the United States in the 1970s as the foundation of TQM. The purpose of TQM is to provide the highest degree of customer satisfac-

---

2. Donald E. Riggs, *Strategic Planning for Library Managers* (Phoenix, AZ: Oryx Press, 1984).

tion by implementing necessary and sustainable changes in organizational culture and operational procedures so as to generate high quality products and services to customers.

Since libraries are service organizations, many public and academic libraries in the United States also adopted TQM. Hwa-Wei liked the idea of TQM because he set high quality library service as one of his management goals.

In the business world, knowledge management has been regarded as strategically important for organizations to gain a competitive advantage and to add value to their products in order to provide greater satisfaction to their customers. In the library world, there is a lesson to be learned from the business world. Knowledge management is as important for libraries as it is for businesses—excepting the competitive, proprietary, and moneymaking aspects. In fact, libraries have had a long and rich experience in the management of information. Much of the knowledge and many of the skills of librarianship can be applied to knowledge management.

For a library to succeed in implementing knowledge management, vision and strong leadership from the top administration are imperative; these can influence the organization's knowledge-sharing efforts in a positive way. According to Hwa-Wei, as libraries enter the "age of knowledge" of the twenty-first century, they should not take a back seat in the development of this field; they, instead, should be in the driver's seat as information technology and systems can provide effective support in implementing knowledge management. Librarians should work together with professionals in information technology to develop the appropriate knowledge management systems for their institutions.

In his book, *Knowledge Management: Theory and Practice,*[3] co-authored with Dr. Xiaoying Dong and Professor Meiyun Zuo, faculty members of the Guanghua School of Management at Peking University, Hwa-Wei asserts that the time has come for libraries to reposition themselves as the central stage for and as a leading player in knowledge management.

4

In January 2000, three months after Hwa-Wei's retirement from Ohio University, he was invited by OCLC to serve as a visiting distinguished scholar with two important assignments, both of special interest to Hwa-Wei. The first assignment was to assist the newly established OCLC Institute in developing its continuing education program. The second assignment was to assist in the outreach of OCLC's Asian Pacific Service in China and Southeast Asia. The former

---

3. Hwa-Wei Lee, Xiaoying Dong, and Meiyun Zuo, *Knowledge Management: Theory and Practice,* Twenty-First Century Library Science Series [in Chinese] (Beijing: Huazhi Publishing, 2002).

was a totally new program initiative with the goal to develop library seminars relating to OCLC's programs and activities, under the direction of Eric Jul.

The second assignment was very familiar to Hwa-Wei because the Asian Pacific Service, under the outstanding leadership of Andrew H. Wang, had already made excellent progress in Asia. Hwa-Wei knew Andrew and his staff very well and had developed a close working relationship with him. By carrying out both of these assignments in a coordinated manner, Hwa-Wei helped in designing appropriate library seminars and conducting them in the East and Southeast Asian countries to promote OCLC's outreach to Asian libraries and library professionals.

It also turned out that Jul was a seasoned specialist on knowledge management. He and Hwa-Wei worked well in conducting library seminars in East and Southeast Asia with knowledge management as part of the course content.

Although the position of visiting distinguished scholar was initially for only one year, Hwa-Wei was retained as a consultant by OCLC for a second and third year—until he accepted the position as chief of the Asian Division at the Library of Congress in January 2003.

During Hwa-Wei's consultancy at OCLC, he was invited by Chiang Mai University in Thailand to work for six weeks, September 9 to October 25, 2001, as a Fulbright senior specialist advising the library science department of Chiang Mai University in designing its new graduate program.

Hwa-Wei still vividly remembers his arrival in Chiang Mai on the evening of Tuesday, September 11, the morning of the 9/11 attacks in the United States. He had just checked in at a local hotel, an arrangement made by Chiang Mai University. At about 10:00 p.m. local time, Hwa-Wei turned on the TV news. He was totally shocked by the news that nineteen militants associated with the Islamic extremist group al-Qaeda had hijacked four airliners and carried out suicide attacks against targets in the United States.

Hwa-Wei saw the photos of the second plane hitting the south tower of the World Trade Center in New York City. The attacks resulted in extensive death and destruction. Over three thousand people were killed during the attacks in New York City and Washington, D.C., on that day. Even though he was very tired from his long trip from Columbus, Ohio, to Chiang Mai, Thailand, Hwa-Wei was unable to sleep and watched the news all night long. America was under unprecedented attack! Hwa-Wei was lucky that his air travel had been completed just a day ahead of the tragic event.

In the following six weeks, despite profound sadness, Hwa-Wei carried out his assignment including the design of the new curriculum and the writing of the final report and the recommendation. He worked very closely with faculty members of the department and other members of the planning team. For a project of such magnitude, six weeks were, indeed, a very short time. Hwa-Wei was very grateful for all the help he received from Professor Ratana Na-Lamphun, head of the Library Science Department, and from her dedicated faculty.

Upon the completion of his six-week assignment, Hwa-Wei co-authored a paper with Professor Ratana Na-Lamphun, a former student at Chulalongkorn University, entitled, "Focusing on Information and Knowledge Management: Redesigning the Graduate Program of Library and Information Science at Chiang Mai University." The paper, which embraces his knowledge management concepts in library education, was published in the March 2002 issue of *Information Development*.[4]

Because of the expressed interest in knowledge management by library professionals in Thailand, Hwa-Wei was invited back to Chiang Mai in March 2003 to attend the "International Conference on Challenges and Opportunities for Libraries and Information Professionals in Knowledge Management and the Digital Age." The conference, organized by the department of Library Science of Chiang Mai University, was held March 20–22, 2003. At the request of the conference organizer, Hwa-Wei gave five presentations on the following topics:[5]

- Libraries in Rapid Transition: Information Management vs. Knowledge Management
- Library Cooperation and Resources Sharing
- Steps in Implementing Knowledge Management
- Promoting Positive Changes in Scholarly Communication: The SPARC Initiative
- Measuring Library Service Quality: The LibQUAL + Tool

Making five presentations at one conference was a first for Hwa-Wei, but he was very pleased and honored by the invitation. He also realized how much the field of library and information science had changed during the fifty years of his library career. There was still much to learn in the rapidly changing field of librarianship.

---

4. Ratana Na-Lamphun and Hwa-Wei Lee, "Focusing on Information and Knowledge Management: Redesigning the Graduate Program of Library and Information Science at Chiang Mai University," *Information Development* 18, no.1 (March 2002): 47–58.

5. "Libraries in Rapid Transition: Information Management vs. Knowledge Management," "Library Cooperation and Resources Sharing," "Steps in Implementing Knowledge Management," "Promoting Positive Changes in Scholarly Communication: The SPARC Initiative," and "Measuring Library Service Quality: The LibQUAL + Tool," *Challenges and Opportunities for Libraries and Information Professionals in Knowledge Management and the Digital Age, 20–22 March 2003, Chiang Mai, Thailand* (papers presented at international conference [Asia-Pacific] organized by the Department of Library Science, Faculty of Humanities, Chiang Mai University), (Chiang Mai, Thailand: The University, 2003), 1–9, 29–32, 84–93, 118–21, 122–28.

CHAPTER 16

The Hwa-Wei Lee Library Annex

When it was proclaimed that the Library comprised all books. . . .
Thousands of covetous persons abandoned their dear natal hexa-
gons and crowded up the stairs, urged on by the vain aim of finding
their Vindication.

—Jorge Luis Borges

1

IN 1978, Hwa-Wei became the first Chinese American to be appointed as a library director of a major American university. He realized the gravity of his
responsibility representing Chinese Americans and his obligation to do well.
The goal he set for himself was very clear—to break the glass ceiling for Chinese
American librarians and to prove that they, too, can do as good a job as other
ethnic groups. After the enactment of the Immigration and Nationality Act of
1965 and the Equal Employment Opportunity Act of 1972, the climate of racial
discrimination and inequality in the workplace had been lessened, and the door
for ethnic minorities to move upward had opened wider.

In addition to working his way up the ladder, Hwa-Wei also served as a
mentor to other Chinese American librarians who were seeking the opportunity for career advancement. There were several such cases where Hwa-Wei's
advice and counsel led to a successful promotion, enabling many of those indi-
viduals to break through the glass ceiling and move into the position of library
director at an American college or university. In sharing his own experience, Hwa-
Wei gave many talks at national and regional conferences of the Chinese American Librarians Association (CALA), such as "Achieving Career Goals: Issues and
Strategies," and "Developing the Core Competences of a Modern Librarian."

Ohio University is the institution that Hwa-Wei served for the longest period
of his library career. From the time he assumed the director's position in 1978 to
his retirement in 1999, he spent twenty-one years at OHIO, where he was first
hired as director and later promoted to dean of Ohio University Libraries.

According to Hwa-Wei, those were the golden years of his career. He was
able to contribute all that he knew and to devote all his effort to accomplishing
his goals and responsibilities. Hwa-Wei was very fortunate to have worked under
two eminent university presidents: Dr. Charles J. Ping and Dr. Robert Glidden.

He also had great satisfaction from working with a very supportive group of university deans, administrators, faculty, and library colleagues. The main source of his pleasure, and what Hwa-Wei most appreciated, was the trust, cooperation, and spirit of teamwork that he received from his library colleagues.

2

During his twenty-one years at Ohio University Libraries, the collection of books more than tripled, from 600,000 volumes to 2,230,000 volumes; the number of serial titles quadrupled, from 5,500 titles to 20,000 titles; and the number of microform materials increased five times, from 600,000 reels to 2,960,000 reels. This fast growth of collections quickly filled the available materials space inside Alden Library.

Ohio University Libraries was not the only library in the state of Ohio to encounter serious spatial problems. Among the eighty member libraries of OhioLINK,[1] representing both public and private colleges and universities, the combined total of books reached 45 million volumes in the mid-1990s.

As Ohio's academic library consortium, OhioLINK served nearly five hundred thousand students, faculty, and staff. When statewide library collections expanded at such a fast pace, space shortage became an imperative issue, and public institutions began seeking state funding for additional storage space. The total costs each year for additions or new buildings were far more than the state of Ohio was able to keep up with or to fund.

As a statewide library consortium, OhioLINK came up with the idea of building five regional storage facilities: one building in each of the northeast, southeast, southwest, northwest, and central regions would provide remote storage for low-circulation materials in order to free up prime space in the main libraries for new acquisitions. Those regional storage facilities were to be shared by libraries in each region.

Seeing the growing spatial needs at OHIO's Libraries, Hwa-Wei decided to seize this funding opportunity by acting first among the many university libraries in the state. He submitted an application to the state government for building a regional storage facility in Southeast Ohio, where Ohio University is located. The government's response was quite favorable, but it required that the university provide the land and the maintenance staff.

Three miles away from the Athens campus on Columbus Road, there happened to be a piece of land for sale, which had originally been used as an auto dealership with a service department. As the owner of the property got older, he decided to close the dealership and sell the land for $500,000.

---

1. About OhioLINK, "History," OhioLINK, https://www.ohiolink.edu/content/history.

Hwa-Wei urged the university to acquire the property for use in building the regional storage facility, as well as a library annex. University President Robert Glidden quickly approved his recommendation. At this time, the state of Ohio was making every effort to promote the building of the five storage facilities and was looking for an exemplar, so Ohio University's proposal was approved and quickly received the initial government funding.

The construction of the new storage facility started in early 1997. Hwa-Wei and his associate dean, Dr. Gary Hunt, oversaw the project throughout all its stages including the application, site selection, planning, design, construction, and opening. The two took turns visiting the construction site to check on the progress. In addition to the high-density shelving area, the new library annex also housed a reading room, the preservation department, the microform production unit, as well as storage for university records, local government records, and manuscripts.

At the completion of phase one, the library annex could hold one million books with sufficient space for building extensions in future years. Each of the future phases, to be built every three or four years as needed, would provide storage capacity equal to phase one. When choosing the location, Hwa-Wei already took projected growth into account, leaving sufficient flexibility for expansion up to five phases.

The front section of the building has two floors. The ground floor consists of a spacious reading room, service area, staff offices, and a lounge equipped with light kitchen facilities. The second floor houses the entire preservation department with ample staff workspace for binding, repairing, microfilming, and the de-acidification equipment.

Behind the front section of the building is the Southeast Ohio Regional Depository area with twenty-one-feet-high ceilings and floor-to-ceiling stacked shelving. The stacks are built extremely well with solid, interwoven steel frames in which the top and bottom frames are firmly fixed in place. A lesson had been learned from other libraries when high stacks collapsed because of failure to bear the weight of high-density book storage, so Hwa-Wei paid special attention to the strength of the design during this stage. To reach the top shelves safely to retrieve books, journals, and other materials, library staff operated mobile lifts, commonly called "cherry pickers," that moved between the shelving units.

Statistics show that at American libraries the average annual storage cost for a single volume including labor, utilities and other maintenance costs is about fifteen dollars. The cost decreases to only fifty cents if it is housed in an off-site storage facility—a significant reduction in storage cost! Furthermore, seldom-used books and other library materials are environmentally secured in such a closed-stack area where the room temperature and humidity are at ideally controlled settings. Materials are also easily located and retrieved through OHIO Libraries' online catalog.

To save shelving space, each book or publication is identified by a unique barcode number. Normally, it will take between four to eighteen hours for materials to be transferred back to Alden Library. In other words, if a book is requested in the morning, it may be available in the afternoon, or if a book is requested in the afternoon, it may be available the next morning. In the case that a user needs a large number of resources, he or she may also go directly to the annex, where he or she can be served immediately. The annex, unlike Alden Library on the main campus, provides ample parking for patrons.

The library construction was scheduled to be completed by June 1999. In March, University Vice President James Bryant spoke to Hwa-Wei seriously: "I heard that you had decided to retire at the end of August. However, because of your familiarity with China, you must take us on a trip to China before your retirement. As you know, my wife, Jean, and I have a travel group of some forty friends. Some of them are Ohio University faculty and staff members. We normally make an international trip once a year in May or June by using our vacation time."

In response to Dr. Bryant's proposal, Hwa-Wei quickly organized a three-week tour that included Beijing, Xian, Three Gorges, Chengdu, Tibet, Guilin, and Hong Kong. Once the trip was announced, some sixty people signed up to join. With the combined expertise of Dr. and Mrs. Bryant and Hwa-Wei, it was very successful. Mary also joined the group trip because she had always wanted to visit Tibet. The trip took place in May of 1999.

By the time the group returned to Athens, the new building was already ready for use. In front of the building was a big sign that read, "Hwa-Wei Lee Library Annex," and a pair of Chinese-style lions carved from white marble. Hwa-Wei was very surprised to see his name on the building. In the United States, university libraries are often named after donors, but seldom after library directors. It was truly an honor.

In order to keep it a surprise, his colleagues and friends came up with the plan to visit China, so Hwa-Wei would be away during the landscaping in front of the new building. This was, indeed, a well-kept secret and a total surprise. He was speechless and deeply touched by what the university had done for him.

The pair of Chinese white marble lions in front of the Lee Library Annex was set on two red brick pedestals to match the building's exterior materials and colors, thereby giving the simple square building a bit of exotic charm.

The New York Public Library on Fifth Avenue also has two stone lions sitting in front of the palatial building. They were initially named "Lady Astor" and "Lord Lenox," respectfully, after the donors. In the early part of the last century,

Mayor Fiorello LaGuardia changed their names to Patience and Fortitude, a phrase that the mayor repeatedly evoked during his Sunday evening broadcasts to encourage the citizens of New York City to get through the darkness of the Great Depression.[2]

As loyal companions of the city through that difficult time, the marble lions, Patience and Fortitude, have earned a special place in the eyes of New Yorkers and of the city's visitors. They indeed symbolize a library's spirit of learning: patience and perseverance.

The two marble lions sitting in front of the Lee Annex add more of a Chinese element than simply their style: stone lions are regarded as auspicious objects in ancient Chinese architecture. As spirit beasts, always found in a pair, they are said to serve the function of protecting a house and bringing good luck, if placed in front of the building. Despite the difference in style between them, both pairs of white marble lions are majestic and awe-inspiring. And their embodied meaning, expressed in the names of New York City's lions, Patience and Fortitude, reaches beyond language and culture and remains the perfect representation of a library's spirit.

Hwa-Wei remembered that the two marble lions were purchased in Shijiazhuang during his 1998 trip to China. He bought them as his retirement gift to the university and had hoped for them to be placed in front of the Vernon R. Alden Library, thinking they would be a perfect match to the pillars at the entranceway. The university president appreciated and approved of the idea.

It did not take long for the stone lions to be shipped to Athens. However, by the end of the year, they were not yet in place. Hwa-Wei often wondered, "The lions have arrived. Why haven't they been placed at Alden Library's entranceway?" The secretary to the president replied with a mysterious smile, "It's a secret." Now, the secret was unveiled. It was completely unexpected, but it was the sweetest and the most thoughtful secret that Hwa-Wei had ever experienced.

3

On August 31, 1999, after his twenty-one years of service at Ohio University Libraries, Hwa-Wei formally stepped down from the dean's position for retirement. He told both the local and university news publications during an interview, "It was my great privilege to work at Ohio University, which allowed me to carry out many innovative programs aimed at achieving the library's strategic plan for excellence in collections and services. I am most grateful to Presi-

---

2. Nicholas A. Basbanes, *The Eternal Library II—Patience & Fortitude* [in Chinese], trans. Chuanwei Yang (Shanghai: Shanghai People's Press, 2011), 22–25. Originally published as *Patience & Fortitude: A Roving Chronicle of Book People, Book Places, and Book Culture* (New York: HarperCollins, 2001).

dent Ping and President Glidden for their counsel, support, and trust, without which many of my accomplishments would not have been possible. I also enjoyed working with the finest group of faculty and researchers in making the library the true center for learning. I must add also that I will miss my wonderful colleagues in the library for their loyalty, hard work, dedication, and comradeship. I will bring with me all these fine memories in my retirement."

In recognition of his superior achievements, the Board of Trustees named the new Southeast Ohio Regional Depository the "Hwa-Wei Lee Library Annex." At the ribbon-cutting ceremony several distinguished guests attended to convey their best wishes for Hwa-Wei's retirement including President Robert Glidden; former presidents, Dr. Vernon Roger Alden and Dr. Charles J. Ping; chair of the Board of Trustees, Ms. Charlotte Eufinger; and former chair, Donald Spencer.

Later on, in recognition of Hwa-Wei's significant contributions in building one of the strongest international collections in the country, the university's administration, with the encouragement of Dr. and Mrs. Alden, decided to renovate the first floor of Alden Library and name it the "Hwa-Wei Lee Center for International Collections." The entire cost of the renovation was covered by President Emeritus Vernon Alden and his wife, Marion.

A few months before his retirement, the planning committee for Hwa-Wei's retirement, chaired by Salinda Arthur, sent letters to alumni and friends soliciting their contributions to establish a library endowment in Hwa-Wei's name. The fundraising drive received enthusiastic response. A total of over $200,000 was raised. Hwa-Wei was deeply gratified when he was later informed of the result.

Mrs. Rene Glidden helped plan a grand retirement party at Baker Center to be given by Ohio University, with a total of over one hundred invited guests including Hwa-Wei's colleagues and friends from the university, the library, the community, and his family members. Among the speakers at the event were Dr. Robert Glidden, university president; Sharon Brehm, provost; James Bryant and Jack Ellis, vice presidents; and Charlotte Eufinger, chair of the Board of Trustees. Many library colleagues, who also spoke, praised Hwa-Wei's remarkable leadership and accomplishments.

In a warm and relaxed atmosphere, the hustle and bustle of Hwa-Wei's twenty-one years at Ohio University became condensed in retrospective reviews by his colleagues and friends, as tranquil as a page in a book being turned over silently by a fingertip. However, the page left by Hwa-Wei held many good memories for him, for his family, for his friends, and for the university and the library, as shown in the commendation from the president of Ohio University and the chair of the Oho University Foundation board.

Hwa-Wei Lee
Professor of Education, 1979–1999
Director of Libraries, 1978–1991
Dean of Libraries, 1991–1999

Distinguished Service
Noted Author and Educator
Advocate of Philanthropy
World Citizen

We salute you for over two decades of exemplary service to Ohio University and the Ohio University Libraries.

During your tenure, library acquisitions grew to over two million volumes; major building renovations were completed; and a regional annex was created. You oversaw the inauguration of ALICE, the computerized card catalog; ensured that the Ohio University Libraries were among the founding members of OhioLINK, a statewide network of academic libraries; and spearheaded a drive for national recognition, culminating in the Ohio University Libraries being named to membership in the elite Association of Research Libraries, one of only 121 facilities so recognized in North America. A tireless fundraiser, you succeeded in building library endowments to over $8 million.

You have been a model for international service. Under your leadership a program for international librarian exchange was created, four countries named our library as their official depository, the Southeast Asia Collection gained national and international renown, and the Chubu University Commemorative Japanese Collection and You-Bao Shao Overseas Chinese Documentation and Research Center were established.

We, the Trustees of the Ohio University Foundation, are honored to have been associated with you, and look forward to our continuing relationship with you.

Done at Athens, Ohio
This twenty-sixth day of February, A. D. 1999

Robert Glidden, President
On behalf of Ohio University

Leonard R. Raley, Executive Director
On behalf of the Ohio University Foundation

James E. Daley, Chairman, Board of Trustees
On behalf of the Ohio University Foundation

The retirement ceremony was touching. Hwa-Wei expressed his gratitude and surprise and thanked his library colleagues for their collective efforts and support throughout the years, and the university's administration for the trust and flexibility that they had given to him and the library. His thanks also went out to those donors who had made generous contributions to the library. He emphasized his belief that the development of a nationally or internationally acclaimed library would have to be the result of a joint effort of various kind-hearted, sincere, positive, and collaborative people. He also stated his willingness to continue his effort to promote the global image of the university in East and Southeast Asia, the region in which he had developed such a good network of library cooperation.

4

In addition to the many recognitions that Hwa-Wei received from Ohio University upon his retirement, he also received special recognitions from the American Library Association (ALA), the Chinese American Library Association (CALA), the Asian-Pacific American Library Association, Ohio Library Council, OhioLINK, OhioNet, the National Library of China, the Library Association of ROC in Taiwan, and the National Central Library of Taiwan.

Additionally, the ALA's executive office passed a special resolution praising his accomplishments and professionalism; Ohio Library Council inducted him into the Ohio Librarians Hall of Fame; Online Computer Library Center (OCLC) invited him to become its Visiting Distinguished Scholar for 2000–2001; and the National Library of China presented him with a plaque, appointed him as its advisor, and thanked him for his "care and support to Chinese librarianship."

Throughout the years, Hwa-Wei has been very active in the American library community where he served as an elected councilor of the American Library Association for eight years, as the chair of its East Asia & Pacific Subcommittee of the International Relations Committee, as a board director of the Ohio Library Council and a number of committees, as its president during the transition from a regional association to a national association on the Chinese American Library Association (CALA), as an Ohio representative to the OCLC Members Council, as a standing committee member of the Academic and Research Library Section of International Federation of Library Associations (IFLA), and as an Ohio delegate to the White House Conference on Library and Information Services.

His extraordinary accomplishments earned him numerous awards and recognitions, including:

- Ohio Hall of Fame Librarian (1999)
- OhioLINK Certificate of Appreciation (1993)
- ALA's Distinguished Service as Councilor Award (1992)
- USIA Certificate of Appreciation (1992)
- APALA's Distinguished Services Award (1991)

In 1987, Hwa-Wei was chosen an Honorary Alumnus of Ohio University as well as the Ohio Librarian of the Year.

At Hwa-Wei's retirement in 1999, the Ohio University Board of Trustees named the library annex in his honor.

Two white marble Chinese lions guard the entrance to the Hwa-Wei Lee Library Annex, which opened in 1999. Participating in the ribbon-cutting ceremony were (*left to right*): Hwa-Wei Lee; Donald Spencer, former chair of the Ohio University Board of Trustees; President Emeritus Charles Ping; Charlotte Eufinger, chairwoman of the Ohio University Board of Trustees; President Emeritus Vernon Alden; and President Robert Glidden.

The first floor of OHIO's Vernon Alden Library was named "Hwa-Wei Lee Center for International Collections" in honor of Dean Emeritus Hwa-Wei Lee.

- ALA John Ames Humphrey Award for Contributions to International Librarianship (1991)
- Chinese Academic & Professional Association in Mid-America (CAPAMA) Distinguished Service Award (1991)
- Library Association of ROC in Taiwan Outstanding Contribution Award (1989)
- Ohio Librarian of the Year Award (1987)
- CALA's Distinguished Services Award (1983)
- Outstanding Administrator Award of Ohio University (1982)

5

Southeast Ohio was once a major coal-mining area, however as the mining declined, the economic condition of the region became depressed in the second half of the twentieth century. The residents in many Southeast counties became poverty stricken. As a consequence, many of these counties were unable to support their public libraries and provide a minimum level of library services to their residents.

As the largest library in the region, although an academic library, Ohio University Libraries was open to the general public and served as the backup library to surrounding public libraries by providing interlibrary loan and reference services, under the commission of the State Library. As an ardent supporter and promoter of library services in Southeast Ohio, Hwa-Wei offered valuable assistance and established good relationships with the county libraries.

Hwa-Wei has always been energetic, but with a calm smiling face. Everything always seemed well under his control, and he readily placed everything in good order. In addition to being the library dean, Hwa-Wei was also a faculty member at the College of Education and served on dissertation committees of some ten doctoral students. His home was always a "home away from home" in Athens to many students and many library interns from mainland China,

Taiwan, and Thailand. On holidays, Mary, one of the busiest housewives in Athens, would prepare a full table of Eastern and Western foods for these students and librarians. Her homemade pineapple coconut punch was her most popular refreshment, leaving every international student with sweet memories about the Lee household.

Once the retirement party was over, Hwa-Wei and Mary returned home. The August evening was already feeling cool; the moonlight was clear like water; the fall colors brewing in the darkness were already peeping out from the tops of the maple and ginkgo trees—celebrating the city's most beautiful season of the year. Although a bit tired, Hwa-Wei, still immersed in the warmth and joy of the party, leaned back against his couch while going through the day's mail. Included was this letter from Shanghai:

Dear Dr. Lee:
Mid-Autumn greetings from Shanghai!
  Please forgive us for leaving Athens without notice.
  Wen-Yuan was offered a tenure-track assistant professor position at Clemson University in Southern Carolina, which will start from September 1. Prior to this, we all came back to Shanghai to visit relatives. Due to our tight schedule, we even did not get a chance to say bye to you. Our sincere apologies!
  Having lived in Athens for as long as twelve years, we have many memories about Athens, our first place in the U.S. we have ever stayed. What we especially feel more proud of is being given such an honor to get to know you, a senior and venerable Chinese American who possesses a thorough knowledge of both Western and Chinese culture. We along with many other Chinese students and scholars, who have been in Athens, were all once taken care of by you and your wife, which truly is a warm chapter in our overseas endeavors. Now, it is time for us to follow your steps and do something good to our people and society. Your impact on us is everlasting.
  Wen-Yuan has already been back to the U.S., and resettled in Clemson. Currently, he is busy with establishing his lab . . . When you and Mary have a chance to come to the south, be sure to visit us.
Respectfully,
Hui-Yi Chen and Wen-Yuan Chen (your students)

Hui-Yi Chen and Wen-Yuan Chen had earned their doctorates from Ohio University and once worked as faculty for the university. Although the couple had been frequent guests at the Lee home, they had not seen the Lees for a while. Hwa-Wei felt happy for them, knowing their life had indeed had some exciting changes. He was happy for every Chinese student who left Athens for a better future. Excited, he got up from the couch; he could not wait to write back to the Chens.

Arriving in Washington, D.C.

We hold these truths to be self-evident, that all men are created
equal; that they are endowed by their Creator with inherent and
inalienable rights; that among these are life, liberty, and the pursuit
of happiness.

—Thomas Jefferson

1

AFTER HIS retirement from Ohio University, Hwa-Wei had a brief period of
rest and relaxation, free of the constant pressure and the heavy workload. Not
only did he gain time to be with his family, but he also had time to take care of
his health, treating his chronic back pain with therapeutic exercises such as
swimming and walking.

Nevertheless, his first retirement did not last very long. Just about two
months after his retirement, Hwa-Wei received a phone call from Jay Jordan,
president and CEO of the Online Computer Library Center (OCLC), inviting
him to be a visiting distinguished scholar for a one-year term. Since this appointment was considered a high honor, Hwa-Wei gladly accepted it.

Back then, OCLC had just established the OCLC Institute with an aim to
provide certified short-term training courses for librarians. Most of these courses
were on the latest developments in the rapidly changing field of library and
information science. It was hoped that through Hwa-Wei's prestige and influence in the region some of these training courses could be offered in Asian
countries—a potentially significant geographic area for the expansion of OCLC's
international outreach.

Hwa-Wei's work schedule at OCLC was quite flexible. The headquarters
of OCLC is located in Dublin, in the northwest corner of Columbus, Ohio. It
is about ninety miles away from Athens. Driving from his home to OCLC
would take less than two hours. Normally, he would travel to OCLC twice
a week and work from home on the other days. A major portion of work-
related communications could be conveniently done through computer and
Internet connections.

Founded in 1967, the Ohio College Library Center (OCLC), in its early years, was a library consortium for developing MARC-based, online-shared cataloging and a unified catalog. Its initial membership, as indicated by its name, was comprised of university and college libraries in Ohio. As the first library consortium in the world, and as a nonprofit entity, the mission of OCLC was to foster collaborative cataloging and resource sharing among member libraries.

OCLC's success in Ohio soon attracted libraries from other states, as well as other nations, to join. By 1977, it had become a national and global center of networked libraries of all types and sizes. To reflect the rapid expansion of its membership composition and geographic coverage, its name was changed in 1981 to the Online Computer Library Center. The new vision was "to be the leading global library cooperative, helping libraries serve people by providing economical access to knowledge through innovation and collaboration."[1]

According to OCLC's 2009–2010 annual report, as of July 2010, there were a total of 72,000 libraries of different types, from 170 countries, using OCLC products and services, of which 26,704 were members. WorldCat, the largest unified catalog and bibliographic database in the world, had 197 million records representing library resources in 479 languages, and an intellectual output of human records that spanned a period of over six thousand years. Between 2009 and 2010, the database had 65 million online visitors and received 10,200,000 interlibrary loan requests.[2]

With Hwa-Wei's assistance, the OCLC Institute, in a short span of two years, organized one or two seminars in each of these Asian countries and regions: China, Korea, Hong Kong, Philippines, Taiwan, and Thailand. All the seminars, led by Institute Director Eric Jul and Hwa-Wei, were well received. In 2001, OCLC extended Hwa-Wei's contract for a second year. The training program was then discontinued due to its failure in cultivating a domestic market. Hwa-Wei became a consultant of OCLC Asia Pacific Services, on recommendation of Director Andrew Wang. In early 2002, Hwa-Wei's contract with OCLC was renewed for a third year.

Late in 2001, Hwa-Wei received a phone call from Dr. Carolyn Brown, director of Area Collections and Services at the Library of Congress (LC), who said, "The position of chief of our Asian Division has been vacant for a long period of time. We would like to invite you to be the interim chief and to assist us in recruiting a permanent chief." Having just renewed his contract with OCLC, Hwa-Wei felt that it was inappropriate to leave, so he recommended his longtime friend, Karl Lo, who had just retired from the University of California at San Diego (UCSD) after years of outstanding service as the director

---

1. OCLC, http://www.oclc.org.

2. OCLC, *Annual Report*, *2010*, http://www.oclc.org/content/dam/oclc/publications/AnnualReports/2010/2010.pdf.

of the University Libraries' International Programs and the head of its East Asian Library.

From Hwa-Wei's point of view, Karl would be the best candidate to be the interim chief of the Asian Division at LC. In fact, Karl was more than qualified to be the chief. Before coming to UCSD, Karl had accumulated twenty-five years of administrative experience as the East Asian library director at the University of Kansas and the University of Washington, consecutively. As an experienced, energetic, and talented leader in the East Asian library community, Karl was recognized as being one of the pioneers in the automation of Chinese, Japanese, and Korean (CJK) materials for East Asian libraries in the United States, and the founder of the Pacific Rim Digital Library Alliance for open sharing of digital and other materials—before such international cooperation in the sharing of digital materials became common.[3] Karl was exactly the person the Library of Congress had been looking for!

At Hwa-Wei's recommendation, Karl was hired by LC and became the acting chief in March 2002. Under his leadership, Karl was able to upgrade outdated computers in the Asian Division and began a training program for the staff to learn the use of these computers for online searches and technical services. In a short span of six months, he succeeded in transforming the division, bringing its old-fashioned operations into the new and exciting world of computer applications. Unfortunately, Karl resigned at the end of his sixth month. Among his reasons for leaving LC, as Hwa-Wei heard later, were the difficulties he encountered with personnel issues and the layers of bureaucratic procedures at LC.

In fact, as a person of action, Karl had left a remarkable legacy at the Asian Division with his efforts in introducing the concept of computer applications for CJK materials during his very short tenure. It was a pity that Karl decided to leave. Shortly after his departure, Hwa-Wei received another phone call from Dr. Brown, inviting Hwa-Wei to apply for the position of chief, not the interim or acting chief. At that time, Hwa-Wei's third-year contract with OCLC was about to end. He was thankful to LC for their repeated invitations and decided to give it a try, despite his age and knowing full well the many challenges that he would face.

Though she had never worked with Hwa-Wei, Dr. Brown was quite aware of his knowledge and expertise in library administration and in Asian library collections. The widely acclaimed reputation of Hwa-Wei was well known in the American library community. Everyone who had had contact with Hwa-Wei through professional activities was impressed by his sincerity, pleasant personality, dedication, and strong sense of mission—all factors behind Dr. Brown's

3. Eugene W. Wu, "Karl Lo – A Tribute" http://www.eastasianlib.org/romax/KarlLoTribute.pdf.

Hwa-Wei was appointed the chief of the Asian Division of the Library of Congress in February 2003.

Hwa-Wei stands inside the Library of Congress Asian Reading Room. One of three buildings housing the LC, the Jefferson Building's ten reading rooms provide public access to the materials and publications of the library's various collections.

Hwa-Wei shows Secretary of Labor Elaine C. Chao one of the rare objects contained within the collections of the library's Asian Division.

offer. She seemed to know from the very beginning that Hwa-Wei had the right qualifications and experience for the position as her decades of administrative experience had taught her that one's characteristics and personality can determine one's performance. Actually, Dr. Brown soon discovered that she had found a very competent and charismatic administrator for the Asian Division.

After he left his post at Ohio University, Hwa-Wei thought that he was ready for retirement. However, his love of the library profession and his accustomed busy life style had become a part of him, things he could not easily change or discard. While his work at OCLC was relatively easy and relaxed, Hwa-Wei knew full well that the position at LC would be very different: the situation at the Asian Division was problematic; it would require major efforts on his part to make the necessary reforms within a short period of time. Because of his character and strong will, that challenge soon became an irresistible temptation to Hwa-Wei. How could he not accept it?

Initially, taking into consideration his age and the condition of his health, Hwa-Wei told Dr. Brown that he planned to work for only three years. But Dr. Brown wanted him to work for at least five years, knowing the difficult and complicated situation at the Asian Division would require a thorough reorganization and reform. Even five years might not be enough time from LC's perspective. Just before leaving LC, Karl Lo had warned Hwa-Wei about the Asian Division and his frustration in overcoming many longstanding bureaucratic and personnel problems, but Dr. Brown was an excellent persuader. Hwa-Wei finally agreed to a five-year term. He was fully aware of the challenges that lay ahead. Fortunately, he was relatively healthy for his age and his chronic back pain was largely gone.

Confucius once said, "At seventy, I would do whatever my heart desires without going beyond what is right." Working at the Library of Congress, the largest and most prestigious national library in the world, would literally be Hwa-Wei's heart's desire: the library was the perfect place to conclude his long and glorious library career. Thus, at the age of seventy-two, Hwa-Wei embarked on the last and, to him, the most challenging phase of his career, facing it as if he were still a young man taking on an exciting and fascinating adventure.

In January 2003, Hwa-Wei and Mary departed from Athens, leaving their house and furniture in the care of good friends, a Chinese couple; the husband, Zhiyong Tian, also worked at the University. In this house Hwa-Wei and his family had lived for over twenty-four years, beginning with their move to Athens in the summer of 1978. There the family had spent joyful and stable years. All of their children, except their second daughter, Pamela, had finished college at Ohio University. (Being a top athlete at Athens High School, Pamela had received a full scholarship from Indiana University.) The Lee family had enjoyed living in this pleasant and comfortable university town, and had thought that they would stay there even longer. The unanticipated invitation from the Library of Congress, however, brought unpredictable changes to their later years.

2

That winter, Washington, D.C., went through numerous bouts of cold weather. People had just returned to work after the holiday break. The entire city, though a bit sluggish, started to hustle and bustle as usual. As the capital of the United States, Washington, D.C., is heavily political. Buildings along the streets downtown house mostly government offices, headquarters of national and international organizations, trade unions, lobbying groups, and foreign embassies. Statues of American founding fathers and other historical figures can be seen everywhere. Most of the city's inner residents are employed by the government, or associated in some way with the business of the government. In addition, numerous national and international tourists come to the city, attracted by the historical sites and interesting museums.

The full name of Washington, D.C., is Washington, District of Columbia. The name was given in honor of George Washington, the first president of the United States. Well situated in the mid-Atlantic region, Washington, D.C., became the nation's capital in 1800. Previously, Philadelphia had been the home of the Continental Congress from 1774 to 1788, and then the capital of the new republic from 1790 to 1800. The capital was moved as the result of a dispute between the northern states, represented by Alexander Hamilton, who favored a strong federal government, and the agricultural, slave-holding southern states, represented by James Madison acting on behalf of Thomas Jefferson. In compromise, Congress decided to place the new capital in a location that acknowledged the interests of both sides.

> On July 9, 1790, Congress passed the Residence Act, which approved the creation of a national capital on the Potomac River. The exact location was to be selected by President George Washington, who signed the bill into law on July 16. The land was to be donated by the states of Maryland and Virginia.[4]

The layout of this capital city is simple and orderly. As many of the city's buildings are named after figures important to the founding and growth of the nation and represent qualities considered integral to the nation's purpose, great care was taken in their placement and their architecture from the city's earliest planning stages, to expound on the founding fathers' idea of this nation: one

---

4. "History," Washington, DC, http://washington.org/DC-information/washington-dc-history. "History of Washington, D.C.," Wikipedia, http://en.wikipedia.org/wiki/Washington, D.C.

based on freedom and democracy. The city's center features the rectangular National Mall. At one end is Capitol Hill; at the other end stands the Lincoln Memorial; between the two is the Washington Monument. All government agencies, museums, and other cultural institutions surround the National Mall. Behind Capitol Hill are two distinctive building complexes: one for the Supreme Court, representing the rule of laws; and the other for the Library of Congress, denoting the governance of the nation with knowledge. The combination is thought provoking.

Capitol Hill acts as the heart of the capital, around which streets reach out to the other parts of the city. Streets and avenues are named after the original thirteen colonies that declared independence from Great Britain. Along the sides of the wide and straight avenues are oak, elm, and cypress trees. Around the Jefferson Memorial and along the Potomac River are stretches of cherry trees. Another unique feature of this capital city, the full cherry blossoms in spring create an indescribably beautiful scene.

All buildings in Washington, D.C., are built lower than the U.S. Capitol, to signify the power of the U.S. Congress. The White House, situated in the city's center, has a low profile in comparison to the surrounding buildings. North of the White House is Lafayette Square. Inside the square mingle groups of street artists and the homeless, many of whom look gaunt and poorly dressed, in sharp contrast to the residents of the White House and the District. Indeed, this contrast also represents the American culture of freedom and tolerance.

There was still some time for Hwa-Wei and Mary to get settled before February 10, Hwa-Wei's official starting date at LC. Over the years, he had preferred to get everything ready before starting a new job. Knowing of his arrival, many staff members at the Asian Division offered their help. It did not take long for them to find a rental apartment in Arlington adjacent to the Washington metropolitan area and close to a Metrorail station, making his commute very convenient.

The Clarendon Apartments in Arlington is situated in a new residential and commercial urban community. There are gardens and fountains, benches, and a playground in the central square. Along the two sides of the square are apartment buildings no more than six floors high, of which the first two floors are commercial shops, with the third and upper floors housing residential apartments. Dining and shopping could be done all within walking distance, simplifying life. The one-bedroom apartment Hwa-Wei and Mary rented was on the sixth floor. As Mary does not like to drive, the location of the apartment proved a great convenience. Right next to their apartment building was a Barnes & Noble bookstore. Being a book lover, Mary had great fun, living right around the corner from one of America's largest bookstore chains.

Still, adapting from the idyllic life in Athens to the urban rhythm of Washington, D.C., would take some time. The good thing was that their apartment, located in the center of Arlington, was conveniently close to bus stops and the Metrorail station. There was no need for them to drive except for special events or visits with friends in the evenings and on weekends.

Also, because there were so many good restaurants specializing in various American and international cuisines, Hwa-Wei and Mary never had to worry about where to eat or what to eat. Having been used to cooking for her big family, Mary found it difficult adjusting to making meals for just two. As the couple started getting older, they started to eat less food and relatively simpler meals. Thus, dining out became very convenient.

3

Hwa-Wei found it almost unbelievable that his life had started again to be as busy as those of the young people in the District; it was as if time had reverted back decades. Every morning, he took the orange line of the Metrorail to work. It was a five-minute walk from his apartment to the Metrorail station, and another twenty-five-minute ride before arriving at Capitol South, the station next to LC's James Madison Memorial Building. After a short walk through an underground passage connecting the Madison Building to the Thomas Jefferson Building, Hwa-Wei entered the Jefferson Building, where the Asian Division and his office were located.

February 10 was Hwa-Wei's first day at the Asian Division. His office, on the first floor of the Jefferson Building, was right behind the Asian Division's reading room and staff offices.

The Library of Congress (LC) is comprised of three buildings named after three presidents: Thomas Jefferson, James Madison, and John Adams. Perhaps, it would be more precise to call the buildings monuments to the three presidents.

Founded in 1800, LC was originally located inside the Capitol building. Its original core collection of three thousand volumes was burned to ashes in August 1814 when British troops set fire to the building. In 1815, Congress approved the purchase of Thomas Jefferson's personal library of 6,487 books for $23,950. This personal collection was comprised of books and journals on a wide range of subjects that Jefferson had collected over a period of fifty years, including his time in Paris as the American minister to France. When donated, it was regarded as the best private collection in the nation. Those books and journals were transported from his residence in Monticello, located near Charlottesville, Virginia, to Washington, D.C., and became a major portion of LC's initial collection.

The Jefferson Building was completed and opened for service in 1897. One of the early government buildings in the District, the Thomas Jefferson Memorial

Building was designed, from the initial stages, with consideration toward both its classical structure and longevity. Built of pure marble in the Renaissance architectural style, the building was expected to last for generations and to be filled with timeless books.

Recognized as one of America's most splendid buildings from the nineteenth century,[5] the Jefferson Building features both an external elegance and an internal strength. The domes and pillars are magnificent, and the frescoes, mosaics, and sculptures, which grace the building, are delicate and luxurious. Along the corridor are eight statues of the Goddess of Wisdom; inside the Main Reading Room stand supporting marble columns to symbolize the connection between civilization and wisdom. Facing toward the Capitol building, the Jefferson Building is one of the top tourist attractions in Washington, D.C., and is visited by thousands of tourists from all over the world, each and every working day.

Located in the center of the Jefferson Building, under a 160-foot-high domed ceiling, is the Main Reading Room, housing some 45,000 volumes of key reference tools, 250 reading seats, and computer terminals.[6] In addition to the Main Reading Room, there are nine special reading rooms: African and Middle Eastern, American Folklife Center, Asian, European, Hispanic, Local History & Genealogy, Microform, Rare Book & Special Collections, and Children's Literature.

The building has two levels, with floors both above and below ground. The underground passage at the lower level, which connects the Jefferson Building with the Capitol, requires a special permit to access. An upper underground level is open to library users and has passages to the other two LC buildings.

The second most important building of LC is the James Madison Memorial Building built in the 1980s. The Madison Building houses LC's administration offices, the Law Library, the U.S. Copyright Office, the Recorded Sound Research Center, and the Veterans History Project Information Center. It is also home to several reading rooms, both of general and special format collections: Copyright Public Records, Geography & Map, Law Library, Manuscript, Motion Picture & Television, Newspaper & Current Periodical, Performing Arts, and Prints & Photographs.

Named after the fourth president of the United States, this gigantic modern building, with a white marble exterior, fills almost the entire block of Capitol Hill. Inside the building, there are also large stacks and reading areas. The entire first level of its basement is like an underground palace, where the most precious American historical materials, such as manuscripts and rare books, are kept. In addition, there are also a large number of print images, photographs, and

---

5. Nicholas A. Basbanes, *The Eternal Library II—Patience & Fortitude* [in Chinese], trans. Chuan-wei Yang (Shanghai: Shanghai People's Press, 2011), 124. Originally published as *Patience & Fortitude: A Roving Chronicle of Book People, Book Places, and Book Culture* (New York: HarperCollins, 2001).

6. Yalan Cheng, *The Moving Scenery—A Library Tour* (Beijing: Beijing Library Press, 2006) 7–8.

maps. Among its map collection of some 20 million items are many Chinese historical maps. Also collected in the Top Treasures Vault is Thomas Jefferson's handwritten note of his presidential inauguration speech along with his lengthy letter to Dr. Benjamin Rush, which contains his firm principle: "I have sworn upon the altar of God, eternal hostility against every form of tyranny over the mind of man."[7]

The third building of LC, the John Adams Building, was completed in 1939, before the Madison Building. While its primary function was for collection storage, it also houses the Federal Research Division and the Science and Business Division, along with division reading rooms.

Eventually, all three LC buildings reached their full capacities due to the rapid growth of the collections. A number of off-site storage facilities were built by the library including the Packard Campus for Audio-Visual Conservation, in Virginia; and the High Density Storage at Fort Meade, Virginia. The Fort Meade facility, which formally opened on November 7, 2002, was designed to maximize the storage capacity. Items sent to the Fort Meade facility are shelved by size in boxes developed to accommodate the specific size of each item. Individual items and storage boxes carry discreet barcodes and are retrieved via the library's computerized Integrated Library System. This cost-effective method of storing under-used library collections is similar to the method used in the Hwa-Wei Lee Library Annex at Ohio University.

4

The first day of Hwa-Wei's work at LC was a daylong orientation for all newly employed staff held by the office of Human Resources. After the general orientation, through special arrangements made by Dr. Brown, Hwa-Wei spent half days during his first two weeks meeting with key administrative heads of the library and visiting most of the other divisions and centers. He also had a special meeting with Dr. James H. Billington, the librarian of Congress, who gave him a warm welcome and encouragement. Winston Tabb, associate librarian, an old friend and an active member of the organizing committee for the China-U.S. Library Cooperation Conference in 1996, also met with Hwa-Wei to offer his welcome and support.

The first thing Hwa-Wei did at his new post was meet with his staff at the Asian Division, both individually and in groups at division or sectional meetings. Hwa-Wei was very pleased that Acting Assistant Chief Philip Melzer was

---

7. Nicholas A. Basbanes, *The Eternal Library II—Patience & Fortitude*, 124–25.

Chapter 17

a seasoned administrator, borrowed from the Acquisitions and Bibliographic Access Directorate during the year prior to Hwa-Wei's arrival.

Through this orientation, Hwa-Wei had a glimpse of the gigantic organization and its complex structure. Under the overall leadership of the librarian of Congress and the deputy librarian of Congress there are seven offices: Office of the Librarian, Congressional Research Service, U.S. Copyright Office, Law Library, Library Services, Office of Strategic Initiatives, and Support Operations.

Acting as the de facto national library, the office of Library Services, under the administration of an associate librarian, oversees four directorates: Collections and Services, Acquisitions and Bibliographic Access, Partnership and Outreach Programs, and Preservation. Among the four thousand library employees, two-thirds are working under the associate librarian for Library Services. The Asian Division is one of the divisions within the Collections and Services Directorate.

During the meeting with his staff in the Asian Division, Hwa-Wei was very impressed by their subject knowledge and professional expertise. Hwa-Wei also learned quickly, either from meetings with the staff or through his own observations, that some of the existing problems were serious and needed to be addressed and corrected as soon as possible. One of the most serious problems was the lack of strong leadership and clear communication from the chief's office. This meant, as the division chief, Hwa-Wei had to begin reform from his own office.

Working closely with Philip Melzer and the office secretary, a series of measures were taken to improve two-way communications, vertically as well as horizontally, among all sections and units. A weekly newsletter for internal communication was issued, and all administrative actions were made more transparent. Staff participation was not only encouraged, but invited, in the development of a strategic plan with clearly stated goals, objectives, and action plans, which stressed the importance of collaboration between, and among, all sections and units.

Before Hwa-Wei's arrival, it was well known that there was frequent conflict, mistrust, and infighting among staff members in and among various sections and units. Since Hwa-Wei is a strong believer in the importance of creating a harmonious working environment, he worked very hard to create an atmosphere where mutual trust and respect were of foremost importance. Starting with himself, Hwa-Wei tried to build such a relationship with his staff. Not only did the door of his office remain open most of the time, he also frequently visited staff members in their offices or workplaces to discuss work-related issues, concerns, and actions.

In the Library of Congress strong labor unions represented various staff groups such as professional librarians, classified staff, police, and security officers. Their representatives often attended staff meetings to observe Hwa-Wei's administrative style and decision-making approach. Hwa-Wei always welcomed and acknowledged their presence at these various meetings.

As a part of his strategic planning process, Hwa-Wei worked through a planning committee to develop the division's mission statement, vision, goals, objectives, and action plans. This planning document was reviewed and updated each year in compliance with the overall vision, mission, goals, and objectives of the entire library. Below, for example, is the division's mission statement:

> The mission of the Asian Division is to establish the collections of the Asian Division as the premier research and scholarly resource of all formats and times on Asia and in Asian languages that is compatible with the dynamics of knowledge and creativity of the twenty-first century; and to make these resources and information services available and useful to the Congress, American people, and the scholarly community nationally and internationally.

5

Over the years, Hwa-Wei had worked for many academic libraries of all sizes, designed primarily for use by faculty and students. The academic atmosphere differed somewhat from that of a government library or, as in the case of LC, a national library. Despite Hwa-Wei's extensive knowledge and experience in library management, he had to make a major adjustment. It was not, however, a difficult one owing to his great adaptability and his willingness to meet new challenges.

After gaining a solid understanding of the challenges and opportunities, as well as the strengths and weaknesses, of the division, Hwa-Wei mapped out his action plans, which included major changes aimed at revamping existing problems or weaknesses and taking on the opportunities to revitalize the Asian Division. His eighteen-point priority actions were the following:

1. Reorganizing the structure of the Division and making it more effective and coherent in collection development and management, as well as in public and scholarly services.
2. Cultivating a new organization culture based on cooperation and teamwork.
3. Modifying the acquisition policy by placing emphasis on acquiring more publications on contemporary subjects and concerns.
4. Acquiring more large-scale digitized bibliographic and full-text databases of research value.

5. Implementing new procedures in stack management.
6. Selecting some three hundred thousand under-used library materials for remote storage at the Fort Meade storage facility.
7. Filling more than a dozen vacant or newly created staff positions.
8. Converting the manual check-in system for journals and serial publications to a computerized check-in operation to facilitate effective bibliographic controls and online applications.
9. Cleaning up long-neglected and uncataloged library material hidden in the stack area and adding them to the collection.
10. Establishing the Asian Division's Friends Society.[8]
11. Opening the Asian Reading Room on Saturdays for the convenience of users.
12. Organizing special events to promote the treasured collections and their use.
13. Creating a website for the Asian Division.[9]
14. Revising and updating the publication, *Library of Congress Asian Collections: An Illustrated Guide,* and placing it on the website for easy online access.[10]
15. Fundraising to support all outreach program activities and other special acquisitions and inventory work.
16. Establishing research fellowships with funds donated by Florence Tan Moeson.[11]
17. Working with national libraries in China, Japan, Korea, and Taiwan to cooperatively digitize the rare book collections for easy online access.
18. Planning for the establishment of an Asian-American Pacific Islander collection.[12]

After consultation with, and approval from Dr. Brown, Hwa-Wei began to charge ahead to implement his ambitious action plans. Hwa-Wei knew full well that most of these plans were major undertakings, and he had only five years in which to carry them out. Fortunately, with the support of Dr. Brown and the enthusiastic participation of all his colleagues, all these ambitious plans were successfully implemented within the five years of Hwa-Wei's tenure at the library.

---

8. Asian Division, "Asian Division Friends Society (ADFS)," Asian Reading Room, Library of Congress, http://www.loc.gov/rr/asian/adfs/.

9. *Asian Collections: 2007 Illustrated Guide* (Washington, D.C.: Library of Congress Asian Division, 2007) http://www.loc.gov/rr/asian/.

10. Ibid.

11. Asian Division, "2015 Florence Tan Moeson Fellowship Program Announced," Library of Congress, http://www.loc.gov/rr/asian/ftm.html.

12. Asian Division, "The Asian-American and Pacific Islander (AAPI) Collection," Library of Congress, http://www.loc.gov/rr/asian/aapi/index.html.

Asian Collections

> To establish the collections of the Asian Division as the premier re-
> search and scholarly resource of all formats and times on Asia and in
> Asian languages that is compatible with the dynamic of knowledge
> and creativity of the twenty-first century, frequently referred to as
> the Asian Century.
>
> —*Vision of the Asian Division, Library of Congress*

1

THOUGH THERE is no formal national library in the United States, there are three national-level libraries: the Library of Congress (LC), the National Library of Medicine (NLM), and the National Agricultural Library (NAL). The LC, the largest and most influential, is regarded as the top national library in the world with a comprehensive collection.[1] Its uniqueness resides in the scope of its collection, which is beyond historical, political, and geographical restrictions. In addition to its ambition of archiving the wide range of American culture and history, the library also has been striving toward covering essential cultural material from all parts of the world.[2]

According to the published statistics of 2012, LC owns a collection of 155 million items in various formats, among which 34 million are books and journals —and the number is rapidly growing at an average rate of ten thousand items per day. It has been said that if the LC's bookshelves were combined, the total length could reach about five hundred miles.[3]

About 40 percent of its impressive collections are in English, while the rest are in a variety of other languages. The size of the collected publications of every country, region, race, and language, in many cases, is the largest outside of those countries of origin. For example, LC's Chinese, Russian, Japanese, Korean, and Polish collections are the largest outside of the source countries. Simi-

---

1. Library of Congress, http://www.loc.gov.
2. Nicholas A. Basbanes, *The Eternal Library II—Patience & Fortitude* [in Chinese], trans. Chuan-wei Yang (Shanghai: Shanghai People's Press, 2011), 125. Originally published as *Patience & Fortitude: A Roving Chronicle of Book People, Book Places, and Book Culture* (New York: HarperCollins, 2001).
3. Library of Congress, http://www.loc.gov.

larly, its Arabic collection is second only to that of Egypt. Meanwhile, it owns the richest Jewish collection and some of the rarest Naxi manuscripts in the world.

Being a de facto U.S. national library, LC collects all government publications published in the country. In addition, U.S. copyright law also requires that two copies of every publication published in the United States be submitted to LC.

LC employs a variety of means to acquire publications of special value not published in the United States through official exchanges and purchases. In order to overcome language barriers, LC has established six field offices strategically located in various regions of the world to acquire, catalog, or microfilm (now digitize) items before they are shipped to the LC.

As an added service to other U.S. research libraries, field offices also acquire additional copies focusing on subjects chosen by those libraries that pay subscription fees to cover the costs. With the language and subject knowledge of their locally hired library staff, all the field offices are able to access valuable publications for LC. The three field offices covering Southeast Asia and South Asia are located in Jakarta in Indonesia, New Delhi in India, and Islamabad in Pakistan. The other three are located in Cairo in Egypt, Nairobi in Kenya, and Rio de Janeiro in Brazil.[4]

2

Since its formation, the Asian Division has gone through several name changes. The Division of Chinese Literature was founded in 1928, thanks to the special efforts of Dr. Herbert Putnam, the LC librarian. Its name was later changed to the Division of Chinese and Japanese Literature in 1931, to the Division of Orientalia in 1932, to the Asiatic Division in 1942, back to the Orientalia Division in 1944, then to the current Asian Division in 1978.

The Asian collection at LC started long before the division was formed. The first batch of Asian language materials at LC was transferred from the Smithsonian Institution in 1865. These books, covering Southeast Asia and the Pacific Islands, had been acquired originally by the Wilkes Exploring Expedition in Singapore from 1832 to 1842. Four years later, in 1869, ten titles, contained in 933 volumes, of Chinese books were presented by Emperor Tongzhi of China to the library. These two separate collections are considered the earliest Asian collections at LC.

The 933 gift books from China cover a variety of subjects such as Confucius, Neo-Confucius, medicine, agriculture, and mathematics; they also include en-

---

4. Cataloging and Acquisitions, "Overseas Offices," Library of Congress, http://www.loc.gov/acq/ovop/.

cyclopedias. An extremely rare item in the batch is the block-printed copy of *Mei's Series* dated 1706. Another block-printed title is the famous pharmacopoeia, *Compendium of Materia Medica*, from 1655–56.

In 1875 the library began its acquisition of Japanese material through an exchange program with the Japanese government.[5] Since then, its Asian collection has had a steady growth with publications from different Asian countries and in various Asian languages. As of December 2010, 135 years later, the size of the collection has grown to over 3 million volumes including 19,241 current journal and serial titles, 62,498 reels of microfilm, 556,931 microfiche, and 10,050 manuscript items.

However, these numbers do not include Asian legal documents, maps, images, photos, and audiovisual materials, which are kept in other divisions such as the Law Library, Geography & Map, Prints & Photographs, Motion Picture & Television, Recorded Sound, and Manuscript.

Another unknown number of non-Asian language materials about Asia are shelved in the Main Reading Room as well as in various other reading rooms, including Microform, Newspaper & Current Periodical, Performing Arts, Science & Business, and Rare Book & Special Collections.

Located on the first floor of the Jefferson Building, adjacent to the Great Hall, the Asian Reading Room is serene and dignified. On two sides of the walls are approximately ten tall narrow windows, brightening the entire space. Between the windows along the walls are large hardwood bookshelves, each with a unique staircase, which one could walk up to fetch books from the top shelf. The spaces between the bookshelves, on both sides, are the reading areas. Readers can fully enjoy the comfort of reading, indulging themselves among the sea of books, while being bathed in the sunlight coming through the windows. The slightly narrow area in the center of the room is for card-catalog cabinets. The room, quiet and spacious, is full of the wisdom and spiritual wealth of Asia. A visit to the room makes one feel as if a gate had opened to the other side of the Pacific Ocean.

The Chinese & Mongolian Collection

As of December 27, 2010, the collection consisted of 1,056,075 volumes of monographs, 5,630 current journal and serial titles, and 10,962 inactive journal and serial titles. Included in the collection are publications in Chinese, Manchu, Mongolian, Naxi (Moso), Tibetan, Uzbek, and a number of minority languages.

---

5. *Asian Collections: 2007 Illustrated Guide* (Washington, D.C.: Library of Congress Asian Division, 2007), 1, 2, 4, 8, http://www.loc.gov/rr/asian/guide2007/. Area Studies Asian Division, "Asian Reading Room," Library of Congress, http://www.loc.gov/rr/asian/.

Also in the collection are Chinese classical books; archival materials from the Qing dynasty, 1644–1911, and the Republic of China, 1911–1949; publications on traditional Chinese medicine; local and regional histories (gazetteers); and contemporary publications from mainland China, Hong Kong, and Taiwan.

The collection also contains some of the rarest and most valuable books from China, Mongolia, and Tibet covering the dynasties from Song (960–1279), Jin (1115–1234), Yuan (1271–1368), Ming (1368–1644), and Qing (1644–1911). It includes a Buddhist invocation sutra, *Yi qie ru lai,* printed in 975 AD, which was recovered from the hollow bricks of the foundation of the Thunder Peak Pagoda when it collapsed in 1924. Also included are forty-one of the four hundred surviving volumes of the 1560 edition of the *Great Encyclopedia of the Ming Emperor Yongle,* and the 1895–98 printing of the *Imperial Encyclopedia of China* in 5,044 volumes.

Collection value is determined by an item's scarcity as well as its uniqueness. Unique materials in the collection include the 3,344 Naxi manuscripts written by the minority group in Yunnan Province. Naxi is the only active pictographic writing system in the world today. Another valuable set is the William Gamble collection of Christian publications that were written in Chinese, or translated from western languages, and published by the American Presbyterian Publishing House in Shanghai and Ningbo in the nineteenth century. Arthur W. Hummel's collection of rare Chinese maps is also one of the division's treasures.[6]

LC also has the richest Tibetan collection in the world, which consists of representative literatures spanning all the years of Tibetan literary development from the eighth century to the present. The subject coverage is all-inclusive, covering religion, history, geography, traditional medicine, astronomy, musical notation, linguistics, sociology, and secular literature. The true riches in this collection are the Tibetan Buddhist scriptures, including more than one hundred volumes of *Kanjur* and about 225 volumes of *Tanjur* (the two core Buddhist canonical works), the latter of which contains precise annotations of original Buddhist scriptures written in Sanskrit from 500 BC to 900 AD.

Some legendary contributors to the early development of the collection were Berthold Laufer, a renowned Tibetologist from the late nineteenth century; William Woodville Rockhill, a U.S. diplomat and Tibetologist who traveled to Mongolia and Tibet during his tenure in China (1888–92, and the early twentieth century); and Joseph Rock, an explorer, adventurer, and scientist, who lived and traveled in China's rugged west for twenty-seven years in the early 1900s.[7]

---

6. "Chinese Beginnings," *Asian Collections: 2007 Illustrated Guide,* http://www.loc.gov/rr/asian/guide/guide-chinese.html.

7. *Beikoku Gikai Toshokan zo Nihon Kotenseki Mokuroku* [Catalog of Japanese Rare Books in the Library of Congress] (Tokyo: Yagi Shoten, 2003).

The Japanese Collection

The collection started in 1875 with the debut of the U.S.-Japan government publication exchange program. It was enriched in 1905 when a significant gift was received from Crosby Stuart Noyes, journalist and editor of the *Washington Evening Star*. The Noyes collection includes 658 volumes of illustrated books published from the mid-eighteenth to the late-nineteenth century.

In 1907, a systematic effort was undertaken by Kanichi Asakawa of Yale University to purchase Japanese books for the Library of Congress including 9,072 volumes on the subjects of Japanese history, literature, Buddhism, Shintoism, geography, music, and the arts. The collection was tripled during Dr. Shiho Sakanishi's term as the chief assistant at the Japanese Section (1930–41). In 2010, the collection included 1,182,073 volumes of books, 6,761 current journal and serial titles, and 9,451 non-current journal and serial titles; all of these publications were collected through a variety of transactions including purchases, donations, and exchanges.

Rare materials in the collection include approximately five thousand titles of publications and manuscript copies that were originally produced before the end of the Tokugawa Shogunate period and the early years of the Meiji period (1868–1912). Among those rare materials is a precious item: the Dharani Prayer Charms dated 770 AD, which is one of the earliest surviving printed materials in the world.

Also noteworthy are a rare complete edition set of the Japanese literary masterpiece, *The Tale of Genji* (Genji Monogatari), published in Kyoto in 1654; and the *Yoshitsune azumakudari monogatari*, printed on movable type sometime between 1624 and 1643.[8] In 2003, Yagi Shoten of Tokyo published a complete catalogue of Japanese rare books at LC.[9]

At the end of World War II, the Washington Documentation Center, a government intelligence agency, transferred to LC a large quantity of historical documents, which had originally come from the former Japanese Imperial Army and Navy, the South Manchurian Railway Company, and the East Asian Research Institute. Many of these documents from the last two agencies were pre-World War II studies on Korea, Taiwan, China, Mongolia, and the Pacific Islands, created in preparation for the war. Also held in the LC collection are microfilmed official documents of Japan's Ministry of Foreign Affairs and the Policy Division of the Ministry of Domestic Affairs; some of these are censored wartime publications.[10]

---

8. "'The Japanese World," *Asian Collections: 2007 Illustrated Guide*, http://www.loc.gov/rr/asian/guide/guide-japanese.html].

9. *Beikoku Gikai Toshokan zo Nihon Kotenseki Mokuroku.*

10. Hwa-Wei Lee, "Building a World-class Asian Collection in the Library of Congress for Area Studies, Culture Preservation, Global Understanding, and Knowledge Creation" (paper), in the

Another important collection is the Inoh Maps, the first modern maps of Japan created originally by Inoh Tadataka from 1800 to 1817. Inoh and his team drew 214 sheets of maps, in fine detail at a 1:36,000 ratio, covering the Japanese archipelago from Hokkaido to the Kyushu Islands. The final comprehensive set was completed in 1821 after Inoh's death in 1818 and consisted of 214 *daizu* (large scale), eight *chuzu* (medium scale) and three *shozu* (small scale).

In the spring of 2001, 207 sheets of the 214 *daizu* maps were rediscovered in LC's map collection. These *daizu*, reproductions made during the Meiji era based directly on the results of the surveys, caused sensational news in Japan since only sixty other *daizu* sheets were known to be extant. (All of the original Inoh maps had been destroyed: The set submitted to the shogunate government was lost in a fire in the Imperial Palace in 1873. The duplicate copy possessed by Inoh's house had burned in the Great Kanto Earthquake of 1923.) At the request of the Japanese government (Japan Map Center), the Inoh maps were digitized by LC. Reproductions of selected pieces of the maps were exhibited at the Kyoto National Museum from October 31 to December 14 in 2003.

The Korean Collection

The Korean collection began in the 1920s with a generous donation from Dr. James S. Gale, a Canadian missionary who spent forty years in Korea from 1888 to 1928. Dr. Gale also helped LC acquire a number of Korean classical materials including rare books from the estate of the Korean scholar Kim To-hui. The collection was further expanded during the Korean War in the 1950s. According to the 2010 statistics, the collection included 273,720 volumes of Korean books, about ten thousand volumes of North Korean publications, twenty thousand volumes of Japanese books, and nine thousand volumes of English language materials on Korea. There are also 1,854 current and 5,598 non-current journal and serial titles.

Also in the collection are 480 titles of Korean rare books in three thousand volumes, written in Chinese characters and printed on mulberry paper. While the Chinese invented clay movable-type printing, the Koreans enhanced this printing technique by replacing the clay type with metal. Some significant rare books are the 1541 edition of *T'oegye sonsaeng munjip* (the collected works of T'oegye); the collected writings of Yi I, a renowned sixteenth-century Confucian scholar and statesman, printed in 1744; and the 1834 reprint of the works of Ch'oe Ch'i-won (857–915), the "father of Korean literature." Rare woodblock-printed materials

Proceedings of the Symposium "The New Horizon of Library Services Toward the Better Understanding of Asia," November 19, 2003 (Kyoto, Japan: National Diet Library, Kansai-kan, 2004), 57–67 (Japanese translation), 150–69 (English paper and slides). Also published in *Collected Works of Hwa-Wei Lee*, vol. 2 [in Chinese] (Guangzhou: Sun Yet-Sun University Press, 2011), 1228–35.

at LC include A History of the Koryo Dynasty (*Koryo Sa*), printed in 1590; and The Law Code of the Choson Dynasty (*Kyongguk Taijon*), printed in 1630.[11]

The Southeast Asian Collection

LC's Southeast Asian Collection started in 1865, predating the other Asian collections. The initial collection of Malay manuscripts and early printed books were acquired in 1842 in Singapore by Horatio Emmons Hale, a philologist in the U.S. Naval Expedition team led by Lt. Charles Wilkes. Hale received assistance from Alfred North, an American missionary in Singapore, in his acquisitions. These materials were first shipped to the Smithsonian Institution, then later transferred to LC in 1865. Included in this acquisition are a unique collection of rare manuscripts written in the script used by the Bugis of South Sulawesi; a manuscript copy of Abdullah's Story (Hikayat Abdullah), a valuable account of the nineteenth-century Malay world, written in Jawi (an Arabic alphabet for writing the Malay language); and an 1840 Mission Press edition of the Malay Annals (*Sejarah Melayu*), the only available account of the Malay sultanate in the fifteenth and early sixteenth centuries, originally written prior to 1536, then modified under the order of Sultan Abdullah Maayah Shah in 1612.

The Southeast Asian collection also includes many palm leaf manuscript copies of the Tipitaka, the basic text of Theravada Buddhism, the majority religion of Cambodia, Laos, Myanmar (Burma), and Thailand. In 1905, a special Thai Tipitaka was presented to the library by King Chulalongkorn (Rama V) of Thailand. In 1949, the library acquired, as gifts of the Burmese government, a large number of Burmese manuscripts written in the Pali language, including a Tipitaka in Pali using Burmese script. The donation also included *The Glass Palace Chronicle,* an important Burmese history written by scholars in 1829.

Other rare resources in the Southeast Asian Collection are materials from the Philippines and Vietnam. Of special note is a set of bamboo tubes inscribed in the old Indic script similar to the ancient scripts used in neighboring Indonesia. The bamboos, fifty-five in prose and twenty-two in verse, provide a intriguing glimpse into the Mangyan (Hampangan) and Tagbanua societies. In addition, the collection holds a few histories of Vietnam dynasties, including texts printed from early woodblocks at the former imperial palace in Hue.[12]

The year of 1938 saw the launch of the Indic Project, aimed to expand the library's Southeast and South Asian Collection, especially in acquisitions of native language publications. The collection grew rapidly during the post-World War II period, as a result of an increasing interest in the United States in the

---

11. "Korean Classics," *Asian Collections: 2007 Illustrated Guide,* http://www.loc.gov/rr/asian/guide/guide-korean.html.

12. "Southeast Asia and the Pacific Islands," *Asian Collections: 2007 Illustrated Guide,* http://www.loc.gov/rr/asian/guide/guide-southeast.html.

region. Today, it contains publications from Brunei, Cambodia, East Timor, Indonesia, Laos, Malaysia, Myanmar, Philippines, Singapore, Thailand, Vietnam, and many South Pacific Islands such as Papua New Guinea.

In 1963, a LC overseas office was established in Jakarta to acquire and process local books, newspapers, and journals. As of 2010, the collection consists of 207,415 volumes of monographs, as well as 2,736 current and 8,462 non-current journal and serial titles, primarily in Southeast Asian languages.

The South Asian Collection

The foundation of the collection was laid in 1904 when the library purchased over four thousand books and other materials from Dr. Albrecht Weber, a German Indologist. The acquisition included Indian religious works in Sanskrit such as *Vedas, Brahman,* and *Upanisads;* an anthology of stories from the Puranas; and other great epic writings including *Mahabharata* and *Ramayana.* Also acquired were Weber's notes on significant early editions of Indian Buddhist scriptures.

In 1938, the Carnegie Corporation made a special grant to LC for development of the South Asian Collection, enabling LC to launch the Indic Project. After World War II, the collection grew dramatically following the establishment of field offices in New Delhi in 1962, and Karachi (later moved to the Pakistani capital, Islamabad) in 1965. Authorized by the Public Law (PL) 480 program, the New Delhi office used rupees from Indian purchases of U.S. agricultural products to buy books and other materials from India and other countries of South Asia.

Statistics of 2010 showed that the collection of materials had grown to more than one hundred languages including Hindi (20 percent), Bengali (15 percent), Urdu (13 percent), and Tamil (11 percent). Other major languages represented are Marathi, Telugu, Malayalam, Gujarati, and Kannada. As of September 30, 2010, there were a total of 269,846 volumes of monographs, as well as 638 current and 2,120 non-current journal and serial titles in the collection.

Among the many rare books and manuscripts in the South Asian collection is a pictorial manuscript of the *Jaina Kalpasutra* (1452), a Jainism scripture from the Gujarati region in Western India. This illustrated text tells the story of Mahavira, the founder of the Jaina religion.

The "Crosby Khotan Fragments" are also among the rare items. During a 1903 journey to Central Asia, Oscar Terry Crosby, an American who later became assistant secretary of the treasury, purchased these manuscripts in Sanskrit at the Taklamakan oasis town of Khotan.

In 1990, the Microfilming of Indian Publications Project (MIPP) was inaugurated at LC's New Delhi field office; the project continued until 2000. Co-funded by the Indian government and the Library of Congress, MIPP aimed to preserve and make accessible out-of-print books listed in the *National Bibliography of Indian Literature: 1901–1953.* The bibliography listed 22,686 publications in fifteen languages, compiled by a group of Indologists based upon the collections of sixty-seven Indian and three non-Indian libraries. The non-Indian libraries were the Library of Congress, the University of Chicago Libraries, and the British Library.[13]

3

In the history of Sino-U.S. book exchange, one very important figure—Caleb Cushing, the U.S. ambassador to China (1843–45)—succeeded in adding the following clauses to the Treaty of Wang Hya (Macau):

> It shall be lawful for the officers or citizens of the United States to employ scholars and people of any part of China without distinction of persons, to teach any of the languages of the Empire, and to assist in literary labors; and the persons so employed shall not, for that cause, be subject to any injury on the part either of the government or of individuals: and it shall in like manner be lawful for citizens of the United States to purchase all manner of books in China.

That passage, included in the official diplomatic document, was truly groundbreaking. It was instrumental in lifting the Qing government's ban on foreigners learning the Chinese language, and in allowing foreigners in China to openly hire Chinese to teach the native languages; it also made it possible for outsiders to freely acquire Chinese books. It thus symbolizes the true convergence of cultural exchange and diplomatic relationship.

During his years in China, Cushing acquired a large quantity of Chinese books in the areas of history, medicine, ancient literature, poetry, and novels. His Chinese collection of 2,547 volumes in 237 titles was later purchased by LC, and is now known as the Caleb Cushing Collection. A handwritten catalog of its titles was produced at the Asian Division. The most valuable resources in the Cushing Collection are ten volumes of Taiping Rebellions publications. Most Taiping books had been burned to ashes at the order of the Qing government after the fall of the Taiping Heavenly Kingdom, with only a very small number preserved outside of China.

Another important event triggering growth in the South Asian collection was China's participation in the St. Louis World's Fair in 1904. Displayed at the fair were 177 titles of Chinese books in the areas of canonical Confucianism, Qing imperial records, philology, phonetics, history, topography, epigraphy, ritual system, criminal law, disaster relief, economics, philosophies, initiation education, mathematics, almanacs, art of war, medicine, poetry, and political

---

13. *The Library of Congress in South Asia, 1960–2002: Celebrating 40 Years of Bibliographic and Cultural Exchanges* (New Delhi: Library of Congress Office, n.d.), 16.

systems. Many of the books had been published by Chongwen Publishing House in Hubei Province, one of four famous late Qing publishers known for the quality of its publications. All of these books were later donated to the U.S. government and added to the early Chinese collection at LC.

The Library of Congress recognized, from its early stages, the value of Chinese gazetteers and openly solicited them in China through a variety of means. This effort was initiated by Dr. Walter T. Swingle, an expert in agriculture and forestry, who was born in Canaan, Pennsylvania, and later lived in the Washington, D.C., area, working for the Department of Agriculture. Through his keen interest in Chinese plants and his research on citrus cultivation utilizing local gazetteers from Fujian and Guangdong Provinces, Swingle grew to value this resource. His advocacy laid a foundation for the library's Chinese gazetteer collection.

Before and after 1918, Swingle, on behalf of LC, made several trips to China to acquire local gazetteers from various provinces. His acquisition efforts continued with the assistance of Yuanji Zhang, of the Commercial Press in China, until 1928. More than half of the old Chinese gazetteers currently held by LC were acquired before 1928. A fabulous Chinese local history collection has been developed outside of China through Swingle's efforts.

The most noteworthy part of the collection is an almost complete set of Shandong gazetteers that were acquired in 1933 from Hongcai Gao (1851–1918), a Wei County magistrate in the province, whose styled name was Hansheng. A Wei County native and epigraphy scholar, Gao devoted over twenty years of his life, exhausting his financial resources, in developing the personal gazetteer collection, among which are many rare editions. Illustrating his ambition, every one of this collection's items was stamped "Wei County Gao Hansheng's Collection of All the Shandong Local Gazetteers at Fu-Zhou-Xian (Prefecture-State-County) Levels." Although the German consulate in Qingdao had wanted to acquire the collection, ultimately, LC succeeded in getting these treasures.

The largest Chinese local gazetteer collections at LC are from the Hebei Province (282 titles), the Shandong Province (279 titles), Jiangsu and Sichuan Provinces (252 titles each), and the Shanxi Province (234 titles). Collections from the provinces of Zhejiang, Shaanxi, Jiangxi, Guangdong, Hubei, and Anhui are also very impressive. While common local gazetteer collections focus primarily on provincial levels, LC's collection is more comprehensive and covers everything from provincial, prefecture, and county materials down to township levels. Many items in the collection are rare gems.[14]

14. Hwa-Wei Lee, "Sinological Resources in the Library of Congress" (keynote speech at the International Conference on Sinological Resources in the Digital Era, December 7–9, 2004, organized by the National Central Library [Taiwan] and Center for Sinological Studies, Taipei, Taiwan), in the *National Taiwan Normal University Alumni Journal* 325 [in Chinese] (February 2005): 4–12. Also published in the *Collected Works of Hwa-Wei Lee*, vol. 2 [in Chinese] (Guangzhou: Sun Yat-Sen University Press, 2011), 1236–43.

Arthur William Hummel Sr., the first Asian Division chief, also played a significant role in building the collection. Born in Missouri in 1884, Hummel went to China in 1915 as an American Christian missionary and taught the English language in Mingyi Church Middle School in Fenzhou (now Fenyang), Shaanxi for ten years.[15] During his years at Mingyi, he studied Chinese language, history, geography, culture, and customs; he became one of the early American sinologists. He also befriended several renowned Chinese scholars including Youlan Feng, Shi Hu, and Jiegang Gu. His son, the famous diplomat, Arthur William Hummel Jr., was born in Fenzhou and served as the U.S. ambassador to China from 1981 to 1984.

In 1928, Arthur W. Hummel Sr. was appointed as the first chief of the Orientalia Division. During his twenty-seven years as chief, the Chinese collection grew from 100,000 volumes to 291,000 volumes and attracted an endless stream of scholars from all over the country for research and thesis writing. In a short period of time, it gained its reputation as a quality Chinese collection and as a cultural salon for Chinese studies.

Arthur W. Hummel Sr., during his tenure, also put a great effort into reorganizing the Chinese rare books; in doing so, he created a Chinese cataloger position with support from the Rockefeller Foundation and the American Council of Learned Societies.

In 1939, by invitation, Chongmin Wang, a renowned Chinese bibliographer, Dunhuang expert, and library specialist, arrived to work on the annotated bibliographies of the library's rare Chinese books, including 624 out of 2,870 titles (thirty-eight out of one hundred boxes) of rare books the Chinese government had deposited in the library for safe keeping during the Sino-Japanese War.

Wang worked at LC until 1947. The handwritten bibliographies that he had completed were brought back to China; they were to be published by Peking University. That plan failed to be implemented, when LC lost contact with Wang and Peking University during the Chinese Civil War and the subsequent change in government.

A photocopied edition of *A Descriptive Catalog of Rare Chinese Books in the Library of Congress* was published in Washington, D.C., instead. The catalog, edited by Dr. Tung-Li Yuan and based on the microfiche copies of Wang's bibliographic scripts left at LC, includes 1,777 titles of Chinese rare books.

---

15. Ibid.

CHAPTER 19

Digital Resources

Visitors will find an amazing place where they will experience highlights of the largest collection anywhere of the world's knowledge
and America's creativity. They will meet the richness of the past,
spark their own curiosity and imagination, and continue the adventure of learning online, at home.

—*James H. Billington, librarian of Congress*

1

THROUGHOUT THE twentieth century the building of Asian collections focused
mainly on printed materials. However, that emphasis began to change in the
early twenty-first century with attention quickly shifting to electronic and web
resources. Large-scale digitization of rare materials was also being launched to
make some of the treasured collections, those with no copyright restrictions,
freely accessible to researchers via the Internet. The approaches taken by Hwa-
Wei after his arrival at LC included subscriptions to selected electronic bibliographic databases; the acquisition of digitized full-text databases of e-books,
e-journals, e-newspapers, and other electronic publications; the digitization of
selected rare books and special collections; and the capture of relevant websites
for the library's Asian portals, which were constructed and maintained by the
Asian Division.

Subscription to Databases

In 2008, forty-five of the library's 219 subscription databases dealt with Asia or
Asian studies. These databases were all accessible in the library's many reading
rooms and included Aardvark, Asian resources for librarians; Asian Development Bank Economics & Statistics of the Economics and Research Department
of the Asian Development Bank; Asian Law Online, bibliographic database
from the University of Melbourne; Bibliography of Asian Studies from the Association for Asian Studies; Country Studies produced by the Federal Research
Division of the Library of Congress; and Treaties and International Agreements by Oceana Publications.

Acquisition of Digitized Full-text Databases

Since Hwa-Wei's arrival in 2003, special efforts had been made to acquire a number of the most important digitized full-text databases from China, Japan, Korea and Taiwan.[1] The following came from China:

- *People's Daily* (electronic version, 1946 to date), a full-text database of this official Chinese newspaper
- China Data Online, a bilingual (Chinese-English) database for statistical data from China at national, provincial, and municipal levels
- CNKI China Academic Journals, a full-text database of over 7,200 academic journals from China
- CNKI China Core Newspaper, a full-text database providing access to one thousand Chinese newspapers
- Superstar Digital Books, which provides access to over one hundred thousand e-Books
- Wanfang China Conference Paper Database, which covers full-text conference papers from three thousand academic conferences held in China each year
- Wanfang China Dissertation Database, which covers full-text theses and dissertations from nearly one thousand institutions of higher education in China

Additional Chinese e-resources from Taiwan were added to the Asian Division collection, including the following:

- *Siku Quanshu,* a Wenyuange edition and stand-alone CD-ROM version
- *Chinese Civilization in Time and Space* by Academia Sinica
- *Taiwan History and Culture in Time and Space* by Academia Sinica
- *Taiwan Electronic Periodicals,* which covers five hundred titles
- *Encyclopedia of Taiwan*[2]

The *Complete Library of the Four Branches of Literature* (Siku Quanshu) was compiled during the years 1773–82 under an edict from Emperor Qianlong in China's Qing dynasty. It included 3,460 works, with a total of more than thirty-six thousand volumes. It covered a wide range of subjects including the classics, history, literature, philosophy, geography, politics, governmental rules and reg-

---

1. Mi Chu and Lily Chen Kecskes, "Reform of the Chinese Section in the Asian Division of the Library of Congress" [in Chinese], *New World Times*, Dec. 9, 2005.

2. Hwa-Wei Lee, "Building a World-Class Asian Collection in the Digital Age at the Library of Congress" (keynote speech at the Symposium on Library Collection in the Digital Age, January 16–17, 2006, organized by the National Chung Hsing University Graduate Institute of Library and Information Science and the National Chung Hsing University Library, Taichung, Taiwan), in *Symposium on Collection Development for Libraries in the Digital Age, January 16–17, 2006* (Taichung, Taiwan: National Chung Hsing University, 2006), 11–29.

ulations, economics, society, astronomy, science, technology, and medicine. The set was the most comprehensive encyclopedia of Chinese scholarship from antiquity to the eighteenth century. Originally seven copies of the *Complete Library of the Four Branches of Literature* (Siku Quanshu), all handwritten, were created, but because of wars and civil upheavals throughout Chinese history, only three complete sets of the original copies exist today. The Wenyuange edition is the first copy, produced in 1782, now kept in Taiwan.[3]

Two core Japanese databases that LC subscribed to were *Directory of Japanese Scientific Periodicals,* covering 13,875 serial titles on science and technology, and *Kodansha Encyclopedia of Japan,* a comprehensive English language encyclopedia with eleven thousand entries.

In addition, full-text databases of several major newspapers from Japan were added including *Mainichi Shinbun, Sankei Shinbu,* and *Yomiuri Shinbun.*

The Asian Division also subscribed to the following Korean databases:

- *Chosŏn Ibo Archive,* the most widely read newspaper in South Korea
- KRpia Korean database, which covers history, literature and traditional medicines
- Korean Studies Information Service System (KSISS), a database of full-text articles from six thousand journals published by 1,200 Korean academic institutions
- DBPia, a searchable database of full-text articles in about seven hundred scholarly journals published in Korea
- Law and Business, Korean law database, which contains articles concerning business law and is available for access in the Law Library reading room

On May 21, 2007, through the leadership of Sonya Lee, head of the Korean area team, the library signed an exchange agreement with the Korean National Assembly Library (KNAL) to acquire access to KNAL full-text databases free of charge. The KNAL databases contained over 8 million items and included monographs, government publications, dissertations in all fields, social science journals, historical newspapers, white papers, and periodical indexes (1910 to date).

2

Digitization of Selected Rare Books and other Collections

During Hwa-Wei's tenure, the Asian Division, besides acquiring a wide range of digital databases, launched several major collaborative projects to digitize its unparalleled Asian collections. With a three-year grant from the Chiang Ching-Kuo

---

3. University Libraries, "E-Research by Discipline," University of North Carolina, http://eresources .lib.unc.edu/eid/.

Foundation (1998–2001), the Chinese and Mongolian team, under the leadership of Dr. Mi Chu, was able to hire Professor Baotian Zhu of the Yunnan Museum in China to review, categorize, and prepare a detailed description of the 3,344 Naxi manuscripts in the collection, and subsequently digitize a portion of this unique collection. This digitized collection is now accessible from LC's website: http://international.loc.gov/intldl/naxihtml/naxihome.html.

On October 1, 2004, the library and the Academia Sinica (Taipei) signed an agreement for the digitization of China-related maps. Through three working visits, subject and digital experts from the Academia Sinica digitized 21,000 maps and 840 aerial photos between 2004 and 2006. These digital files became available online from the website of the Geography and Map Division of the Library of Congress, as well as being incorporated into the Chinese Civilizations in Time and Space (CCTS) database, supported by a historical geographic information system with spatial-temporal applications created by the Academia Sinica.

In May 2005, the library and the National Central Library (Taipei) signed an agreement for the digitization of Chinese rare books. A team of technical specialists from Taiwan worked onsite at the Library of Congress for four years to digitize selected titles in the Chinese rare book collection. These rare books were first selected and reviewed by a Chinese rare book expert, Bangjin Fan, under the supervision of Dr. Chu and other members of the Chinese and Mongolian area team, for authentication and annotation. The library's Conservation Division then inspected these books to determine their physical condition. Mr. Fan's employment, preparing for the digitization, was funded by the Chiang Ching-Kuo Foundation for 2005 and 2006. The goal of this collaborative project was a digitized database of Chinese rare books shared by the two libraries, making those books easily and freely accessible to researchers worldwide.[4]

In close collaboration with the International Research Center of Japanese Studies (Nichubunken), the Asian Division digitized four titles—*Shizuka, Homyo Doji, Shigure,* and *Soga Monogatari*—from the Nara Ehon Collection, consisting of two thousand digital images, including 173 color illustrations, available through the Library of Congress Online Catalog at http://catalog.loc.gov/.

Nara Ehon is a type of colorfully illustrated manuscript or hand-printed book of stories and tales produced from the Muromachi period (1333–1573) through the mid-Edo period (1615–1868). It is considered to be the earliest popular picture book in Japan. Another Japanese rare book, *The Tale of Genji,* a complete sixty-volume set of the 1654 edition, was also digitized in 2007. The digital files have been made available via the Library of Congress online catalog at http://lcweb4.loc.gov/service/asian/asian0001/2005/2005html/20050415toc.html.

---

4. Guo-Dong Zhang, "Plan of the National Library of ROC in Taiwan for the international cooperation in digitizing rare book collections—the case of working with the U.S. Library of Congress" [in Chinese], *Taiwan Library Management Quarterly* 5, no. 4 (October 2010): 99–110.

The Japanese Ukiyo-e Collection in the Prints & Photographs Division also benefited from collaboration with Nichibunken. Under the agreement signed by the library and Nichibunken in February 2005, a team of Japanese art historians visited the library for three weeks and completed their work in identifying and describing some three thousand prints. The library completed the scanning of the Ukiyo-e prints collection in 2006, with financial support from Nichibunken, and made the collection available through the library's Prints & Photographs online catalog (http://lcweb2.loc.gov/pp/pphome.html) and Nichibunken websites.

In cooperation with the Japan Map Center of the Geographical Survey Institute in Japan, the Geography & Map Division digitized the only surviving set of 207 large-scale Japanese maps made between 1816 and 1819 by the famous mapmaker Inoh Tadataka; these became available in June 2005 through the library's webpage: http://www.loc.gov/rr/geogmap/.

In May 2007, the Library of Congress also signed an agreement with the National Library of Korea (NLK) on a collaborative project that involved the preservation of the library's rare Korea-related maps and atlas holdings in its Geography & Map Division. The library's Korean maps and atlas collections include both manuscript copies and the rarer and more valuable woodblock impressions. The collections range from the 1760s to 1896, with many items having grown brittle due to age.

The National Library of Korea agreed to support the conservation of the maps and atlases; in turn, the library agreed to digitally scan selected maps and atlases and to provide free Internet access of these electronic versions via the library's website. Before Hwa-Wei's retirement from LC, the library also participated in the final review of the agreement with the NLK to digitize selected rare Korean books in the Asian Division.

3

Capture Relevant Websites

As a part of the library's effort to provide more and more specialized resources online such as the American Memory (http://memory.loc.gov/) and the Global Gateway (http://international.loc.gov/intldl/intldlhome.html), the library's portals also served as a gateway to selected web resources on a variety of subjects and world areas (http://www.loc.gov/rr/international/portals.html). The portals of the Asian Division (http://www.loc.gov/rr/asian/area_AD.html) were created and regularly updated by subject specialists, and those portals increasingly became a useful source of materials on all Asian countries and regions.

Planning was also initiated to begin a cooperative web capture project for at-risk web contents. This project addresses the problem that web content, which is important for future research, is now disappearing before being collected—and that many smaller institutions may not have the resources and/or the budgets for collecting websites. The Library of Congress was to work with select partner institutions to identify sites for content preservation. The Asian Division was focusing on two specific topics: North Korea and Islam in Asia. The collaborative effort was to ensure that online information needed by researchers would be preserved for posterity.

Online Reference Services

The library also took the lead in the development of QuestionPoint, a worldwide online reference service operating twenty-four hours daily, seven days each week by the Online Computer Library Center (OCLC). QuestionPoint enables library users anywhere to send their reference questions from their local libraries through the OCLC online global network to the Library of Congress for reply by reference librarians and area studies specialists (http://www.oclc.org/questionpoint). Library users may also use the service of "Ask a Librarian" to get reference assistance from librarians in the Asian Division.

4

The Chinese rare book collection at LC's Asian Division is regarded as both unique in quality and in quantity outside China and Taiwan. Most of the items in the collection had been cataloged, but the descriptive information about many of them was incomplete especially in regard to an item's rarity, value, and edition, due largely to the lack of expert knowledge about rare Chinese materials among LC's catalogers and subject specialists. Through the persistent effort of several former chiefs, together with colleagues in the Chinese and Mongolian area team, outside experts from China were invited to help in evaluating and describing several special collections. These experts, who came in the collection's early years, included Professor Shijia Zhu for gazetteers and Professor Zhongmin Wang for selected rare books. In more recent years, experts included Professor Xiaocong Li for older maps and Professor Baotian Zhu for the Naxi manuscripts. Three excellent catalogs were published as a direct result of their work:

- Zhu, Shijia. *A Catalog of Chinese Local Histories in the Library of Congress.* Washington, D.C.: Library of Congress, 1942.
- Wang, Zhongmin. Edited by Tung-Li Yuan. *A Descriptive Catalog of Rare Chinese Books in the Library of Congress,* 2 vols. Washington, D.C.: Library of Congress, 1957.

- Li, Xiaocong. *Descriptive Catalogue of the Traditional Chinese Maps in the Library of Congress.* Beijing: Wen Wu Publishing Co., 2004.

A Descriptive Catalog of Rare Chinese Books in the Library of Congress was started by Wang, then completed by Dr. Tung-Li Yuan, and provides a very useful bibliographic tool for digitization. However, because of the scarcity of Chinese rare books, access to them was restricted and inconvenient for researchers. Soon after the reorganization of the division was completed, and more new staff was added, Hwa-Wei began his effort to digitize Chinese rare books, to allow those valuable resources in the Asian Division to be more easily accessed in electronic format via the Internet by both on-site and remote researchers.

At first, Hwa-Wei tried to obtain approval from LC's library automation unit to handle the digitization within LC. However, he found that there were already too many projects, previously approved and waiting to be digitized. Chinese rare books would have to wait in line for many years before that unit could work on them.

Considering the short time span that he had before reaching his five-year tenure at LC, Hwa-Wei knew that he had to find a more expeditious way to digitize the rare books collection. Because of the size of the collection and the special care required in digitizing them, the cost of digitization would be prohibitively high.

At that time, Hwa-Wei knew about ongoing digitization projects undertaken by both the National Library of China in Beijing and the National Central Library (NCL) in Taipei. He explored the possibility of collaboration in digitization with the directors of both of these national libraries. At that time, in 2004, the National Library of China did not have extra funds to extend its own digitization project. However, during a visit to the National Central Library in Taiwan, Hwa-Wei, in meeting with the director, General Dr. Fang-Rung Juang, learned that the library was very much interested in collaborating with the Library of Congress.

Hwa-Wei also learned that Dr. Juang was to lead a delegation from the Library Association of China (Taiwan) to attend the annual conference of the American Library Association in Washington, D.C. He immediately extended an invitation to Dr. Juang and his delegation to visit the Library of Congress during, or after, the conference. The invitation was accepted.

In June 2004 when Dr. Juang and his delegation visited LC, they were warmly welcomed and invited by Dr. James H. Billington to a formal luncheon in the Whittall Pavilion, which was used only for very special guests. After the luncheon, Hwa-Wei and Dr. Juang agreed to work out the details for collaboration in digitizing the Chinese rare books at LC and in sharing the digitized databases of both libraries.

At that time, Hwa-Wei learned that NCL had just completed the digitization of its own rare books, a collection far larger in size than the Chinese rare books collection at LC. The work had been completed by a contractor who specialized in the digitization of rare books. Since NCL had funding for more digitization work, it was willing to extend the project by including the digitization of Chinese rare books at LC. A draft agreement was worked out between Dr. Juang and Hwa-Wei, but, because of LC's internal policies and procedures, the agreement took one year to be approved; it was signed by LC in May 2005.

Soon after the approval of the agreement, a team of four technical specialists and a set of equipment arrived at LC. Hwa-Wei provided a room next to his own office for the team to begin their digitization work. All of their expenses were paid by NCL.

According to the agreement, books were scanned and produced in the same size as the originals, with the digital images saved in a tiff format at a resolution of 300 dpi and a 24-bit color depth. After review and correction, the images were burned onto DVDs.[5] The Chinese rare book specialist not only checked each book to be digitized with the holdings of NCL to avoid duplication, but also prepared bilingual (Chinese-English) metadata and bibliographic records for the books that were to be digitized.

Over three years, 2005 to 2008, 1,215 copies of rare books were scanned into 583,166 digital images, and five hundred metadata records were created. Among those scanned rare books were manuscript (codex) and printed copies from the Song, Yuan, Ming, and Qing dynasties, as well as copies made using the Korean movable-type printing technique.[6] A total of 3,043 bibliographic records from *A Descriptive Catalog of Rare Chinese Books in the Library of Congress* were added to NCL's Rare Book Image Search System. In addition, two batches of bibliographic records for Chinese rare books (1,700 in August 2004 and 1,200 in December 2006) were loaded into NCL's *Chinese Rare Book Catalog* for public access on the Internet.

Unlike the LC, whose images were scanned in black and white, NCL used color-imaging devices. In addition to the unique charm of the original paper's texture, Chinese rare books often contain annotations made by other scholars in red ink that have become an important addition to the originals. Only color image scanning could capture the quality and style of these books and annotations while maintaining their authenticity.

To be scanned by the LC's department, a book had to be taken apart for digitization. This risked damage to these Chinese rare books, many of which were several hundred years old. Because of the brittle condition of the paper,

---

5. Ibid.
6. Ibid.

the technical specialists from Taiwan came up with a solution that completely avoided this harmful treatment, giving these ancient treasures preservation-quality care by utilizing modern technologies. The NCL team shared this digitization process in the cross-cultural collaboration.

Because of the relatively low cost and more efficient way of digitization by the Taiwanese specialists, the Korean area team, with funding from the Korean government, decided to hire the specialists from Taiwan to digitize its special collection. Likewise, the Japanese area team also contracted them for digitizing some of the Japanese rare books. This collaborative digitization project with the NCL was thus extended from 2005 to 2012.

Based on the success of this collaboration between LC and Taiwan, Hwa-Wei went on to promote a wider collaboration in the digitization of rare Chinese research materials among major libraries in the United States, China, Hong Kong, Macau, and Taiwan, continuing this work after his retirement from LC.

In November 2010, at the "Eighth Conference on Cooperative Building and Sharing of Chinese Publications and Resources," organized by the Sinological Research Center of the National Central Library and held in Taipei, Hwa-Wei gave a speech, by invitation, on "Opportunity for Sharing Chinese Digital Resources and Possible Considerations."[7] The conference was well attended by library representatives and key Chinese studies librarians from many parts of the world.

In recent years, the digitization of Chinese resources has been carried out vigorously in mainland China with strong support from China's Ministry of Culture. Because of the government's support, specialized digitalization projects have been done throughout the nation. Every provincial, municipal, or county library has joined the national network, allowing all Chinese rare books digitized by the National Library of China and other valuable materials from other libraries, to become shared resources. Any reader from one of over 2,900 county libraries can gain remote access to these resources. Currently, the resource-sharing project is being expanded to the township level. Having the privilege of access to these valuable resources will soon become reality for every reader in China.

7. Hwa-Wei Lee, "Opportunity for Sharing Chinese Digital Resources and Possible Considerations" [Chinese and English, in PPT format], (paper presented at the Eighth Conference on Cooperative Building and Sharing of Chinese Publications and Resources), in *Proceedings of the Conference* (Taipei: Sinological Research Center, 2010), 17–36.

CHAPTER 20

Reorganization

Determine that the thing can and shall be done,
And then we shall find the way.

—Abraham Lincoln

Surround yourself with the best people you can find, delegate authority, and don't interfere as long as the policy you've decided upon is being carried out.

—Ronald Reagan

1

THE SECOND week after taking office at LC, Hwa-Wei encountered his first problem. That morning, shortly after his arrival, he heard two staff members arguing in loud sharp voices, as if they were getting into a fight. The argument was over trivial things. Hwa-Wei found later that this type of outburst was quite common among staff in the Asian Division.

During his third week, Hwa-Wei was advised about another serious personnel issue involving the dismissal of one of the library's technicians in the division. The case, which was handled by his acting assistant chief, was about the technician's frequent conflicts with other co-workers.

The process of firing an employee at LC is complex. There are many time-consuming procedures and paperwork involving negotiation with an employee's labor union. Hwa-Wei was asked to schedule a meeting with the employee and the representative of the union to hear their appeal. Because his acting assistant chief had already spent quite a lot of time on this case, Hwa-Wei knew it was simply too late to reverse that action. So he went ahead with the meeting and fired the employee. It was the first time in Hwa-Wei's long administrative career that he fired one of his staff.

Due to the absence of strong leadership for such a long time, the division was very much divided and in serious disarray. The staff was demoralized, often complaining and distrusting one another. Any small conflict was easily amplified. At divisional meetings, Hwa-Wei reiterated the urgent need for the division to rebuild its image through rededication, unity, mutual respect, trust, and organizational change. The frequent clashes and in-house fighting had to be stopped immediately.

Hwa-Wei knew that the first thing he needed to do was to reorganize the division and guide the staff with new plans that included a vision, a mission, goals, objectives, and action plans. Luckily, his new colleagues had already recognized Hwa-Wei's leadership and management skills. At the same time, Hwa-Wei had recognized through close interactions that most of his colleagues were excellent library professionals possessing strong subject knowledge as well as good service attitude. All they needed was a change in the organizational culture guided by strong leadership. Most staff members had been extremely unhappy about the status quo and had wanted to have someone like Hwa-Wei bring in fresh ideas to lead the division in a new direction.

There were many things Hwa-Wei needed to take care of; one of these was an ongoing lawsuit filed against LC for racial discrimination by two Chinese American librarians from his division. Despite their seniority and meritorious performance, the two had not received any promotions: one librarian for over two decades, the other for ten years. This was the result of poor leadership in the Chinese Section: the head had failed to give due recognition to them.

After filing complaints to the office of Human Resources at LC and to the Equal Employment Opportunity Commission (EEOC), the two eventually filed a lawsuit with LC as the defendant. While the case remained open, Hwa-Wei was under pressure to resolve the case from both the library administration and the two employees. Since the head of the Chinese Section was responsible for the program, Hwa-Wei first began by talking to the head and advising him that his management style and performance should be improved. However, the section head, who had worked at LC for more than forty years, did not take Hwa-Wei's advice seriously.

According to Hwa-Wei, the division was in need of a complete reorganization. He knew full well that it would not be an easy task to accomplish in a huge government agency such as LC. It would require great effort to go through the rigorous procedures and complicated rules and regulations. Hwa-Wei, with the encouragement and support of Dr. Brown, decided to go ahead and make an organizational change.

2

The Asian Division was originally structured in four regional sections: Chinese, Japanese, Korean, and South Asian. Each section was responsible for collecting assigned language materials in their respective geopolitical regions. Under the chief were the following staff: one assistant to the chief; one secretary; and the personnel of the four regional sections, including one office administrative assistant. While each of the four sections consisted of a number of regional scholars, specialists, librarians, and staff, only the Chinese Section, at that time, had a section head. Work-related disputes were often the result of a lack of both a clear division of labor and cross-sectional coordination and collaboration.

There were no formally appointed section heads for any of the other three sections because of their small size. LC's administrative rules stipulated that only a section with ten or more staff could have an appointed head. None of the sections in the Asian Division, the Chinese Section included, had more than ten staff members. The lack of section heads was one of the causes for the ineffective operation within each section, and the insufficient collaboration among sections.

After careful consideration, Hwa-Wei came up with a new organizational structure based upon a "Matrix Model" that established, under the division chief, two administrative sections and five area teams. The two administrative sections were Scholarly Services and Collection Management. The five area teams were the Chinese and Mongolian team, the Japanese team, the Korean team, the Southeast Asian team, and the South Asian team.

In the two-dimensional Matrix Model, the two administrative sections each had a head and were in vertical lines of management; the five area teams each had a team leader and were in horizontal lines of management. In an operational sense, Scholarly Services administered and coordinated the work on user-oriented services of all five area teams, whereas, Collection Management administered and coordinated the work on collection management of all five area teams. Both of these section heads were appointed by an open search and through formal recruiting and hiring procedures.

The Matrix Model transformed the original hierarchical structure to a flattened one. Based on each of their area specialties and preferences, all professional and technical staff were assigned to different area teams.

Five area teams replaced the original four regional sections. Since Mongolia is an independent country, the name of the Chinese Section was changed to the Chinese and Mongolian area team; the Japan Section and Korea Section renamed as the Japanese area team and the Korean area team. In view of the growing importance of the Southeast Asian geo-political region, the Southeast Asia area team was created. The former South Asian Section was renamed the South Asian area team, but it no longer included Southeast Asia.

Professional staff, with dual or multiple-area expertise, could be cross-assigned to multiple area teams as per their interests and desires. Each area team could elect its own leader for a one-year term, subject to re-election.

Based on the new organizational structure, the work of all five area teams was better coordinated by the two administrative section heads. Each was responsible for the planning and execution of one of the two key functions of the division: scholarly services and collection management. Weekly meetings were held by the chief, his office staff, and the heads of both sections. Both section heads also had regular joint meetings with the five team leaders. In addition, monthly meetings for the entire staff were held, chaired by the chief. All these meetings were designed to maximize internal communication in all directions. A weekly newsletter, *Intercom*, was issued from the chief's office for internal communication.

In addition to the two administrative sections and the five area teams, there were a number of standing committees and task forces. Among the standing committees were strategic planning, budget allocation, and special acquisitions. Many of the task forces were for special events and activities. The membership of each standing committee and task force consisted of staff members from all area teams.

At LC, before the conclusion of each fiscal year, there were unspent acquisitions funds to be reallocated for the purchase of major collections. Each division was asked to submit proposals with a very short deadline because these surplus funds had to be spent before the end of the fiscal year. Each proposal had to be prioritized and justified. In order to take advantage of such surplus funds, most of the divisions kept a "wish list" of special items to be purchased. One of the standing committees in the Asian Division compiled such a "wish list" for special acquisitions and always kept it handy.

Hwa-Wei's plan for reorganization was somewhat unusual at LC. It was also a major undertaking. Hwa-Wei was very lucky to have the full support of Dr. Carolyn Brown, who even hired a retired senior staff from the office of Human Resources to assist in reviewing position classifications of every employee in the division and in rewriting the job descriptions. Such special help was invaluable to Hwa-Wei and sped up the entire process. After nearly a year of hard work, the whole of the reorganization package was approved in record time and was ready to be put into operation without any challenge or objection from the labor unions.

While reorganizing the department, Hwa-Wei corrected a mistake of the past by bringing the Tibetan Collection from the South Asian area team back to the Chinese and Mongolian area team. The original decision to place the Tibetan Collection in the South Asian Section was made in 1992 by proposal of the head of the South Asian Section, whose justification was based on the location of the Tibetan government's exile in India. The truth is, however, Tibet had been part of China for centuries, and was recognized as such by the U.S. State Department. Unfortunately the Chinese Section, at that time, did not raise any objections to this change.[1] Hwa-Wei felt it was time to correct this mistake.

1. Mi Chu and Lily Chen Kecskes, "Reform of the Chinese Section in the Asian Division of the Library of Congress" [in Chinese], *New World Times* (Dec. 9, 2005).

Reorganization of the entire division took eight months, much faster than had been expected. Hwa-Wei was very happy about its completion, but he was exhausted from the effort required for such a major task. In order not to lose momentum, Hwa-Wei immediately began to implement the new plan. In addition to placing each employee in his or her new position, Hwa-Wei also received approval from Dr. Brown to fill eight vacant positions and add three new positions. The new positions were for two new section heads and an automation specialist.

According to LC's personnel procedure, all new and vacant positions needed to be advertised nationwide to attract the best qualified applicants. A search committee was established for each position. Because of the library's reputation, and its better than average salary and benefits, each position attracted a very large number of applicants. Hwa-Wei's goal was to fill each position with the most qualified candidate. One replacement was for the position of an assistant to the chief, after the Acting Assistant Chief Philip Melzer returned to his previous position in the Acquisitions and Bibliographic Access Directorate.

For the open search on the two section heads, the application pool was very large. Among those applicants for the two senior positions were the two librarians from the Chinese and Mongolian area team who had a pending lawsuit against the library. Since both of them were among the most experienced and qualified applicants, the search committee for each section head selected each of them as one of the three finalists for the respective positions. After going through the interview process for all finalists, the two were selected to head the two new sections.

Seeing that their long years of loyal and meritorious service at the Asian Division were finally recognized and rewarded, the two immediately withdrew their three-year pending lawsuit against LC. The restructured Asian Division revived their hopes and passion. The removal of the racial discrimination case was a big relief to the entire library. Dr. James Billington, the librarian of Congress, was very pleased to see this positive solution come about as a direct result of the department's reorganization.

As a part of the plan, the former Chinese Section was changed to the Chinese and Mongolian area team. The head of the Chinese Section was removed and replaced by a team leader, who was to be elected by team members on an annual basis. The former Chinese Section head was allowed to keep the same pay grade, but not his former title. However, he decided to retire instead.

3

The Asian Division had been undergoing a drastic change since Hwa-Wei's arrival, with a scope and speed beyond anticipation. Subtle changes came about in the office atmosphere with the return of a harmonious working relationship among staff members; mistrust and in-fighting were disappearing. Even though the workload had increased, everyone was happy, cheerfully doing their job in the best way possible. Also manifested was a strong sense of comradeship. All the newly hired staff could be integrated into the workforce to learn from experienced staff. They all shared a common goal and aspiration: to build a new Asian Division that would make everyone proud.

In spite of that progress, the U.S.-China Economic and Security Review Commission (USCC) called upon Hwa-Wei to attend a hearing concerning the reorganization of the Asian Division and rumors about the dismantling of the Chinese Section. The purpose of the commission, created on October 30, 2000, by Congress, was, as stated on its website:

> to monitor, investigate, and submit to Congress an annual report on the national security implications of the bilateral trade and economic relationship between the United States and the People's Republic of China, and to provide recommendations, where appropriate, to Congress for legislative and administrative action.
>
> The Commission is composed of twelve members, three of whom are selected by each of the majority and minority leaders of the Senate, and the speaker and the minority leader of the House. The Commissioners serve two-year terms . . . The commissioners are supported by policy and administrative staff with extensive backgrounds in trade, economics, weapons proliferation, foreign policy, and U.S.-PRC relations. Some are fluent or proficient in Chinese (Mandarin), and most have significant prior working and traveling experience in China and Taiwan.[2]

In September 2005, Hwa-Wei attended a formal hearing, held in one of the congressional hearing rooms, for the first time in his professional career. He was accompanied by Dr. Brown to explain LC's position on the reorganization. After the opening statement by the chair of the Commission, Dr. Brown and Hwa-Wei each presented prepared statements and responded to questions from the commissioners.

Peculiarly, the former head of the Chinese Section was also there and requested to speak at the hearing. His prepared statement, full of criticism about the departmental changes, faulted Hwa-Wei for abolishing the Chinese Section and dismantling the Chinese collection. In response, both Dr. Brown and Hwa-Wei strongly objected to his accusation, answering that the reorganization had been aimed at achieving a greater operational efficiency and improvement in the Chinese collection and services of the Asian Division.

Hwa-Wei also stated that even though the changes had been implemented only two years ago, remarkable improvements had been made in both collection

2. U.S.-China Economic and Security Review Commission, fact sheet, http://www.uscc.gov/about/fact_sheet.

and services. The new acquisitions had included a wide range of publications on contemporary China, which were of special interest to researchers and other watchers of recent developments in China. The most noticeable increases were in journal subscriptions and the purchase of major electronic and digital databases. Working closely with the Acquisitions Department, subject specialists from the Chinese and Mongolian area team were able to visit major book fairs held annually in China, Hong Kong, and Taiwan in order to gain firsthand knowledge of new publications, and to obtain access to politically sensitive publications not normally available through book dealers.

One year after the first hearing, USCC called for a follow-up hearing, held right at the Asian Division. The members of the Commission came prepared with a long list of hundreds of core Chinese journals. They wanted to see with their own eyes the latest Chinese collection development in the division. The results were quite surprising—the size of the Chinese journal holdings, both in title and volume counts, far exceeded the lengthy inventory that they had prepared. Facts speak louder than words. The commissioners also inspected the book and journal stacks of the Chinese collection and were very impressed with the well-maintained Chinese collection. During and after the second hearing, Hwa-Wei received many compliments for his good work.

4

Hwa-Wei was very pleased with all the new hires. All worked very well with other colleagues, and their enthusiasm and dedication were contagious. Some of the new staff became leaders of their teams. A positive and enduring new commitment, to work together harmoniously to achieve excellence in collections and services, had developed within the organization.

The new head of Collection Management, Judy Lu, was most commendable in carrying out her area of responsibilities. With the support of area teams, she was able to tackle several long overdue tasks including:

1. Implementing new procedures in stack management, so that most of the collections are properly shelved and easily retrieved.
2. Selecting some three hundred thousand under-used library materials for remote storage at the Fort Meade facility in order to make room for new acquisitions.
3. Converting the manual check-in system for journals and serial publications to a computerized check-in operation to facilitate effective bibliographic controls and online applications.
4. Cleaning up neglected and uncataloged library material hidden in the stack area and adding them to the collection.

5. Assisting the chief in establishing the Asian Division's Friends Society.
6. Helping the chief in fundraising activities and securing a sizable donation from Florence Tan Moeson.

Likewise, the new head of Scholarly Services, Dr. Mi Chu, carried out the following programs with the support of area teams:

1. Opening the Asian Reading Room on Saturdays for the convenience of users.
2. Working with a contractor to revise and update the publication, *The Library of Congress Asian Collections: An Illustrated Guide,* and placing it on the website for easy online access.
3. Advising and assisting the John W. Kluge's scholars in residence and research fellows, and the Florence Tan Moeson's research fellows. Two distinguished Kluge scholars who spent a great deal of time researching at the Asian Division were Dr. Jing Wu and Dr. Ying-Shih Yu.
4. Securing financial support from the Chiang Ching-Kuo Foundation to inventory Chinese rare books in preparation for digitization.
5. Working with the National Central Library in Taiwan to cooperatively digitize the rare book collections for easy online access.

Dr. Anchi Hoh, the new assistant to the chief, was very energetic and methodical, and assisted Hwa-Wei in managing the Asian Division Friends Society and its outreach activities by organizing many special events to promote the treasured collections and their use, and by taking care of routine office business. With his expert knowledge and skill, the new computer specialist, Tien Doan, was responsible for the application of computer technology in the division including the creation and maintenance of the division's website and portal.

In addition to the staff newly hired through national searches, there were colleagues from other LC divisions who had also applied for positions at the Asian Division. One day, Hwa-Wei received a transfer application from a Japanese American librarian from another division who had been working at LC for twenty years and had once filed a complaint of racial discrimination to the union against her division. Having carefully reviewed her application and resume, Hwa-Wei felt that her knowledge of Japan and the Japanese language could be useful to the Asian Division.

However, an interdivision transfer for librarians at LC was extremely difficult, especially if it was a one-way transfer, because the original unit could permanently lose the professional position unless the Asian Division would agree to swap the position status. At that time, all vacant positions at the Asian Division were already filled. By talking to the chief of the other division, Hwa-Wei was very lucky to complete the transfer and thereby gain another position. It turned out the woman was an excellent worker and became a valuable addition to the Japanese area team.

An experienced administrator needs not only a keen eye to identify talented employees, but also the ability to create the right environment for them to ensure the full use of their talents. Hwa-Wei was extremely pleased to have a group of highly competent and dedicated colleagues in the division. All of them were enthusiastic and committed to their work assignments. In order to promote a positive working environment, Hwa-Wei not only delegated maximum authority to all his colleagues in each of their areas of responsibility, but he also provided them with the necessary encouragement and support, including recognition and reward. Suddenly, there seemed to be a gust of fresh air blowing in, uplifting everyone. The Asian Division, once the sleeping lion, had finally woken up.

CHAPTER 21

Convenience for Readers

I have always imagined that Paradise will be a kind of library.

—*Jorge Luis Borges*

1

FOLLOWING THE September 11, 2001, terrorist attacks on the United States, the entire country took extreme caution to prevent any recurrence. All government buildings in Washington, D.C., including the Library of Congress, tightened their security measures. Surrounding the three buildings of LC were cement blocks and fenced gates to prevent possible terrorist vehicles from getting close to the buildings.

As a safety precaution, open lawns and parking lots around the Jefferson Building were carefully guarded. When entering any of the buildings, all library staff and patrons had to pass security checks similar to those at airports. Because of the lack of public parking and the tight security checkpoints, the number of library visitors reduced drastically, so many of LC's spacious and luxurious reading rooms were often empty.

As a result, the library's audit office proposed closing some of the divisional reading rooms and combining those rooms into a larger one in order to save manpower and operating costs. A rumor also spread that congressional members and their staff might begin using some of those rooms as additional office space. Luckily, this proposal was not approved by the library administration, but it did cause serious concerns and called for appropriate action. Because the diversity and size of LC's collections are in a variety of formats, subjects, languages, and geopolitical regions, the separate reading rooms are staffed by knowledgeable librarians and subject specialists, who were essential in serving both the Congress and the public.

At regular meetings, chaired by Dr. Brown for chiefs of the various area and special collections, the issue of increasing readership was raised and discussed. Each chief was encouraged to come up with appropriate measures to bring back patrons and researchers.

Hwa-Wei thought there might be another cause of low readership. At LC, the Main Reading Room was open six days a week and closed on Sunday; all other reading rooms were only open Monday through Friday from 8:30 a.m. to 5:00 p.m. They were closed on weekends—the days most of the general public would have time to use the library. Based on conversations with many of the patrons at the Asian Reading Room, Hwa-Wei determined the need to extend the room's open hours to include Saturdays was evident: providing service on weekends would be a beneficial change.

In order to find a way to extend those hours, Hwa-Wei had to overcome a number of administrative issues. First he received approval from Dr. Brown to experiment with the extension of service for a six-month trial period, which was easily obtained. However, there was one condition—the extension had to be without additional staff or funding.

Hwa-Wei was grateful to his staff for their whole-hearted support of the experiment. Hwa-Wei made it clear from the beginning that anyone who worked on Saturday would take one day off during the week; his or her work schedule would continue to be five days per week for a total of forty hours. The Saturday rotation was totally voluntary, so there was no opposition from the unions. Many staff members told Hwa-Wei that they did not mind working Saturdays. They thought that it was great to have a weekday off, allowing them to avoid weekend crowds when banking, shopping, and taking care of other business matters.

It turned out that Saturdays were the busiest day of the week at the Asian Reading Room. The number of patrons increased dramatically after the new hours were widely publicized in the local newspapers.

In addition to the successful extension of the hours, Hwa-Wei encouraged all area teams to plan special exhibitions and events in the Asian Reading Room and foyer to promote their treasured collections and attract more readers. Hwa-Wei frequently appeared at many professional and community gatherings in and around the Washington, D.C., area to give talks on the Asian collections at LC. It was learned that many of the new patrons were unaware that the reading rooms were open to the public, and few knew of the rich resources available at LC.

As a result of the many outreach activities, the number of readers who visited the Asian Reading Room during the weekdays increased. Statistics showed that during 2006, the first year of the intensive promotion, the number of readers doubled from the previous year. The trend continued in the second and the third year. Once this increase in the number of readers became known to the library administration, Hwa-Wei's changes were cited as a good model for increasing library readership in other divisions. After the six-month trial was successfully completed, the division staff decided to continue Saturday hours indefinitely. Not only were the hours extended, visitors could also sense the change in staff attitude toward service. "Readers came first" was the way patrons felt they were treated.

For the promotion of the Asian collections, area teams in collaboration with embassies, cultural organizations, and ethnic groups in the Washington, D.C., area organized a number of significant cultural events. These events were all held at LC and included the "International Symposium on the Significance of Admiral Zheng He's Voyages (1405–1433)," held on May 16, 2005; "In the Footsteps of Marco Polo: An International Symposium" and "A Special Book Exhibit on Italy-China Cultural Exchange in the 13th–17th Centuries," held on March 23, 2006, in cooperation with the Italian Embassy; and "A Bridge between Cultures: Commemorating the Two-Hundredth Anniversary of Robert Morrison's Arrival in China," held on March 15, 2007, in a joint sponsorship of the Asian Division, the Oxford Centre for the Study of Christianity in China, and the Confucius Institute at the University of Maryland.[1] The costs for holding all those events came from external funding sources—not from LC's budget.

The "International Symposium on the Significance of Admiral Zheng He's Voyages (1405–1433)" was well received by the academic community. Nearly two hundred historians, scholars, and specialists from many countries participated. Gavin Menzies, the international bestselling author of *1421: The Year China Discovered the World* and *1434: The Year a Magnificent Chinese Fleet Sailed to Italy and Ignited the Renaissance,* gave the keynote speech.[2] Among the other speakers was Charlotte Reeds, who spoke about her findings on the "Secret Maps of the Ancient World."[3]

Speakers at the international symposium "In the Footsteps of Marco Polo," and its accompanying exhibit, included Dr. Piero Corradini, a well-known Italian historian, whose presentation was titled, "Marco Polo and other Italians in China in the XIV Century;" Rev. John Witek, professor of East Asian History at Georgetown University and a well-known Italian historian, whose paper was titled, "Through an Italian Lens: Viewing Books on Sixteenth and Seventeenth-Century China in the Library of Congress;" and Dr. Kam-Wing Fung, from the University of Hong Kong, who spoke on, "Lexicography, Cartography, and Instrument Making: Matteo Ricci and Jesuit Science in China." In conjunction with this symposium and exhibit, hundreds of manuscripts and books on the history of Jesuit science in China were displayed.

Another symposium, "A Bridge between Cultures: Commemorating the Two-Hundredth Anniversary of Robert Morrison's Arrival in China," was

---

1. Mi Chu and Lily Chen Kecskes, "Reform of the Chinese Section in the Asian Division of the Library of Congress" [in Chinese], *New World Times* (Dec. 9, 2005).

2. Gavin Menzies, *1421: The Year China Discovered America* (New York: William Morrow, 2003). Menzies, *1434: The Year a Magnificent Chinese Fleet Sailed to Italy and Ignited the Renaissance* (London: HarperCollins, 2008).

3. Charlotte Reeds, *Secret Maps of the Ancient World* (Bloomington, IN: Author House, 2008).

co-sponsored by the Asian Division, the Oxford Centre for the Study of Christianity in China, and the Confucius Institute at the University of Maryland. The Asian Division distributed an annotated catalogue of nineteenth-century missionary work in China entitled, "Christianity in China," which was compiled for the symposium by Dr. Mi Chu and Dr. Man Shun Yeung.

In addition to these special academic activities organized by the Chinese area team, other area teams in the division also organized academic and culturally significant events. All of these brought the division to the attention of scholars and researchers interested in Asian studies and raised the reputation of the Asian Division and its treasured collections. The enthusiastic participation of the division staff in the planning and conducting of these successful events also brought them a sense of professional satisfaction and pride.

3

Another major effort aimed at improving reader services was the complete rearrangement of the book stacks, so books and journals that were requested by readers could be retrieved quickly. Located inside the Adams building, the Asian Division's stack area was in disarray when Hwa-Wei first arrived in 2003. Books were scattered everywhere—on the floors or stuck on shelves in double layers—making it very difficult to find and retrieve books for readers. Some of the books simply could not be found. This problem was caused, to a great extent, by not having enough shelf space. Furthermore, there were unopened boxes of unknown books that had not been inventoried for decades due in part to a lack of manpower—or simply because they had been forgotten. In one corner of the stacks were stored relatively new acquisitions with simple barcodes attached to them that were waiting to be cataloged. These books were piled next to each other, row after row, leaving only those in the front visible. It was extremely difficult to find a requested book.

Having noticed the problem, Hwa-Wei started to embark on the clean-up effort. He insisted that library materials must be well organized. Every book had to have a designated location either with a call number or with a barcode, so the book could be readily located whenever it was needed.

As soon as Judy Lu, the new head of the Collection Management, was appointed, Hwa-Wei discussed with her the best action strategy to reorganize the book stacks. Judy was the perfect person for the position because of her leadership and management skills. She worked closely with both librarians and technicians in the five area teams to clean up the stack area. Despite her huge workload, Judy was seen in the stacks working with her colleagues every day. By leading the project for nearly a year, great progress was made, and the stacks had a totally new organization.

A procedure was created to ensure that every book was checked and shelved. Uncataloged items, if they were worth keeping, were sent to the department of Cataloging. Underused materials were sent to offsite storage in Ft. Meade in order to create much-needed space for new books and journals. Within two years, the stack area had a completely new look, and books and journals were all shelved in good order.

While in the process of cleaning up the stacks, some dusty treasures were accidentally uncovered including 170 boxes of books and other materials that had been confiscated by U.S. military intelligence in Japan after World War II. The boxes contained library collections from Tokyo's branch library of the South Manchuria Railway Company and had been stored in the back of the stacks for sixty years without being inventoried.

The South Manchuria Railway Company had had a long history. It was founded in the Empire of Japan in 1906, having been seized after the Russo-Japanese War (1904–5), and operated within China in the Japanese-controlled South Manchuria Railway Zone. Headquartered in Dalian, the company served not only as a railway company, covering seven hundred miles in northeastern China, but also as a spy agency for Japan to gather intelligence information on China, Korea, Southeast Asia, and the Pacific in preparation for economic control and military invasion.

It was estimated that, at the time of the Japanese surrender in 1945, a total of one hundred thousand volumes of books and journals were stored at Tokyo's branch library of the railway company, among which thirty thousand were Western language materials. Of the sixty thousand volumes sent to LC, twenty-five thousand were added to its Japanese Collection, and thirty-five thousand, mostly Chinese, Korean, and Western language materials, were added to various collections including Chinese and Korean, and other LC divisions, such as Law Library, Geography & Map, Prints and Photographs, Motion Picture & Television, and Recorded Sound. Duplicate copies were given to other East Asian libraries in the United States and Ryukyu. The books in the 170 boxes were mostly older Chinese classics that had been put aside for processing, but then forgotten.

Hidden in the stacks for over sixty years, those thirteen thousand volumes of older Chinese books and journals were finally sorted by Dr. Jeffrey Wang of the Chinese and Mongolian area team at the request of Hwa-Wei. A large amount of this material was sent to Cataloging, and later a complete inventory list was published on the Asian Division's website.

Another service for readers was the conversion of nearly twenty thousand journals in Chinese, Japanese, and Korean languages that were held in the Asian Division from a manual check-in system to an online check-in system. The creation of online records of these journals made it easy for readers to search online and to obtain the latest holding information. With the allocation of $250,000 from Dr. Deanna Marcum, associate librarian for Library Service, the division was able to contract an experienced outside vendor to complete the task, under the supervision of Judy Lu. The conversion project not only sped up the check-in process for journal titles, but it also made searches easy for library patrons, especially those searching for library holdings remotely from around the world.

4

Aside from work, there was a lighter side to Hwa-Wei's life in Washington, D.C., that included his love of Chinese food, in particular, steamed water turtle. During workdays, Hwa-Wei often went to a nearby Chinese restaurant, China Dynasty, only a ten-minute walk from his office in the Jefferson Building. Because it was located very close to Congress, many congressional members and their staff, government officials, and tourists were frequent customers of the restaurant. After becoming acquainted with the owner, Hwa-Wei was treated to their specialty dish, steamed water turtle, which was prepared only on special occasions.

Whenever this dish was available, Hwa-Wei would receive a phone call from the owner asking him to come by for dinner before going home. The steaming of the whole water turtle, stuffed with Chinese ginseng and other ingredients, takes four hours to prepare, so the restaurant served the dish only occasionally. Normally Hwa-Wei would eat this special treat once or twice a month.

Gradually, many staff learned about Hwa-Wei's special treat and began to tease him, "No wonder our chief is full of energy. It should be credited to the steamed water turtle. What an unfair thing to us, who have had no chance to enjoy the dish." Hwa-Wei was amused, "Don't be jealous. Everyone could have the dish. I will treat all of you one of these days, so we all could have more energy." To keep his promise, he made a special order with the owner of the China Dynasty—to prepare half a dozen water turtles for him and his colleagues.

A few days later, the owner called and informed Hwa-Wei that the steamed water turtles were ready. Hwa-Wei invited five of his office staff to join him for the turtle feast.

The water turtle feast was very lively, with a lot of jokes and bursts of laughter made about the steamed whole turtles. Each turtle was served in a big bowl. Hwa-Wei gave a demonstration of the correct way to eat water turtle. No doubt, for those who had never tasted water turtle, it was quite an experience. When paying the bill, Hwa-Wei seized the opportunity to say, "Now that the water turtle dinner is over, we are all equal, aren't we?" With another round of laughter, the last batch of guests left the China Dynasty restaurant.

CHAPTER 22

The Friends of the Asian Division

The Library—my refuge, my shelter, my source, resource, joy—
where I browsed hungrily through the stacks, finding my teachers,
my inspiration, my companions.

—*Tillie Olsen*

1

TO BETTER serve their users, all libraries need to establish a close and pleasant relationship with their readers. In addition to developing rich and up-to-date collections, libraries must provide their readers with good services by helping readers find the information that they want and by creating an environment conducive to lifelong learning. Books are for reading; that is where their value resides. Books are lifeless when left on shelves, but can be brought back to life through being read.

As a government agency, the Library of Congress (LC) inevitably seems, to members of the general public, distinct from other libraries; the public might not even know that the library is accessible to them. Thus, it is particularly important that LC take the lead in reaching out to a broader range of users. Only when feeling the openness and friendliness of the library, will the public feel comfortable walking in and using its collections and services.

Building on his long years of experience in academic library management, Hwa-Wei spared no effort to revitalize the library's dual role as both the Library of the Congress and the national library.[1] One of his priorities was the establishment of the Asian Division Friends Society (ADFS) at LC in 2004. Considering the success of the Friends of the Libraries at Ohio University (OHIO), Hwa-Wei was confident that LC needed a Friends group, one that would serve as a public relations and outreach arm of the Asian Division to the external community and readers. By using the successful OHIO model, the preparation and formation of ADFS moved ahead expeditiously, with the support of the top administration.

---

1. Yan Li, "Let Books Be Alive Again: Interviewing Hwa-Wei Lee, the Chief of the Asian Division at the Library of Congress," (Washington D.C.) *Washington Observer*, no. 41, 2005. Also in *How2USA*, v.7, issue 5, May 2006, 8–10.

Already in existence were the James Madison Council, which was connected to the librarian of Congress, and a small number of Friends organizations established by other departments and divisions, such as the Law Library and the Geography and Map Division. According to the website of the Library of Congress:

> The James Madison Council mission is to bring the world's largest and most inclusive collection of human knowledge and creativity, the Library of Congress, to people all over the country and the world. The council, the library's first private-sector advisory council in its 210-year history, is comprised of individuals who are visionaries, champions, and ambassadors on the library's behalf. This dynamic collaboration between the public and private sectors is helping the Library of Congress grow into a truly vital and active treasure house of knowledge and an even more awe-inspiring institution for future generations.[2]

Beginning in late 2003, Hwa-Wei was already making contacts with many prominent academic, civil, and political leaders and inviting them to serve as a honorary board of directors of ADFS. In addition, he also tried to identify founding members of the ADFS board of directors. Through his efforts, the founding members of the ADFS honorary board of directors consisted of many influential leaders including Senator Daniel Akaka, Ambassador Julia Chang Bloch, Mme. Anna Chennault, Ambassador David Dean, Dr. Fred Harris, Congressman Mike Honda, Dr. Cho-Yun Hsu, Dr. Michael Pillsbury, Senator John D. Rockefeller, Dr. Daniel Kung-Chuen Shao, and Dr. Warren M. Tsuneishi.

Ms. Judy Lu, the head of Collection Management, introduced Hwa-Wei to Madam Anna Chennault, widow of General Claire Lee Chennault, an aviator best known for his heroic action in leading the American Air Force's Flying Tigers in China during the Sino-Japanese War. A charming and talented member of Washington, D.C. high-society, Madam Chennault was once a journalist and gifted writer in China. After her husband passed away in July 1958, she settled in the Washington, D.C., area with her two daughters. There, she became an influential political figure who was highly respected in the United States, China, and Taiwan.

Hwa-Wei paid a special visit to Madam Chennault, who lived in a wealthy residential area on the bank of the Potomac River. Her gorgeous home was full of treasures from China. Her daily activities were taken care of by two young Chinese assistants. In her eighties, Madam Chennault was graceful, charming, elegant, energetic, and in good health, looking much younger than her years. She warmly welcomed Hwa-Wei and Judy, and praised Hwa-Wei for his effort

---

2. Support the Library, "James Madison Council," Library of Congress, http://www.loc.gov/philanthropy/madison.php.

Meetings of the Asian Division Friends Society (ADFS) were often held inside the Asian Reading Room.

Many of Hwa-Wei's colleagues were members and supporters of the Asian Division Friends Society (ADFS).

in establishing ADFS. Not only did she agree to serve as the chair of the ADFS honorary board of directors, but she also introduced Hwa-Wei to other celebrities in the area including Ambassador Julia Chang Bloch, the first U.S. diplomat of Chinese heritage, who had served as the American ambassador to Nepal during the administration of President George H. W. Bush.

Hwa-Wei also went on to meet several members of Congress, who were very active in Asian affairs and had a strong interest in the Asian Division at LC. Congressman Mike Honda, who chaired the Congressional Asian Pacific-American Caucus and served on several important congressional committees, was a victim of ethnic discrimination, having spent several years of his childhood in an internment camp for Japanese Americans in the United States during World War II. Congressman Honda, the U.S. representative for California's seventeenth congressional district (also known as Silicon Valley), had been a strong voice for Asian Americans in Congress and maintained a close relationship with the Asian Division. Despite his busy schedule, Congressman Honda accepted Hwa-Wei's invitation to serve as one of the founding members of the ADFS' honorary board of directors.

It did not take long for ADFS to gain its blaze of fame. Due to Hwa-Wei's experience from OHIO Libraries, the focus of the group's activities was on various outreach-based scholarly events. Hwa-Wei showed up at all kinds of gatherings, taking these opportunities to promote the Asian Division and its collections. A wide range of relationships was developed between his division and various Asian ethnic communities and embassies.

Khasbazaryn Bekhbat, the Mongolian ambassador and a famous historian, was attracted to the Mongolian Collection and to ADFS's scholarly events. Almost every week, he would find time to use the Mongolian historical documents in the Asian Division Reading Room. As a frequent reader, he became a Friend of the division.

The Asian Division was soon turned into an Asian American cultural center at Capitol Hill, promoting and preserving the cultural heritage of that ethnic minority. The division provided that precious service by offering a wide range of weekly lectures, exhibits, and scholarly activities in order to build a strong link between the public and the library. As a result the attendance at the Asian Reading Room increased dramatically.

2

One day, an unexpected visitor, speaking with a strong Chinese accent, walked into Hwa-Wei's office, bypassing his secretary who tried to ask if there was anything that she could do for him. Even though Hwa-Wei was busy at that time, he invited the visitor into his office to talk with him.

Hwa-Wei soon learned that this visitor, a first-generation Chinese immigrant, was a restaurant owner in Washington, D.C. He had read in a local Chinese newspaper about the Asian Division and the newly established Asian Division Friends Society. He told Hwa-Wei that he didn't have much education, but he did like books and reading. He wanted to join the Friends Society and would like to make a small donation. He handed a check for $1000 to Hwa-Wei. Hwa-Wei was deeply touched by the generosity of this humble, yet sincere, donor whose gift was far more significant than its monetary value.

Through Mr. and Mrs. Paul Ho, his LC colleagues, Hwa-Wei was introduced to Florence Tan Moeson, a LC retiree of Chinese origin who was interested in making a donation to the Asian Division. Accompanied by Judy Lu, another good friend of Mrs. Moeson, Hwa-Wei visited Florence at her apartment in a retirement home in Maryland. The three had a pleasant conversation.

Having finished her college education in China, Florence Moeson came to the United States for graduate studies under church funding and received a master of education degree from the University of South Florida. Later, she also earned a master in library science (MLS) from The Catholic University of America in Washington, D.C.

Before her retirement in 2001, she had worked in LC's Cataloging Department for over thirty years. Although she had some unpleasant experiences while working in the Cataloging Department, and despite the fact that she didn't attend her retirement party, she was very grateful to LC. Since her husband had died years earlier, and the couple had no children or close relatives except for an adopted son who was already independent, Mrs. Moeson was thinking of donating her estate for a good cause as a way of returning her favor to society.

Her admiration for Hwa-Wei increased as their conversations continued. Seeing him as a shining star among Chinese Americans, she expressed her willingness to make a one-time donation of $30,000 to the Asian Division. She asked Hwa-Wei to send her a proposal specifying how the Asian Division would use her donation. In response to her request, Hwa-Wei prepared four proposals with justifications for her to choose from—each requesting a total amount of $30,000. They were as follows:

- Establishing a number of research fellowships each year to support scholars researching at LC using the collections of the Asian Division.
- Establishing a special acquisition fund for purchase of special Asian collections.
- Establishing a special fund to support the inventory of uncataloged collections found in the stacks by hiring part-time qualified specialists.
- Establishing a travel fund to partially subsidize the expenses of sending subject specialists to visit major book fairs in East Asian countries, which were not covered by LC's field offices.

It happened that Mrs. Moeson liked the first three proposals and wanted to support all three instead of choosing just one. She therefore increased her donation from a one-time $30,000 donation to $300,000, which would be paid over a ten-year period. Thus, her initial wish of donating $30,000 was multiplied tenfold.

Throughout the many years of Hwa-Wei's fundraising experience, Florence Moeson has stood out as a special donor. She had been widowed and led a simple and thrifty life. Different from most wealthy donors, her money had been saved through prudent investment. A grateful person, Hwa-Wei felt she would "give the shirt off her back" to others, a trait he found truly noble and admirable.

To Hwa-Wei and the Asian Division, Florence Moeson's donation couldn't have come at a better time, since each of these three funds addressed one of the top priorities of the division. To Mrs. Moeson, it was a fulfillment of her life-long desire to give back to society. She passed away soon after Hwa-Wei's retirement, but she left a legacy at LC, which will long be remembered.

3

During his tenure at LC, Hwa-Wei kept a very busy schedule on behalf of ADFS. His everyday workload was far beyond what a person in his mid-seventies would usually take on. His dedication and hard work set a good example for his colleagues. Everyone was motivated by him to do likewise in his or her job, including work in fundraising. Within LC, an anonymous colleague from another division donated $10,000 seed money to enable the establishment of an ADFS fund within LC's official business accounts. A good friend of Hwa-Wei from California also joined ADFS by donating $10,000. For the establishment of the Asian-American Pacific Islander Collection, a colleague in the Japanese area team, upon learning that Hwa-Wei had donated $10,000, also, with her husband, made a generous donation of $10,000.

ADFS's most significant business donor, however, was the U.S. corporate office of the Japanese company, Hitachi, Ltd., which had more than thirty affiliate companies and subsidiaries spread across the Americas. The director of the U.S. corporate office was Takashi Ohde, who Hwa-Wei had met at one of the social events. Through their conversation, he learned that Ohde had two offices, one in Washington, D.C., and one in Los Angeles. Ohde had also served as a board member of the Los Angeles Public Library Foundation, and had provided financial support to that library. Knowing that Ohde had a strong interest in libraries and library collections, Hwa-Wei invited him to visit LC to see the treasured Japanese Collection at the Asian Division. Ohde gladly accepted the invitation, telling Hwa-Wei that he had heard about the Japanese Collection and would like very much to see it.

Before long, as promised, Ohde visited Hwa-Wei in his office. The team leader of the Japanese area team, Eiichi Ito, gave a detailed description of the Japanese Collection and showed him a number of rare items from the collection. Ohde was very impressed. He asked if he could bring other top executives from the company to visit LC in the future—whenever they had a chance to be in Washington, D.C. Hwa-Wei replied positively to his request, then used this opportunity to invite Ohde to serve as a board director of ADFS, an invitation Ohde gladly accepted.

Ever since the visit, Hitachi has become a corporate member of ADFS, paying annual dues of $10,000. Ohde was later elected president. Through his efforts, many other Japanese companies also became donors and sponsors of ADFS.

4

Decades earlier, the Korean Foundation and the South Korea government made a significant grant of $1 million to LC to establish Korean collections within the Asian Division. This grant was instrumental in the expansion of the Korean collections and services at LC. However, most of that grant had been used up before Hwa-Wei even arrived at LC. In order to renew that relationship, Sonya Lee, the leader of the Korean area team, with encouragement from Hwa-Wei, made fruitful efforts to re-establish contacts with the Korean Foundation and the Korean Embassy in Washington, D.C. As a direct result of Ms. Lee's efforts, new funding was received to support many of the events and activities organized by the Korean area team.

The Southeast Asian and South Asian area teams also both initiated contacts with their respective communities and embassies. Many of their community leaders actively took part in planning and conducting special cultural events at the Asian Division. They also joined ADFS and served as board directors.

At the 2005 annual meeting of ADFS, a group of special guests from the Indian community dressed in their national costume and performed a Bharatanatyam, a classical Indian dance that is usually seen on festive occasions dedicated to shrines. The swaying saris, tinkling anklets, and mysterious fast beat made the performance extremely exhilarating for the ADFS members.

ADFS served the Asian Division in outreach and fundraising. Underlying its formation was a simple premise: once people knew about the division and its collections and recognized its value, they would naturally be willing to offer their support. The division always had sufficient funds for activities through donations and sponsorship, and, in most cases, even had surplus money, a big shock to other divisions at LC. It seemed hard to believe that hosting events could make money.

The generous support from Florence Tan Moeson, several Japanese corporations, and many other individual donors provided critical finances for ADFS during its formative period. Taking advantage of LC's reputation, the Asian Division soon attracted support from the embassies of different Asian countries. These embassies seized the opportunity to collaborate with the Asian Division to promote their national culture by co-sponsoring various activities. For Hwa-Wei and his division, funding was no longer a problem and success came quite naturally.

With the rising fame of ADFS, the Asian Division, and its treasured collections, many ADFS members also served as volunteers in a variety of services, including planning and organizing special exhibits and events and helping in collection inventory. Each year, an average of five volunteers, including some retired librarians, came to the Asian Division regularly to contribute their labor without compensation. The contribution of labor by these volunteers was most commendable and much appreciated.

Asian American and Pacific Islander Collection

When I was young, I lived at Camp Amache, a Japanese American internment camp in southeast Colorado during World War II. One of the first lessons I learned was that being Japanese carried a negative connotation in America. My parents raised me talking about the injustices of camp, how it was a violation of the Constitution, and how Japanese Americans had been mistreated. I've since followed in their footsteps by advocating for social justice and publicly serving communities that do not have a voice. The reason we were sent to camp is because no one in Washington said no. I'm here in Congress to make sure that never happens again to any community in America.

—Congressman Mike Honda,
California's Fifteenth Congressional District

1

THE LAST contribution Hwa-Wei made before he left LC was to create and build the Asian American and Pacific Islander (AAPI) Collection. This priority turned out not to be as easy as he had anticipated due to the opposition of the new director of the Collections and Services Directorate, who replaced Dr. Carolyn Brown when she became the director of the Office of Scholarly Programs and the John W. Kluge Center.[1]

There were several reasons why Hwa-Wei wanted to establish such a collection at LC:

1. As one of the key minority groups in the United States, Asian Americans and Pacific Islanders have made significant contributions to the development of this nation. However, despite their far-reaching contributions, no organized effort had been made in LC to systematically collect and preserve historical documents about them.

---

1. The John W. Kluge Center of the Library of Congress brings together scholars and researchers from around the world to stimulate and energize one another, to distill wisdom from the library's rich resources, and to interact with policymakers and the public. The John W. Kluge Center, Library of Congress, http://www.loc.gov/loc/kluge/.

2. Unlike the Asian Americans and Pacific Islanders, there had been organized efforts in collecting and preserving historical documents in LC for other ethnic groups such as: African American History and Culture; Hispanic American Studies; Latin American Heritage; and Native Americans. No organized efforts were made for the AAPI collection.

3. Because of the sufferings of Asian Americans and Pacific Islanders from a long history of racial discrimination and mistreatment in the past, many historical documents have been destroyed or lost due to neglect.

Another reason that prompted and reinforced Hwa-Wei's desire to move ahead in creating an AAPI collection within the Asian Division came from Congressman Mike Honda.

Soon after taking his post at LC, Hwa-Wei had an opportunity to meet with Congressman Mike Honda, the chair of the Congressional Asian-Pacific American Caucus (CAPAC), in his office. Congressman Honda, who had been a strong supporter of the Asian Division, gave Hwa-Wei a warm welcome and assured him of his support to expand the Asian collections in the Library of Congress.

During that time, the congressman also asked Hwa-Wei to check into the possibility of establishing a strong Asian American and Pacific Islander collection within the Asian Division. It was obvious to Hwa-Wei that the congressman, a major champion in Congress for Asian-Pacific Americans, knew the importance of having such a collection. The time to begin it, he felt, was now!

A third-generation Japanese American, Honda's grandfather came to the States in the late nineteenth century. During World War II, after the Japanese raid on Pearl Harbor, the American government took a precautionary measure by ordering the internment of 120,000 Japanese Americans. Heavily armed soldiers guarded all internment camps.

Born in 1941, Congressman Honda spent his childhood in one of those camps with his family and suffered from racial discrimination. Forty years later, in 1988, the U.S. government made a formal apology to all Japanese Americans who were once detained in the camps and offered compensation to the victims and their families, most of whom had lost all their property and belongings.

That first generation of Asian-Pacific Americans, who had arrived as immigrants to the United States in the nineteenth century or earlier, actively participated in this country's early development. However, the way they were treated was very different from the treatment received by their European counterparts. Not only did they not receive adequate recognition, they were also subjected to extreme discrimination, oppression, humiliation, and other unfair treatment. Such biased treatment was finally stopped by the 1943 Magnuson Act (Chinese Exclusion Repeal Act) and the Immigration and Nationality Act of 1965 (Hart-Celler Act). From then on, Asian-Pacific Americans were afforded, under law, the same protections and impartial treatment granted to the majority of Americans.

After generations of struggle, Asian-Pacific American immigrants, through perseverance, education, and hard work, were able to enhance their social status and to play an increasingly important role in American society. However, in LC, the systematic collecting and archiving of historical documents about this ethnic group in the United States had not been seriously undertaken—commensurate to the improved recognition and respect due to them.

Hwa-Wei was deeply touched by Congressman Honda's concern about the absence of a strong and well-organized Asian American and Pacific Islander Collection at LC. While LC's Asian Division was designated to systematically collect and preserve relevant publications and other valuable human records from Asia and in Asian languages, nothing was done to include important historical documents on Asian-Pacific Americans, despite a strong cultural link between Asians and Asian Americans in the United States. Hwa-Wei felt it was logical to establish the Asian American and Pacific Islander Collection as a new focus among the collections in the Asian Division; he found it particularly important because no other division or unit showed an interest in doing so.

After his meeting with Congressman Honda, Hwa-Wei came up with a plan about building the collection, thinking it would greatly benefit current and future generations of Asian-Pacific Americans. A history of the United States would not be complete without acknowledging the role played by these Americans, nor would an Asian collection be complete without holdings devoted to the group.

As soon as Hwa-Wei had made up his mind, he carefully drafted a proposal with the blueprint that the Asian Division would not only create and build a strong AAPI collection but would also play a role in coordinating the various scattered AAPI collections in the country. By creating a national union catalog of these collections through OCLC's WorldCat, all such collections could be made known and accessible to researchers nationally and internationally. In his proposal, Hwa-Wei recommended six immediate actions:

1. Creating a new position for an AAPI collection librarian within the Asian Division.
2. Seeking a three-year budget to support the formation of the AAPI collection.
3. Conducting an inventory of existing AAPI collections scattered in various parts of LC.
4. Checking with OCLC about the possibility of creating an online union catalog for AAPI collections, held by OCLC member libraries worldwide.
5. Planning for a national conference to discuss and map out the national network of AAPI collections.

6. Beginning the collection efforts through acquisitions and solicitation of donations from Asian communities.

Along with the initial proposal was a working budget for the first three years, submitted to LC administration in 2005.

2

Unfortunately, the approval of his proposal was delayed. The library's budget was being cut at the same time that the role of the Asian Division was expanding, causing a difficulty in finding additional funds. Hwa-Wei had stated that the AAPI collection did not need to reside in the Asian Division, if there was an alternative responsible unit in LC with interest in it.

To Hwa-Wei, the Asian Division at LC seemed the most appropriate unit to collect and house the AAPI materials. However, at that time, the collection scope for the division was defined as books, journals, and other materials from Asia and in Asian languages. It excluded documents from the community of Asian immigrants and their descendants in the United States and publications about them in the English language. Hwa-Wei felt this kind of collection policy was clearly improper and out of date. The Asian Division, he believed, should collect all kinds of materials about Asia without being limited by language.

After waiting for more than a year, through several repeated inquiries, Hwa-Wei still had received no sign of approval on his proposal. He had no choice but to report back to Congressman Honda about his inability to move the project forward. He also made a special appeal to Dr. Deanna Marcum, associate librarian for Library Services, for her support.

Soon after, Congressman Honda wrote to Dr. Billington, librarian of Congress, to urge his support. The letter from Congressman Honda represented the voice of the Congressional Asian-Pacific American Caucus (CAPAC), consisting of nearly eighty out of 435 members of the House of Representatives. In addition to his work on CAPAC, Congressman Honda served on the House Committee on Appropriations and commanded a strong influence on Capitol Hill.

Perhaps that letter triggered Dr. Marcum's response. She informed Hwa-Wei that he could use one vacant position from the Asian Division to hire an AAPI Collection librarian, giving a very clear indication that his proposal to create an AAPI collection within the Asian Division was approved.

While the search for an AAPI librarian was in progress, Hwa-Wei began to plan and organize a conference, "National Conference on Establishing an Asian-American Pacific Islander Collection in the Library of Congress," in order to announce the creation of the AAPI collection at LC and to seek input and advice from the AAPI community in the country. The date of the national conference was set for October 4–5, 2007, just five months from Hwa-Wei's intended retirement.

Hwa-Wei was very fortunate in that he was able to invite many distinguished AAPI political leaders to speak at the conference. They included Elaine I. Chao, secretary of the U.S. Department of Labor; Congressman Michael M. Honda, chair of the Congressional Asian-Pacific American Caucus; Norman Y. Mineta, former secretary of the U.S. Department of Transportation; Congressman David Wu; and Congresswoman Mazie K. Hirono.

In addition, the following AAPI leaders and scholars agreed to attend and to speak at the conference:

- Rama Deva, Indian American community leader and former publisher of the *Indic Magazine* for the Indian American community in the United States
- John L. Fugh, major general of the U.S. Army (Retired) and chair of the Committee of One Hundred
- Ginny Gong, national president of the Organization of Chinese Americans
- Katy Goring, executive director of the United States-Indonesia Society
- Reme A. Grefalda, author and APA activist
- Evelyn Hu-DeHart, professor of history and the director of the Center for the Study of Race and Ethnicity in America at Brown University
- Prem Kurien, associate professor in the Department of Sociology at Syracuse University
- Gorky Lee, dubbed the "undisputed and unofficial Asian American photographer laureate"
- Marjorie Lee, librarian of the Asian American Studies Center at the University of California, Los Angeles
- Michael C. Lin, executive director of the Organization of Chinese Americans
- Juanita Tamayo Lott, supervisory survey statistician at the U.S. Census Bureau
- Krystyn Moon, assistant professor of History and American Studies at the University of Mary Washington
- Don T. Nakanishi, director and professor of the Asian American Studies Center at the University of California, Los Angeles
- Franklin Odo, director of the Asian-Pacific American Program at the Smithsonian Institution
- Kent A. Ono, professor of Asian American Studies at the University of Illinois, Urbana-Champaign
- Stephen Y. S. Shey, musician and "concert-cultural artist"

- Larry H. Shinagawa, director of the Asian American Studies Program at the University of Maryland
- Frank Joseph Shulman, bibliographer, editor, and consultant for Western-language reference publications in Asian Studies, and president of ADFS
- Betty Lee Sung, chair of the advisory board of the Asian American Asian Research Institute, and professor emerita and former chair of the Department of Asian Studies in City College in New York
- Ling-Chi Wang, associate professor of Asian American Studies in the Department of Ethnic Studies at University of California in Berkeley
- Frank H. Wu, dean and professor of law at Wayne State University Law School in Detroit
- Jeremy Wu, program manager of the U.S. Census Bureau and former national ombudsman of the U.S. Department of Energy

Hwa-Wei was especially grateful that Dr. James H. Billington, librarian of Congress, and Dr. Deanna Marcum, associate librarian for Library Services, attended the conference and delivered the greetings and welcoming remarks. Their presence was undoubtedly a symbol of approval for the establishment of the Asian American and Pacific Islander Collection in the Library of Congress.

The beautifully printed conference program contained congratulatory letters from Secretary Elaine L Chao, Congressman Mike Honda, and Secretary Norman Y. Mineta. In the published welcoming letter, Hwa-Wei wrote of the importance of having such a national AAPI collection:

> Asian-Pacific Americans are not only growing in number in this country but also continue to make significant contribution to the building of our nation and our democracy. During the past half-century especially, many of them have excelled in government, education, medicine, science, technology, business, arts, and sports. They set the example of living up to the American dream. The time has come to collect, organize, and preserve the recorded history of Asian-Pacific Americans, a history that has become a vital part of our national identity. Some of the older historical records are already at risk if not collected and preserved promptly through concerted efforts.

Congressman Mike Honda wrote in his greeting letter, also published in the program:

> It is an honor for me to extend my warmest greetings to the attendees of the "National Conference on Establishing an Asian-American Pacific Islander Collection in the Library of Congress"—it is no secret that every office on Capitol Hill relies upon the Library of Congress for information, and this institution routinely and capably obliges.
>
> One significant fact that can be found within the library's volumes is the rapid rate at which our country's Asian-American Pacific Islander (AAPI) pop-

ulation is growing; it is expected to reach 20 million by 2020, and 33.4 million by 2050. As logically follows, issues involving AAPIs are gaining importance in the U.S. Congress, reflected by the inception of the Congressional Asian-Pacific American Caucus in 1994. And yet, nowhere is there a centralized, comprehensive AAPI collection.

As chairman of the Congressional Asian-Pacific American Caucus and also as a teacher, I commend the attendees of this conference for recognizing the need to develop and coordinate such a national collection. This is a necessary and appropriate progression for the Library of Congress, one that will centralize the AAPI experience.

Thank you to all of you who share this vision. Your energy, enthusiasm, and determination for establishing a comprehensive AAPI collection will help to preserve a very important part of our nation's history.

This strong message from Congressman Honda undoubtedly set the tone of the conference, providing an impetus with which to move ahead. After a great deal of discussion, the conference participants made many recommendations. Conference attendees were also treated to a display in the Asian Reading Room titled, "Don't Worry, Yoshio—You Are an American," which featured a selection of children's books by Japanese American authors and illustrators. Hwa-Wei was very pleased that the conference had turned out to be so successful.

3

On Saturday afternoon in January 2007, about one hundred guests attended the Asian Division Reading Room to celebrate the one-hundredth birthday of a Filipino member of ADFS. Hwa-Wei got to know the birthday lady, Ms. Mima Remedios Cabacungan, through her daughter, Reme A. Grefalda, an active member of ADFS. When Reme learned about the plan to begin an AAPI collection at LC, she immediately volunteered to help.

Ten years ago, Reme had been a government employee, but she had taken an early retirement to stay home and take care of her aging mother. While at home, she started a quarterly online literary arts journal for the Filipino diaspora titled, *Our Own Voice*. The Filipina Women's Network (FWN) selected her as one of "the one hundred most influential Filipina woman in the U.S." under the category of Innovators & Thought Leaders.

In 2006, *Our Own Voice* partnered with ADFS to hold the Carlos Bulosan Symposium at LC. A talented and award-winning author of a full-length play and short film, Reme was one of the most welcome volunteers for ADFS.

The birthday party for her mother was to raise money for ADFS; her mother had been a well-known actress and community leader in her younger years with many followers. Even at her one-hundredth birthday, she looked happy, radiating her charm among friends. In 2005, when her mother was ninety-eight years old, Reme suggested to Hwa-Wei that, if a birthday party could be held in the back of the Asian Reading Room, she would ask each of her mother's friends to write a check for $98 to ADFS, as their contribution.

The birthday event was a success—some $4000 was raised. This was repeated in 2006, when each friend wrote a check for $99. In 2007, each check was made out for $100. In addition to the fundraising effort and other volunteer work, Reme helped Hwa-Wei in the planning of the "National Conference on Establishing an Asian-American Pacific Islander Collection" and designed the conference's beautiful program.

The centenarian's birthday party was auspicious and festive. Hwa-Wei made a toast to the mother, wishing her a long life. He then turned to Reme, informing her privately of the good news about the AAPI librarian position, which would soon be the focus of a nationwide open search. Hwa-Wei added with a smile, "It is a perfect position for you. We welcome you to apply."

The national search for the AAPI librarian position attracted many applications. As one of the applicants, Reme stood out from several finalists who were invited for onsite interviews. Being talented, energetic, enthusiastic about public activities, and popular with others, Reme was considered a good fit for the position by all members of the search committee.

Hwa-Wei got to know Reme by chance. Once he had discovered her talents, he offered her an opportunity, allowing her passion and strengths to be put to good use. Hiring her for the AAPI collection proved a smart decision.

4

After getting the approval to establish the AAPI collection within the Asian Division, the need arose to find and solicit donations of major and well-known AAPI collections. Between 2005 and 2008, several valuable collections from private donors were acquired. The most important one, regarded as a treasure trove among AAPI collections, was the sizable lifelong collection of a Chinese American, Dr. Betty Lee Sung. Her collection consisted of her eight publications, one hundred conference proceedings, yearbooks, directories, historical photographs, and newspaper clippings, some dating as far back as the beginning of the twentieth century and continuing up through 2005. Also included were early newsletters of Asian American organizations.

The older newspapers came from a number of cities; some were very scarce, by representing publications that had very short runs or only first issues. Many represented the only records from those early time periods and the only clues to scholars in providing a glimpse into Asian American activities, especially those

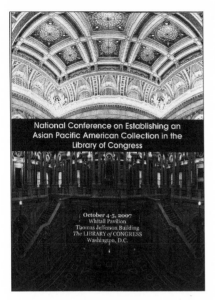

One of Hwa-Wei's goals at the Library of Congress was to establish an Asian-American Pacific Islander Collection. Its creation was announced at a national conference held during October 2007.

Ms. Mima Remedios Cabacungan graciously donated the gift monies she received on her ninety-eighth birthday to the Asian Division.

of Chinese Americans. The main focus of the Sung Collection was on the sociological impact of Chinese assimilation into the American mainstream. This included discussions and reports tangential to ethnic intermarriage and its resultant issues; generational conflicts; the proliferation of Chinatowns as either conclaves, ghettos, or communities; the fight for Asian American studies in university curricula; the group's empowerment through social and fraternal organizations; and Chinese American contributions to the U.S. economy.[2]

Dr. Sung, born in the United States on October 3, 1924, to poor Chinese immigrant parents from Guangdong, had experienced the full gamut of struggles, discrimination, experiences, and achievements of Chinese Americans. She grew up in Washington, D.C., but, during the depression years, her father took the family back to his hometown of Toishan. Dr. Sung returned to the United States shortly before Guangdong fell into Japanese hands during World War II.

In the United States, she attended the University of Illinois, graduating with a B.A. in Economics in 1948. Coming to New York, she worked as a scriptwriter for the Voice of America. One of her weekly programs was on the activities of the Chinese in the United States. It was at this time that she discovered the paucity of information about the Chinese, and learned of the mistaken images that American people held of her people. She vowed to correct that image.

This vow led to her pioneer work in her first book, *Mountain of Gold*, published in 1967 by Macmillan, which chronicled the history of the Chinese in America. Its publication led to an invitation to initiate Asian American Studies at the City College of New York in 1970. These courses were the first of their kind in the Eastern United States. Dr. Sung taught at City College until her retirement in 1992, advancing to chair of the Department of Asian Studies.

She followed her first book with seven other titles on Chinese Americans: *The Story of the Chinese in America*, 1971; *The Chinese in America*, 1972; *A Survey of Chinese-American Manpower and Employment*, 1976; *An Album of Chinese Americans*, 1977; *Statistical Profile of the Chinese in the United States: 1970 Census*, 1979; *The Adjustment Experience of Chinese Immigrant Children in New York City*, 1987; and *Chinese American Intermarriage*, 1990. Despite her full schedule of teaching and writing, Dr. Sung completed a doctorate from City University of New York in 1983.

In 1994, she completed a database of Chinese immigrant records at the National Archives in New York City with grants from the Chiang Ching-Kuo Foundation and the National Endowment for the Humanities. The database has since become a fertile source for genealogical research. In 1996, she was

---

2. The Asian-American Pacific Islander (AAPI) Collection, Asian Reading Room, Asian Division, Library of Congress, http://www.loc.gov/rr/asian/aapi/index.html.

Chapter 23

awarded an honorary doctorate of letters from the State University of New York, Old Westbury.[3]

Another important acquisition by the AAPI collection was the Carlos Bulosan Archive. This consisted of presented papers from the Carlos Bulosan Symposium titled, "America Is in the Heart in the 21st Century," held at the Library of Congress in April 2006. The contents of the archive included the original publication of "The Power and The Glory," an insert in a Canadian newspaper; a copy of "Freedom From Want" from the *Saturday Evening Post*; the *Local 37 Cannery Workers Yearbook,* edited by Bulosan; a DVD of Ma-Yi Theater Company's production of *The Romance of Magno Rubio;* the redacted document from FBI files of a letter written by Bulosan on Luis Taruc; a copy of the inventory of the Bulosan papers in the archives of the University of Washington Libraries, Special Collections; and copies of Carlos Bulosan's short stories and poems originally published in *Town & Country, Harper's, Poetry,* and other magazines from 1936 to 1946.[4]

Carlos Bulosan, an English-language Filipino novelist and poet, was born in a rural farming village near the town of Binalonan in Pangasinan Province on the island of Luzon. He was the son of a farmer and spent most of his upbringing in the countryside with his family. Like many families in the Philippines, Carlos's family struggled to survive during times of economic hardship. Many families were impoverished, and many more families would suffer because of conditions in the Philippines due to U.S. colonization.

Rural farming families experienced severe economic disparity due to the growing concentration of wealth and power in the hands of the economic and political elite. Determined to help support his family and further his education, Carlos decided to come to America.

Traveling by ship, Carlos arrived in Seattle on July 22, 1930, at the age of seventeen, with very little money. Having had only three years of education, Carlos spoke little English. Desperate to survive, he soon began taking various low-paying jobs including servicing in hotels, harvesting in the fields, and working in the Alaskan canneries. During his struggles to find employment, Carlos experienced much economic difficulty and racial brutality, which resulted in significant damage to his health.

As the result of several years of racist attacks, starvation, and sickness, Carlos underwent surgery for tuberculosis in Los Angeles, including three operations in which he lost most of his ribs on his right side and the function of one lung.

---

3. Chiamonline, "Betty Lee Sung," http://www.chiamonline.com/People/QU/bettyleesung.htm.

4. The Asian-American Pacific Islander (AAPI) Collection, Library of Congress, http://www.loc.gov/rr/asian/aapi/index.html.

During his recovery, he stayed in the hospital for about two years, where he spent much of his time reading and writing.

The discrimination and unhealthy working conditions Carlos had experienced propelled him to participate in the labor movement along the Pacific Coast of the United States and to edit the 1952 yearbook of the Union Local 37 International Longshoremen Worker Union, a predominantly Filipino American cannery trade union, then based in Seattle.

Carlos become a self-educated and prolific writer determined to voice the struggles that he had undergone as a Filipino immigrating to America, and those that he had witnessed of other people. His best-known work today is the semiautobiographical *America Is in the Heart,* but he first gained fame with his 1943 essay titled, "The Freedom from Want," published in the *Post* as one of a group of articles on the "Four Freedoms." The following year, *Laughter of My Father* became a bestseller, establishing Bulosan as an important writer. Due to the resurgence of Asian American Pacific Islander activism in the 1970s, his unpublished writings were discovered in the library at the University of Washington, which led to posthumous releases of several unfinished works and anthologies of his poetry.

As a labor organizer and socialist writer, he was blacklisted. Denied a means to provide for himself, his later years were ones of flight and hardship, which probably included alcoholism. He died in Seattle from an advanced stage of bronchopneumonia and was buried at Queen Anne Hill in Seattle.[5]

In *America Is in the Heart,* Bulosan wrote of his vision for the future:

> We in America understand the many imperfections of democracy and the malignant disease corroding its very heart. We must be united in the effort to make an America in which our people can find happiness. It is a great wrong that anyone in America, whether he is brown or white, should be illiterate or hungry or miserable.[6]

5. Carlos Bulosan Centennial, http://www.bulosan.org/.

6. Cynthia Mejia-Giudici, "Carlos Bulosan, Writer," HistoryLink.org., www.historylink.org/index.cfm?DisplayPage=output.cfm&file_id=5202. Sources cited include Susan Evangelista, *Carlos Bulosan and His Poetry: A Biography and Anthology* (Seattle: University of Washington Press, 1985); "Carlos Bulosan" in *Asian American Biography,* vol. 1, ed. by Helen Zia and Susan B. Gall (International Thomson Publishing Co., 1995), 24–27; "Bulosan, Carlos," in *Current Biography,* ed. by Anna Rothe (New York: H. W. Wilson Co., 1946), 82–83; Chris Mensalves, "Reporting for Carlos Bulosan," *Daily Peoples World,* December 28, 1956. "Carlos Bulosan," Wikipedia, http://en.wikipedia.org/wiki.Carlos_Bulosan.

CHAPTER 24

Sunshine Beach

The day returns, but nevermore
Returns the traveler to the shore,
And the tide rises, the tide falls.

—Henry Wadsworth Longfellow

1

HWA-WEI AND Mary moved to Cypress Village, a senior community in Jacksonville, Florida, after his retirement from LC in March 2008. The 120-acre retirement community is owned and operated by Brookdale Senior Living, the largest of such companies in the United States, which operates over one thousand such communities in forty-plus states.

At Cypress Village, there are several different types of housing accommodations built to meet the needs of senior residents. Around the three lakes in Cypress Village are three hundred houses for independent elderly, all varying in size and design. The community, as a whole, is well landscaped with lakes that are surrounded by trails, trees, flowers, gardens, docks, and a pavilion. For those residents who enjoy outdoor activities, there are also a putting green and a croquet court.

There are also five hundred apartments in a seven-story main building, each apartment containing one to three bedrooms. These apartments provide independent living, assisted living, skilled nursing, memory units for Alzheimer's care, and the Health Care Center. Residents can choose the type of accommodation best suited to their individual needs and health conditions.

In addition to the apartments, the first floor of the main building holds these facilities: a dining room, bistro, beauty salon, fitness center, computer station, bank, library, exercise rooms, and an auditorium. This building also serves as a venue for a variety of daily activities such as musical performances and variety shows, allowing residents to get just about everything they may need without walking outside. A large indoor swimming pool is located adjacent to the main building. Regular transportation services are also provided for residents to go shopping, take tours, or to go to the movies, concerts and dining.

The new home that Hwa-Wei and Mary purchased is a two-bedroom duplex with a bright and spacious living room, a kitchenette, and a patio. As Hwa-Wei decided to convert the patio into an air-conditioned office space, glass windows replaced the screens. A quiet and cozy place, the office has an excellent view of the banana and loquat trees in the backyard, behind which are tall pine trees and a wetland, providing a natural privacy fence from the golf course in the other side of the campus.

At Cypress Village, the most beneficial facility is the nearby Mayo Clinic, one of the nation's top three medical centers, only a five-minute drive from Hwa-Wei's home. After retirement, Hwa-Wei had a comprehensive physical examination at the clinic, and was told that he had serious blockage in his main arteries. The two stents that had been implanted in 2005 in Washington, D.C., were also blocked. His cardiologist at the Mayo Clinic wanted to schedule a cardiovascular bypass surgery immediately. After learning that his patient was planning to travel to China for a conference in September, the doctor said, very seriously, "China? No! No! You must have the surgery first."

The surgery, performed on June 25, 2008, went very well. After a two-month post-surgical recovery period and a three-month cardiopulmonary rehabilitation, Hwa-Wei was ready to return to his retirement life.

However, in March 2009, Hwa-Wei accepted an invitation from the University of Illinois at Urbana-Champaign to serve as the project evaluator for the newly created U.S.-China Librarians Professional Exchange Program, funded by the U.S. Institute of Museum and Library Services in cooperation with the Chinese Ministry of Culture. The exchange program was officially launched on May 28, 2009, at the National Library of China in Beijing. Hwa-Wei and an official delegation from the United States attended the ceremony. The project added a new stimulus to Hwa-Wei's retirement: he made two to three trips a year to China between 2009 and 2011. Each of these trips covered three provinces in China and took three weeks.

Aging remains an inevitable fact of human life. Growing old can result in a gradual decrease in one's health. Hwa-Wei does not deny that he is aging, but he stays active and engaged, despite his heart ailment and age-related illness. He wants to enjoy his retirement with Mary in a meaningful way—and Mary knows full well that Hwa-Wei is not ready for full retirement just yet, even though he is in his eighties.

2

Jacksonville is a large city near the Atlantic Ocean located in northeastern Florida, with year-round beautiful sunny skies and a moderate, warm to hot, climate.

Except for the hot summer months, the rest of the year, especially the winter season, is quite mild. Owing to its geographical location, the city is generally not directly affected by hurricanes, which often bypass Jacksonville, and leave it unscathed except for some heavy rains.

In the center of the community of Cypress Village is a large lake. On one side of the lake is a pavilion with several corridors. Fish and water turtles in the lake are very friendly with the residents, because they often feed the animals bread and crackers. Whenever residents walk along the dock, these water turtles, large and small, stick their heads out, anxiously waiting to be fed.

There are also a large number of fish waiting to get their share of food. Because water turtles move rather slowly, those fast-moving fish are able to snatch the food before the water turtles. One or two young alligators also reside in the lake, cohabiting peacefully with the fish and turtles. It is said that young alligators, before reaching age seven, will not attack humans or other animals. These alligators just sprawl there, sometimes motionless, occasionally coming to get a bite of the bread, but seeming nonaggressive.

Cypress Village is home to many talented elderly people. Hwa-Wei and Mary attended a family concert organized by one resident, a ninety-eight-year-old lady. She played piano; her daughter sang opera; and her granddaughter, a ballet dancer, also sang beautifully. The three delivered a one-hour, high-quality show. And the ninety-eight-year-old lady looked gorgeous.

The residents have organized all kinds of clubs. Some even tried to persuade Hwa-Wei to organize a mahjong club, believing all Chinese love to play mahjong. Ironically, Hwa-Wei has rarely played mahjong, and shows no particular interest in it since retiring.

Among all the clubs at Cypress Village, Hwa-Wei is most passionate about the Computer Club, of which he was elected secretary in 2012; and the monthly community news publication, the *Cypress Log,* edited and published by the residents, which he serves as associate editor of photography.

Another club both Hwa-Wei and Mary enjoy is the Line Dancing Club. The club is led by Lloyd Lohaus, a ninety-year-old neighbor, who resides in the other half of the Lees' duplex. Lloyd has lived in Cypress Village for twenty-four years—arriving soon after the opening of the retirement community. He is among the three residents who have lived in Cypress Village the longest. Being an excellent dancer, Lloyd led the club for more than eighteen years with dedication and devotion. Lloyd Lohaus served as a pilot in the U.S. Navy and later became an engineer. Although he had heart valve replacement a decade ago, he remains active.

Both Mary and Hwa-Wei enjoy being members of the Line Dancing Club because they are able to get to know and be friends with some of the wonderful residents. One of them is Ms. Bernie Gamble, a ninety-eight-year-old lady, who, despite being nearly blind, walks without the use of a cane. She is a very graceful dancer and believes the secret to longevity is to stay active, be kind to others, and be happy.

Another member, Ms. Harriett Hodges, who is only a few months younger then Bernie, had a most outstanding and unparalleled lifetime achievement. Harriett's late husband was an American military attaché stationed in South Korea for more than two decades in the 1960s and 1970s. During that time, Harriett saw many Korean children with heart defects die from lack of any medical facility. Harriett took it upon herself to arrange for these children to come to the United States for heart surgery.

Not only did she contact doctors and hospitals willing to perform the surgery free of charge, she arranged with Korean Airlines to fly these children and their parents to the United States for free. She also found American families who were willing to provide accommodations for these children and their parents, during the surgery and recovery period. Over time, Korean doctors came to the United States for training and then American doctors went to Korea to train Korean doctors. In all, Harriet had helped more than three thousand children have their surgeries either in the United States or in Korea.

Because of her kind heart, every morning outside her residence in Seoul, South Korea, parents with their sick children waited to see Harriett, begging for her help. In recognition of her good deeds, she received prestigious Medals of Honor from both the president of South Korea and President Ronald Reagan. Two Korean universities also conferred honorary doctorate degrees upon her.

3

Hwa-Wei and Mary chose to retire in Jacksonville, Florida, because they wanted to be close to their daughter, Shirley, whose family was then residing in Jacksonville. However, soon after Hwa-Wei bought the house at Cypress Village, Shirley's family moved to Rockledge, Florida, about 150 miles south of Jacksonville—still only a two-and-a-half hour drive away. Shirley and her family come to visit quite often during weekends and holidays. Occasionally, Hwa-Wei and Mary drive to Rockledge to visit them also.

Their other five children live quite a distance away in Maryland, Ohio, Wisconsin, and Iowa. During the summer months, when it is too hot in Florida, Hwa-Wei and Mary often fly north to visit them. In the winter months, the Lee children will organize a family reunion in Florida to enjoy the warmer weather. As the Eastern seashore in Florida is a preferred vacation area, it holds plenty of resorts, villas, or condos for weekly rental; some are large enough that the whole family can stay together. Family gatherings used to be arranged by Mary

After Hwa-Wei retired from the LC, the Lees purchased a duplex in Cypress Village, Jacksonville, Florida.

Mary and Hwa-Wei's daughter, Shirley, and her family live in nearby Rockledge, Florida, and visit frequently.

One of the features of their retirement community is a series of lakes. Mary enjoys riding in their golf carts within the community.

and Hwa-Wei; now, their children arrange them. When the whole family gets together, the total number exceeds twenty-four people, not counting nieces, nephews, and friends.

Hwa-Wei often compares his big family with that of his parents. They share many similarities, especially in terms of the harmony and intimacy among family members. Owing to his mother's love, Hwa-Wei and his six siblings have been very close to each other. Because of the early death of his oldest brother, Min Lee, Hwa-Wei has become the pillar of the family. His migration to the States led the way for his other siblings to follow: Hwa-Chou, his younger sister, followed him to the States for graduate studies at the State University of New York in Binghamton, then pursued her doctoral studies at Columbia University. Hwa-Tsun, his youngest brother, also attended the University of Pittsburgh, completing his Ph.D. in physics, and then taught at Point Park University in Pittsburgh until his retirement; and Hwa-Ming, his younger brother, was a certified accountant who worked as the CFO for a company in New York until his retirement. His oldest sister, Hwa-Yu, lives in a retirement home in Little Rock, Arkansas, close to her daughter Jean who works at the University of Arkansas at Little Rock.

Still living in Taiwan is his second youngest brother, Hwa-Nin, who after graduating from the Asian Institute of Technology (AIT) in Thailand with a master's of civil engineering, returned to Taiwan and became a professor, then later a department chair, at National Chung Hsing University. Upon his retirement, Hwa-Nin served for many years as the chief executive of T. Y. Lin International Taiwan, a major civil engineering consulting firm founded by Tung-Yen Lin, an internationally renowned structural engineer.[1]

After she graduated from Columbia University, Hwa-Chou married Dr. Tsing Yuan, the youngest of the three children of Dr. Tung-Lin Yuan, who was a pioneer in modern librarianship in China and served with distinction as the director of the National Library of China before 1949.

Dr. Tung-Lin Yuan moved to the United States in 1949 and served as the chief bibliographer of the Stanford Research Institute and later worked at the Library of Congress, as the consultant in Chinese Literature. While at the Library of Congress, he edited a descriptive catalog of rare Chinese books, which had been started by Zhongmin Wang prior to his return to China in 1949.[2] Dr. Yuan was a productive scholar. During his time at LC, he published several highly useful bibliographical works.[3]

---

1. Tylin International Group, http://www.tylin.com/region/Taiwan.
2. Zhongmin Wang, *A Descriptive Catalog of Rare Chinese Books in the Library of Congress*, two vols., ed. Tung-Li Yuan (Washington DC: Library of Congress, 1957).
3. Tsing Yuan, "Tung-li Yuan (1895–1965): Founding Father of the National Library of China and Cultural Communicator between the East and West," in Chinese American Librarians Association,

To honor his dedication and accomplishments, the T. L. Yuan Memorial Scholarship was established at the School of Library Service at Columbia University in 1966.[4] Furthermore, the family of the late Tung-Li and Hui-Hsi Yuan established an endowment fund in memory of their parents to provide an award to students enrolled in the School of Information and Library Science at the University of North Carolina.[5]

4

Hwa-Wei and Mary celebrated their golden wedding anniversary on March 14, 2009. In their fifty years together, the couple raised six children: Shirley, James, Pamela, Edward, Charles, and Robert. Their respective Chinese names, given them by Hwa-Wei are Yu-Hua, Shu-Yi, Shu-Fen, Shu-Qian, Shu-Zhen, and Shu-Tai. The word "shu" in Chinese means "book." The children now have their own careers, families, and children, a total of eleven grandchildren altogether—four girls and seven boys. The oldest is Kristen, who is already twenty-seven years old and works as a registered nurse. The youngest is Avery, a six-year-old boy with red hair.

Each Lee family member—children, grandchildren, daughters-in-law, and sons-in-law—has a Chinese name, given by Hwa-Wei. Each of Hwa-Wei's sons and daughters has also received from him a stone seal with their Chinese name carved on it. Hwa-Wei had these made for them during his trips to China. Because of their father's origin, they all have a connection with China on the other side of the world.

March signals the beginning of spring in Columbus, the capital of Ohio, which is also the home city of Hwa-Wei's sons, James and Robert, his nephew Steve, and his niece Qing Wang. Steve, the son of Hwa-Nin, is a dentist with his own clinic near Columbus. Qing is the granddaughter of Hwa-Wei's uncle, Dr. Tiao-Hsin Wang. Both Steve and Qing stayed with Hwa-Wei and Mary during their arrival in the United States for study. Steve completed high school in Athens, his bachelor degree from the University of Cincinnati, and his doctorate in dentistry from Ohio State University. Qing attended Hocking Technical College and earned a master in computer science degree from Ohio University. Her husband, Zhigang, owns a large furniture store and warehouse in Columbus.

Bridging Cultures. Chinese American Librarians and Their Organization: A Glance at the Thirty Years of CALA, 1973–2003, eds. Shijia Shen, Liana Hong Zhou, and Karen T. Wei (Guilin: Guangxi Normal University Press, 2004), 174–87.

4. Mengxiong Liu, "T. L. Yuan: a Tribute, 1967," from "The History and Status of Chinese Americans in Librarianship," *Library Trends* 49, no. 1, (2000).

5. University of North Carolina School of Information and Library Science, "Gift Fund Descriptions," http://www.ils.unc.edu/development/fund_descriptions.html.

With so many family members living in Columbus, the children decided to celebrate their parents' golden wedding anniversary there. To Hwa-Wei and Mary, it was truly a precious time, for all their children were able to attend.

The couple's fifty-six years of marriage have been happy and harmonious. They had a clear division of responsibilities: Hwa-Wei took care of external business, while Mary was in charge of the family affairs. She saw the family as the most important part of her life and devoted her full attention to raising the children and supporting Hwa-Wei's career.

Mary wanted Hwa-Wei to succeed and has done her best to help him achieve his goals; she knew that her husband, as a first-generation immigrant of Chinese origin, would have to confront and withstand tremendous pressure in order not only to gain a foothold in American society, but also to excel. She was also a great help to Hwa-Wei with her kindness, charm, and friendly personality, which earned friendship from Hwa-Wei's staff, university administrators, faculty members, and their spouses. She took great delight in helping international students and visiting librarians.

An easy-going and accommodating person, Mary has been loved by everyone, which was very helpful to Hwa-Wei in his effort to maintain a pleasant and harmonious working environment. Over the past decades, friends and family members of Hwa-Wei, visiting Chinese librarians, and international students from mainland China and Taiwan stayed temporarily with the Lee family. Mary was always hospitable and attentive, bringing kindness and love to the guests.

After she married Hwa-Wei, Mary dreamed of raising a big family, and her children were born one after another. With her master's of education degree, she would have been able to get a teaching job at a school. However, she chose to stay at home and take care of their children. Fortunately, Hwa-Wei's career has been good, and his income, higher than average in this country, was sufficient to support the big family.

Things at home, especially the home care and education of their children, were all under Mary's discretionary management. Hwa-Wei not only accepted, but also followed, her guidance. There were barely any household disputes between them. In fact, Hwa-Wei fully trusts his wife, valuing her highly rational and loving personal traits. Especially noteworthy is the fine mother-child relationship that Mary has developed with their children. Even after having their own families, the children still call Mary frequently, with endless conversations. While Mary's success lies at home, Hwa-Wei's victory has been his career. This has been very important to both of them.

Fifty-eight years ago, in 1957, Hwa-Wei flew across the Pacific Ocean for the first time and landed in this country, alone with little money in his pocket

In 2009, Mary and Hwa-Wei celebrated their fiftieth wedding anniversary in Columbus, Ohio.

In 2010, the Lee family attended the wedding celebration of Pam Lee and her partner, Beth (*seated front center, right to left*) in Iowa.

Nieces Elizabeth Lee (*fifth from left*) and Elizabeth Yuan (*seventh from left*) pose with Mary and Hwa-Wei and their six children.

Mary and Hwa-Wei enjoy the relaxing atmosphere of Cypress Village.

and full of uncertainty about his future. The only thing he had at that time was his determination to overcome whatever challenges he would face, even though he knew full well that doing so would not be easy. Looking back on the long road that he had traveled—it had not been that difficult after all. He considered himself very fortunate to have met Mary and to have tied their two lives together. Now it is time for them to enjoy their senior years in the sunshine state of Florida, where they can breathe fresh air on the beaches of the Atlantic Ocean.

CHAPTER 25

A Lovely Family[1]

by Mary Frances Lee

Kindness in words creates confidence.
Kindness in thinking creates profoundness.
Kindness in giving creates love.

—*Lao Tzu (604BCE–531BCE)*

ON A SEPTEMBER day in 1957 on the twenty-seventh floor of the Cathedral of Learning at the University of Pittsburgh, the world changed for Hwa-Wei and for me. After fifty-five years of marriage, Hwa-Wei told me that his world had changed for the better on the day that he met me. Before that, he felt that his life had been very unlucky because of the serious troubles and hardships surrounding his youth and the war. Afterward, from then on, that changed and all manner of good and fortunate things happened for him, things he never imagined could be possible. How could he even have thought of one day being chief of the Asian Division in the U.S. Library of Congress?

For me, I felt the coming to an end of a restless searching for a future that might hold love and family plus adventure and travel. I wanted more than being a schoolteacher in a small Pennsylvania town. That I could end up married to someone as loving, generous, and caring for others as Hwa-Wei, and one day have the opportunity to travel around the world five times was beyond my imagination.

Family

Our family is not an average American family. We don't fall into any of the usual types of being, such as:

- Conservative with a small-town traditionalist worldview
- Materialistic, status conscious, conventionally religious, focused on the immediate

---

1. This chapter was originally written by Mary Frances Lee in an effort to explain a little about American life to a Chinese readership as the book was originally written for publication there.

- Totally involved in a political agenda at local or national levels
- Strongly naturalistic, focusing on the ecology and the back-to-nature trend

That's what we're not. What we are is what I would call futuristic. We're independent thinkers, very liberal, deeply involved in the study of the past, even the ancient forgotten past, in order to think ahead and act for the future. Hwa-Wei has done this through his constant contact uniting the East and the West; developing technologies to bring librarianship into the future; and, lastly, by enabling so many librarians and administrators to travel and broaden their worldview.

My independent lifelong studies have given me a worldview that is a little ahead of our times. I see reality as more than just the material world, and I see undercurrent threads that run from the past into the future. My children and I study how the human body is still evolving, and we see the future as an expanded dimensionality.

That is a big, general, overall view. I need to emphasize that I am meticulous about not belonging to any organization, religion, or movement. And, I don't automatically believe everything I read. I look into any author's background, the organization to which he or she belongs, and the agenda they have. My views and perspectives, after reading all I can find on any subject, are my own by choice. And other than my six children, I don't share my views or try to influence anyone else, even Hwa-Wei. As we stand outside any organized religion, it was necessary to give the children "something to live by" besides any example that we might set for them ourselves. At the end of this book, honoring how their father influenced their lives, are letters from our children.

In order to share some of my knowledge with them, if I find any book of real significance in presenting an answer to questions we have asked, I buy six additional copies, underline important passages in each and every book, and then send them to the children in the hope that some time in their busy lives they will find time to read them. I know from talking with them that they do. Usually, the only time that we are able to talk one-on-one is when they are driving me around—when no one else is around, and there is nothing else to do. That has been the best time for long conversations.

Before I begin writing about the children, let me give just a few notes about the mainstay of our family unit, our marriage. Our marriage works well because Hwa-Wei and I found that we have the same basic goals and values. Neither of us places value on material things. We're both very practical, so if something is still working, or in good shape, we don't care about replacing it for something new.

We avoided a lot of conflict and clash of cultures, because from the beginning, we both agreed that Hwa-Wei's career came first, and whatever he wanted, or needed to do, was fine with me. Likewise, he agreed to allow me to make decisions about the house and the children. Finances he also left to me, mainly because he was too busy with work, but also because he knew that I was never extravagant with money.

My only hobby or source of pleasure is my library of books. Besides my main roles in life as wife, mother, and teacher, my only other interest has been on my chosen "path of wisdom" through knowledge. This did necessitate purchasing many books and using any free time I had in reading. I'm grateful Hwa-Wei has never complained about that expense or the time I spend in that pursuit.

Personality-wise, Hwa-Wei and I do differ. In contrast to Hwa-Wei's Confucian nature, I am more a follower of Lao-Tze's way; whereas Hwa-Wei is one to take immediate action on anything that comes up, I, on the other hand, am a quiet soul who is prone to reflection and contemplation rather than action; where Hwa-Wei is disciplined, organized, and methodical, keeping his work and our household and finances in perfect order, I am the opposite and always have "my head in the clouds" looking to the future, and to the past, for the big overall picture— not placing too much importance on day-to-day affairs. I also dislike strict schedules, perfect order, and set plans for each and every day. This combination has worked out well for us.

Most of the children's growing-up years were in Thailand. They were very healthy the seven years that we lived there with lots of sunshine, swimming, and soccer every day. For pre-kindergarten and kindergarten, our children Pamela, Edward, and Charles went to Twinkle Star Nursery School, where I taught pre-kindergarten classes for two years. I stopped right before Robert was born.

The older two children, Shirley and James, went to the International School of Bangkok. After school, American military personnel organized baseball and soccer teams; James was old enough to take advantage of that. Also, one of the military wives held drama classes and the three older children attended. Shirley, being a little older, often went to the Teen Club that was set up for the teenage crowd.

On weekends we all went for lunch and swimming at the Royal Bangkok Sports Club, where we were members. On holidays, the club had a family day with games and races for each age group. Our children always came home with two or three gold medals around their necks.

When Hwa-Wei was home, no office work was ever brought home with him to do. We often all went out to dinner to eat at excellent Chinese restaurants, and we went a lot to children's movies. Of course, we also did the usual tourist sightseeing such as the Chao Phrya River cruises; the fruit plantations by canal; and the crocodile farm where we couldn't make noise because the newborn crocodiles have such an undeveloped nervous system that any loud noise can kill them. There was also the Grand Palace and the wats (or temples) with beautiful marble walls and gold-leaf trim on every door, window, and wainscoting. The Thai people "made merit" by buying squares of gold leaf to rub onto statues and by lighting tall, thin, sticklike incense. The floating market was interesting in that, on both sides of the big canal, there were shops where you could get out of your boat and shop. The two shops that we laughed about were a photo shop where you could go in your wedding gown to take your wedding pictures; and also a place where you could buy a new motorcycle, but you had to take it home by boat.

Road trips on the main highway were dangerous because not only do the Thai people drive on the opposite side of the road than we do, but they also do not believe in following the rules. Even worse was that we had our big American station wagon, with the steering on the wrong side for driving there, so I had to watch and tell Hwa-Wei when he had enough time to pass cars and trucks. We did manage a trip north to Chiang Mai and south to the beach at Pattaya.

On holidays, we weren't too lonely for home because all the other families faced the same situation. It led to us happily getting together to celebrate each other's holidays. In our compound the children had the opportunity to make friends with international neighbors: Japanese, Italian, Lebanese, Burmese, English, and Indian. Even though they couldn't communicate in the same language, they did form a soccer team and played against the children in the neighboring compounds.

We gave a Halloween party for everyone. Of course, the children enjoyed dressing up in costume and playing games, but the interesting thing was when mothers of the two youngest ones exchanged native costumes: the Japanese mother wore the Indian sari, and the Indian mother wore her kimono. It was very heartwarming to see their friendship and to watch them share in the fun.

The last two years in Thailand were at the newly built AIT campus "up" country and "in" the countryside at Rangsit. Other than the campus, there was only the one tiny village of Rangsit. We moved into one of the eight prefabricated houses donated to the school by New Zealand. We even were able to design our own Chinese-style furniture that was to be made for us. His Majesty the King and Her Royal Highness the Queen of Thailand came to the opening of the campus.

At the AIT campus, the children joined in all the student activities such as picnics, sing-a-longs around the campfires in the evenings, and dance festivals.

Our house there ended up with a slight tilt to it after an earthquake in China rippled across the ground to our yard and shook the entire house enough that the clothes in the closets all started swinging, and the water in Bobby's bathtub splashed out onto the floor. Afterward, the upstairs hall sloped downward slightly. The AIT engineering faculty and students all came to study our yard and house.

The Children

Shirley

Our "Jade Treasure," Shirley Yu-Hwa, was always a dainty little lady. She was born in Oakland near Pittsburgh, Pennsylvania. When she was still little, we moved from our apartment on Coltart Street to government housing near the University of Pittsburgh's football stadium. My father brought us three rooms of furniture in his big station wagon. Our third-floor apartment had painted cement floors and open shelving in the kitchen, but we were glad to have the space and three bedrooms.

As Shirley grew older, our neighbors often sat outdoors in front of their building and liked watching Shirley play in the yard or try roller-skating down the sidewalk. She became much like me in nature, but like Hwa-Wei in stature. In that way, she was like Hwa-Wei's mother and his Aunt Phyllis, both of them petite. Shirley, being the oldest, became close to Hwa-Wei's Aunt Phyllis. Our new apartment was very near the Health Sciences Library at Pittsburgh, and we were often able to join her for lunch in the cafeteria there. She loved Shirley and always had chewing gum for her in her pocket.

Shirley was also close to my mother. She stayed with her for several weeks during her illness with cancer and was with her in the hospital when she died. She was also there when my mother asked me if I knew what happened when you died. I didn't know anything for certain, but, most fortuitously, when Shirley and I went to the hospital gift shop, there on a swivel bookrack, among all the novels and inspirational books, was the one book that helped answer my mother's question. That started me on my quest for more books. Shirley often mentioned to me that our family was always lucky and seemed to be blessed with good fortune. Things just fell into place in our lives when there was a need.

Shirley grew up like military children in that she attended school in five different cities beginning with kindergarten in Dormont, when Hwa-Wei was working at Duquesne. At Edinboro, she went to the school conducted by the College of Education. Being on campus, she could travel to and from school with Hwa-Wei and often visited him in the library, where he gave her bookmarks to cut out. She's the child who remembers the most about Edinboro such as walking in the woods behind our house, going for walks around Edinboro Lake, and always buying penny candy at the little store there on the shore.

After the big city streets of Pittsburgh, we all appreciated the countryside in Edinboro. Our house was on a state route with no sidewalks. All our neighbors, along that row of eight houses, had back lawns that ran together with no fencing or bushes in between. When the neighbors brought foods to welcome us to the neighborhood, they informed us that the children in the neighborhood were all free to walk through or play anywhere along the back of the eight houses. Also behind us were small lanes to other rows of houses where Shirley could safely ride her bicycle for the first time.

Going to Bangkok was an even greater change for us all. Shirley was only eight years old. She started fourth grade at the largest international school in the world at that time, over 3,600 students in grades kindergarten to high school. Also new for her was having to wear a uniform—safari shirts and pants of any color—and riding a bus to school.

As Shirley was very athletic, she joined teams in track and volleyball. She had some interesting experiences at International School Bangkok (ISB). Thailand has many elephants that do a lot of the heavy lifting in the countryside; sometimes, trained elephants were brought to ISB, where two teams of elephants could play soccer. Shirley has photos of that and another of a baby elephant, standing in front of the school. She also has a photo of herself riding on a big elephant in one of the parks. After she was married and had her daughter Kristen, she often showed these photos to her daughter. One day, Kristen's nursery school teacher saw Shirley in the street and told her how Kristen told the class during "show and tell," that her mother rode to school on elephants when she lived in Thailand!

After three years of high school in Fort Collins, Colorado, we uprooted Shirley once again to move across the country to Athens, Ohio. One of those lucky moments for her, and for us, was when we learned that Shirley and all of our children could get an 80 percent tuition waiver at Ohio University. This was a blessing from heaven with a family of six children! Shirley was happy to live at home while attending classes, a benefit for me, because we were still able to have her at home with us—and later, have the other children at home during their adult years—where we could be close and communicate as adults.

Shirley earned her degree in business, majoring in marketing. After graduating, she married Jay Kennedy, who was also in business, and a pilot who trained people for piloting licenses at the Ohio University airport. They were married at Ohio University's Galbreath Chapel the third week of October, when the autumn leaves were at their most colorful. Both the local Catholic priest and Rev. Paul Offenhiser, Hwa-Wei's sponsor at the First Baptist Church in Pittsburgh, officiated at the wedding.

Shirley and Jay lived in several cities in North Carolina, where Shirley managed an import store, before moving to Florida, where they ended up in Rockledge, near Cocoa Beach and Cape Canaveral. She was a communication and marketing manager for Eastern Florida State College, before her most recent position as an outreach coordinator for the Brevard County Elections Office. Her hobbies are now fencing and horseback riding. She and her family are also into hang gliding and skydiving.

She and Jay have two children, Kristen and Kyle. As happens sometimes in a relationship, Shirley and Jay grew apart and have gone their separate ways. She is now the marketing and program manager for SimpleQuE, James' firm.

James

James (Shu-Yi—lover of books) was also born in Pittsburgh. As a youngster, he was big and strong. In our Hill District third floor apartment, he gave our neighbors below us headaches when he raced around with his walker over the cement floors, which sounded like loud unending thunder to the people below. Fortunately, he took his first step at nine months—and just kept going on his own two feet ever since.

James has his Dad's dark hair, but, while in his teens when he went for a haircut, his barber once asked him how he got copper-colored hairs among the black ones, "Oh, you have to see my mother to understand that," he said.

When we flew to Thailand, James was only six, Pamela was four, Edward was three, and Charles was two. James also went to ISB and became an expert in soccer, so that when we returned to Fort Collins, Colorado, he was a leading scorer at Lesher Junior High School, and later at Athens High School in Athens, Ohio.

In Fort Collins, he was old enough to take advantage of skiing in the Rocky Mountains. One of our family reunions, at a later time, was skiing at Copper Mountain in the Rocky Mountains.

James was mature and very responsible at an early age. At fourteen, he worked at a local Chinese restaurant. Later, he and Shirley helped manage a cheese company in the local mall. When we lived in Athens, James was the family chauffeur. We enticed the children a little during their college years at Ohio University by promising them each a new car if they lived at home.

Jim got into difficulty with his Japanese-made Toyota that we bought for him after graduation with his degree in electrical engineering, when he had a two-year internship with General Motors. He felt uncomfortable parking his Toyota among all the American cars in the parking lot. He experienced a lucky break, when a truck loaded with metal pipes backed up and, not seeing his low car, rammed the pipes right into his driver-side window. James is tall and heavy. He had difficulty escaping over the raised middle console, but he did manage to get out through the other door. He never bought a small car again.

Jim remembers another time when we, fortunately, escaped a car accident in Colorado. We went to visit Mesa Verde where the Anasazi, a prehistoric American Indian tribe, had built multistoried dwellings within the rocky canyon walls. From its 8,572 feet elevation, you could see the "four-corner-states" of Utah, Colorado, New Mexico and Arizona.

Shirley and her family.

James, his wife, and their three children.

Pam and Beth.

Late afternoon, on that Easter holiday Sunday, as we started to drive the deep decline that led down from the plateau we could hear a rattling sound in one of our tires. There was no place to stop, no other cars were around, and no guardrails over the steep drop-offs, so Hwa-Wei had to just keep on going. We couldn't believe the miracle that at the bottom there was a garage right there, which usually wouldn't have been open on a holiday. Even more miraculous, the owner himself was there. He told us that we were very fortunate because the bolts on one tire were loose, and it could have come off. Needless to say, the tire was flat, and the rim was bent. The owner offered to drive Hwa-Wei to where he knew that he could get another tire and rim. When they came back, the owner replaced the rim and tire, but when Hwa-Wei tried to pay him for his time and services, he refused to take any money. The children all remember that day.

After General Motors, James worked ten years for Huffy Bicycle where he traveled internationally for four years, and then for six years he made trips to Asia. He met his wife Lisa at Huffy. Their son Christopher was born there in Dayton, Ohio. Then the family lived four years in Colorado where their sons, Tyler and Austin, were born.

Jim now owns his own quality consulting and training company, Simple QuE. The family had lived in Westerville, Ohio, where Lisa was the executive secretary to the president at Otterbein University. She is now office manager for SimpleQuE. They split their time between their lake house in Apple Valley, Howard, Ohio, and their new condominium near Shirley in Rockledge, Florida.

Pamela

Of all our children, Pamela (Shu-Fen—fragrant book) looks the most like Hwa-Wei. She was born with a full head of black hair—even with bangs. She is also most like Hwa-Wei in her determination and work ethic. She began life having to be a little more independent, when a doctor's mistake left me unable to be on my feet or sit for more than one-half hour at a time. So I couldn't hold her much. She quickly learned how to hold her own bottle.

Once as a toddler, my mother saw her sitting up on a tree branch while the other children played underneath, and said that she looked like an independent little bird ready to fly out on her own. And fly away she did. In high school, she was an all-around athlete with fourteen letters in softball, basketball, volleyball, and track. She earned a "full ride" to Indiana University in Bloomington for an athletic scholarship in softball as well as an academic scholarship. She broke many records there, and when her team played in the national championships, we went to watch her games. After college, she was an assistant coach at Indiana University. Later, Coach Blevens asked her to be an assistant coach, again, at the University of Iowa. She went on for a master's degree in athletic administration, and then a master's degree in physical therapy at Iowa.

Pam and her partner of twenty-five years, Beth Beglin, designed and helped build their new house in North Liberty, Iowa. They even included a gym and a pool in the basement to keep up with their athletic training. Beth, a three-time Olympian in field hockey, was head coach of the Iowa field hockey team for eleven years. Continuing their educations, Beth completed her law degree and is now a prosecuting attorney for Johnson County, Iowa; and Pamela is now a physical therapist at the University of Iowa Hospital and Clinic, specializing in spinal injuries.

In 2010, Pamela and Beth were finally able to have their wedding ceremony, which was then made legal by Iowa law. Both had their entire families fly in to celebrate with them and their many friends. One very unusual "sign from above" was on a photo Pamela took a week before their wedding of a double rainbow (one on top of the other) that ended right over their house. Even more astounding was that the day after the ceremony Hwa-Wei took a photo of Pamela and Beth standing at their front door, just before dusk, and there again was another double rainbow over their house.

Edward

Edward (Shu-Chen—true book) was born in Erie, Pennsylvania, when we were living twenty miles south in Edinboro. He looked the most like me. When I looked for him through the nursery window, I couldn't tell him apart from the other babies there. He is the most like me in temperament, also.

His schooling began in Thailand with me as his teacher. Pamela had gone to Twinkle Star Nursery School two "sois" (streets) away from our apartment. The principal asked me to teach there when Edward was ready to start school. I was happy to do it, as I had brought or bought at the PX (U.S. military post exchange) more books, records, and learning materials than the school itself had. I taught for two years until right before Robert was born.

Edward was eleven when we returned to the States to Fort Collins. He remembers the first Fourth of July there. Our children were so glad to be back in the States that they organized a parade with all the other neighborhood children. They decorated their bicycles and Robert's wagon with red, white, and blue, and a big sign that said, "Glad to be back in the U.S.A." It was also heartwarming to be a part of the city's celebration: everyone went to the city park; to the picnic where the band played; and then stayed on for the fireworks that were set to go off at nightfall. We missed having this typical Fourth of July celebration during the years abroad.

After we moved to Athens, Edward had an unusual experience that led us into another area of study. During very light anesthesia for dental work, he had an out-of-body experience: he was up against the ceiling looking at himself in the chair down below. That led us into out-of-body studies.

Edward, with his wife and daughters.

Charles, his wife, and their two children.

Robert, with his wife and sons.

Edward was always interested in music and art. He remembers fondly how we all gathered around the spinet piano, which I bought at the PX, while I played, and we all sang. From junior high school onward, Edward played trumpet in the school band.

When Edward entered college at Ohio University, he studied design and computer-aided design. He went on toward a master's degree in architecture at Miami University of Ohio. There he met his wife, Amy, who was studying and got her degree in occupational therapy.

Since Amy's family was from Wisconsin, after graduation, they moved there to be married. We all flew to Green Bay, where Amy's family lived, for the wedding. Hwa-Wei and I are so far away from their home in Appleton that we don't see them very often. We are happy that Edward has become an integral part of Amy's big family there. Interestingly, Amy's sister married Edward's best friend, so he also already had a good friend there.

Edward is now a facility CAD specialist with Schneider National and owns his own company, Entasis Designs, Inc. He also enjoys teaching design part-time at the University of Wisconsin at Stevens Point. He and Amy have two daughters, Hannah and Elissa. We consider it special when they are able to travel the 1,700 miles to join our family reunions in Florida.

Charles

Charles (Shu-Chien—thousands of books), like Edward, was born in Erie, Pennsylvania. He was born with a smile on his face and a happy disposition. From the beginning, he was always happy and with a sense of humor. He continues to be so even now. Hwa-Wei's parents lived with us for several months, when Charles was two, and they delighted in this toddler who would run to their room to grab their hands and bring them to dinner.

He was only two years old when we left for Thailand. With so many children, and the large crowds at tourist sites, we often dressed the children in red shirts, so they would be easy to spot. It helped when once Charles got lost at a large weekend open market. Thais running the stalls saw us looking for him, and one by one, they kept pointing out the way that they had seen Charles go.

One of the synchronicities, or strange coincidences, of life occurred for Charles when we lived in Athens. It illustrated the saying "Be mindful to entertain strangers for you may be entertaining angels unawares." Hwa-Wei had invited a female Chinese librarian from New York to spend the weekend in our home. She called to ask if she could also bring her daughter and son-in-law. We said, "Of course," so they came. After they arrived and were sitting in our living room, Charles came back from delivering newspapers for his paper route—up the steep Mulligan Road hill. Charles was very tired and perspiring heavily.

The visiting Chinese son-in-law, a medical researcher, looked at him and said, "Maybe I've been too involved in my research for the last six months on hyperthyroidism, but I'm certain your son shows all the symptoms of having it. I really want you to let me go with you to see a doctor tomorrow." He was right. Charles' teacher had told us earlier that something seemed wrong, but when we asked our local doctor he said that it was nothing; it was healthy to be so thin; it's better than being fat. So, we miraculously had had our "angel" walk right into our living room.

In spite of his condition, Charles went on to play high school football. He played the position of "monster back." His job was to sack the quarterback before he could throw the ball. He was very successful because something changed in his mind when he played: he saw everything happening in slow motion and could see the openings to run through to get to the quarterback. He also was able to have a "runner's high." When he ran track, his body took over automatically, so he didn't have to extend much effort near the end of a race.

Charles went on to college at Ohio University where he got his BBA in business, and later, his MBA from George Washington University. He worked five years at True Software, where he developed a program to convert computers for the year 2000 Y2K switchover. For the last thirteen years, he has been with Blackboard, a company specializing in online educational systems, as director of solution engineers and customer success.

Charles' wife, Erika, is a lawyer, who was appointed by the White House as chief privacy and civil liberties officer in the U.S. Department of Justice. Charles and Erika both work in Washington, D.C., but live in Potomac, Maryland. They have a daughter, Madison, and a son, Owen.

Robert

Robert (Shu-Tai—Thai book) was born in Thailand at the U.S. Fifth Army Field Hospital. As he was born five years after Charles, the other children were able to enjoy him as their baby brother. He became everyone's baby. We came back to Fort Collins when he was four. Robert had one year of school in Fort Collins before we moved to Athens. He's the only one of our children who had most of his schooling in one city.

He became quite well known in Athens when many students and townspeople saw him injured in a high school football game. Unfortunately, a player from the opposite team was injured only one play before, so the ambulance, which is always in waiting, was gone taking him to the hospital. Robert lay on the cold, hard ground for half an hour, while they tried to find another ambulance. His legs were paralyzed because he had hit another player head-on, helmet-to-helmet, and injured his spine. Because it was a spinal injury, they didn't dare to try to move him.

Hwa-Wei and I had been at a wedding in Dayton three hours away. We had planned to stay overnight, but instead, we decided to drive home. In a half sleep, I remember thinking about O'Bleness Hospital and just walking through it. I didn't know why. As we passed the football field, we saw that the lights were still on, and the game was still being played at 11 o'clock at night.

We stopped, and someone said to us, "How is Bobby?" We said, "You tell us. What happened?" They told us to go see the coach, who said "Now go right away to the hospital, but don't drive so fast [that] you yourself have an accident." That's what they tell you, when something is extremely serious.

Fortunately, it was once again, one of those "blessings from above." When we got to the hospital, Robert was able to move his legs, and they found that his spinal cord was just bruised, not severely injured. That ended his football-playing days. He then concentrated on his studies and editing the school newspaper. Robert was later honored by his classmates when he was asked to give the commencement speech.

He went on to college at Ohio University, where he earned two BA degrees, one in journalism and one in sports administration. After he spent a year in Taiwan teaching English at Feng Chia University as an exchange student, he earned his MA in sports administration, also from Ohio University.

He feels very lucky that he was able to have an internship, as he had wanted, with the Olympic training center in Colorado Springs, Colorado. He lived with James and Lisa in Denver, during that time, and commuted to Colorado Springs. He also was overjoyed to get his graduate internship with the Denver Broncos, a National Football League (NFL) team, where he did public relations and broadcasting, and was assistant video director. After that, his first real job was with the New Orleans Saints, another NFL team.

Robert has always been interested in his Chinese heritage. When he read the book about Zheng He, *1421: The Year China Discovered America,* written by Gavin Menzies,[2] he was so impressed and wanted to know more. He also wanted to share it with his friends, so he chose that book to give to his best man at his wedding as a valued memento.

Robert now lives in Westerville, Ohio, only three miles from James and Lisa. He also lives close to his two cousins, Steven Lee and Qing Wang, who had lived with us for short times in Athens. Robert is now director of communications and marketing at Columbus Academy, a very reputable private school, kindergarten to high school. It is one of the few schools that very early on started teaching Chinese, bringing teachers from China, and sending their students there. His wife, Cara, works with child-care policy for the state of Ohio. Her office oversees day-care centers, ensuring that they meet all state regulations. They have two sons, Seth and Avery.

2. Gavin Menzies, *1421: The Year China Discovered America* (New York: William Morrow, 2003).

Mary, Hwa-Wei, and his siblings gathered together for a family reunion in Columbus during August 2012. Shown (*left to right*): Hwa-Ming, Mary Lee, Hwa-Wei, Hwa-Chou, Tsing, Hwa-Nin, Hwa-Tsun, and Su.

During the reunion, members of the family visited the first floor of the Vernon R. Alden Library Hwa-Wei Lee Center for International Collections.

In Our Retirement

All our family members were glad to see Hwa-Wei retire (for the second time) in 2008. In 2005, while he was still working at the Library of Congress, Shirley helped me search for a place to retire in Jacksonville, where she was living at that time. Cypress Village attracted me because the streets are lined with tall, old, broad-leaf sycamore trees, and the houses had red brick for their bottom half. This is very unusual for Florida. It looks like any street you might see up north. Besides being only a few miles from the beach, it is also right next to the Mayo Clinic, one of the best medical facilities in the country. Hwa-Wei concurred with our choice, and after seeing it for himself, bought our little retirement house here.

It turned out that living next to the Mayo Clinic was a blessing in that soon after we moved to Jacksonville, Hwa-Wei experienced a serious heart illness and had to have quadruple bypass heart surgery. It was done conveniently at Mayo by some of the very top cardiology specialists.

Hwa-Wei celebrated his eightieth birthday in 2011. He continues to exhibit boundless energy and vigorous enthusiasm. Since he is happy, as we have all learned all these years, we are happy, too. Nothing seems to be able to slow him down. Despite his busy activities, Hwa-Wei continues to be a good father and a good husband. We love him dearly, even though he still works all the time. When we visit our youngest grandchild Avery, if he sees Hwa-Wei sit down at the computer, his parents have coached him to yell, "No work, Poppy!"

Letters from the Children[1]

> Mid pleasures and palaces though we may roam,
> Be it ever so humble, there's no place like home;
> A charm from the sky seems to hallow us there,
> Which, seek through the world, is ne'er met with elsewhere.
> Home, home, sweet, sweet home!
> There's no place like home, oh, there's no place like home!
>
> —*John Howard Payne, "Home, Sweet Home"*

From Shirley

MY DAD and mom have always been a strong positive presence in my life. They are with me in celebrating the good times and support me with their love and strength even when times are not so good.

So it is not surprising that of the many life lessons my parents passed on to me, the most important was to love and cherish family. As the oldest of six children, I saw the devotion, time, and love my parents put into raising such a large family. And usually our numbers were increased with cousins, relatives, and students who shared our home for various reasons and lengths of time. We were used to sharing bathrooms and bedrooms and preparing big portions of food. This family loves to eat!

There are twelve years between my youngest brother and me, with the others filling in the years in-between. So I helped with raising my siblings—dressing and feeding them when they were little and guiding them as they grew older. We all pitched in to help my mother, who was very organized at running a big household. A large family meant having others to play and hang out with. Even today when we get together, we love to play cards and games, and now our children join in the fun! The best holidays are the ones when we can all arrange to be together, but it's not easy because most of us live in separate states.

My father always made sure we had opportunities to travel and explore the world and other cultures. From this and the example of my parents, we learned to be open and accepting of other ideas, religions, and lifestyles. We also learned the importance of photography. My dad took his camera everywhere and took pictures on every occasion. There are thousands! When we were young we

---

1. This chapter is composed of letters written by Hwa-Wei's children.

A Lee family reunion was held in Orlando, Florida, during 2011. Standing (*left to right*) are: Edward, Shirley, Hwa-Wei, Mary, Pam, James, and Robert.

didn't appreciate stopping for pictures at every scenic location. Now, as adults, we cherish those pictures and memories. At family gatherings there are usually at least four or five cameras clicking away as we carry on the tradition.

By exposing us to Chinese history, language, culture, and food my dad helped us to embrace our heritage. Although we were born in America, each of us was inducted into this world with a Chinese middle name. Since he was a librarian our names had to do with books. My mother's love of books also ensured that we spent a lot of time reading and in libraries.

In 1986, I had the opportunity to learn more about my dad's boyhood and heritage by traveling with my parents to China. We visited nine regions and I will always remember that amazing experience and the thousands of years of history and culture that makes me proud to be my father's daughter and half Chinese.

My most strong wish is that my children are also able to travel and experience the world. I am glad my son Kyle had the opportunity to accompany my dad on one of his business trips to China, and then, later, after his sophomore year in college, was able to spend three months in China learning Mandarin and acquiring a minor in Asian Studies.

From James

I received a great treasure of traveling around the world four times by the age of thirteen; seeing the Vatican, the Parthenon, the Taj Mahal, and other famous marvels of the world. I got my entrepreneurial spirit indirectly through my dad and this travel experience.

I say that because I've always had the "travel bug," and it was through my international work experience that I met many influential entrepreneurs, most of them Chinese. I saw what they did in starting and building their businesses. I've had the desire to have my own business for a long time but it wasn't until 2001 that I was presented with those opportunities.

Our family talked about what we could do as a family business, but my mom always rejected the idea because she saw the negative side to a family business that could tear families apart. She didn't want to risk that possibility with our family.

I've always been driven by goals that I set for myself. When I was twenty-five I set the goal to be a vice president by the age of thirty-five. I didn't achieve that goal, but at thirty-five I became a director with Emerson Electric, a $15 billion corporation. By the age of forty, I was an executive vice president and chief operations officer of a small company (Eagle Registrations) and I also became an entrepreneur by investing in another small company (ACLASS Corporation). At the age of forty-one, I became president of Eagle. I started my current company at the age of forty-three and sold ACLASS in 2009 to ANSI-ASQ National Accreditation Board. For the last six years, I've owned SimpleQuE, a quality consulting and training company.

The strong work ethic is imperative for an entrepreneur and his family. Family is important in supporting an entrepreneurial venture, since there often has to be an imbalance between family and work. If I didn't have the support from my wife, Lisa, I would not have been able to do what I wanted and take the risks required. With my current business, we had to sell our big new house and newer cars to make sure we had enough cash flow to sustain our family while starting the business. We were willing to risk it all. During the recession of 2009, my wife even went back to work full-time so we could get medical insurance and a little extra income.

As an individual and entrepreneur there are several things that I attribute to my dad: the "travel bug," a strong work ethic, and a friendly character. From my mom, I attribute going after what you want, and family.

From Pam

I love my dad. There are many memories of our childhood, of our family being together in Thailand and traveling all over the world. We all had the opportunity to pursue our passions. For me it was always sports. I loved to compete. My dad also had a love of athletics and particularly basketball. Between him and my siblings, we played games and competed against each other and the neighborhood kids. We actually called it the Olympic Games. The Lee family was Team China. I believe we competed in every sport imaginable.

I felt the support from my parents all the way through my childhood and in the sports I wanted to play. I remember getting to meet the Taiwan national women's basketball team during our travels.

When we moved to Colorado my focus turned to playing softball. It would become my best sport and love. My team was the Colorado Buckaroos. We traveled all over the country playing softball with the full support of my parents. It became my ticket to college, eventually earning me a college softball scholarship at Indiana University.

During high school in Athens, Ohio, I played volleyball, basketball, and softball and ran track. I earned fourteen varsity letters in my four years at Athens High School. That said, we, The Lee Kids, all felt the need to be the best we could be in our studies in school. It was expected that we would excel in our grades. I graduated in the top 10 percent of my class so I was able to have both a sports and an academic scholarship, which is called a "full ride" at Indiana University.

When it came to deciding about college, our dad had the tuition scholarship from Ohio for all of us kids. I was the only one who didn't go to college at Ohio University. That decision was due to a combination of my dreams to play college softball and a need to move out on my own. Even though it was a financial hit to the family, my parents were very supportive. They told me they would make it work and give me whatever I needed to pursue my dream. I can never thank them enough for this.

It takes years of practice to become good at something. The pursuit of excellence was a trait we Lee kids all learned from our dad and our mom. We saw how hard our dad worked to provide for us. He was at the top of his profession with three advanced degrees after arriving in the States with no money and being able to speak little English. His is an amazing story of dedication and pursuit of excellence. Mom gave us an education in life with every educational opportunity taken advantage of. I took the lessons learned and made the most of my opportunity.

I now work in the University of Iowa Hospitals and Clinics as a physical therapist. I brag about my dad all the time. I am proud to be his daughter.

From Edward

My father has given our family so much to be thankful for, throughout his entire life. He has provided so many unique experiences to engage us, so many accomplishments and accolades to inspire us, and so many personal traits to influence us. For me, the most valuable gifts that I received from my father have been a love of teaching and a dedication to a lifetime of learning. Undoubtedly, my siblings were influenced by my father's scholarship to some degree as well, as evidenced by the fact that each one of his children attained at least one bachelor's degree, and that all of them also went on to pursue graduate degrees.

On occasion, my design students will ask me what is needed in order to be a good designer. I believe that in order to be a good designer, you should be a "well-rounded" person. It is always beneficial for a designer to have some amount of artistic ability and technical skills. However, a good designer should have a large pool of interests and experiences to draw from during the design process. So I tell my students that they should endeavor to read, talk, travel, learn, and basically experience as much as possible of what life has to offer. This is when I most appreciate that my father's remarkable life has provided me with many of these opportunities for learning and growth. I do not mean to suggest that I am a great designer because of my life experiences. But it makes me more appreciative of the fact that my father has laid a solid foundation for me to be a "well-rounded" individual, and hopefully a better designer and educator. Oliver Wendell Holmes once said, "The mind, once stretched by a new idea, never regains its original dimensions." I feel that the many countries we have visited, the cultures we have observed, and the unique experiences that we have been exposed to through my father's life and academic career have done the same for me.

I firmly believe that my decision to enter the design field was greatly influenced, at an early age, by our family's travels throughout Europe and Asia. Very few people that I have known or met in my life have had opportunity to climb amongst the impressive ruins of the Acropolis in Athens, Greece, attend the 1970 World Expo in Osaka, Japan, or witness the desperate human conditions in Bombay (Mumbai), India. How can you visit architectural marvels such as the Coliseum in Rome, or the temple complex of Angkor Wat and not be inspired and influenced by them? How can someone who gazes upon these magnificent edifices not be inquisitive about the cultures that constructed them? I don't know of any of my classmates that could say that they had actually been to many of these ancient places when we watched the slide presentations in our architectural design and history classes.

Living in Bangkok, Thailand, for seven years was another wonderful life experience, and it served as a base for our travels to other countries in Europe and Asia. This rare opportunity to be completely immersed in other cultures and customs has given me a unique perspective on the topic of diversity. The focus in education recently has been to recognize and address the various aspects of diversity in today's student populations. I feel that spending seven years as a foreigner in a different country was one of the best ways to gain insight into some of the challenges facing foreign students, inside and outside of the classroom.

So much of my father's life has been devoted to teaching and to a variety of academic pursuits. He has earned many degrees and well-deserved awards and accolades. I have always been proud of my father's accomplishments and the recognition that he has received. He is a wonderful example of what a life of hard work, integrity, and dedication can produce. My life and my own sense of self have been greatly influenced by his example. My father's accomplishments, both academic and professional, are a great source of pride, admiration, and respect for me. I strive in my own academic and professional pursuits to match the high standards that he has always set for himself. As I have become more involved in teaching at the college level, I draw on my father's commitment to education. He instilled in me a desire to not only succeed in my chosen profession, but to share my knowledge and experience with future designers. And my father's emphasis on continuing education and lifelong learning while I was growing up is something that will continue to drive me in my role as an educator and as a designer.

I owe so much of who I am, and what I have become, to my father's guidance and quiet influence. The example that he has set through his life of learning and teaching will always be a rich resource for me to draw upon as I continue to grow, as a teacher, as a professional, and as a father to my own children. I can only hope that I will have as profound an effect on their lives as my own father has had on mine.

From Charles

My dad taught me a lot during my life. He is a principled and deeply caring father who demonstrates his commitment by the examples he sets in everyday life. Even after retiring (for the second time), he continues to be an extremely hard worker. He has extraordinary leadership skills, and he is excellent at coaching those around him. He has always been generous and giving to those in need. His passion to succeed at work and to support his immediate and extended family is always evident. Perhaps that is why he never had time to develop many hobbies? He loves his work and his family. His passion for success in work and family life is infectious. I am one of many who are proud to have been influenced by a great man who also happens to be my dad.

Some of the most important lessons my dad taught me:

1. Find work that you are passionate about, and the work is never hard.
2. Lead by example.
3. Be generous.

I like the Winston Churchill quote that he often references in his email signature:

We make a living by what we get, but we make a life by what we give.

From Robert

One of the things that I remember most about my childhood was the steady stream of guests we had staying in our house. Even with six children to feed, shelter, and send to college, my parents were generous enough to allow others to live with us and be a part of our family.

Some of these guests were in fact related to us from my father's side. Many of them were not. All of them, however, were coming from China or Taiwan to study in the United States with the hope of bettering their lives. They were taking a big leap, and we were their first landing spot.

As the youngest in the family, I never knew anything but a full house. I was very close to my brothers and sisters, so it was hard for me when they grew older, had other interests, and eventually moved out for college and to start their careers. When my siblings weren't around, it was the houseguests—these Chinese graduate students—who played games with me and kept me occupied at times. I grew very fond of them, too, and missed them after they moved on.

Years later, I grew to appreciate what my father had done for these young immigrants. He had offered them a chance to get started in the States, much like his Aunt Phyllis had done for him when he was a foreign graduate student at the University of Pittsburgh, where he met my mother and began his library career.

This taught me a great lesson: when someone has been generous to you, pay it forward as many times as you can. My father has done this in both his personal and professional lives. I never knew how truly respected my father is around the world until I spent a year teaching in Taiwan. I met many people who knew him and had been helped by him. It was eye-opening for me and inspiring.

My one regret is that I have never traveled to China with my father. I work for a school called Columbus Academy that has a longstanding exchange program with the Hefei school district, so there is a good chance I will be able to join a group of teachers and students for a visit there in the coming years. (Bob did get to go in 2013.)

I'm hopeful that my two young sons, Seth and Avery, will eventually be able to take part in the exchange program when they reach high school. My ultimate dream, however, would be if I could take my wife, Cara, and both of my sons to China while my father is still able to travel with us. That may never be possible, but I hold out hope that it will … because it would be a truly unbelievable and unforgettable experience for us all.

Important Dates and Events
in the Life of Hwa-Wei Lee

1931   Hwa-Wei is born January 25, 1931, at Kuang Xiang He Maternity Hospital in Guangzhou, China, where his father, Luther Kan-Chun Lee, serves as governor of Shihui County, Guangdong Province.

1932   Kan-Chun Lee is appointed to the Ministry of Interior in the National Government. The Lee family moves to Nanjing.

1937   Hwa-Wei starts first grade in Nanjing.

1938   The Lee family moves to Guilin, Guangxi Province. Due to the Japanese invasion, Kan-Chun is appointed chief education officer in the Provincial Cadre Training Corps.

1939   To protect them from the dangers of the war, including daily bombing raids by the Japanese, members of the Lee family—Hwa-Wei, his mother, Hsiao-Hui Wang, and his five siblings—are sent to Haiphong, Vietnam, where his youngest sister is born. Kan-Chun remains in Guilin.

1941   The Lee family moves back to Guilin where schooling is frequently interrupted by the war.

1943   Hwa-Wei graduates from elementary school. The Lee family moves to Chongqing, the wartime capitol.

         Hwa-Wei starts junior high school at the National Number Two High School for Overseas Chinese in Wufuchang, Jiangyin District, Sichuan Province.

1946   With the end of World War II, the Lee family moves back to Nanjing. Hwa-Wei is enrolled in the ninth grade at the First Municipal Middle School.

         Kan-Chan Lee is transferred to Beijing. The family joins him, leaving Hwa-Wei in Nanjing.

1947   Hwa-Wei graduates from junior high school at the First Municipal Middle School in Nanjing.

         With the outbreak of the Chinese Civil War, the Lee family returns to Guilin; Hwa-Wei enrolls in the tenth grade at the National Han-Min High School.

1949   Due to the defeat of the Nationalist army by Communist forces, the Lee family is forced to flee Guilin, settling in Taichung, Taiwan.

         Hwa-Wei enrolls as a senior in the Provincial Taichung First High School, Taiwan.

1950   Hwa-Wei graduates from Taiwan Provincial Taichung First High School, passes the college entrance examination, and enrolls in the Provincial Taiwan Teachers College (renamed National Taiwan Normal University), majoring in education.

1954   Hwa-Wei graduates from the National Taiwan Normal University and receives thirteen-months of ROTC training at the Army Officers Academy.

1955   Hwa-Wei completes his ROTC training and is commissioned as a first lieutenant reserve officer.

He passes the National Civil Service examination and is assigned to the Affiliated Experimental Elementary School of the Provincial Taipei Teachers College, where he serves as dean of students.

1956   Hwa-Wei returns to National Taiwan Normal University to serve as a teaching assistant and is then assigned to work in the office of Dean of Students in charge of student organizations.

1957   Hwa-Wei passes his examination to study abroad and receives a scholarship to the University of Pittsburgh to work toward a master's degree in education.

In one of his classes at the University of Pittsburgh, Hwa-Wei meets Mary Kratochvil.

1958   Hwa-Wei begins work as a library student assistant at the University of Pittsburgh Library.

1959   Both Mary and Hwa-Wei receive their Master of Education (MED) degrees.

On March 14, 1959, Hwa-Wei and Mary are wed in Jeannette, Pennsylvania, at the First Methodist Church.

Hwa-Wei is employed as a full-time librarian trainee in the University of Pittsburgh Libraries and enrolls in the Master of Library Science (MLS) degree program at Carnegie Institute of Technology (later Carnegie Mellon University).

1961   Hwa-Wei receives his MLS degree from Carnegie Institute of Technology.

Hwa-Wei is hired by the University of Pittsburgh Libraries as the first assistant in the Acquisitions Department, and begins his doctoral studies in education at Pitt.

1962   Hwa-Wei is hired by Duquesne University Library, Pittsburgh, as the head of Technical Services and the Africana Special Collection librarian.

1965   Hwa-Wei completes a Ph.D. degree in Education, majoring in Educational Administration with a minor in Library Science, from the University of Pittsburgh.

Hwa-Wei is hired by Edinboro State College to serve as deputy library director with the rank of assistant professor.

1967   At Edinboro, Hwa-Wei is promoted to library director with the rank of associate professor.

1968   Hwa-Wei is hired by Colorado State University to serve as the director of the Library (later Library and Information Center) at the Asian Institute of Technology, established in Bangkok, Thailand, under the sponsorship of the U.S. Agency for International Development.

The Lee family, Hwa-Wei, Mary, and their five children, move to Bangkok, Thailand, where they live for seven years.

1970   Hwa-Wei is appointed an adjunct professor by the Department of Library Science, Chulalongkorn University, Bangkok, to teach a course, Introduction to Library Automation, the first of its kind in Asia.

1975   The Lee family returns to the U.S., with Hwa-Wei's appointment at Colorado
        State University, Fort Collins, as the associate director of the Colorado State Uni-
        versity Libraries with the rank of professor of Library Administration.

1978   Hwa-Wei is hired by Ohio University in Athens, Ohio, as the director of University
        Libraries.

1979   Hwa-Wei establishes the International Librarians Internship Program at OHIO
        Libraries.

        Hwa-Wei is appointed an adjunct professor of curriculum and instruction in the
        College of Education.

1982   The International Development Research Centre of Canada invites Hwa-Wei to
        join a team of library experts for a two-week workshop, Management of Scientific
        and Technical Information Centers, in Kunming, Yunnan Province, China. This is
        Hwa-Wei's first visit to China since 1949.

        Ohio University honors Hwa-Wei with the Outstanding Administrator Award.

1983   Luther Kang-Chun Lee (b. September 22, 1893, d. March 1,1983) passes away in
        Taichung at the age of eighty-nine.

        Hwa-Wei receives the Distinguished Services Award from the Chinese American
        Librarians Association.

1984   Hsiao-Hui Wang (b. May 27, 1894, d. August 6, 1984) passes away in Taichung at
        the age of ninety.

1987   Hwa-Wei is named the Ohio Librarian of the Year.

1989   The first international conference of Chinese and U.S. libraries, "Application of
        New Information Technology in Libraries," is jointly organized by Ohio Univer-
        sity and Xian Jiaotong University in Xian, China. The conference is held Septem-
        ber 8–11.

        Hwa-Wei receives the Outstanding Contributions Award from the Library Associa-
        tion of China, Taiwan.

1991   Hwa-Wei receives three service awards: the American Library Association (ALA)
        John Ames Humphrey Award for contributions to international librarianship, the
        Distinguished Services Award from the Asian Pacific American Librarians Associa-
        tion, and the Distinguished Service Award from the Chinese Academic & Profes-
        sional Association in Mid-America.

        Hwa-Wei's formal title is changed from library director to the dean of Ohio Uni-
        versity Libraries.

1992   Hwa-Wei is honored for his distinguished service as a councilor by the American
        Library Association.

        Hwa-Wei receives a Certificate of Appreciation for Distinguished Service from the
        United States Information Agency.

1993   Hwa-Wei receives an OhioLINK Appreciation Award.

1996   The First China-U.S. Library Conference is held on August 21–23 at the National
        Library of China, Beijing. The conference theme is "The Global Storage and Re-
        trieval of Information: Challenges and Opportunities."

1999   After twenty-one years of service, Hwa-Wei retires from Ohio University and is honored with the title of dean emeritus of Ohio University Libraries.

By a resolution of the Board of Trustees, Ohio University names the Southeast Ohio Regional Depository the "Hwa-Wei Lee Library Annex."

Ohio University names the first floor of the Vernon R. Alden Library the "Hwa-Wei Lee Center for International Collections."

Ohio Library Council recognizes Hwa-Wei as a Hall of Fame Librarian.

2000   Online Computer Library Center (OCLC) invites Hwa-Wei to serve as a visiting distinguished scholar.

The First International Conference of Libraries and Research Institutes on Overseas Chinese Studies is organized and held at Ohio University on March 24–25.

2001   At Chiang Mai University, Chiang Mai, Thailand, Hwa-Wei serves as a Fulbright senior specialist to help design the graduate program in the Department of Library Science.

2002   Hwa-Wei is appointed a consultant for OCLC Asian Pacific Services.

2003   Hwa-Wei is hired by the Library of Congress to serve as the chief of the Asian Division.

2005   Hwa-Wei is selected as an Honorary Life Member of the Library Association of China.

2008   Hwa-Wei retires from the Library of Congress and moves to Jacksonville, Florida.

2009   Hwa-Wei and Mary celebrate their fiftieth wedding anniversary.

University of Illinois at Urbana-Champaign asks Hwa-Wei to serve as the project evaluator for the China-U.S. Librarians Collaboration Project (2009–2011). The project is funded jointly by the U.S. Institute of Museum and Library Services and the Chinese Ministry of Culture.

2011   Hwa-Wei celebrated his eightieth birthday.

Collected Works of Hwa-Wei Lee, a 1,565-page, two-volume publication, is released by Sun Yat-Sen University Press, Guangzhou, China, in both English and Chinese (ISBN 978-7-306-04025-7).

A 305-page biography, The Sage in the Cathedral of Books: The Distinguished Chinese American Library Professional Dr. Hwa-Wei Lee, written by Yang Yang, is published by Guangxi Normal University Press, Guilin, China, in Chinese (ISBN 978-7-5495-0881-5).

A 233-page biography, The Choice of a Sage: Biography of Dr. Hwa-Wei Lee, written by Hong Lu, is published by Science Press, Beijing, China, in Chinese (ISBN 978-7-03-032686-7).

In memory of his aunt, Phyllis Hsiao-Chu Wang (Xiao-Chu Wang), Hwa-Wei establishes the Wang Xiao-Chu Memorial Scholarship Fund at the Graduate Institute of Library and Information Studies at Sun Yat-Sen University.

A symposium, The Library Thoughts and Contributions of Hwa-Wei Lee, is held at Shenzhen Library November 17, 2011, jointly organized by Sun Yat-Sen University Libraries, Shenzhen Library, Guangdong Provincial Zhongshan Library, and the Public Library Research Institute.

2012   Ohio University confers an Honorary Doctor of Letters degree on Hwa-Wei during commencement, June 9, 2012.

2013   As part of its fortieth-anniversary celebration, the Chinese American Librarians Association publishes *Spotlight on CALA Members: Dr. Hwa-Wei Lee*. The ninety-one-page publication, edited by Shali Zhang and designed by Sai Deng, is released at the CALA annual conference June 30, 2013, in Chicago, Illinois (http://cala-web.org/files/spotlight/DrLee.pdf).

A seventeen-minute video, *The Life of Dr. Hwa-Wei Lee*, is released by Sai Deng (http://youtube/7qwiUNF111Q).

The National Taiwan Normal University Library honors Hwa-Wei with a special symposium, The Development and Trends of Academic Libraries, held on December 12, 2013. The library also displays a three-week special exhibition of his lifelong achievements.

2014   A 455-page Taiwan edition of the biography, *Sage in the Cathedral of Books: The Distinguished Librarian Dr. Hwa-Wei Lee,* written by Yang Yang, is published by Showwe Information Science and Technology, Ltd., Taipei, Taiwan (ISBN 978-986-5729-03-5).

2015   Hwa-Wei is awarded the Melvin Dewey Medal by the American Library Association recognizing his "creative leadership of high order" in "library management, library training, cataloging and classification, and the tools and techniques of librarianship."

Publications by Hwa-Wei Lee

Books

"Educational Development in Taiwan under the Nationalist Government, 1945–1962." Ph.D. diss., University of Pittsburgh, 1964, 333 pgs.

Edited with Sally C. Tseng and K. Mulliner. *Areas of Cooperation in Library Development in Asia and Pacific Regions: Papers presented at the 1983 Joint Annual Program of the Asian/Pacific American Librarians Association and Chinese American Librarians Association, June 28–29, 1983, Los Angeles, California.* Athens, OH: Chinese American Librarians Association, 1985. 63 pgs.

Librarianship In World Perspective: Selected Writings, 1963–1989. [In English and Chinese.] Taipei: Student Book Company, 1991. 332 pgs.

Library Development, Resource Sharing, and Networking among Higher Education Institutions in Papua New Guinea. Final Report and Recommendations. Port Moresby, Papua New Guinea: Commission for Higher Education, December 1991. 48 pgs.

With Gary A. Hunt. *Fundraising for the 1990s: The Challenge Ahead: A Practical Guide for Library Fundraising: From Novice to Expert.* Canfield, OH: Genaway and Associates, 1992. 183 pgs.

Modern Library Management. [In Chinese.] Taipei: San Min Book Co., Ltd.,1996. 257 pgs.

With Weihan Diao and Andrew H. Wang. *An Introduction to OCLC Online and CD-ROM Cataloging.* [In Chinese and English.] Shanghai: East China Normal University Press, 1999. 222 pgs.

With Xiaoying Dong and Meiyun Zuo. *Knowledge Management: Theory and Practice.* [In Chinese.] Twenty-first Century Library Science Series. Beijing: Huazhi Publishing, 2002. 471 pgs.

Collected Works of Hwa-Wei Lee. 2 vols. [In English and Chinese.] Library of Library Scientists. Guangzhou: Sun Yat-Sen University Press, 2011. 1565 pgs.

Papers, Reports and Presentations

"Africana at Duquesne University Library." In *African Studies Bulletin* 6, no. 3 (October 1963): 25–27.

"Africana—A Special Collection at Duquesne University." In *The Catholic Library World* 35, no. 4 (December 1963): 209–11.

"Real Issues and Problems Encountered by Foreign Students in the U.S.—Notes from Attending the Conference of Midwest Universities on Reviewing Foreign Students Applications." [In Chinese.] In *China Newsweek*, no. 834 (April 18, 1966), 12–15.

"The Recent Educational Reform in Communist China." In *School and Society* 46, no. 2311 (November 9, 1968): 395–400.

"Computer Application in Library and Information Services: The Current AIT Experiments and Future Plans." Paper presented at the First Computer Applications Symposium jointly sponsored by the Computer Science Laboratory, Chulalongkorn University and U.S. Educational Foundation in Thailand, Bangkok, June 23–25, 1969.

"Asian Institute of Technology." [In Chinese.] In *The Scooper Monthly*, October 1969, 76–81.

"Planning for Computer Applications in the AIT Library." Paper presented at the 1969 annual conference of the Thai Library Association, Bangkok, December 15–19, 1969.

Proposal for a Regional Information Center for Science and Technology at the Asian Institute of Technology. Bangkok, Thailand: Asian Institute of Technology, January 1971. 13 pgs.

"Fragmentation of Academic Library Resources in Thai University Libraries." In *International Library Review* 3, no. 2 (April 1971): 155–67.

"Library Mechanization at the Asian Institute of Technology." In *International Library Review* 3, no. 3 (July 1971): 257–70.

"Regional Cooperation in Scientific and Technical Information Service." In *Proceedings of the Conference on Scientific and Technical Information Needs for Malaysia and Singapore, Institute Teknoloji Mara, Kuala Lumpur, September 24-26, 1971*, 97–105. Kuala Lumpur: Persatuan Perpustakaan Malaysia and Library Association of Singapore, 1972.

"A New Engineering Library Emerging in Asia." In *Libraries in International Development*, no. 41 (December 1971): 103.

"The Information Technology—New Tools and New Possibilities for Information Storage, Retrieval, and Dissemination." Paper presented at the Regional Seminar on Information Storage, Retrieval and Dissemination organized by the Asian Mass Communication Research and Information Centre in cooperation with the National Research Council of Thailand, Bangkok, March 26–30, 1973. 10 pgs.

Asian Information Center for Geotechnical Engineering. Progress Report, January to June 1973. Bangkok, Thailand: Asian Institute of Technology, July 1973. 16 pgs.

"Partner for School Library Development in Thailand." In *T.L.A. Bulletin* 17, no. 5 (September/October 1973): 443–48.

"Considerations in the Establishment of a National Network for Books and Other Information Resources." [In Chinese.] In *Central Daily News* (Taipei), February 26–27, 1974.

"Possibilities in Employing Computer and Other Information Technologies to Further Library and Information Services in Southeast Asia." In *Network* 1, no. 3 (March 1974): 10–12, 24–28.

With S. W. Massil. *Library Automation at the Asian Institute of Technology—Bangkok*. The Larc Reports vol. 7, no. 3. Peoria, IL: The Larc Press, 1974. 35 pgs.

"Regional Cooperation in Scientific and Technical Information Service." In *Survey of Automated Activities in the Libraries of Asia and the Far East*. World Survey Series, vol. 5, 11–17. Peoria, IL: The Larc Press, 1974.

"The Application of Information Technology to Close the Information Gap." Paper presented at the First Conference on Asian Library Cooperation, Tamsui, Taipei, August 19–22, 1974. 12 pgs.

"User and Use Analysis: A Case Study of the Information Utility by Geotechnical Engineers in Asian Countries." In *Information Utilities: Proceedings of the 37th Annual Conference of the American Society for Information Science in Atlanta, Georgia, on October 13-17, 1974*, vol. II, edited by Pranas Zunde, 133–36. Washington D.C., 1974.

With S. W. Massil. *Proposal for Library Development at Prince of Songkla University in Southern Thailand*. Prepared at the request of the University Development Project Office, Prince of Songkla University. Bangkok: Asian Institute of Technology, 1974. 23 pgs.

With S. W. Massil. "Scholarly Publications: Considerations on Bibliographic Control and Dissemination." In *Scholarly Publishing in Southeast Asia, Proceedings of the Seminar on Scholarly Publishing in Southeast Asia, sponsored by the Association of Southeast Asian Institutions of Higher Learning, University of Malaya, Kuala Lumpur, January 16-18, 1975*, edited by Beda Lim, 212–18. Kuala Lumpur, 1975.

With Jane C. Yang. "International Standard Numbering for Books and Serials and the Standardization of Bibliographic Descriptions." [In Chinese.] In *Journals of Library and Information Science* 1, no. 1 (February 1975): 60–66.

"The Experience of a Specialized Information Service in Asia—AGE." Paper presented at the Round Table Conference on Documentation Problems in Developing Countries, Khartoum, Sudan, April 10–11, 1975, sponsored by FID/DC and FID National Member in Sudan. In *Journal of Library and Information Science* 1, no. 2 (Oct. 1975): 82–93.

"Recent Important Developments in the Library World." [In Chinese.] In *Bulletin of the Library Association of China*, no. 27 (December 1975): 34–36.

The Possibility of Establishing a Regional Centre for the International Serials Data System in Thailand. (SC-76/WS/7.) Paris: UNESCO, 1976. 43 pgs.

"The Third Conference of Southeast Asian Librarians." In *Leads* 18, no. 1 (March 1976): 3–4.

"Proposal for the Establishment of an ISDS Regional Center for Southeast Asia in Thailand." In *Leads* 18, no. 2 (July 1976): 4–5.

"Cooperative Regional Bibliographic Projects in Southeast Asia." Paper presented at the Library Seminars of the International Association of Oriental Librarians held in conjunction with the 30th International Congress of Human Sciences in Asia and North Africa, Mexico City, August 3–8, 1976. 17 pgs. In *UNESCO Bulletin for Libraries* 31, no. 6 (Nov.–Dec. 1977): 344–51, 370.

"Regional Cooperation for ISDS." In *Proceedings of the Third Conference of Southeast Asian Librarians, Jakarta, Indonesia, December 1–5, 1975*, edited by Luwarsih Pringgoadisurjo and Kardiati Sjahrial, 159–66. Jakarta: PDIN-LIPI for Ikatan Pustakawan Indonesia (Indonesian Librarians Association), 1977.

With Marjorie Rhoades. "Approaches to Development of Water Resources Scientific Information Systems." In *Water Knowledge Transfer: Proceedings of the Second International Conference on Transfer of Water Resources Knowledge, Colorado State University, June 29–July 1, 1977*, vol. 2, 625–44. Fort Collins, CO: Water Resource Publications, 1978.

"Sharing Information Resources Through Computer-assisted Systems and Networking." In *Resource Sharing of Libraries in Developing Countries: Proceedings of the 1977 IFLA/UNESCO Pre-session Seminar for Librarians from Developing Countries, Antwerp University, August 30–September 4, 1977*, 208–16. Munchen: K. G. Saur, 1979. Also in *Journal of Library and Information Science* 4, no. 1 (April 1978): 14–24.

"The Millionth Volume." *The Library Scene* 8, no. 4 (December 1979): 24.

"The Current Status of Academic Library Administration in the U.S." [In Chinese.] Paper presented at the Annual Meeting of Directors of Academic and Research Libraries, Taipei, December 1, 1979. 10 pgs.

"Online Revolution and Libraries." [In Chinese.] In *Library Planning and Media Technology, Library Workshop Proceedings, November 28–30, 1979*, 14–17. Taipei: National Taiwan Normal University Library, 1980.

With K. Mulliner and Lian The-Mulliner. "International Information Exchange and Southeast Asia Collections—A View from the U.S." Paper presented at the 1980 Meeting of the International Association of Orientalist Librarians, Manila, August 17–23, 1980. 17 pgs. In *Journal of Educational Media Science* 18, no. 2 (Winter 1980): 3–18.

"Impact of International Information System and Programs on NATIS." (SCP/4252-25.) In *Regional Cooperation for the Development of National Information Services: Proceedings of the Fourth Congress of Southeast Asian Librarians, Bangkok, Thailand, June 5–9, 1978*, 133–46. Bangkok: Thai Library Association, 1981.

"A Sketch for a Computerized National Library and Information Network." Paper presented at the International Workshop on Chinese Library Automation in Taipei, Taiwan, on February 14–19, 1981. 11 pgs.

Edited and compiled, with K. Mulliner. *Acquisitions from the Third World.* Special thematic issue of *Library Acquisitions: Practice and Theory* 6, no. 2 (1982): 79–238.

With K. Mulliner. "Library Acquisitions from the Third World: An Introduction." In *Library Acquisitions: Practice and Theory* 6, no. 2 (1982): 79–85.

"Recent Breakthroughs in Library Automation in Taiwan." In *Journal of Educational Media Science* 19, no. 2 (Winter 1982): 119–36.

With K. Mulliner. "International Exchanges of Librarians and the Ohio University Internship Program." Paper presented to the International Relations Round Table of the American Library Association at the Annual Conference in Philadelphia, July 1982. In *College & Research Libraries News* 43, no. 10 (November 1982): 345–48.

"Challenges for the Library and Information Profession." In *Bulletin of the Library Association of China*, no. 35 (1983): 235–46.

With K. Mulliner, E. Hoffmann-Pinther, and Hannah McCauley. "ALICE at One: Candid Reflections on the Adoption, Installation, and Use of the Virginia Tech Library System (VTLS) at Ohio University." In *Integrated Online Library Systems Second National Conference: proceedings*, Atlanta, Georgia, September 13–14, 1984, edited by David C. Genaway, 228–42. Canfield, OH: Genaway & Associates, 1984.

With M. Beckman and Jianyan Huang. "Management of Scientific and Technical Information Centres: Aspects of Planning a Course Sponsored by IDRC (Canada) and ISTIC (China)." Paper presented at the International Federation for Information and Documentation (FID) Pre-Congress Workshop on Curriculum Development in a Changing World, The Hague, September 3–4, 1984. 19 pgs.

"International Library Internships: An Effective Approach to Cooperation." Paper presented to the annual program of the Asian/Pacific American Librarians Association and the Chinese American Librarians Association, in conjunction with the American Library Association Annual Conference, Los Angeles, June 28–29, 1983. In *Areas of Cooperation in Library Development in Asian and Pacific Regions*, 21–27. Athens, Ohio: Chinese American Librarians Association, 1985. Revised in *International Library Review* 17, no. 1 (1985): 17–25.

Lecture Notes and Suggested Readings on Modern Library Management and Automation. Athens, OH: Ohio University Libraries, 1985. 87 pgs.

With K. Mulliner. "Educating for International Interdependence: The Role of the Academic Library—Ohio University and Malaysia." Paper presented at the First Annual Tun Abdul Razak Conference in Malaysia. Athens, Ohio, May 10, 1985. 9 pgs.

With K. Mulliner. "Funding the Southeast Asia Collection and Research Resources at Ohio University." Paper presented at the Annual Meeting of the Association for Asian Studies in Chicago, Illinois, March 21, 1986.

"International Exchanges and Internships for Librarians." Paper presented at the Library Association of the City University of New York (LACUNY) Institute '86, New York City, April 4, 1986.

"The Current Status and Future Trends of American Libraries." [In Chinese.] *Newsletter of Fujian Provincial Library Association*, no.1 (1986): 34–38. Notes taken by Yang Jin based on recording.

"Principles and Issues on National Library and Information Policy." In *Papers of the Library Cooperation and Development Seminar*, August 17–18, 1986, 5.1–5.22. Taipei: National Central Library, 1987. Also in *Journal of Library and Information Science* 13, no. 1 (April 1987): 1–16.

"Applications of Information Technology in an American Library—The Case of Ohio University Libraries." In *First Pacific Conference: New Information Technology for Library and*

Information Professionals: Proceedings, Bangkok, Thailand, June 16–18, 1987, edited by Ching-Chih Chen and David I. Raitt, 155–64. West Newton, MA: MicroUse Information, 1987.

"Library Automation at Ohio University Library: Past, Present and Future." In *Collection of Essays Honoring Chiang Wei-Tang on his Ninetieth Birthday,* 47–72. Taipei: Library Association of China (Taiwan), 1987.

Edited with Zhiyou Zhang. *Proceedings of the International Symposium on New Techniques and Applications in Libraries, Xi'an, China, September 8–11, 1988.* [In Chinese and English.] Xi'an: Xi'an Jiaotong University Press, 1988. 576 pgs.

"Trends in Automation in American Academic Libraries: Ohio University's Experience." Educational Resources Information Center, ED 315 081, ERIC Clearinghouse, May 1989. 20 pgs. In *Journal of Educational Media & Library Sciences* 27, no. 1 (Autumn 1989): 1–23.

"Planning Process and Considerations for a Statewide Academic Libraries Information System in Ohio," In *Proceedings of the Second Pacific Conference on New Information Technology for Library and Information Professionals and Educational Media Specialists and Technologists,* Singapore, May 29–31, 1989, edited by Ching-chih Chen and David I Raitt, 203–10. West Newton, MA: MicroUse Information, 1989. Also in *Journal of Educational Media & Library Sciences* 27, no. 2 (Winter 1990): 127–38.

"Major Milestones of Library Automation in American Libraries." [In Chinese.] Speech delivered at the National Central Library in Taipei on June 2, 1989. *National Central Library News Bulletin* 11, no. 4 (Nov. 1989): 4–7.

New Concepts and New Technology in Library Services. [In Chinese.] Library Lecture Series, no.10. Kaohsiung, Taiwan: National Sun Yat-sen University, 1989. 25 pgs.

Final Report of the INNERTAP Project Review. Consultant report on the Information Network on New and Renewable Energy Resources and Technologies for Asia and the Pacific, commissioned by the International Development Research Centre. Ottawa, Canada: IDRC, 1990. 33 pgs.

With Anne S. Goss. "Medical Librarianship in China: Recent Developments." In *Asian Libraries* 1, no.1 (March 1991): 80–84.

"New Visions in Library Automation and Networking—Ohio's Approach to the 1990s." In *Proceedings of the International Conference on New Frontiers in Library Information Services,* May 9–11, 1991, 361–82. 2 vols. Taipei, Taiwan: National Central Library, 1992. Also in *Journal of Academic Libraries,* no. 59 (1992): 38–45. Translated by Ping Bao and Xiaoyan Zhang. [In Chinese.]

"Contributions of International Faculty to International Education on Campuses." Paper presented at the 1992 Ohio Chinese Academic and Professional Association, Columbus, Ohio, April 1992. 15 pgs.

"The Future Begins Now: Ohio's Library Automation, Information Services and Networking." Paper, with abstract. In *Proceedings of the International Seminar on Collection Development and Resource Sharing in Modern Libraries,* May 17–20, 1992, Xian, China, edited by Yu Chen, 59–60. Shanghai: Shanghai Scientific & Technical Publishers, 1992.

With Judith Sessions and Stacey Kimmel. "OhioLINK: Technology and Teamwork Transforming Ohio Libraries." In *Wilson Library Bulletin* 66, no. 10 (June 1992): 43–45.

With John Evans. "Developing Higher Education Libraries in Papua New Guinea." In *Information Development: The International Journal for Librarians, Archivists and Information Specialists* 8, no. 2 (November 1992): 221–27.

With Gary Hunt. "The Ten Principles for Successful Fundraising." In *The Bottom Line* 6, no. 3/4 (Winter 1992/Spring 1993): 27–33. Also in *Sponsoring fur Bibliotheken,* edited by Rolf Busch, 130–41. Berlin: Deutsches Bibliotheksinstiut, 1997.

"Advancing Information Technologies: The Role of National Libraries." Paper presented at the International Conference on National Libraries, "Toward the 21st Century," sponsored by the National Central Library, Taiwan, Republic of China, April 20–24, 1993.

"Ohio Academic Libraries Prepare for the 21st Century." In *Library in the '90s: Selected Papers of the International Symposium on the Latest Development in Technologies of Library Service, September 6–10, 1992, Beijing, China*, edited by Chengjian Sun and Bingxin Jiang, 292–308. Beijing: International Academic Publishers, 1993.

"Managing Information Technology—The Experience of Ohio Academic Libraries." Paper presented at the IX Congress of Southeast Asian Librarians (CONSAL) in Bangkok, May 2–7, 1993, and the Seminar on National Academic Library Networking, May 12–14, 1993, Chiang Mai, Thailand. In *CONSAL IX Papers: Future Dimensions and Library Development*, B45–B62. Bangkok: CONSAL IX Secretariat, 1993.

"Expanding Ties between Ohio and Chinese Libraries." *Ohio Libraries* 6, no. 4 (Fall 1993): 22–23.

"Managing Information Technology—The Experience of Academic Libraries in Ohio." [In Chinese.] *Newsletter of the Graduate Institute of National Cheng-chi University*, no. 7 (November 1993): 1–11.

"Managing Information Technology—the Experience of Ohio Academic Libraries." In *Chiang Mai University Library Journal* 4 (1994): 20–43.

"Networked, Electronic and Virtual Library—Libraries of the 1990s." In *Proceedings of the International Seminar on Information Technologies and Information Services*, October 20–24, 1994, Shanghai, China, vol. 2, 167–72. Beijing: China Social Sciences Publishing House, 1994. Also in *Journal of Educational Media & Library Sciences* 32, no. 2 (Winter 1995): 119–29.

With Kent Mulliner. "Southeast Asia Collection Growth in the United States: Ohio University's Experience." In *Information Challenge: A Festschrift in Honor of Dr. Donald Wijasuriya*, edited by Ch'ng Kim See, 87–103. Kuala Kumpur: Knowledge Publishers, 1995.

"Global Information Access: Libraries as Citizens' Gateway to the World." In *Proceedings of the Chubu University-Ohio University Conference on Lifelong Learning for the 21st Century: Local and Global Dimensions*, October 4-6, 1994, Kasugai, Japan, 75–82. Kasugai: Chubu University, 1995.

Program CPR/91/420 Basic Education: Administration and Teachers Training. Consultant Report. Submitted to United Nations Educational, Scientific, and Cultural Organization, June 30, 1995. 13 pgs. "Sharing of Library and Information Resources: the OhioLINK Model." In *Proceedings of the 1996 International Symposium on Information Resources and Social Development*, September 3–6, 1996, Wuhan, China.

"American Contributions to Modern Library Development in China: A Historic Review." In *Proceedings of the China-U.S. Conference on Global Information Access: Challenges and Opportunities*, held in Beijing, China, August 21–23, 1996. 14 pgs. Also in *Journal of Information, Communication, and Library Science* 4, no.4 (Summer 1998): 10–20.

"Maximizing Information Access and Resource Sharing: The OhioLINK Experience." In *Proceedings of the 10th International Conference on New Information Technology*, March 24–26, 1998, Hanoi, Vietnam, edited by Ching-Chih Chen, 149–56. West Newton, MA: MicroUse Information, 1998.

"Maximizing Information Access and Resources Sharing: The OhioLINK Approach." In *Proceedings of the International Conference on New Missions of Academic Libraries in the 21st Century*, October 25–28, 1998, Beijing, China, 283–87. Beijing: Peking University Press, 1998.

"Library Cooperation and the Development of a Library Network—The OhioLINK." In *Proceedings of the Seminar on Library Cooperation, Resource Sharing, and the Development of Networks,* August 19–20, 1999, Bangkok, Thailand, organized by the Rajabhat Institute Bansomdejchaopraya, 1–27. Bangkok: Rajabhat Institute Bansomdejchaopraya, 1999.

"The Success of OhioLINK for Information Access and Resources Sharing in a Networked Environment—OhioLINK." In *Bulletin of Library and Information Science,* no. 30 (August 1999): 1–17.

"OhioLINK for Information Access and Resources Sharing in a Networked Environment." [In Chinese.] In *Proceedings of the Seminar on Modern Library Services and Management,* September 13–15, 1999, 5–12. Hangzhou, China: Zhejiang University Library, 1999.

"Library Cooperation and Resources Sharing in the Networked Environment." [In Chinese.] In *Proceedings of the Symposium on Internet and Library Development, December 4, 1999, National Central Library,* 3–44. Taipei, Taiwan: Library Association of China, 1999.

Ohio University Libraries 1998–99 Annual Report. Athens, OH: Ohio University Libraries, 1999. 33 pgs.

"Libraries in the Digital and Networked Knowledge Age of the Twenty-First Century." In *Proceedings of the Seminar on 21st Century Public Libraries: Vision and Reality,* May 1–3, 2000, Taipei, Taiwan, organized by the Central Taiwan Office of the Council for Cultural Development of ROC, 43–68. Taichung, Taiwan: National Taichung Library, 2000.

"Knowledge Management and the Role of Libraries in the New Century." In *Prospects of the 21st Century,* 397–436. Taichung, Taiwan: Feng Chia University and Liao Ying-Ming Cultural and Educational Foundation, 2000.

"Does Library have a Role in Knowledge Management?" In *Global Digital Library Development in the New Millennium,* proceedings of the 12th International Conference on New Information Technology, May 29–31, 2001, Beijing, China, edited by Ching-Chih Chen, 145–52. Beijing: Tsinghua University Press, 2001.

"Strategic Direction of Libraries in Knowledge Management." In *New Technology of Library and Information Service,* no. 93, 2002: 13–17.

With Ratana Na-Lamphun. "Focusing on Information and Knowledge Management: Redesigning the Graduate Program of Library and Information Science at Chiang Mai University." *Information Development* 18, no. 1 (March 2002): 47–58.

"Implementing Knowledge Management, Providing Quality Services, and Promoting Knowledge Advancement." In *Proceedings of the Symposium on Knowledge Management: Opportunity and Challenge for Libraries, May 19–22, 2002, Beijing, China,* organized jointly by the Information and Documentation Center of the Chinese Academy of Science and National Library for Science and Technology. Beijing: Chinese Academy of Science Press, 2002, 90–94. Also in *Progress in Library and Information Work* [in Chinese], no. 4, 2002: 2–6.

With Peggy Shu-Te Liu. "The Cooperation of Non-profit Organizations in Publishing and Marketing Electronic Periodicals: The Case of Bio-One by SPARC and OCLC." [In Chinese.] In *Bulletin of the Library Association of China,* no. 68, (June 2002): 14–25.

"Who should be in Charge of Knowledge Management, Librarians/Libraries or Someone Else?" In *Journal of Academic Libraries* 20, no. 5 (2002): 79–84. Special issue for the International Symposium on the Current Status and Future Development of Libraries in the Digital Age, Oct. 23–25, 2002. Centennial Celebration on the Funding of the Peking University Library.

"Libraries in Asia: New Life for Libraries in the Digital Age." In *Harvard Asia Pacific Review* 6, no. 2 (Fall 2002): 22–24.

"Knowledge Management: The Role of Libraries." [In Chinese.] *Tianjin Library Journal* 78, no. 1 (2003): 1–5.

With Liren Zheng. "First Decade of the Dr. Shao You-Bao Overseas Chinese Documentation and Research Center at Ohio University (1993–2003)." In *Proceedings of the Second International Conference of Institutes & Libraries for Chinese Overseas Studies. "Transnational Networks: Challenges in Research and Documentation of the Chinese Overseas, March 13–15, 2003, Hong Kong,"* organized jointly by the Chinese University of Hong Kong Libraries and Ohio University Libraries. Hong Kong, 2003. 17 pgs. Also in *Chinese Overseas: Migration, Research and Documentation,* edited by Chee-Beng Tan, Colin Storey, and Julia Zimmerman, 275–95. Hong Kong: The Chinese University Press, 2007.

With Hongqin Lou. "Issues on the Performance Appraisal of Library Services." [In Chinese.] In *Journal of Academic Libraries* 21, no. 5 (2003): 18–22.

"Libraries in Rapid Transition: Information Management vs. Knowledge Management," "Library Cooperation and Resources Sharing," "Steps in Implementing Knowledge Management," "Promoting Positive Changes in Scholarly Communication: The SPARC Initiative," "Measuring Library Service Quality: The LibQUAL+ Tool." In *Challenges and Opportunities for Libraries and Information Professionals in Knowledge Management and the Digital Age, 20–22 March 2003, Chiang Mai, Thailand,* proceedings of the international conference (Asia-Pacific) organized by the Department of Library Science, Faculty of Humanities, Chiang Mai University, 1–9, 29–32, 84–93, 118–21, 122–28. Chiang Mai, Thailand: Chiang Mai University, 2003.

"Building a World-class Asian Collection in the Library of Congress for Area Studies, Culture Preservation, Global Understanding, and Knowledge Creation." Keynote address. [In Japanese and English.] In *Proceedings of the Symposium "The New Horizon of Library Services Toward the Better Understanding of Asia," November 19, 2003.* [Japanese translation, 57–67; English paper and slides, 150–69.] Kyoto, Japan: National Diet Library, Kansai-kan, 2004.

"Building a World-class Asian Collection in the Library of Congress." In *Information Services across the Digital Age: Collected Essays in Celebrating the 70th Birthday of Professor Margaret Chang Fung,* 17–30. Taipei: Wen Hua Library Management Co, 2004.

"Ching-chih Chen: A Shining Star and Model of Chinese American Library and Information Science Professionals." In *Bridging Cultures: Chinese American Librarians and Their Organization: A Glance at the Thirty Years of CALA, 1973–2003,* edited by Zhijia Shen, Liana Hong Zhou, and Karen T. Wei, 9–25. Chinese American Librarians Association. Guilin: Guangxi Normal University Press, 2004.

"Sharing the Treasures of the Asian Collections in the Library of Congress." In *Proceedings of the Second Shanghai International Library Forum—City Development and Library Services,* Shanghai Library, October 12–15, 2004, 157–165. Shanghai: Shanghai Scientific and Technological Literature Publishing House, 2004.

"Historical Resources on Northeast China and Japan in the Library of Congress." [In Chinese and Japanese.] Paper presented at the International Conference of the Historical Resources for the Studies of Northeast China and Japan held at Niigata University in Japan, October 27–30, 2004.

Overseas Chinese and Overseas Chinese Studies—Dr. Shao You Bao Overseas Chinese Documentation and Research Center at Ohio University, U.S.A. Athens, OH: Ohio University Libraries, 2004. 34 pgs.

"Sinological Resources in the Library of Congress." Keynote speech at the International Conference on Sinological Resources in the Digital Era, December 7–9, 2004, organized by the National Central Library (Taiwan) and Center for Sinological Studies,

Taipei, Taiwan. 13 pgs. [In Chinese.] In *National Taiwan Normal University Alumni Journal*, no. 325 (February 2005): 4–12. Also in *Culture Communication* [in Chinese], nos. 17 (July/August 2005): 2, and 18 (September/October 2005): 3.

"Chinese Resources for Zheng He Studies in the Library of Congress." In *Maritime Asia and the Chinese Overseas, 1405–2005*, proceedings of the Third International Conference of Institutes and Libraries for Chinese Overseas Studies, Singapore, August 18–21, 2005. Also in *The Collected Works of Hwa-Wei Lee*, vol. 2, 1244–52. Guangzhou: Sun Yat-sen University Press, 2011.

"Building a World-Class Asian Collection in the Digital Age at the Library of Congress." Keynote address. In *Symposium on Collection Development for Libraries in the Digital Age, January 16–17, 2006*, organized by the National Chung Hsing University Graduate Institute of Library and Information Science and the National Chung Hsing University Library, Taichung, Taiwan, 11–29. Taichung, Taiwan: National Chung Hsing University, 2006.

"Asian Collections in the Digital Age at the Library of Congress." *Shenzhen Library Newsletter*, no. 14 (no. 1, 2007): 3–11.

"Asian Collections in the Library of Congress: A Historical Overview." In *Over a Hundred Years of Collecting: The History of East Asian Collections in North America*, October 18–19, 2007, University of California, Berkeley. 25 pgs.

"Building a National Asian Pacific American Collection in the Library of Congress, USA." In *Proceedings of the Fourth International Conference of Institutes and Libraries for Overseas Chinese Studies*, jointly organized by Jinan University and Ohio University, May 9–11, 2009, Jinan University, Guangzhou.

"A History of the East Asian Collections in the Library of Congress: A Bibliographic Guide." In *Collecting Asia: East Asian Libraries in North America, 1868–2008*, edited by Peter X. Zhou, 22–31. Asia Past and Present: New Research from AAS, no. 4. Ann Arbor, Michigan: Association for Asian Studies, 2010.

"Major Milestones in Library Automation in American Libraries in the Past 50 Years." [In Chinese.] *Academic Library Work* 30, no. 135 (No. 1, 2010): 3–7.

"The Development and Effects of the Chinese Collection in the Library of Congress." [In Chinese.] In *Proceedings of China-US Cultural Exchange and Library Development and the Opening Ceremony of the T. H. Tsian Library, October 31-November 4, 2007, Nanjing*, edited by Zhiqiang Zhang and Yuan Zhou, 189–201. Nanjing: Nanjing University Press, 2010.

"The Collections of Contemporary Historical Documents on Northeast China and Japan at the Library of Congress." [In Chinese.] In *Chinese Studies in North American—Research & Resources*, edited by Haihui Zhang, 787–94. Beijing: Zhonghua Books, 2010.

"New Concept for Implementing Knowledge Management in University Libraries." [In Chinese, PPT format.] In *Proceedings of Global Perspective—University Library Directors Forum, June 1–3, 2010*, 32–43. Shanghai: Shanghai University of Finance and Economics Library, 2010.

"Opportunities and Discussions on Sharing Chinese Digital Resources." [In Chinese and English, PPT format.] In *Proceedings of the Eighth Conference on Cooperative Development and Sharing of Chinese Resources—Conference on Digital Archives of Chinese Library Resources*, November 3-4, 2010, Taipei, 17–36. Taipei: Sinological Research Center, 2010.

Yang Yang

YANG YANG attended Ohio University, Athens, where she received a master's degree in Communication and Development Studies from the Center for International Studies and a Master of Business Administration from the College of Business. When employed by China Central Television (CCTV) in Beijing, China, she was in charge of program planning for *Time and Space in the East* and directed the program *Sincerity - Communication*. Since 2008, she has collaborated consecutively with the Discovery Channel in the United States and Granada TV in the U.K. in making a full-length documentary film, *The Ultimate Olympics*; and with the National Geographic Channel in making *The Ancient Warrior Queen*. She also directed the documentary film series *Tea* for CCTV. Currently, she is responsible for the production of a series of public educational programs for the News Center of CCTV.

Dr. Ying Zhang

DR. YING ZHANG is a research librarian for Asian Studies at the University of California, Irvine. Prior to this, she worked at Rutgers, The State University of New Jersey, as the interim East Asian librarian for three years; and at Sun Yat-Sen University Libraries as a research librarian and, later, a webmaster for twelve years, during the course of which she spent six months at Ohio University as a visiting scholar. In her early career, she was a lecturer at Shanghai Fishery College, now Shanghai Ocean University. Dr. Zhang has earned her bachelor of science from Shandong College of Oceanography, Qingdao, now the Ocean University of China; a master's of information management from Sun Yat-Sen University; and a doctorate of library and information science from Rutgers University. Besides her career, she enjoys reading, listening to music, and traveling with her family and friends.